T0264252

Microsoft Virtualization
Master Microsoft Server, Desktop, Application, and Presentation Virtualization

Microsoft Virtualization
Master Microsoft Server, Desktop, Application, and Presentation Virtualization

Thomas Olzak

Jason Boomer

Robert M. Keefer

James Sabovik

Kenneth Majors, Technical Editor

ELSEVIER

AMSTERDAM • BOSTON • HEIDELBERG • LONDON
NEW YORK • OXFORD • PARIS • SAN DIEGO
SAN FRANCISCO • SINGAPORE • SYDNEY • TOKYO
Syngress is an imprint of Elsevier

SYNGRESS.

Syngress is an imprint of Elsevier
30 Corporate Drive, Suite 400, Burlington, MA 01803, USA
Linacre House, Jordan Hill, Oxford OX2 8DP, UK

Microsoft Virtualization: Master Microsoft Server, Desktop, Application, and Presentation Virtualization

Notices
Knowledge and best practice in this field are constantly changing. As new research and experience broaden our understanding, changes in research methods, professional practices, or medical treatment may become necessary.

Practitioners and researchers must always rely on their own experience and knowledge in evaluating and using any information, methods, compounds, or experiments described herein. In using such information or methods they should be mindful of their own safety and the safety of others, including parties for whom they have a professional responsibility.

To the fullest extent of the law, neither the Publisher nor the authors, contributors, or editors, assume any liability for any injury and/or damage to persons or property as a matter of products liability, negligence or otherwise, or from any use or operation of any methods, products, instructions, or ideas contained in the material herein.

Library of Congress Cataloging-in-Publication Data
Application submitted

British Library Cataloguing-in-Publication Data
A catalogue record for this book is available from the British Library.

ISBN: 978-1-59749-431-1

Printed and bound by CPI Group (UK) Ltd, Croydon, CR0 4YY

For information on rights, translations, and bulk sales, contact Matt Pedersen, Commercial Sales Director and Rights; email m.pedersen@elsevier.com

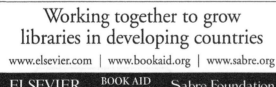

Working together to grow
libraries in developing countries

www.elsevier.com | www.bookaid.org | www.sabre.org

ELSEVIER   BOOK AID International   Sabre Foundation

For information on all Syngress publications visit our Web site at www.syngress.com

Acknowledgments

The authors acknowledge Pomeroy IT Solutions and CDW for supplying the hardware used in the writing of this book, and Andrew Page of Microsoft for providing technical validation of the Microsoft Virtualization products.

Contents

About the Authors

Thomas Olzak is an IT professional with over 26 years of experience in programming, network engineering, and security. He has an MBA and is a CISSP. He is currently the director of information security at HCR ManorCare, an Ohio-based leading provider of short- and long-term medical and rehabilitation care with more than 500 locations in 32 states. At HCR ManorCare, he is responsible for managing the corporate security program, change management, and business continuity planning. He is also the CEO of a security training company. Prior to his current job, he held positions as a network and server engineer, director of infrastructure engineering, director of technical operations, and programming manager at a variety of manufacturing and distribution companies. Before joining the private sector, he served 10 years in the United States Army Military Police with 4 years as a military police investigator. He has written a book, *Just Enough Security*, and various papers on security management.

Jason Boomer is a senior network engineer with HCR ManorCare. He currently provides senior-level strategic and technical support for all Microsoft Server and Client devices in the HCR ManorCare enterprise. His specialties include server- and client-side automation solutions; Active Directory design, implementation, and support; application packaging and deployment; and operating system deployment automation. Jason's background includes positions as senior technical consultant for Pomeroy IT Solutions, as a senior system administrator for La-Z-Boy Incorporate, as a senior systems engineer for Sequoia, and as a senior systems engineer at InaCom.

Robert M. Keefer (MCSA + Messaging, MCSE Windows Server 2003, Security+, C|EH) is a security analyst for HCR ManorCare. He currently works to maintain and improve the security stance of the company by identifying and investigating issues, reviewing and recommending new products, and monitoring systems for policy violations as well as performing risk assessments and penetration tests. His specialities are in vulnerability assessment and ethical hacking. Robert's background includes positions in IS management and as a senior network engineer for a systems integrator in Ann Arbor, MI. He currently resides in southeast Michigan.

James Sabovik is the manager of production operations at HCR ManorCare, where he has also served as the manager of network engineering and database administration. He is an IT veteran with more than 15 years of experience, including designing, deploying, and maintaining such things as Active Directory, Exchange, and server and network infrastructures. In addition, he has managed teams of engineers responsible for more than 600 servers, both physical and virtual, and 15,000 client devices spread out across the majority of the United States.

James holds a bachelor's degree in computer and information science from Ohio State University's College of Engineering.

TECHNICAL EDITOR

Kenneth Majors (MCSE, MCITP, ITIL v3, Project+, VMware VCP, Citrix CCEA, CCA) is a vice president of systems architecture for Choice Solutions LLC, a systems integrator headquartered in Overland Park, KS. Choice Solutions provides IT design, project management, and support for enterprise computing systems. He is a key contributor to defining best practices for Microsoft technologies, including Windows Server, Hyper-V, and Systems Center; Citrix XenApp, XenServer, and XenDesktop; VMware vSphere and View; and development of documentation standards. He develops technology solutions and methodologies focused on improving client business processes. These technology solutions touch every part of a system's life cycle—from assessment, blueprint, construct, and deployment on projects to operational management and strategic planning for the business process.

Kenneth holds a bachelor's degree from Colorado Technical University. He currently resides in Olathe, KS, with his loving and supportive wife, Sandy, and near their daughter, Tabitha, and their grandsons, Wesley ("Peanut") and Austin. Their son, Keith, is currently on active duty with the US Navy.

Introduction

The intention of this book is to provide a thorough reference for those considering a migration into the virtualized world. The majority of our target readers will likely be seasoned system administrators and engineers who grew up in and still manage primarily a hardware-based server environment containing a large assortment of both newer and legacy applications. As much as we attempt to outline the granularities of Microsoft virtualization as a whole, done properly, the combinations and possibilities are truly endless. The IS world is nearing, and in some cases, has already passed the point of no return when it comes to large-scale virtualization implementations. Virtualization has evolved from something fun for ultra-geeks to play with in their spare time, to a solid development tool widely used by everybody from high-school students to goliath software development companies. The inevitable result of this evolution is a new way of looking at enterprise management, for not only the datacenter but also all of the components used by IS to provide the solutions required by the business it supports. The stigma once placed on the use of virtualization by industry leaders is diminishing, and rightly so.

We stress throughout the book the importance of proper research and documentation. These are two terms common to the IS world, but rarely used properly. Failure to fully research, understand, and document your virtualization strategy can easily turn what should be an enjoyable and very successful transformation into a nightmare for all involved.

We cover the broad spectrum of Microsoft virtualization in a way that will help the IS professional begin using virtualization in both theory and practice. Whether you are just beginning your IS career, or you are a seasoned professional, we hope you find this book useful in not only understanding the technology itself but also in learning how to best prepare to use the technology in everything from a small home-based test lab to a large enterprise production environment.

We knew from the beginning that this book would be written to target our fellow IS peers. The majority of the topics in this book focus on the use of virtualization in day-to-day operations of an enterprise-level IS organization. We do not sell Microsoft virtualization as the silver bullet to cure all of your IS problems; however, we do feel that the proper use of its collective technologies can help to alleviate a high amount of inadequacies that plague a large number of data centers today. From the small family-owned businesses to the largest of mega corporations, there is an aspect of virtualization that can help you to become a more successful IS professional. Whether it be something as simple as using Disk2VHD to create a backup of an office computer for use in the event of an unforeseen disaster, or something as complex as the full implementation of Microsoft System Center as the framework for managing thousands of servers, there are benefits to researching the use of virtualization in your environment.

The true benefits of virtualization are often underappreciated, and in some cases, not obvious at all to anybody outside of the technical professional who implements and manages it. This can make the adoption of virtualization a hard sell to those responsible for managing costs. We discuss this topic at length in an effort to provide some tools that the IS professional can use to promote the implementation of virtualization through the benefit of increased efficiency and life cycle cost savings.

Using this book as a reference, you can begin your dive into the world of virtualization and start to understand the benefits that it may provide for your environment. The book will provide you the tools and explanations needed to allow you to create a fresh virtualization environment. We will walk you through step-by-step instructions on everything from building a Windows 2008 server to installing and configuring Hyper-V and App-V.

We provide examples of how to publish applications in various configurations, as well as detailed explanations on how to migrate existing servers into the virtual world, but we will not be able to show you how to configure your environment. Every virtualization environment will be different. A properly built virtualization strategy must take into account everything from the way you configure and manage your servers to how your company does business. Be wary of anybody who promises a shrink-wrapped, plug-and-play virtualization design for your company; you must embrace the process of moving into the virtual world, and you must be prepared to dig in and ask the questions that others may be afraid to ask or simply not know whom to ask. Virtualization technology is truly awe inspiring, which is likely one of its own biggest enemies. Before virtualization became a mainstream technology, it was much easier for managers and others responsible for budgets to understand the cost of a data center, but the days of easily comparing the number of physical servers with the number of applications or users is quickly becoming a thing of the past. As this evolution continues, you will begin to see budget decision makers become more and more dependent on their IS staff to provide reliable information. Be thorough and concise, and understand that others will not likely be able to comprehend the true nature of a virtualized environment as you will.

Here is a quick outline of each chapter.

- *Chapter 1: Introduction to Virtualization*—In this chapter, we discuss the basics of virtualization that every IS professional and their management should understand before jumping in head first. We talk about the role of virtualization in the changing landscape of the traditional data center and its benefits.
- *Chapter 2: Understanding Microsoft Virtualization Strategies*—In this chapter, we discuss the strategies of virtualization, and how to begin your approach. We talk about changing the data center from its traditional cost center to a true asset. We touch on the definitions common to any virtualization discussion and explain how virtualization extends far beyond the walls of the data center.
- *Chapter 3: Installing Windows 2008 Server Core and Hyper-V*—In this chapter, we cover the step-by-step process used to build a Windows 2008 server, whether you choose the traditional GUI method or the newer command line (GUI-less) "core-install." With the

operating system installed, we explain the steps taken to install Hyper-V and get it ready for use.

- *Chapter 4: Managing Hyper-V*—In this chapter, we dive into the process of configuring and managing a Hyper-V infrastructure. We examine the various tools included in Hyper-V and how they can benefit you. We cover the configuration and use of virtual networks, and why you would want to configure them in different modes. And we discuss the different disk modes available in Hyper-V.

- *Chapter 5: Installing and configuring Virtual Machine Manager 2008*—In this chapter, we talk about Virtual Machine Manager (VMM) and all of the underrated functionality it provides. We discuss proper VMM library structure and Hyper-V consoles that can be installed and used on nonserver operating systems.

- *Chapter 6: Hyper-V and High Availability*—In this chapter, we discuss one of the most highly discussed topics associated with the use of virtualization—Microsoft's approach to high availability and how the proper combination of Microsoft tools can be put together in order to provide a very reliable and highly available virtualization infrastructure.

- *Chapter 7: Creating Virtual Machines and Templates*—In this chapter, we explain virtual machines and how to best create them. We discuss the importance of proper planning specific to this functionality, and why you will want to be especially careful when creating virtual machines and templates.

- *Chapter 8: Performing Physical-to-Virtual and Virtual-to-Virtual Migrations*—In this chapter, we discuss the most referenced and talked about function of virtualization; namely, the migration of physical servers to virtual servers. We talk about the best practices, the importance of vendor support, and how to prepare for the migration itself.

- *Chapter 9: Securing, Monitoring, and Managing a Virtual Infrastructure*—In this chapter, we discuss the methods you will want to understand in securing and managing your Hyper-V environment. We cover the varying opinions regarding the need for security within the Hyper-V environment, and how you should approach researching and applying this security in your data center.

- *Chapter 10: Creating a Dynamic Data Center with Microsoft System Center*—In this chapter, we discuss the "Dynamic Data Center" concept and how you can get there using the Microsoft System Center suite of tools and concepts. We revisit the importance of proper planning and research and discuss how virtualization for the sake of virtualizing is a bad idea.

- *Chapter 11: Application Virtualization*—In this chapter, we go into granular detail of setting up an application virtualization platform. From the step-by-step build of the server itself, to understanding the prerequisites of your App-V farm.

- *Chapter 12: Deploying App-V Packages*—In this chapter, we demonstrate the ease of creating and publishing a virtual application within App-V. We talk about the different options available when publishing an application and how the different options might apply to different scenarios.

- *Chapter 13: Presentation Virtualization (Terminal Services)*—In this chapter, we discuss the highly renovated Microsoft Terminal Services and how this newer generation can provide more efficient traditional use, as well as new functionality that may have otherwise gone unnoticed. We discuss the Terminal Services "role" in detail and provide some insight into how it may help you with managing your data center.

■ *Chapter 14: Integrating Application and Presentation Virtualization*—In this chapter, we discuss the new RemoteApp function available within the latest generation of Terminal Services. We talk about how RemoteApp can be used in association with Web Access to provide access to applications across the Internet.

■ *Chapter 15: Desktop Virtualization*—In this chapter, we conclude the book with a discussion of desktop virtualization and all of the potential it provides for a much more streamlined and efficient enterprise landscape of tomorrow. We explain how the technology, although complex, is relatively easy to implement today, and why you should consider it.

That is our book in a nutshell. We hope you enjoy reading and using it as much as we enjoyed researching and writing it. Remember that proper research and documentation are not just the key to a successful virtualization implementation, but key to the success of any job. Implementing and using virtualization are as dynamic as the technology itself, and virtualization is a world that truly defines the phrase "it's only as successful and complex as you choose to make it." As the use of virtualization becomes easier for the end user, it will undoubtedly become more complex for those who support it, so research the technology regularly and always verify with peers and vendors that the approach you followed yesterday is still the right approach to take today.

Chapter

1

What is virtualization?

CHAPTER OUTLINE

This chapter is not intended to expose you to the tedium of a step-by-step exploration of virtualization. We assume anyone picking up this book already understands the value of this emerging technology. Instead, we provide a quick overview of virtualized servers and end-user devices. We also provide information useful for making a business case for shifting IT budget dollars in that direction. Finally, we provide you with a list of things to consider during virtualization strategy discussions.

The chapter is short, to the point, and only introduces a short delay before we jump into the reason you bought this book—implementation of Microsoft virtualization technology.

EVOLUTION OF VIRTUALIZATION

In the 1970s, mainframes ruled the datacenter. Partitioning ensured both optimum use and efficient sharing of resources. This was a great way to get the most for the many, many dollars organizations spent to acquire, implement, and manage these behemoths.

All processing was performed on a single computer with data retrieved from and stored to storage located in the datacenter. Access to the datacenter was tightly controlled. In many cases, users received reports from the computer operators through a window or slot. They accessed electronic information with dumb terminals with no local processing capabilities. The terminals were simple devices which collected keystrokes and presented data in green-screen text.

Distributed processing began in the 1980s, with personal computers finding their way to the desktop. These were fat clients which participated in client/server configurations and connected to the mainframe's smaller cousin, the minicomputer. Although many companies still performed the bulk of their business processing in a centralized environment, both applications and data began to drift out to endpoint devices.

During the 1990s, another shift in business processing architecture took place with the advent of layered system technology. This included building applications with presentation and data access logic layers. Data resided in database servers in the datacenter. Still, fat client endpoint devices continued to run applications, and more data than ever before found its way to local hard drives. This was also a time when malware writers began perfecting their art. Attacks that eventually spread across entire enterprises often started on an unprotected—or weakly protected—personal computer.

In the twenty-first century, IT managers began to realize that traditional methods of managing desktop and laptop systems were no longer effective in dealing with changes in business requirements, user demands regarding technology implementations, and black hat hackers transitioning from fun and games to an organized crime business model. Demands for the rapid turnaround of application installation or upgrade requests, the need to quickly apply security patches to operating systems and applications, and many other management headaches are driving a new approach to endpoint and server processing and management—virtualization. Figure 1.1 shows a timeline for the development of virtualization technology.

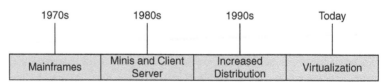

■ **FIGURE 1.1** Evolution of virtualization timeline.

VIRTUALIZATION DEFINED

As with all emerging technologies, there are several definitions or perceptions of what constitutes virtualization. To remove ambiguity, it is important to understand what virtualization means within the context of this book. Let us start with the definition provided by Amit Singh, author of kernelthread.com, in "An Introduction to Virtualization":

Virtualization is a framework or methodology of dividing the resources of a computer into multiple execution environments, by applying one or more concepts or technologies such as hardware and software partitioning, time-sharing, partial or complete machine simulation, emulation, quality of service, and many others [1].

This is an accurate definition, but it fails to consider business drivers. It should be more specific about expected outcomes. Integrating outcomes, we arrived at the following:

Virtualization is the configuration of servers or clients which results in the division of resources into multiple, isolated execution environments, by applying one or more concepts or technologies to reduce costs and enhance flexibility associated with the acquisition, implementation, management, expansion, and recovery of critical business systems.

Our definition takes virtualization beyond the realm of "cool technology" and places it where you can make a case for allocating IT budget. Virtualization, if properly planned and positioned, can quickly demonstrate return on investment (ROI) while improving your ability to agilely react to new solution requests from business managers.

HOW VIRTUALIZATION WORKS

How our definition is implemented depends on a vendor's view of the world. As you might expect—since this is a book on how to implement Microsoft's virtualization solutions—we move virtualization from concept to reality using Microsoft's virtualization toolbox. In this chapter, we provide a high-level overview. In Chapter 2, we examine Microsoft's complete virtualization strategy.

The Microsoft virtualization toolbox contains solutions for both server (Hyper-V) and client (App-V and Virtual PC/MED-V) platforms. Each solution is implemented in a way that closely aligns with the virtualization business and technology drivers reviewed later in this chapter. We focus on App-V in this chapter, because it appears to be Microsoft's preferred method of virtual application delivery. Chapter 15 is dedicated to Virtual PC and MED-V.

Server virtualization

Figure 1.2 is a simple depiction of how to get the most from your server hardware with Hyper-V. Building a Hyper-V virtual environment begins with a hardware platform designed for Windows compatibility. It must be capable of 64-bit operation and be virtual technology enabled. Installed on top of the hardware layer, and abstracting it from future virtual machines (VMs), is the hypervisor.

The hypervisor "decouples" hardware from the production operating systems running in the VMs. Configured and managed via the parent VM, it oversees hardware resources by

- Supporting the creation and deletion of VMs
- Managing memory access and security rules

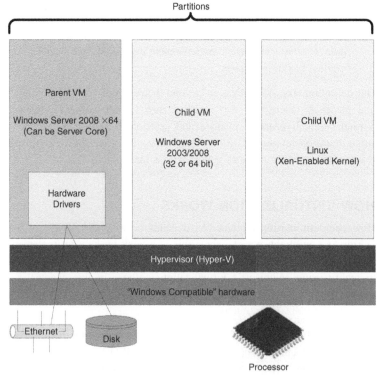

■ **FIGURE 1.2** Hyper-V concepts.

- Enforcing CPU usage policy
- Scheduling and managing processor usage
- Managing attached/installed device ownership

VMs in a Hyper-V world live in partitions. The first partition created contains the parent VM, which must run Windows Server 2008 ×64 or Windows Server Core. Once the parent partition is in production, you can create child partitions which contain your business server environments.

Note
All partitions share the following characteristics:
- Each partition is configured with one or more *virtual* processors
- Each partition participates in hardware resource sharing
- Each partition hosts software known as a *guest*

Client virtualization

Microsoft's approach to client virtualization focuses on efficient, controlled, and safe distribution of applications from a central point. Based on technology acquired during Microsoft's purchase of SoftGrid, App-V technology has evolved into a powerful solution for organizations of any size.

Before going into how App-V works, we think it is important to understand how Microsoft's approach to application virtualization compares to other solutions. Figure 1.3 shows three primary methods used today.

Instead of permanently installing applications on users' endpoint devices, they are installed in virtualized server environments, on blade servers (with each blade corresponding to a single desktop device), or by using thin clients which access terminal services. These are fundamentally examples of server-based computing, which still leaves a significant amount of computing resources unused on enterprise desktops.

Note
In Windows Server 2008 R2, Microsoft has renamed Terminal Services. It is now called Remote Desktop Services (RDS). The terms terminal services and RDS are used interchangeably throughout this book.

Microsoft also supports desktop virtualization. See Chapters 2 and 15 for the "what and how."

Figure 1.4 depicts a basic Microsoft App-V-enabled desktop. Each application runs in an isolated environment. Although the applications share OS services and hardware resources, components unique to each application (e.g., registry entries, dynamic link libraries, COM objects, etc.) are private—running within the application "sandbox." App-V does not virtualize the OS, just the applications.

The second piece of an App-V solution for endpoint availability and security management is centralized distribution and management of applications. There are two ways to do this. First, entire applications can be downloaded to virtualized runtime environments. Second, only those components necessary for initial load and execution of the virtualized

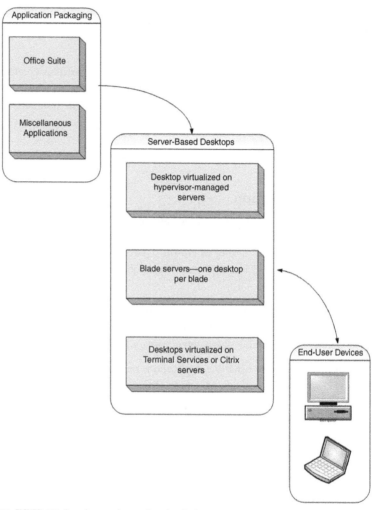

■ **FIGURE 1.3** General approaches to client virtualization.

applications are downloaded. App-V supports both methods and downloads additional application components as needed.

Hyper-V, App-V, Virtual PC/MED-V, and RDS are the basic building blocks of Microsoft virtualization. In subsequent chapters, we drill deep into how they work and explore optional implementation strategies.

Tip
Do not virtualize because it is cool or just because you can. You are more likely to get management support—and budget—if you can clearly state why and how virtualization will benefit the business.

BUILDING A BUSINESS CASE FOR VIRTUALIZATION

Transitioning from a traditional computing environment to one based on strategic use of virtualization is not free. New servers are usually required to support multiple VMs or to implement, manage, or monitor App-V

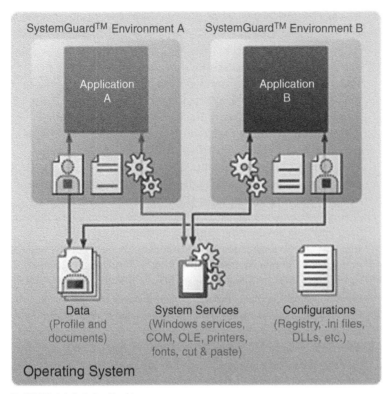

SystemGuard™ Environment A   SystemGuard™ Environment B

Application A

Application B

Data
(Profile and documents)

System Services
(Windows services, COM, OLE, printers, fonts, cut & paste)

Configurations
(Registry, .ini files, DLLs, etc.)

Operating System

■ **FIGURE 1.4** Basic App-V architecture.

rollouts. And let us not forget training for IT staff. So why should management shift dollars from other projects to fund virtualization?

Virtualization provides a long list of benefits to the business, including:

- *Consolidation of workload to fewer machines.* Server consolidation is usually one of the first benefits listed when IT begins to discuss virtualization. Although a definite benefit, you will probably only virtualize a subset of your datacenter—for reasons which will become obvious—resulting in limited ROI.
- *Optimized hardware use.* Most servers are underutilized. Placing multiple VMs on expensive server hardware drives processor, memory, disk, and other resources closer to recommended utilization thresholds. For example, instead of an application server using only 5-10% of its processing capability, multiple application servers on the same platform can drive average processors upto 40% or 50%. This is much better use of invested hardware dollars.

- *Running legacy applications on new hardware.* Any organization which has been around a few years has old applications it can not live without. Rather, it has applications its users must have or civilization as we know it will collapse. As the software stands fast, and hardware and operating systems evolve, you might find it difficult or impossible to run legacy applications on replacement platforms. Server and client virtualization provide opportunities to continue to run older environments on hardware with which they are incompatible. This is possible due to the abstraction of operating environments from the underlying hardware components.
- *Isolated operating environments.* Have you ever needed to run two versions of an application at the same time on the same device? If so, isolated environments are a great way to facilitate this. Further, each operating environment can have its own registry entries, code libraries, etc. So application incompatibilities are rare. Finally, failures or corruption in one environment will not affect other applications or data. Isolated environment capabilities in App-V can sometimes be a bigger selling point than server consolidation.
- *Running multiple operating systems simultaneously.* You do not have to make the leap to Linux to have the need to run multiple server operating systems. Most organizations do not upgrade all servers to the latest version of Windows Server at the same time. So there are often various versions in the datacenter, running critical applications. Hyper-V partitioning allows you to consolidate servers running operating systems at various version or patch levels, without the risk of incompatibilities. If you are gradually introducing other operating systems into the datacenter, they can all happily coexist with current operating systems—in "sibling" partitions on the same hardware platform.
- *Ease of software migration.* Application streaming, coupled with isolated operating environments, makes end-user application deployment much easier. Using Hyper-V, new application rollouts or upgrades to existing applications are easy and centrally managed.
- *Quick buildup and tear-down of test environments.* Testing is a big part of any internal development process, but rapid test environment builds are difficult to achieve. With virtualization, engineers create virtual image files which are quickly deployed when relevant system testing is required. Image files are also a great way to refresh a test environment when changes do not quite work as expected.

We believe this list represents the major reasons why an organization would want to move to virtualization, except for one. The final reason, improved business continuity, is so important we decided to give it special attention.

Virtualization and business continuity

Business continuity is an important consideration in system design, including both system failures and datacenter destruction scenarios—and everything in between. Traditional system recovery documentation provides instructions for rebuilding a system using the hardware which is no longer accessible or operational. The problem is that there are usually no guarantees your disaster recovery or hardware vendors will be able to duplicate the original hardware.

Using different hardware can result in extended rebuild times as you struggle to understand why your applications do not function. Even if you can get the same hardware, you need to rebuild the environment from the ground up.

Finally, interruptions in business processes occasionally happen when systems are brought down for maintenance. You understand the necessity, but your users seldom do.

Virtualization provides advantages over traditional recovery methods, including:

- *Breaking hardware dependency.* Since the hypervisor provides an abstraction layer between the operating environment and the underlying hardware, you do not need to duplicate failed hardware to restore critical processes.
- *Increased server portability.* If you create virtual images of your critical system servers, it does not matter what hardware you use to recover from a failure—as long as the recovery server supports your hypervisor and, if necessary, the load of multiple child partitions. Enhanced portability extends to recovering critical systems at your recovery test site, using whatever hypervisor-compatible hardware is available.
- *Elimination of sever downtime (almost).* You may never reach the point at which maintenance downtime is eliminated, but virtualization can get you very, very close. Because of increased server portability, you can shift critical virtual servers to other devices while you perform maintenance on the production hardware. You can also patch or upgrade one partition without affecting other partitions. One way to accomplish this is via clustering, failing over from one VM to another in the same cluster. From the client perspective, there is no interruption in service—even during business hours.
- *Quick recovery of end-user devices.* When a datacenter goes, the offices in the same building often go as well. Further, satellite facilities

can suffer catastrophic events requiring a complete infrastructure rebuild. The ability to deliver desktop operating environments via a centrally managed virtualization solution can significantly reduce recovery time.

It might seem that virtualization is an IT panacea. It is true that it can solve many problems, but it also introduces new challenges.

THE OTHER SIDE OF VIRTUALIZATION

Any new technology brings with it changes to the process. Virtualization is no exception. Although there are challenges, they are usually outweighed by the benefits—assuming you understand and address them up front. The following is a list of common issues which must be considered when developing a virtualization strategy.

- *License management.* It is somewhat easy to track operating system and application licenses in a traditional datacenter or across user desktops. However, licensing in a virtualized world is different and often confusing. Make sure you understand how your vendors license virtual instances of their products and ensure your engineers adhere to licensing policy. It is very easy to bring up VMs without thinking about license availability.
- *New skill sets.* Configuring, monitoring, and managing virtualized environments require skills not typically found in in-house resources. This is a challenge easily met with training and new hiring requirements.
- *Support from application vendors.* The big question? Will your application vendor support its software within your selected virtual environment? Does the application even run virtualized? Does the vendor know or care?
- *Additional complexity.* It should not be a surprise that virtualization adds another layer of complexity to your infrastructure.
- *Security.* Security on VMs is not very different from standard server security. However, the underlying layers (i.e., the hypervisor and related services) require special consideration, including adjustments to antivirus solutions. Apart from technology differences, the ease with which engineers can build VMs can result in explosive growth of unplanned, unmonitored, and insecure servers. Make sure your change management process is adjusted, policies updated, and staff trained on what is and is not acceptable behavior.

- *Image proliferation.* This might not be a bad thing unless the images you keep on the virtual shelf are rife with weak configurations or other challenges you might not want spreading like a disease across your datacenter.
- *Ineffectiveness of existing management and monitoring tools.* As we hinted in the security bullet, your tried and true monitoring and management tools might not include the intricacies of virtualization management.
- *Inability of the LAN/WAN infrastructure to support consolidated servers.* What happens to your switch when you replace several single traditional servers with one or more beefy hardware platforms running multiple VMs? If you can not answer this or other similar questions, you are not quite ready to make the leap to virtualization.

And these are just the thought-provoking issues we could come with. You may have your own set, which reflect the unique way you do business.

FINALLY, DROP THE HAMMER

I am sure you have heard the adage, "If the only tool you have is a hammer, every problem looks like a nail." This is a very wise statement, and fits very well what some organizations try to do with server virtualization. After you address the list of potential "gotchas," you still have one very important question to answer as you evaluate each server. Does it make sense to virtualize this environment?

For example, a server with average process utilization of 50% or more is probably not a good candidate for virtualization. However, two or more servers, each with less than 10% processor capacity used, are excellent candidates. In addition to processor capacity, pay attention to NIC (network interface card), disk, and memory utilization. A VM running a specific application will use the same resources as a stand-alone server. Do not consolidate servers when performance hits far outweigh budget savings. Figure 1.5 shows a sample worksheet for evaluating virtualization candidates.

Tip
The total processing power required in a virtualized hardware platform is roughly equal to the sum of the processing resources used by the target applications on the nonvirtualized servers.

Server	Component	Current	Supported by Hyper-V
Domain Controller	CPU	20% use of single 2 GHz processor	Depends on host hardware
	Memory	2 GB	Yes
	Disk space	20 GB	Yes
	NIC	5% use of single gigabit Ethernet	Yes
	OS	Windows Server 2008	Yes

■ **FIGURE 1.5** Virtualization worksheet.

As a general rule, you should leave database servers until last. It is usually a bad idea to virtualize database environments unless they contain little-used tables. Your biggest gains when developing your strategy will likely result from considering the following:

- Application servers
- File servers
- Print servers
- Domain controllers
- Web servers
- Testing servers
- Development servers
- Business recovery environments

Virtualization planning documents are available from Microsoft, for both servers and end-user devices, at http://tinyurl.com/Microsoft-IPD. We refer to these resources throughout the design and setup chapters.

SUMMARY

Virtualization was an inevitable result of the increasing capability of datacenter technology and the continuing pressure to reduce technology costs; hardware use is optimized, recovery times are reduced, and IS is able to react quickly to changing business-user demands. However, virtualization is not an answer for every system in your datacenter.

Not every application behaves well—and not every vendor for that matter—in a virtualized environment. A careful analysis of current hardware utilization, application constraints, and vendor support is a critical first step, even before you put together your business case for virtualization. It is difficult to understand business value when you do not understand how many of your applications are candidates for aggregation. Once you have this information, you can begin working to get virtualization technology into your IS budget.

Finally, virtualization is not a panacea. It introduces new challenges which you must consider in order to adapt security and operational monitoring and controls.

REFERENCE

[1] Singh A. An introduction to virtualization, kernelthread.com; 2004 [cited January 2010]. Available from www.kernelthread.com/publications/virtualization/.

Chapter 2

Understanding Microsoft virtualization strategies

An easy to manage virtualization environment uses a single solution set to create, manage, and deploy images and applications. This is Microsoft's objective:

> *Our goal is to help customers make IT systems more self-managing and dynamic so that they can gain more control of their IT systems, and enable their businesses to respond faster and stay ahead of the competition. We're doing this by:*

- Providing a complete set of virtualization products that span from the desktop to the datacenter
- Helping manage all IT assets—both physical and virtual—from a single platform [1]

Note

Virtualization should move IT from a cost center to a business enabler and provider of significant business value.

Microsoft's stated goals are not hype, considering the array of products available from the software maker. Based on Gartner's Infrastructure Maturity Model, MIT's Architecture Security Model, industry best practices, and its experience with customers, Microsoft has developed a collection of virtualization products that support an incremental IT maturity model. The intent is to move IT beyond a cost center to a provider of significant business value.

In this chapter, we describe each of the products in Microsoft's virtualization toolkit and how each fits into the company's overall dynamic datacenter and desktop strategy. In the following chapters, we demonstrate how to implement them while avoiding common pitfalls.

MICROSOFT'S IT MATURITY MODEL

Microsoft's maturity model consists of four levels: Basic, Standardized, Rationalized, and Dynamic. Each level above Basic steps IT closer to the role of strategic asset.

- *Basic*—This is a fire-fighting mode. Most organizations find themselves at this level, with IT agility and cost containment constrained by complete reliance on manual, uncoordinated implementation and management of resources.
- *Standardized*—IT managers, realizing the futility of using manual processes to dislodge IT from its traditional role of electronic data processing, begin to automate critical processes to enable the business to compete more effectively. They also implement enterprise monitoring and management tools.
- *Rationalized*—Technology begins to remove itself as a business constraint. Instead, IT is able to quickly react to changes in strategic or operational business requirements. IT teams no longer struggle to stay ahead of the changing business environment. In fact, they actually begin to drive business process improvements.
- *Dynamic*—The final stage in Microsoft's model is IT's arrival as a strategic asset. No longer perceived as a hole into which management dumps budget, it is seen by business units as a partner in the development and maintenance of competitive advantage.

Figure 2.1 depicts the model, adding two additional elements. The first is our addition of "Continuous Improvement." Arriving at the final maturity

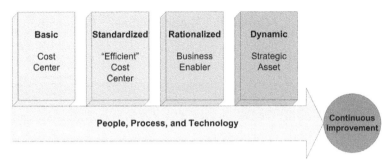

■ **FIGURE 2.1** Microsoft's IT maturity model (modified).

level should never result in a sense of completion, secure in the knowledge that we have "arrived," while the business moves forward and our position as a strategic asset rests on an increasingly unstable foundation. There is always room to improve, with new opportunities and challenges arising every day.

Tip
Achieving the highest maturity level is not the end. There is always more work to do.

The second is the triumvirate comprising the foundation upon which an organization drives IT improvements: people, process, and technology. It is not enough to throw virtualization and additional management tools at a struggling IT environment. People must be convinced of the need for change. Maturing an IT organization requires more than intent. It also requires changes in IT culture.

Processes are often documented and never reviewed again, even if they are followed religiously. Managers and staff should regularly assess each process by asking the following questions:

1. Is every task in the process necessary? Are we doing things because of reasons we can no longer remember?
2. Are we doing enough to meet customer or stakeholder expectations?
3. Are we doing more than expected, incurring unnecessary costs?
4. Can someone else do it cheaper or with better outcomes?

The final element is technology. One of the building blocks of a dynamic IT organization is the proper use of virtualization. To help organizations move along the maturity continuum, Microsoft provides virtualization across all components of the IT infrastructure, as shown in Figure 2.2. Using these tools helps arrive at a dynamic datacenter with centralized, optimized desktop management.

■ **FIGURE 2.2** Microsoft virtualization components.

BUILDING A DYNAMIC DATACENTER

Evolution of IT to a strategic asset is impossible unless your datacenter is configured and managed to react quickly to changing business needs. In addition to agility, the cost of maintaining a mature datacenter should fall well below that associated with traditional datacenter infrastructures. Finally, the dynamic datacenter must minimize business impact when critical systems fail. Server virtualization plays an important role in reaching these objectives by providing the following:

Note
Virtualization plays a major role in achieving a dynamic datacenter.

- Increasing utilization of server processing, memory, input-output (I/O), and storage resources
- Decreasing server sprawl by aggregating applications on fewer hardware platforms
- Improving IT service levels by enabling quick deployment of new servers and operating systems while providing the means to recover failed systems well within maximum downtime constraints
- Supporting legacy systems by allowing older software solutions to run on newer hardware platforms
- Streamlining management and security
- Reducing challenges associated with application compatibility, hardware or other applications
- Improving time to recovery during business continuity events

Virtualization layers in a dynamic datacenter

Microsoft's vision of a virtualized datacenter consists of three layers above the physical layer, as shown in Figure 2.3. Positioned immediately above the hardware layer is Hyper-V, abstracting hardware resources from future VMs. Above Hyper-V is the application layer in which virtualization-capable operating systems and applications come together to form a collection of VMs. The Model layer comes last, providing the

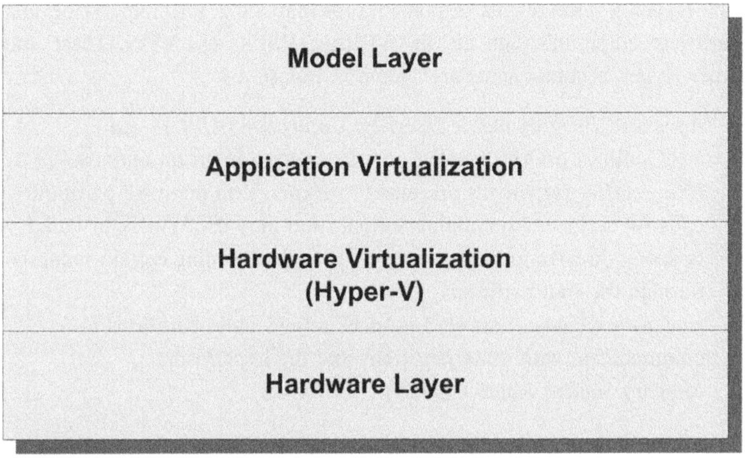

Model Layer
Application Virtualization
Hardware Virtualization (Hyper-V)
Hardware Layer

■ **FIGURE 2.3** Layers of a dynamic datacenter.

tools and processes necessary to bring together the other three layers, configure them in a standard way, and create a cohesive processing environment. Tools used in the Model layer include System Center Operations Manager (SCOM), System Center Virtual Machine Manager, System Center Configuration Manager (SCCM), and Visual Studio development tools.

Hardware virtualization layer

The hardware virtualization layer is created by installing Microsoft Hyper-V on one or more compatible hardware platforms. Hyper-V, Microsoft's entry into the hypervisor market, is a very thin layer that presents a small attack surface. It can do this because Microsoft does not embed drivers. Instead, Hyper-V uses vendor-supplied drivers to manage VM hardware requests.

Warning
Hardware targeted for virtualization must support virtualization, as specified in Chapter 1.

Each VM exists within a partition, starting with the root partition. The root partition must run Windows 2008 Server ×64 or Windows 2008 Server Core ×64. Subsequent partitions, known as child partitions, usually communicate with the underlying hardware via the root partition. Some calls directly from a child partition to Hyper-V are possible using WinHv (defined below) if the OS running in the partition is "enlightened." An enlightened OS understands how to behave in a Hyper-V environment. Communication is limited for an unenlightened OS partition, and applications there tend to run much more slowly than those in an enlightened one. Performance issues are generally related to the requirement for emulation software to interface hosted services.

Note
Enlightened-capable operating systems include Windows Server 2003/2008, Windows Vista, Windows XP, and SUSE Enterprise Linux.

The Hyper-V components responsible for managing VM, hypervisor, and hardware communication are the VMBus, VSCs, and VSPs. These and other Hyper-V components are shown in Figure 2.4.

- *Advanced Programmable Interrupt Controller (APIC)*—An APIC allows priority levels to be assigned to interrupt outputs.
- *Hypercalls*—Hypercalls are made to Hyper-V to optimize partition calls for service. An enlightened partition may use WinHv or UnixHv to speak directly to the hypervisor instead of routing certain requests through the root partition.
- *Integration Component (IC)*—An IC allows child partitions to communicate with other partitions and the hypervisor.
- *Memory Service Routine (MSR)*

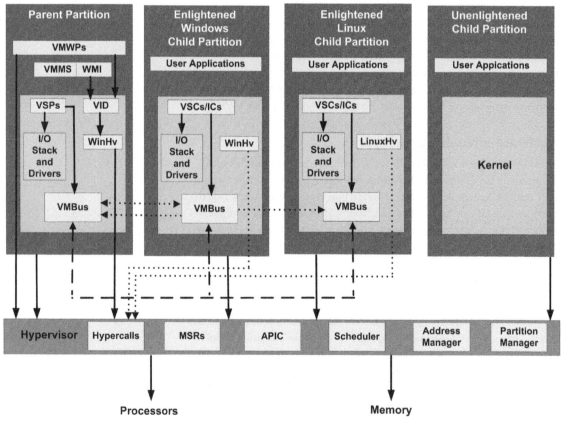

■ **FIGURE 2.4** Hyper-V components.

- *Virtualization Infrastructure Driver (VID)*—The VSD provides partition management services, virtual processor management services, and memory management services.
- *VMBus*—The VMBus is a channel-based communication mechanism. It enables interpartition communication and device enumeration. It is included in and installed with Hyper-V Integration Services.
- *Virtual Machine Management Service (VMMS)*—The VMMS is responsible for managing VM state associated with all child partitions. A separate instance exists for each VM.
- *Virtual Machine Worker Process (VMWP)*—The VMWP is a user-mode component of the virtualization stack. It enables VMMSs for the root partition so it can manage VMs in the child partitions.
- *Virtualization Service Client (VSC)*—The VSC is a synthetic device instance residing in a child partition. It uses hardware resources provided by VSPs. A VSC and VSP communicate via the VMBus.
- *Virtualization Service Provider (VSP)*—The VSPs reside in the root partition. They work with VSCs to provide device support to child partitions over the VMBus.
- *Windows Hypervisor Interface Library (WinHv)*—The WinHv is a bridge between a hosted operating system's drivers and the hypervisor. It allows drivers to call the hypervisor using standard Windows calling conventions when an enlightened environment is running within the partition.
- *Windows Management Instrumentation (WMI)*—The WMI exposes a set of APIs for managing virtual machines.

Note
Hyper-V relies primarily on vendor-supplied drivers to communicate with the underlying hardware.

Application virtualization layer

The application layer consists of operating systems and business applications that run in Hyper-V partitions. Again, not all software behaves well in a virtualized environment. However, Microsoft puts candidate applications and operating systems through a certification process. Applications that pass are listed at www.windowsservercatalog.com.

Note
Key resources to implement and manage the application layer include:
- System Center Virtual Machine Manager
- System Center Operations Manager
- System Center Data Protection Manager

System Center Virtual Machine Manager

Once you select the right applications, you have to manage them. The traditional method of sliding an installation CD into the server's CD/DVD drive is not a good practice for a virtualized environment. To take full advantage of the fast server build and process migration capabilities inherent in

Microsoft's virtualization strategy, you need to manage your VMs and hardware resources from a central console. Out-of-the-box management of your VM environment is possible with server manager. However, as the sophistication of your virtualization environment increases, management becomes more challenging. Managing more complex VM and host environments is the role of System Center Virtual Machine Manager (VMM).

Figure 2.5 shows a simple VMM configuration. All components of VMM communicate with each other and with host systems via the VMM Server. The VMM Admin Console is an MMC snap-in that allows the performance of the following:

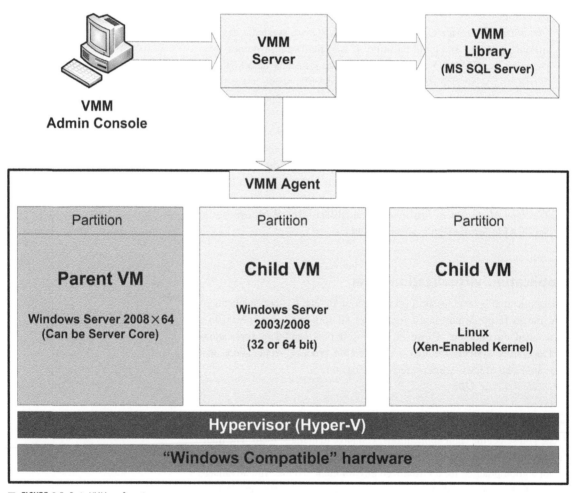

■ **FIGURE 2.5** Basic VMM configuration.

- Configuration of the VMM environment
- Creating, deleting, starting, and stopping VMs
- Conversion of physical servers to virtualized systems
- VM monitoring

The VMM Library contains the profiles used to create VMs, including templates, virtual disks, and CD/DVD ISO images. In addition to access by the VMM Server, the library is also accessed by the VMM Self-Service Portal (not shown in the diagram). The portal is used by IT staff to create and manage VMs using predefined profiles. Portal rights and permissions are configurable to control who can access and what they can do.

The VMM Agent resides on Hyper-V hosts. The VMM Server uses the agent to effect changes to the virtualization environment and to monitor its health.

Centralized management is not possible in a heterogeneous environment. For example, some datacenters might house both Microsoft and VMware VMs. To ensure a single management solution, Microsoft has designed VMM to support the following:

- MS Virtual Server
- Hyper-V
- VMware ESX

VMM also supports Powershell scripting. In fact, any operation you perform with VMM—including ESX operations—can be automated with Powershell scripts.

Other capabilities supported by VMM include:

- Analysis of which server is the best choice for a new VM
- Assessment of the impact of a workload migration
- Automation of workload migration
- Automation of VM cluster placement when high availability is specified

Finally, VMM integrates with SCOM.

System Center Operations Manager

SCOM allows the administrator to monitor physical and virtual environments from a single console, including:

- Overall performance
- Processor
- Memory
- I/O

Tip
Use the VMM Self-Service Portal to allow IT staff to create new VMs with predefined profiles.

Tip
You can use VMM to manage your VMware ESX instances.

Tip
All Virtual Machine Management operations can be automated using Powershell scripts.

System Center Data Protection Manager

Data Protection Manager (DPM) plays a key role in the dynamic datacenter by backing up critical systems. Using Microsoft Volume Shadow Copy (VSS), it is capable of performing block-level synchronization of VMs in as little as 2-3 min, with a repeat cycle as short as every 30 min. In addition to VMs, DPM also backs up nonvirtual machines.

To enable backups, a DPM agent is placed on each target device. The nature of the desired backup and restore determines where the agent is installed. Agent installation options include:

- *In the VM*—This allows backup of the virtual workload only. The administrator can restore the backups to the same VM or to another protected location.
- *On the virtual host*—Placing an agent on the virtual host enables backup of the VMs themselves, allowing an administrator to restore an entire VM if necessary.

CENTRALIZED, OPTIMIZED DESKTOP MANAGEMENT

Datacenters are often what we think of when someone mentions virtualization. However, servers lined neatly in racks with resource usage optimized do not provide all the value possible with a comprehensive virtualization strategy. In fact, datacenter issues can often seem small in the face of managing hundreds or thousands of end-user PCs. Challenges include:

- *Updating tracking*—As the number of applications increases across a growing number of end-user computers, many organizations cannot effectively determine which systems are up-to-date. This is a significant issue when the untracked updates are either security patches or mandatory changes to a critical business application.
- *Controlling help desk costs*—Unless a standard image is deployed to all PCs, the number of help desk calls can be huge. Even when standard configurations are used, the pressure to allow user-provided applications causes many companies to provide local administrator capabilities to laptops and desktops for installation and desktop configuration purposes. Conflicts between these changes and business critical applications can result in significant costs in both lost productivity and IT support.
- *Security patch cycles that seem to take forever*—When vendors release security updates, the length of the PC update cycle mirrors the organization's appetite for risk. Since most business managers are more concerned with business continuity issues than with "possible" security issues, cycle times can be rather long. And even when patching is approved, engineers face a time-consuming rollout—a rollout during which making sure every system is patched can be very difficult if not impossible.

■ *Application incompatibilities*—In addition to potential conflicts when patches or PC software are installed, new applications mandated by management can also cause havoc when new or replaced operating system components cause failures in existing applications. Examples include dynamic link libraries (DLLs), Java versions, ActiveX controls, and other shared components or services. Add to these challenges the possible changes to registry controls, and you have conditions for widespread business disruption.

■ *Spread of malware*—In today's business environment where every device is connected to every other device, malware infestations are often able to run rampant across enterprise networks. Further, eliminating malware from end-user devices often means reimaging or replacing them with freshly imaged systems.

■ *Data leaks*—Traditional fat client PC drives are often full of sensitive information. Local storage of information might be intentional or incidental to application execution. Intentional data storage results from users making a conscious decision to store information on their local disk. Incidental storage occurs when application information is cached locally to meet processing requirements. In both cases, information is liable to theft or loss.

■ *Controlling access to applications*—Once an application is installed on a user's computer, it can be all but impossible to remove access.

■ *Providing application/data access to mobile users*—The problem here goes beyond access, which can be provided by many solutions, such as SSL VPN. Rather, maintaining mobile device patches and application updates can be difficult.

Microsoft offers an impressive set of solutions or solution combinations to ease these burdens, including:

■ App-V
■ App-V for RDS
■ MED-V and Virtual PC

Table 2.1 shows how these products fit into an overall desktop virtualization strategy.

Table 2.1 Microsoft Desktop Virtualization Solutions

Solution	Product	Licensing
Application virtualization	App-V	Microsoft Desktop Optimization Pack
Desktop virtualization	Med-V	Microsoft Desktop Optimization Pack
Presentation virtualization	Windows Server Terminal Services	Terminal Services Client Access Licenses (CALs)

Application and presentation virtualization

App-V improves implementation of both application and presentation virtualization frameworks. Figure 2.6 shows a typical configuration. Note that the user delivery vehicle can be either the user's desktop or Terminal Services.

At a high level, the application to be virtualized is installed on the sequencer. The resulting virtualized application package is delivered to

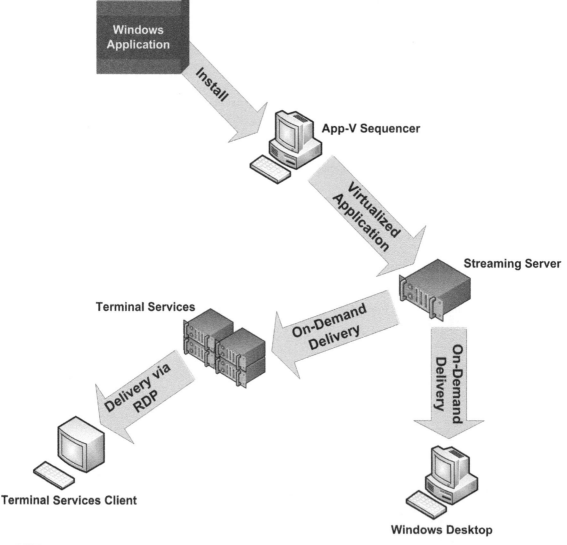

■ **FIGURE 2.6** App-V framework.

the streaming server from where it is delivered on demand—per user access rights and permissions—via Terminal Services or directly to a Windows desktop. Another method, not shown in the figure, is delivery of packages using SCCM.

Details about how to prepare applications for streaming and how to deliver them to user desktops are found in Chapters 11-14.

Desktop hardware virtualization

If application streaming is not in your future, then maybe the answer is desktop hardware virtualization. This approach is similar to virtualizing server hardware.

Virtualization of desktop hardware begins with installation of Virtual PC. Virtual PC has hardware requirements similar to those of Hyper-V, specifically a processor that supports either the Intel Virtualization Technology or AMD-V. Desktop images are centrally managed and delivered to virtualized desktops using MED-V.

While we are working on this book, Microsoft Windows XP Mode (XPM) for Windows 7 Professional, Ultimate, and Enterprise is in beta. It is intended to help ensure compatibility between Windows 7-based PCs and legacy Windows XP applications. You can download XPM from http://tinyurl.com/WinXPM. Like other Microsoft virtualization solutions, XPM requires virtualization-enabled hardware.

How to install Virtual PC as well as how to create, deliver, and manage desktop images is detailed in Chapter 15.

Additional tools

Not all organizations are ready to jump into enterprise-wide desktop virtualization, but they may have specific requirements that may be excellent candidates for limited centralized solutions. Furthermore, compatibility issues may arise when trying to assimilate older systems into a virtualized environment. Microsoft provides two solutions that help overcome these challenges—Virtual Desktop Infrastructure (VDI) and Windows Fundamentals for Legacy PCs (WinFLP).

Warning
In our opinion, neither VDI nor WinFLP should be considered for enterprise implementation of virtualization.

VDI

VDI enables users to access virtualized instances of Windows desktops running in the datacenter from any network-connected Windows machine. Although VDI might look like a viable option for App-V or MED-V, it falls short of achieving the same business benefits. We do not recommend this solution for general enterprise desktop virtualization. Rather, it is a problem-specific solution.

We do not cover VDI in this book. For more information about this technology, visit http://tinyurl.com/MS-VDI.

WinFLP

WinFLP is offered by Microsoft so that you can enable legacy PCs to take advantage of a newer, supported Windows operating system functionality.

Based on Windows XP SP2, WinFLP provides limited functionality. For example, PCs running WinFLP cannot run productivity applications like Office. What they can do, however, is run the following:

- Microsoft Remote Desktop Client, Citrix's ICA Client
- Security software
- Management software
- Back-up and recovery software
- Terminal emulation software
- Web browsers
- Media players
- Instant messaging clients
- Document viewers (e.g., Office, Acrobat)
- .Net Framework
- Third-party Java Virtual Machine

We included WinFLP here because it can enable older, irreplaceable PCs to take advantage of your virtualization framework. WinFLP is not covered in detail in this book, and use rights are only provided under specific licensing agreements. For more information, visit http://tinyurl.com/WinFLP.

SUMMARY

Microsoft's virtualization strategy is based on a datacenter and desktop maturity model. The model helps organizations move IT from a cost center to a strategic asset. The dynamic datacenter and centralized desktop management are two key components of reaching this goal.

The dynamic datacenter is characterized by agility and cost containment, both of which are facilitated by server virtualization. Server virtualization is enabled using Microsoft Server 2008 and Hyper-V. Management of the virtualized environment is possible using System Center Virtual Machine Manager and SCOM, with System Center Data Protection Manager providing VM and VM workload backup and recovery services. Implementation of these solutions is governed by an administrative model that determines when, how, and what to virtualize.

Microsoft's strategy for virtualizing an enterprise continues from the datacenter to the desktop. Centralized development of images or installation packages is supported by on-demand delivery of those applications to the users' Windows PCs. Distribution of applications is supported by application streaming (App-V) directly to the desktop or to Terminal Services sessions. Organizations can also choose to actually virtualize desktop hardware with Virtual PC, distributing desktop images via MED-V.

There are many solutions in the Microsoft virtualization toolbox, and we think we have spent enough time describing them. So let us get to the how-to stuff found in the rest of this book.

REFERENCE

[1] What is Microsoft's strategy for virtualization? Virtualization with Hyper-V: FAQ, Microsoft.com; 2010. Available from http://tinyurl.com/hyperV-FAQ.

Chapter **3**

Installing Windows Server 2008 and Hyper-V

In this chapter, we touch on the differences between Windows Server 2008 Standard and Core editions, and the advantages and disadvantages of each for Hyper-V. We discuss the hardware and software requirements, and walk you through an install of the Hyper-V role on Windows Server 2008, and how to connect to a finished install using your Windows Vista or Windows 7 client. Finally, we bring up BitLocker as an option to secure your Hyper-V installation (a subject we discuss in greater detail in Chapter 9).

WINDOWS SERVER 2008 AND SERVER CORE

Any discussion about Hyper-V should begin with the recommended hypervisor OS layer. Hyper-V requires Windows Server 2008, or Windows Server 2008 Server Core. Server Core is a minimal installation of Windows Server 2008, with only those applications and services required for operation. Even Windows Explorer is not available in a default install of Server Core. This means that an "out of the box" installation is highly secure, with only those services enabled that you absolutely require. The only direct interface available is a command-line window.

Note
Server Core is not available on separate media. Instead, it is an installation option on your Windows Server 2008 Standard or Enterprise DVD.

29

The lack of a GUI can also be a significant barrier to entry for learning a new technology such as Hyper-V. We are much more familiar with the traditional graphics-based method of server management that Microsoft has developed over the years. Even if you have experience in UNIX or other command-line centered operating systems, you still need to learn your way around the command syntax of Windows Server Core. (This gets better with Windows Server 2008 R2 with the introduction of the SCONFIG utility.) Rather than present you with roadblocks to understanding Hyper-V and the other technologies we present in this book, we made the decision to use Windows Server 2008 Standard Edition for our server.

INSTALLATION REQUIREMENTS FOR HYPER-V

In this section, we will discuss hardware and software requirements for installing Hyper-V.

Hardware requirements for Hyper-V

Note
Intel calls its virtualization technology Intel-VT, and AMD calls its AMD-V. Most current CPUs on the market have this function installed, although few motherboard manufacturers enable it by default. This can be enabled in the motherboard BIOS. Consult your manufacturer's documentation for details.

The hardware requirements for Hyper-V are not much different from the base requirements for Windows Server 2008. Windows Server 2008 is available in both 32-bit and 64-bit configurations, while Windows Server 2008 R2 is 64-bit only. Hyper-V, however, is only available on the 64-bit editions of Windows Server. The CPU must have the necessary virtualization extensions available and turned on in the BIOS. Both the major processor manufacturers (Intel and AMD) have CPUs with these extensions available.

In addition, the CPU must support hardware-enforced Data Execution Prevention, or DEP. For Intel processors, this requires enabling the XD bit; for AMD processors it is the NX bit. These functions are found in your computer's BIOS settings.

Memory is another consideration. In addition to the underlying (or "host") Operating System, the virtualized (or "guest") operating system also requires its share of RAM; the more guests you plan to run simultaneously, the more memory you need. A good minimum to aim for is 4 GB of RAM, as this leaves sufficient memory for the guest and one or two hosts. HP has a sizing tool available at http://g3w1656g-vip.houston.hp.com/SB/Installs/HyperV_SizingTool.zip. Again, this is a minimum number. We seem Microsoft recommendations as high as 8 GB.

For hard drive space, you similarly want to consider the needs of the host and each guest operating system. In the case of the guests, you need enough disk space to accommodate all of the installed guests, applications, and data simultaneously, regardless of how many you intend to run at the same time.

For best results, Hyper-V requires a minimum of two physical network adapters: one for hypervisor management and one for VM to network connectivity. If you plan to cluster your devices, install a third adapter.

Software requirements for Hyper-V

Hyper-V is installed as a role. (A role is a predefined function for a server, such as DNS, Active Directory Controller, or Hyper-V.) Before you can install the Hyper-V role, you must install the Hyper-V update packages for Windows Server 2008 (KB950050), as well as the Language Pack for Hyper-V (KB951636). Hyper-V v2 comes preinstalled in Server 2008 R2; you simply have to enable it.

Note

In addition to the patches already listed, install the Update for Windows Server 2008 (KB952627) on the Vista workstation if you plan to remotely administer the Hyper-V server from a workstation with Windows Vista SP1.

SUPPORTED GUESTS ON HYPER-V

You can install both 32-bit and 64-bit guest operating systems on Hyper-V. While many Operating Systems may install on a virtual machine instance, the following list is officially supported by Microsoft, meaning—among other things—that they can be "enlightened" (see Chapter 2 for a definition of an enlightened OS):

- Windows Server 2000, 2003, and 2008
- SUSE Linux Enterprise Server 10
- Windows Vista and Windows 7 Business, Enterprise, and Ultimate
- Windows XP Professional

INSTALLING HYPER-V

The installation process for Hyper-V is similar to adding other roles to Windows Server 2008. From the Server Manager console, select the Roles icon on the left-hand window. On the right, click the *Add Roles* link (see Figure 3.1).

This will launch the Add Roles Wizard. The first screen informs you of the process. The next page is a list of checkboxes: Check the *Hyper-V* role and select *Next* (see Figure 3.2).

In the next window, select *Next* to move on to the Virtual Networks creation screen (see Figure 3.3).

For performance and security reasons, it is recommended that you reserve one network adapter for remote management. You can, of course, select multiple adapters; one virtual network will be created for each of them.

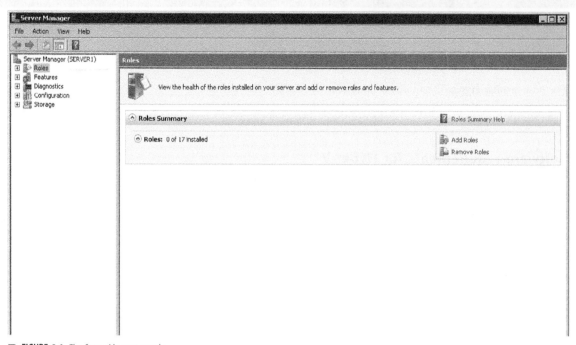

■ **FIGURE 3.1** The Server Manager console.

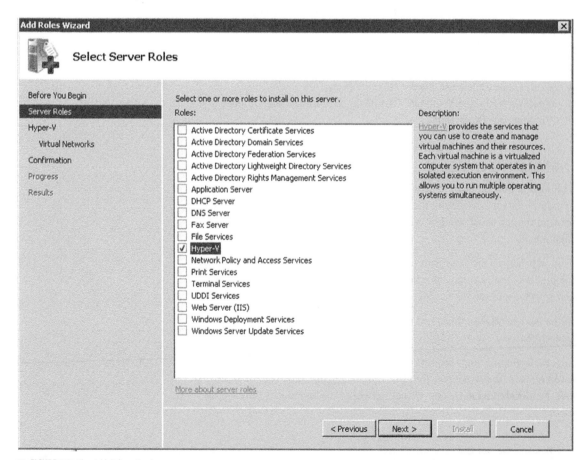

■ **FIGURE 3.2** The Add Roles wizard.

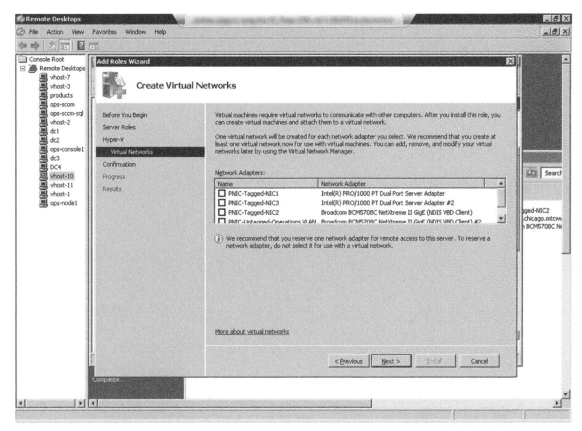

■ **FIGURE 3.3** The Virtual Networks creation screen.

Select *Next* and review the selections you have given. If you like what you see, proceed with the install. When the installation process is complete, you will see a screen similar to the one shown in Figure 3.4.

Select *Close* and reboot the server when prompted.

On reboot, the Hyper-V role is installed and available for management.

INSTALLING THE HYPER-V MANAGEMENT CONSOLE ON A WORKSTATION

If Hyper-V is installed on Windows Server 2008 Standard or Enterprise, the management console is available on the server after reboot. However, you may be using Server Core, or simply prefer to manage your Hyper-V installation remotely by installing the management console on a Windows Vista

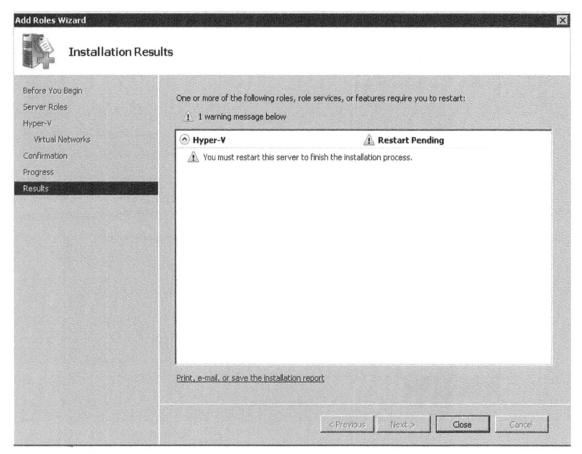

■ **FIGURE 3.4** Installation results.

or a Windows 7 workstation. To enable remote management, the server must be able to accept management connections through the firewall.

On Windows Server 2008 Standard/Enterprise, the installation of the Hyper-V role also enables the inbound connections for client-side management. Enable *Network Discovery and Browsing* for full functionality. If the server has been used for any file or print sharing previous to being used for Hyper-V, this will already be enabled. Otherwise, the easiest method is to open up the Network browsing window, and follow the prompts.

Download and install the Hyper-V management tools for Windows Vista, also called KB952627. You need to validate your installation of Windows

Vista before you will be allowed to download the tool. After the installation of the management console (if you are running Microsoft Vista SP2 or later), you also need to download and install KB970203. When the installation completes, you will have a new Hyper-V Manager shortcut in your Administrative Tools menu. Launch the console as a user with permissions to access the server, typically a domain or server administrator (see Figure 3.5).

From the Action menu, select *Connect to Server*. Choose to connect to Another Computer and either browse to the server running Hyper-V or enter the name or IP address of the server (in our case the name is Server). A successful connection will give you a screen similar to the one shown in Figure 3.6.

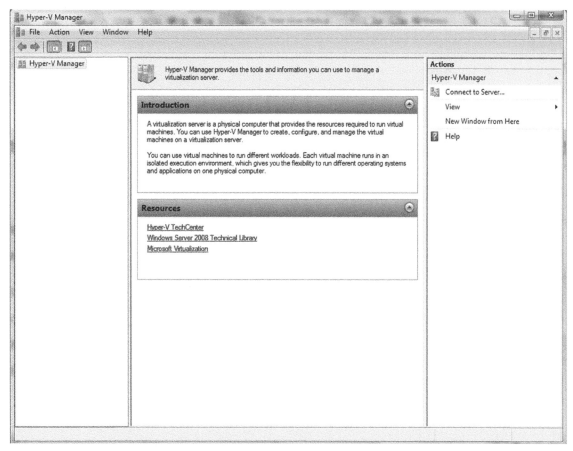

■ **FIGURE 3.5** Hyper-V Manager.

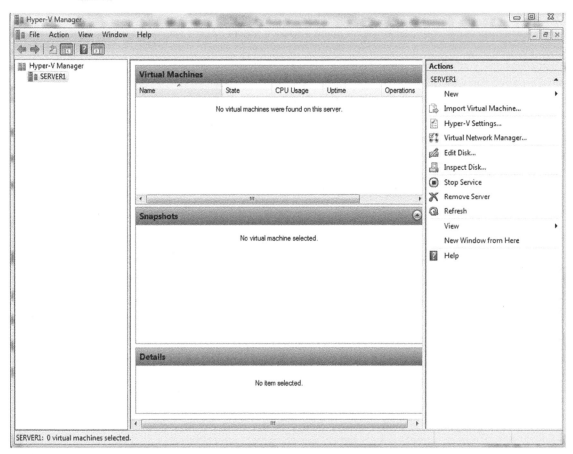

■ **FIGURE 3.6** The Action menu.

BITLOCKER AND HYPER-V

BitLocker works with the Trusted Platform Module (TPM) chip in supported systems to encrypt the data partitions of your hard drives. A Virtual Hard Disk (VHD) or virtual machine configuration can be placed on a BitLocker encrypted partition to allow the data contained on the VHD to benefit from this security as well—regardless of the guest operating system. This allows you to extend the protection of BitLocker to incompatible and legacy Windows operating systems. Once BitLocker is enabled on your host system, and the drives prepared and encrypted, the only step required is creation of the virtual devices on the encrypted drive.

SUMMARY

Although Windows Server 2008 comes with a core-install option, be sure you have the time to commit to learning the un-Linux/Unix like command-line interface. If not, just go with what you know; a security hardened, traditional Windows Server installation.

Hyper-V is quickly installed. We did not encounter any undocumented challenges. Just be sure your hardware meets the minimum processor and memory requirements.

Finally, setting up a remote management workstation is quick and easy. We used Vista in this chapter, but there are no significant differences when using Windows 7.

Chapter 4

Managing Hyper-V

Now that we have a working Hyper-V installation, we need to manage it. This chapter introduces you to the Hyper-V Management console and walks you through several of its management functions. We will configure the various options of the Hyper-V system, including the creation of virtual networks. Finally, we take an installed virtual machine and configure several common options.

INTRODUCTION TO THE HYPER-V MANAGER SNAP-IN

The Hyper-V snap-in is installed automatically on the Windows 2008 Server when the Hyper-V role is installed, provided the role is installed on a Standard or Enterprise edition. Server Core, as previously discussed, does not have a GUI, and so the snap-in is not available.

If you wish to install the Hyper-V Management snap-in on a client machine, you can do so by simply downloading and installing the application from Microsoft. Remember from Chapter 3 that KB970203 must be installed on the workstation as well if it is a Vista machine (Windows 7 does not require the patch). The Hyper-V Management application can be found by searching for KB952627.

We used the snap-in directly on the server with Hyper-V installed. You will find it in the applications menu.

The left-hand pane of the window allows you to manage multiple Hyper-V server installations, and choose between them. The middle pane

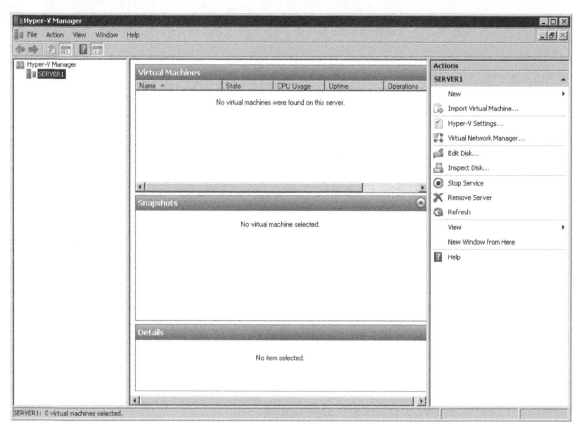

FIGURE 4.1 The Hyper-V Management console.

allows you to manage the individual virtual machines and the snapshots of each individual machine. The right-hand pane shows the actions available to manage the Hyper-V server, virtual machines, and related virtual drives, as well as those used to manage the Hyper-V services (see Figure 4.1).

VIRTUAL NETWORKS

Virtual networks allow the virtual machine to communicate with the rest of your network, the host machine, and other virtual machines. With the Virtual Network Manager, you can create the following types of virtual networks:

- *Private network*—allows a virtual machine to communicate only with another virtual machine on the host.
- *Internal network*—sets up communication between the host system and the virtual machines on it.
- *External network*—connects virtual machines and the host physical network. This allows the virtual machine to communicate on the same network as the host, operating as any other node on the network.
  1. You can create and manage virtual networks by clicking on the Virtual Network Manager link on the right-hand page (as shown in Figure 4.2). This brings up a wizard similar to the one shown in Figure 4.3.

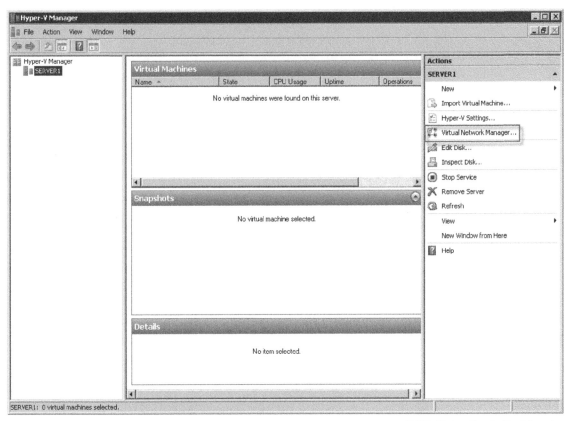

■ **FIGURE 4.2** Launching the Virtual Network Manager.

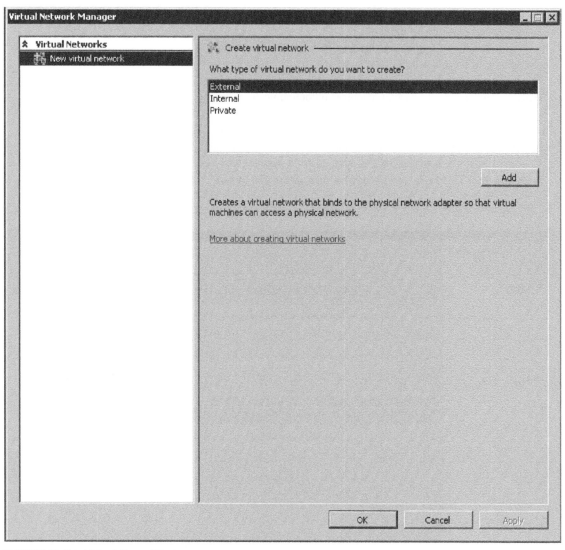

■ **FIGURE 4.3** Virtual Network Manager Wizard.

2. In this case, you want your new virtual machine to talk on your network, so you will select *External* and click *Add* (see Figure 4.3).
3. Give the virtual network a name, one that is easy to identify. The notes field can also help to identify the virtual network's intended function. On the Connection type, you should choose *External*, since you want to use it to connect to your physical network

in the lab. You have to choose a physical network card in the host server from the drop-down box (remember to leave one card dedicated to management!), and finally you have the option to enable Virtual LAN identification, with the number of the VLAN you want to use (see Figure 4.4). Virtual LANs are used as a security control to segment data within a switched network; discussion of the pros and cons of VLANs are beyond the scope of this book.

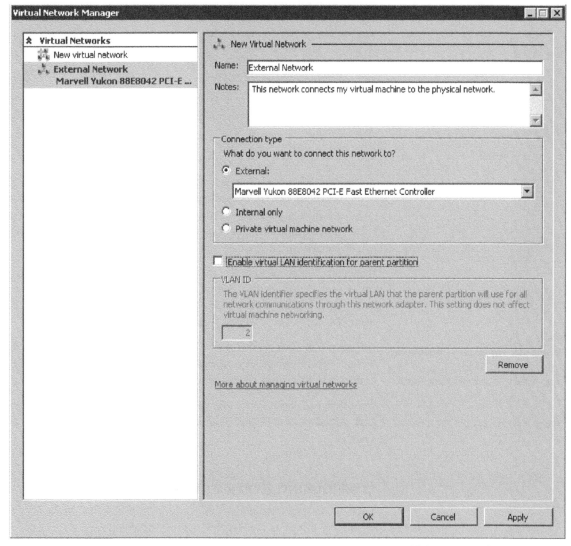

■ **FIGURE 4.4** Creating the Virtual Network.

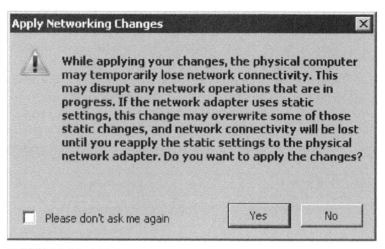

FIGURE 4.5 Network Warning.

4. You acknowledge the warning in the pop-up shown in Figure 4.5 and click *Yes*. (If, by now, you have seen this pop-up window more times than you can remember, you can check the box to never be asked again. Just do not be surprised when you lose your network connection on that card temporarily!)

Remember when we told you to dedicate a network card to managing the server? If you decided against that, and are using remote desktop to manage the Hyper-V server, you just lost your connection for a short while. Do not panic; it will be back soon.

Note
Internal Networks may also use VLAN identification. Private Networks do not—they are only used for virtual machine to virtual machine communication.

Now that you have created your virtual network, you can use the same Virtual Network Manager to change it to an Internal or Private network. Simply select the proper radio button, as shown in Figure 4.4.

Now that you have a network, you can use it when you create your first virtual machine. The creation of virtual machines is covered in Chapter 7.

CONFIGURING HYPER-V OPTIONS

Clicking the *Hyper-V Settings* link on the right pane of the Manager (see Figure 4.6) brings up the Hyper-V Settings window:

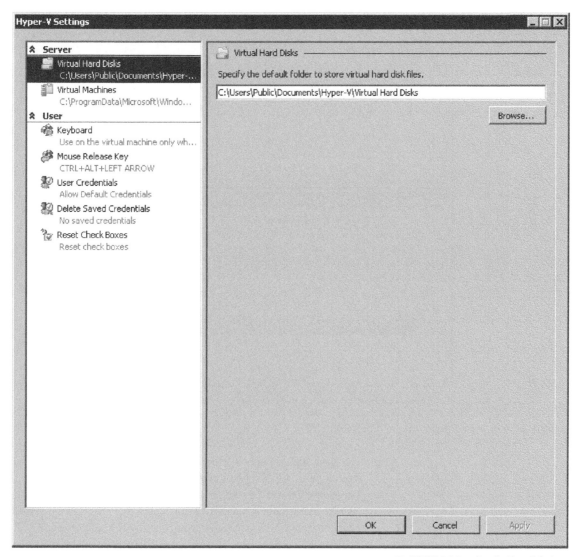

You can set two options for the server itself and five for each user connecting to the virtual machines (see Figure 4.7):

■ The Virtual Hard Disks and Virtual Machines options allow you to set a path for the virtual hard disk files and virtual machine files, respectively.

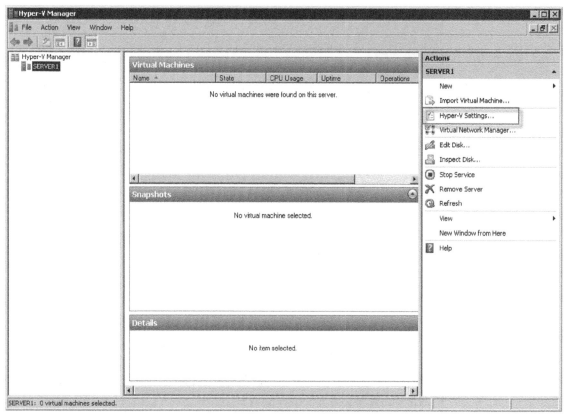

■ **FIGURE 4.7** Hyper-V Settings Wizards.

- The Keyboard user option determines when Windows key combinations (such as ALT + TAB) pass through the virtual machine.
- The Mouse Release Key option lets you set which keys you must press to take the mouse pointer out of the virtual machine window in the Virtual Machine Connection application. Note that if you have the virtual machine drivers installed on the virtual machine (in other words, you are running an "enlightened OS"), you will not need to use the key combination to release the mouse—it will operate on whichever desktop it is currently hovering over. If you have not installed the virtual machine drivers, Chapter 7 walks you through the process.
- The User Credentials check box determines if you use the currently logged on user to log in to the virtual machine as well, in a "pass-thru" arrangement. With this box checked, you will not need to log in to the virtual machine when it starts up; it will use the credentials you used to log in to the management system. Unchecked, you will need to log in to the virtual machine once it is up and running.

- Delete Saved Credentials does just what is advertized: it deletes any saved user log-ons you have in the virtual machine. Cached user log-ons are vulnerable to being captured by attackers—remember, just because the machine is virtual, it does not mean that it is secure! This option makes it easy for you to remove any and all cached log-ons that may be residing on the virtual machine.
- Finally, the Reset Check Boxes option reverses all the work you did to ensure the annoying pop-up windows do not pester you anymore. Clicking the *Reset* button will allow you to once again see the warning messages before confirming certain actions.

The next option we explore is the Edit Disk option. Figure 4.8 shows you where this option is located. Selecting this launches the Edit Virtual Hard Disk Wizard.

Warning

Only run the Edit Virtual Hard Disk Wizard on virtual disks that are *not currently in use.*

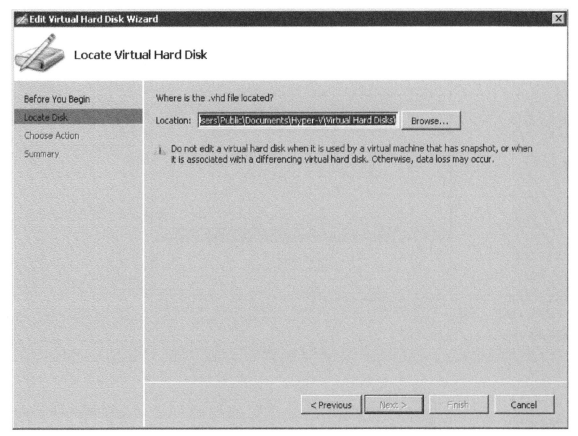

■ **FIGURE 4.8** Launching the Edit Disk Wizard.

1. After the typical introductory screen, you are asked to locate the virtual hard disk image, which is a .vhd file. (Of course, you need to have a .vhd file before you can edit it; Chapter 7 walks you through the process of creating a Virtual Machine.

2. Browse to the .vhd file you wish to alter, as shown in Figure 4.6 and select *Next* (Figure 4.9).

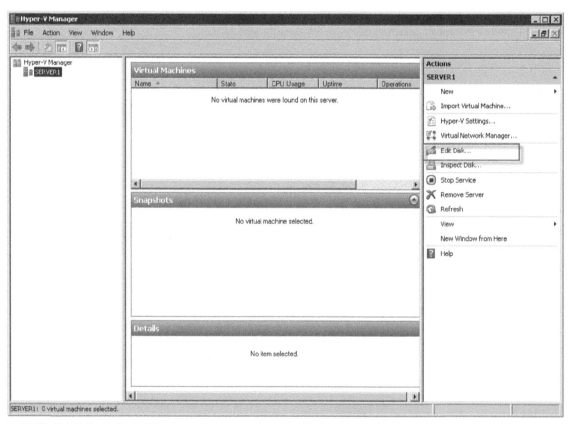

■ **FIGURE 4.9** Beginning the Edit Disk Wizard.

3. Figure 4.10 shows you the three available actions:

- The *Compact* option allows you to shrink a dynamic disk by removing any blank space that might exist from deleting files within the virtual machine.
- The *Convert* option allows you to change the virtual disk from a fixed to a dynamic disk, or vice versa. It does this by copying the contents of the current .vhd file to a new one of the type you wish to convert to. This means you will need enough free disk space to contain both the old .vhd file and the new one on the physical drive. Once the conversion is completed, the old file is removed.
- The *Expand* option is primarily useful for fixed disks and allows you to expand the maximum size of the virtual disk.

Note

The differences between a dynamic disk and fixed disk are essentially that a dynamic disk starts at a particular minimum size and grows as the amount of data on the virtual machine grows. A fixed disk begins at a particular size and stays there. The third type of disk is called differencing, and is used to create a copy of an existing disk. The differenced disk then records the changes made to the original disk, instead of the original being changed. Chapter 7 goes into much greater detail on the advantages and disadvantages of each.

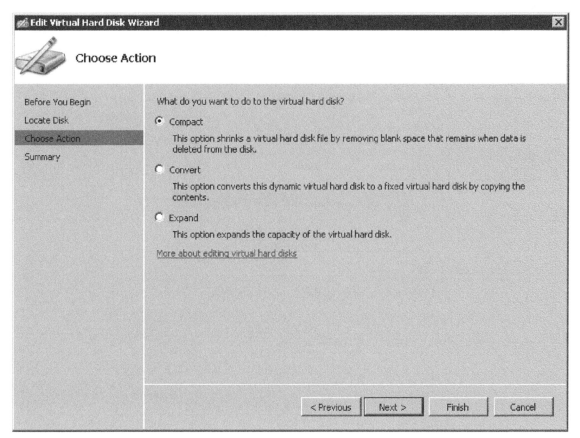

■ **FIGURE 4.10** Edit Disk options.

If you have a differencing disk attached as well, you have two more options available to you in this wizard: *Merge*, which takes the changes recorded on the differencing disk and writes them to the parent disk; and *reconnect*, which is only available if the parent disk cannot automatically be found. The reconnect function will prompt you for the new location of the parent disk.

4. Once you select your action, click *Next*. For the Convert option, you are asked for the location of the new disk; for Reconnect you will be asked to locate the parent disk. Click *Finish* and set the wizard to work. You will see a progress bar, as seen in Figure 4.11.

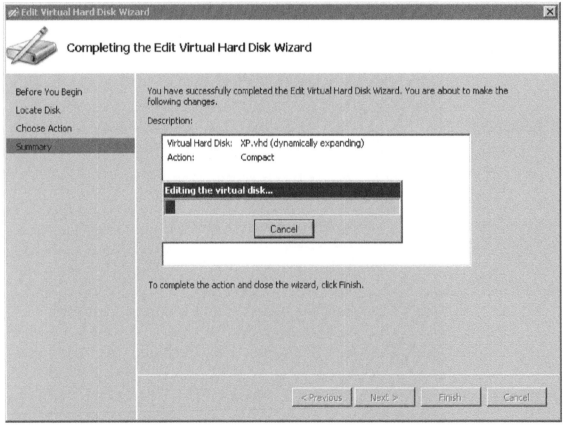

■ **FIGURE 4.11** Edit Virtual Disk Wizard goes to work.

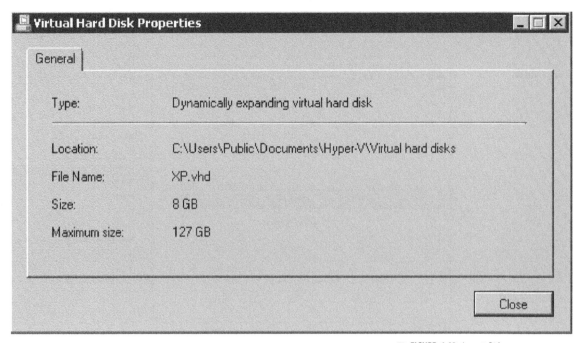

■ **FIGURE 4.12** Inspect Disk.

Another function available to you in the Hyper-V Management console is the Inspect Disk option as seen in Figure 4.12. The Inspect Disk option prompts you to locate the .vhd file you wish to inspect. It then connects to the disk and displays the properties in a window similar to Figure 4.13.

Type, location, name, size, and max size are listed (see Figure 4.13).

The next two Management console options, Stop Service and Remove Server, are shown in Figure 4.14.

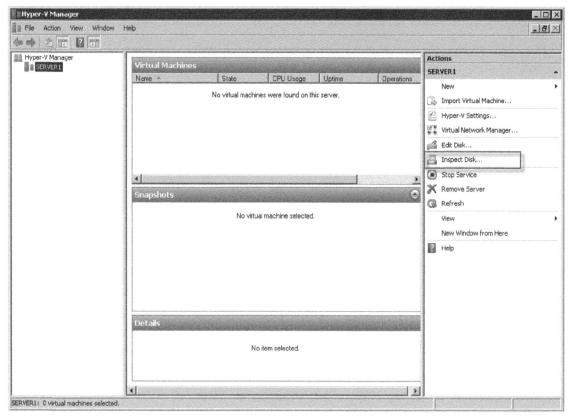

■ **FIGURE 4.13** Virtual Disk properties.

- *Stop Service* will stop the Hyper-V services on the host machine, turning off any running virtual machines and disabling the virtual network connections.
- *Remove server* takes the currently selected server off the list of servers available to manage in the Hyper-V Management console.

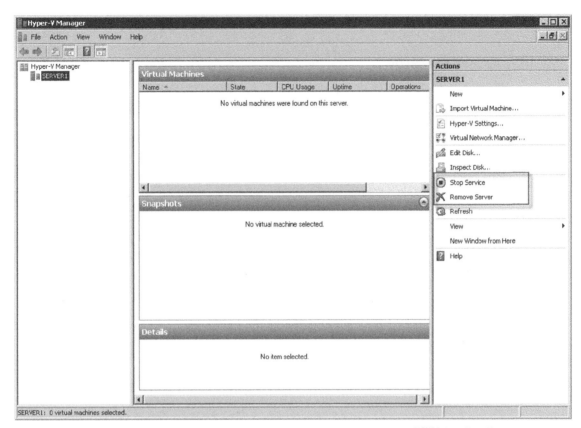

CONFIGURING VIRTUAL MACHINE OPTIONS

There are several options available to alter the behavior and setup of your virtual machines. You access the settings options by selecting the virtual machine you wish to manage from the list in the middle column of the Management console, as shown in Figure 4.15, and then clicking *Settings*

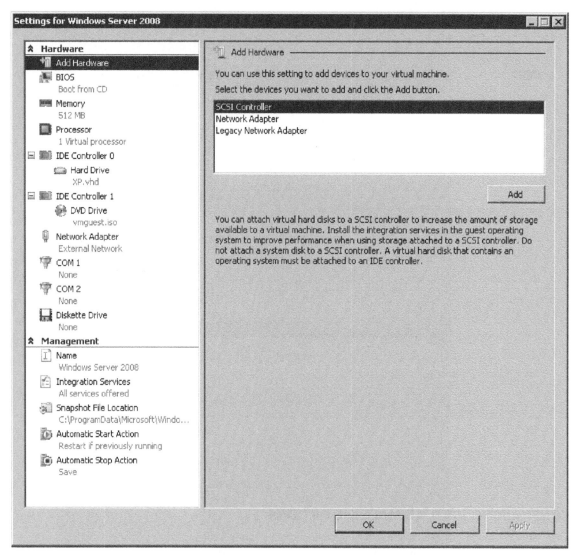

■ FIGURE 4.15 Created Virtual Machines can be found here.

in the right column. You will see a window like the one shown in Figure 4.16.

Several options are available on the left, with the right pane changing to give you the various options available for each action.

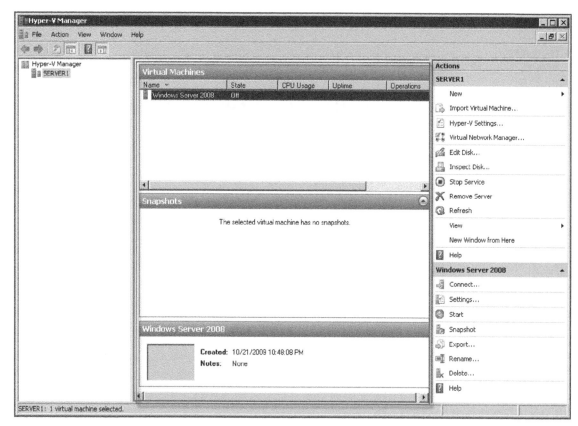

To begin with, Add Hardware allows you to create another virtual SCSI Controller, Network Adapter, or Legacy Network Adapter. Selecting any of these names will launch the appropriate wizard.

The *BIOS* option shown in Figure 4.17 allows you to change the boot order of the virtual devices. This option also enables you to toggle the Num Lock function on or off while booting.

The Memory panel allows you to configure the available RAM for the virtual machine, up to the maximum installed in the host machine (i.e., after the host operating system's own needs are met).

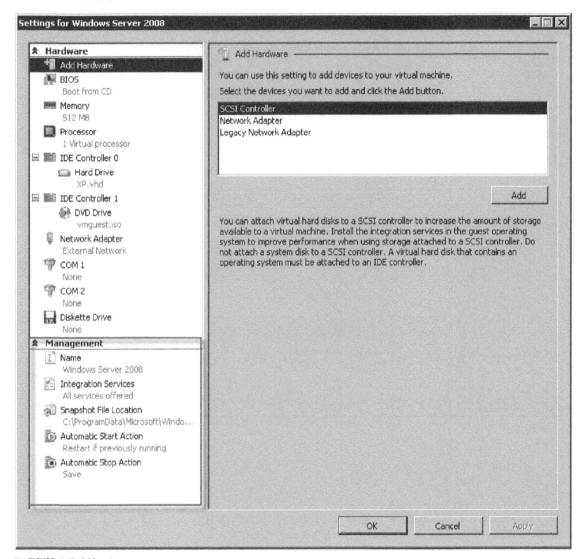

■ **FIGURE 4.17** BIOS option.

The Processor option in Figure 4.18 allows you to change the number of virtual processors available to the virtual machine, as well as configure other resource options. Note, you cannot assign more logical processors than you have processor cores available in the host.

Virtual Machine Reserve and Virtual Machine Limit refer to the amount of host resources reserved for the virtual machine's exclusive use and

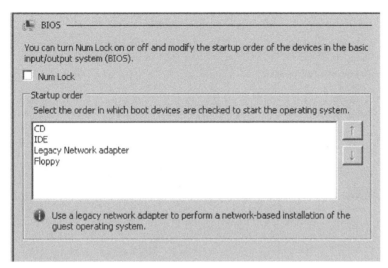

■ FIGURE 4.18 Processor and resource control.

the maximum it can consume, respectively. Relative weight comes into play when multiple virtual machines are running on the same host and essentially gives a priority value to each virtual machine.

Use these options to maximize the performance of a given virtual machine, typically at the expense of the other virtual machines on the host, as well as at the expense of the host itself. By increasing the reserve, you force the host to dedicate more resources (CPU, RAM, disk I/O time, etc.) to the virtual machine, and by increasing the limit, you allow the virtual machine to consume more of the available resources. By decreasing these values, of course, you limit the amount of resources it can consume. Decreasing the relative weight will make it wait behind other virtual machines for a given resource if it is busy.

The other hardware options allow you to configure virtual analogs of the physical hardware you are familiar with. The configuration screens for each present the appropriate options, so for the COM ports, you will have the ability to change communication speeds and the like, add and remove virtual devices to the SCSI controllers, etc. Figure 4.19 shows you the options available.

The Name option (in the Management section of the pane) shown in Figure 4.19 allows you to change the name the virtual machine displays in the Management console, as well as add and edit the notes for it.

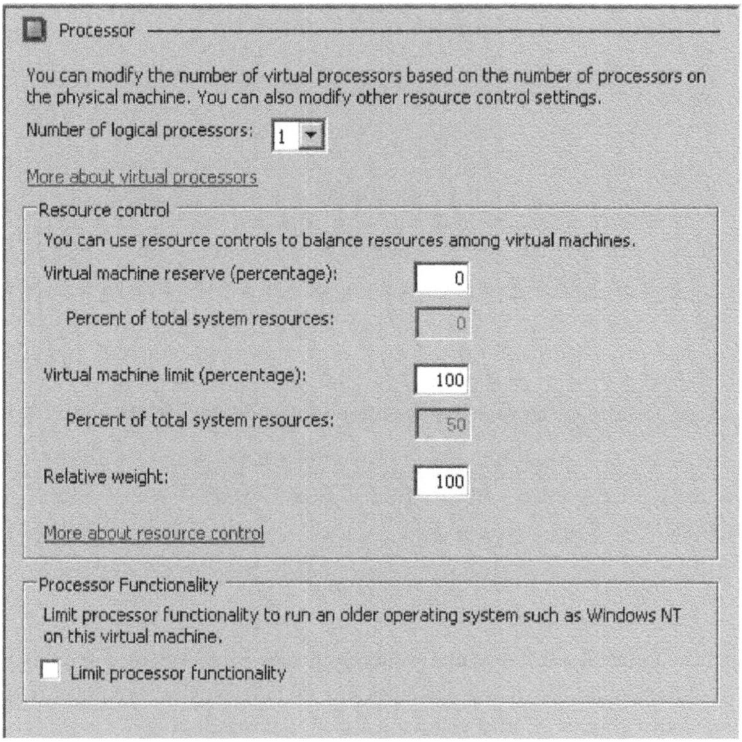

Processor ──────────────────────────────────

You can modify the number of virtual processors based on the number of processors on the physical machine. You can also modify other resource control settings.

Number of logical processors: [1 ▼]

More about virtual processors

┌─Resource control ──────────────────────────────────
│ You can use resource controls to balance resources among virtual machines.
│ Virtual machine reserve (percentage):   [0]
│   Percent of total system resources: [0]
│ Virtual machine limit (percentage):   [100]
│   Percent of total system resources: [50]
│ Relative weight: [100]
│ More about resource control
└──────────────────────────────────

┌─Processor Functionality ──────────────────────────────────
│ Limit processor functionality to run an older operating system such as Windows NT on this virtual machine.
│ ☐ Limit processor functionality
└──────────────────────────────────

■ **FIGURE 4.19** VM Management pane.

The Integration Services option shown in Figure 4.20 gives you a series of checkboxes to turn on and off the various Integration options available to enlightened virtual machines. The Integration Services and their installation are covered in detail in Chapter 7.

Snapshot File Location allows you to set the folder where snapshots are saved for this virtual machine. Snapshots are useful for backups. For instance, when you are about to install a service pack that may render your virtual machine unusable, snapshots allow you to revert to the previous state.

The Automatic Start Action determines what the virtual machine does when the host machine is first booted. The selections are:

- *Nothing*
- Automatically start if it was running when the service stopped

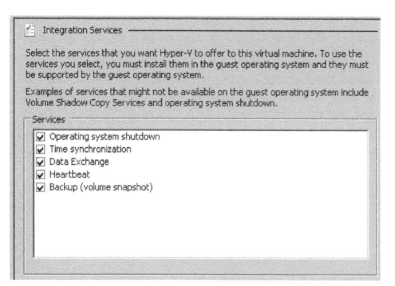

■ **FIGURE 4.20** Integration services.

- Always start this virtual machine (The Automatic start delay allows you to pause the startup of the virtual machine, so that multiple automatically starting machines are not contending for resources.)

The Automatic Stop Action is very similar. It determines the behavior of the virtual machine when the host machine is shut down. The options here are:

- Save the virtual machine state
- Turn off the virtual machine
- Shut down the guest operating system

The last two are the most confusing; Turn off the virtual machine does not make an effort to shut down the operating system gracefully, while the other does.

Warning
The Automatic Stop Action cannot take place if the host machine is shut down unexpectedly.

SUMMARY

In this chapter, we installed the Hyper-V Server Manager on a Windows 7 or Vista desktop, as well as on a Windows 2008 Server. We examined the various tools at your disposal to manage the Hyper-V server itself, including the creation and management of virtual networks. These networks can be used to communicate between the host and the virtual machine, between virtual machines, or the virtual machine and the network.

Virtual disks can be shrunk, expanded, and changed from one type to another. Differencing disks can be merged and, if necessary, reconnected.

Finally, we went through the various options available to manage the virtual machine itself. From adding or removing new hardware, to changing the usage of host resources, there are many ways to configure and optimize your virtual machines.

Now that you are familiar with the Hyper-V management, you will want to create or import your own virtual machines. You can do that in Chapter 7.

Chapter **5**

Installing and configuring Virtual Machine Manager 2008

CHAPTER OUTLINE

Virtual Machine Manager (VMM) 2008 is part of Microsoft's comprehensive System Center system management suite. VMM enables you to manage your virtual environment from one central console with the tools needed to get the most out of your data center. Leveraging VMM facilitates maximization of physical server resources, improves agility and virtual machine deployment, and allows your company to continue to leverage the skill sets of your existing IT staff.

INTRODUCTION TO VIRTUAL MACHINE MANAGER

If you are responsible for a medium-sized to a large virtualized enterprise, then at some point you will likely realize that the management of multiple virtual host machines can be very cumbersome and time-consuming when using the standard console for each machine. VMM simplifies their management by consolidating everything you need into one console. In fact, you can manage your Hyper-V, Virtual Server, and even VMware ESX hosts all via VMM.

If you are already using System Center Operations Manager (SCOM), you can use the data it collects via its monitoring capabilities to further advantage. Performance and Resource Optimization (PRO) leverages it and recommends actions to be taken to improve the performance of your virtual machines. You can even configure it to automatically make certain

61

adjustments on your behalf in order to maintain the level of performance your customers require.

VMM not only consolidates the functionality built into Hyper-V but also adds to it. With VMM performing, physical-to-virtual (P2V) migrations are greatly simplified and can be done without service interruption. VMM will also convert your VMware machines to VHDs using a similar technique called virtual-to-virtual transfers.

For development and testing environments, VMM provides a self-service Web portal you can configure to delegate virtual machine provisioning while maintaining management control of the VMs.

By implementing a centralized library for the storage virtual machine components, you can leverage these building blocks to quickly stand up new virtual machines as demand dictates.

You can also create scripts to increase your level of automation, because VMM is built on Windows PowerShell. The various wizards included in VMM are typically just a pretty interface to generate a PowerShell script. VMM provides the functionality to view the code behind these scripts to help expand your knowledge of the scripting language.

This chapter not only provides you with a high-level synopsis of what VMM can do to help you with managing your enterprise but also helps to illustrate how easy it can be to leverage and exploit to your advantage.

SYSTEM REQUIREMENTS

Before designing your VMM architecture, you should decide whether you want to implement VMM on a single server or share the load of VMM's multiple components across separate servers. As a rule of thumb, if you need to support 20 or fewer virtual machine hosts, you can use a smaller single processor server. If you suspect you will eventually have a greater number, up to 150 or more servers, then consider a multiple processor server. If you will be supporting groups of virtual machine hosts in diverse locations, you might want to use a multiple server approach. For a complete list of hardware requirements and software prerequisites for either deployment option, visit the TechNet Web site at http://www.microsoft.com/systemcenter/ virtualmachinemanager/en/us/system-requirements.aspx#Server.

ACQUIRING AND INSTALLING VMM

VMM is not included with Windows Server 2008—unlike most of the products in this book—and must be purchased and licensed separately. VMM is available from the Microsoft Volume License Services Web site (https://www.microsoft.com/licensing/servicecenter/). You can download a trial version from http://technet.microsoft.com/en-us/evalcenter/cc793138. aspx. In either case, you must download the VMM ISO file and burn it to a DVD. The DVD contains the installation media for all of the components of VMM whether you intend a single server implementation or plan to use multiple machines to handle the load.

1. Let us start with the machine where you intend to install the VMM Server itself. If you intend a single server deployment, then the choice is simple. Place the DVD in the server's drive and you are greeted by the System Center VMM installation launch screen, as shown in Figure 5.1. Selecting the *Setup Overview* will present you with the latest information on system requirements and other information and updates about VMM.

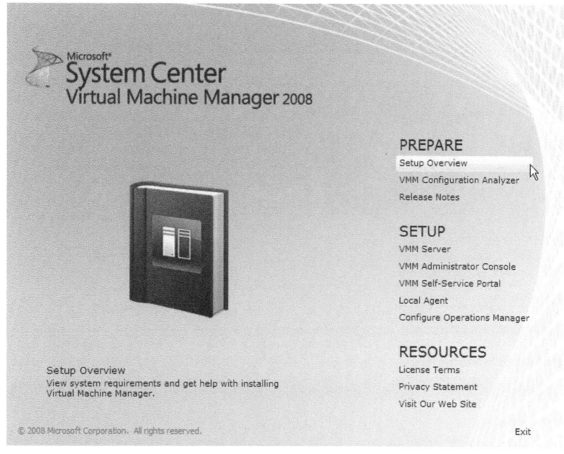

■ **FIGURE 5.1** The System Center Virtual Machine Manager Installation Launch Screen.

2. Selecting the *VMM Configuration Analyzer* assists in downloading and running a program to inspect and evaluate your server to determine if it has all of the prerequisites needed to install VMM. Using this tool helps avoid issues and troubleshooting later. You will be required to download and install an application locally on your server for the validation process. This selection is shown in Figure 5.2.

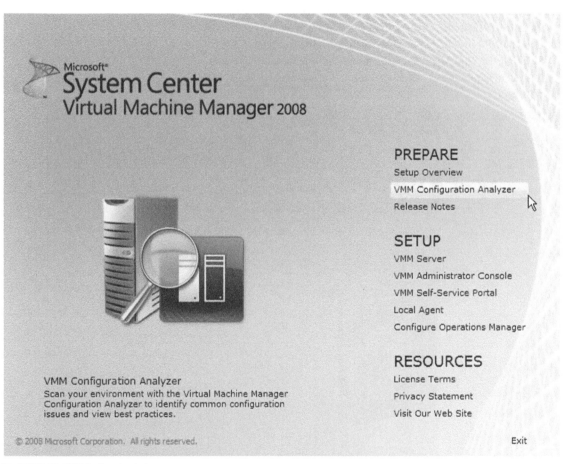

■ **FIGURE 5.2** VMM Configuration Analyzer.

3. The Release Notes option simply displays the VMM release notes, shown in Figure 5.3.

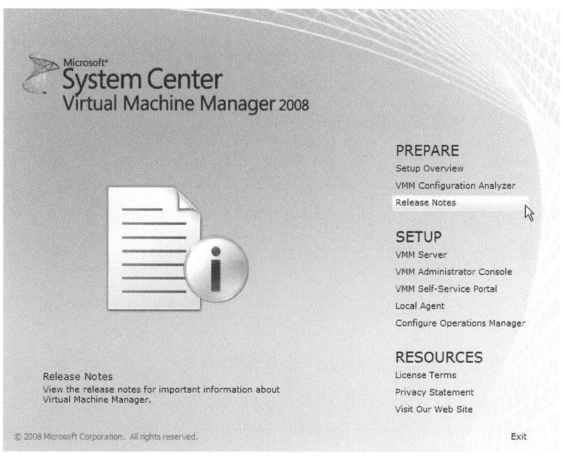

Release Notes
View the release notes for important information about
Virtual Machine Manager.

■ **FIGURE 5.3** Access to the Release Notes.

4. The options under Resources, as shown in Figure 5.4, are License Terms, Privacy Statement, and Visit Our Web Site. These options enable users to display the terms of the license agreement, view the details of the privacy statement, and get direct access to the VMM Web site, respectively.

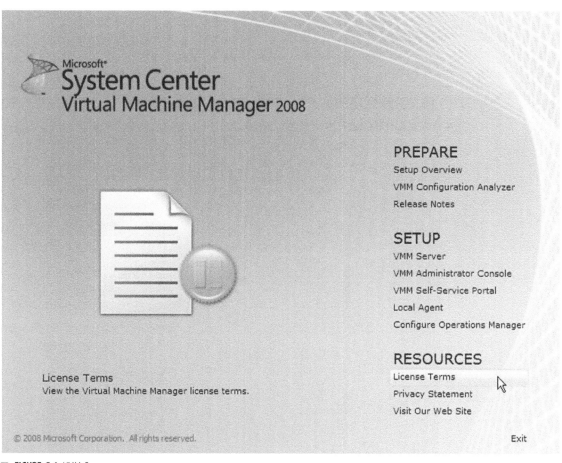

■ FIGURE 5.4 VMM Resources.

5. Let us get started. Under *Setup* you will see *VMM Server*. Clicking this option, as depicted in Figure 5.5, starts the installation process for VMM Server itself.

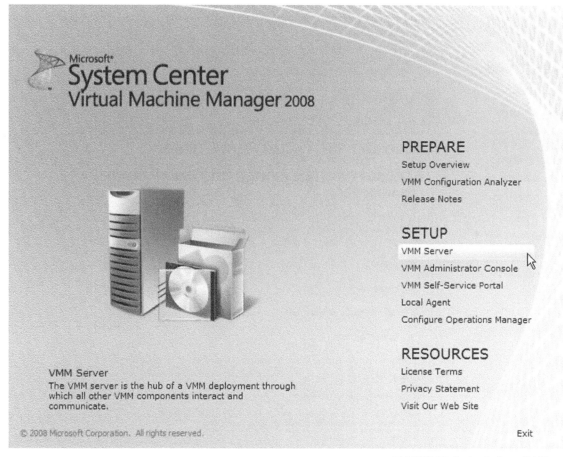

■ **FIGURE 5.5** Starting the Setup of VMM.

6. The VMM installation process follows a series of steps listed in the left-hand pane of the setup window. See Figure 5.6. Step 1, as you might expect, is the acceptance of the license terms. Once you feel comfortable with the fine print, select *I accept...* and click *Next*.

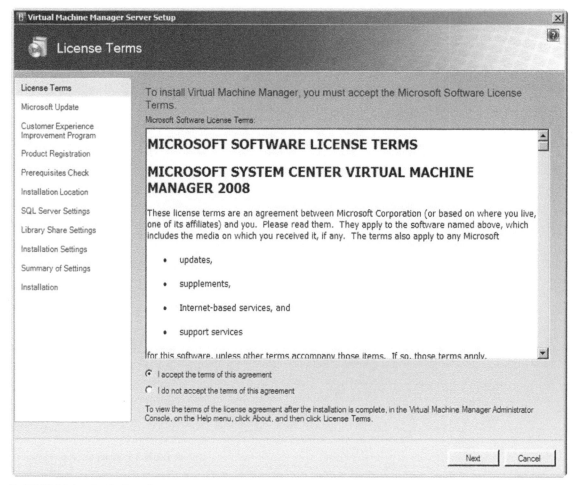

■ **FIGURE 5.6** Accepting the License Terms.

7. If you want to leverage Microsoft Update to help keep your
VMM server current on patches, select the appropriate radio
button shown in Figure 5.7. If you plan to keep VMM current on
patches by other automated means or by manually applying updates,
select *I don't want to use Microsoft Update*. Click *Next*.

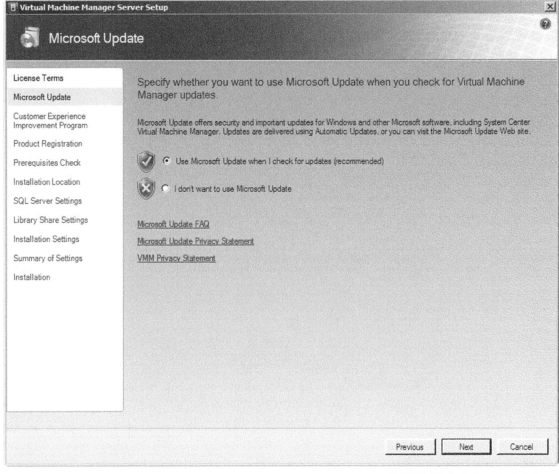

■ **FIGURE 5.7** Configuring Microsoft Update.

8. Joining the Microsoft Customer Experience Improvement Program is a personal decision. It is an attempt to constantly better their solution offerings by having you fillout periodic surveys. Read the page as shown in Figure 5.8, make your selection, and click *Next*.

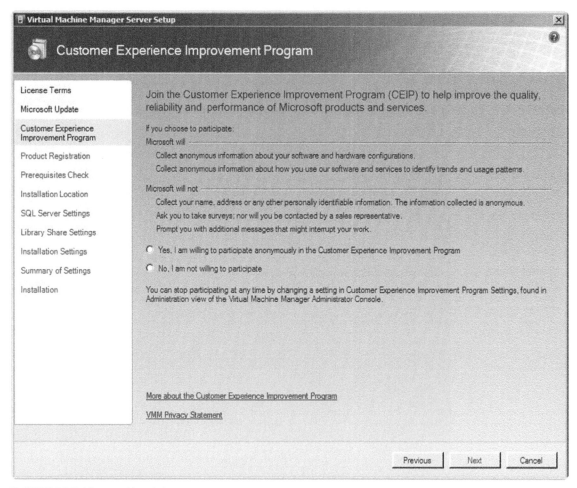

■ **FIGURE 5.8** Deciding to participate in the CEIP.

9. Product registration is next on the list. Go ahead and enter in your
information in the fields shown in Figure 5.9 and click *Next*.

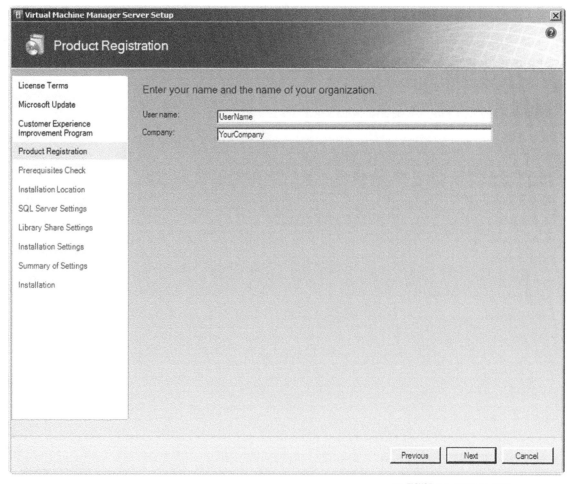

10. The installation process runs a Prerequisites Check on your machine instead of just allowing the install to bomb out. If you get all green check marks, as shown in Figure 5.10, click *Next* to continue. If you see red checks, follow the advice displayed in the window and install any missing components. There is a *Check Again* button that you can click after you get your server up to speed. This assumes that you did not have to reboot and start the VMM installation over again.

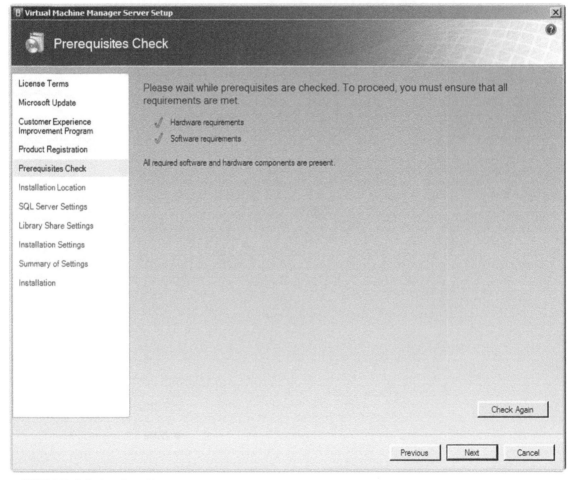

■ **FIGURE 5.10** Performing a Prerequisites Check.

11. The next step is to choose your install location in the field shown
in Figure 5.11. You can simply accept the default or choose a different
location, perhaps on a drive other than your system partition. Click
Next when you are ready.

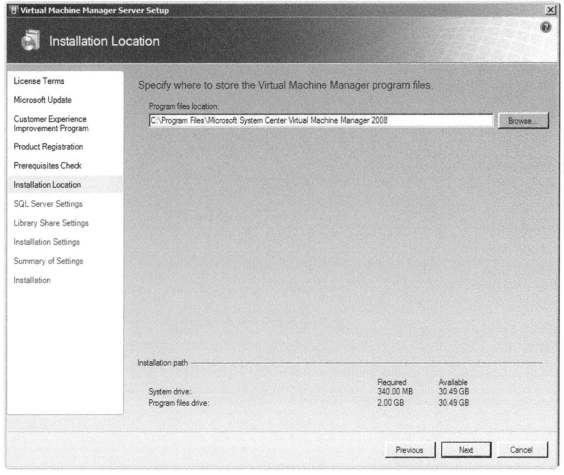

■ **FIGURE 5.11** Selecting an Installation Location.

12. Refer to Figure 5.12. The information you enter here depends on how you intend to leverage SQL Server.

   ❑ If you select the default configuration, you will install SQL Server 2005 Express Edition with Service Pack 2 locally on your VMM server in a folder location of your choice. Again, you may want to select a location other than your system drive.

   ❑ If you do not feel that Express Edition meets your requirements or you already have full SQL Server implemented on a dedicated server and would prefer to use it, you can easily choose to do so. Select the "Use a supported version of SQL Server" radio button and enter the name of your existing SQL server in the appropriate text box.

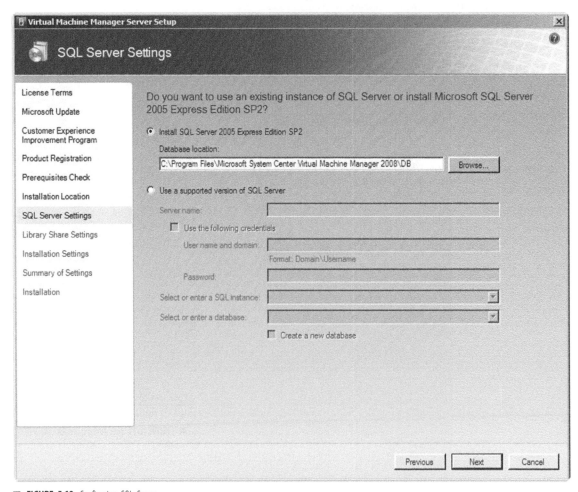

■ **FIGURE 5.12** Configuring SQL Server.

13. VMM stores all the resources used in the creation of virtual machines in the VMM library. Your enterprise must have at least one library server. In the default setup, each VMM server contains a library server and share (Figure 5.13). If you already have an existing library server, point this VMM server to it. In our example, we assume this is your first VMM server. So let us create a new one locally on this server. You can change the share name, location, and/or description all from this window. When ready, click *Next*.

Warning
You cannot move or remove a library server or share once setup is complete. So give some thought to where you place them before completing the installation.

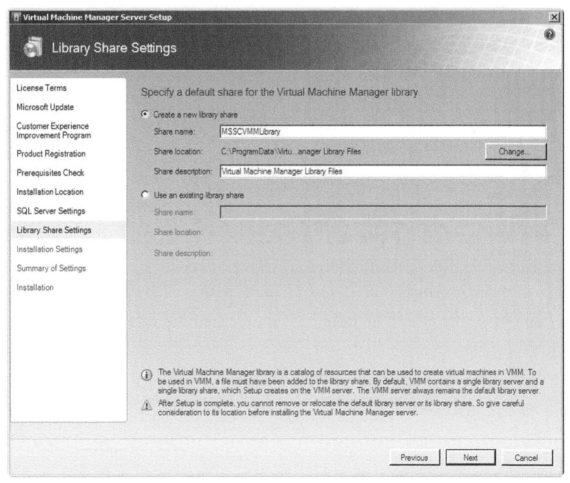

■ **FIGURE 5.13** Configuring the Library Share.

14. At this point, we will configure some important installation parameters. See Figure 5.14. VMM uses three ports for communication:

- ❑ One for communicating with the Administrator Console
- ❑ One for communication to agents and library servers
- ❑ One for transferring files to agents and library servers

You are presented with default port assignments, but you can change them to conform to your environment and security policies and procedures. You may want to jot down any changes in port assignments for easy reference

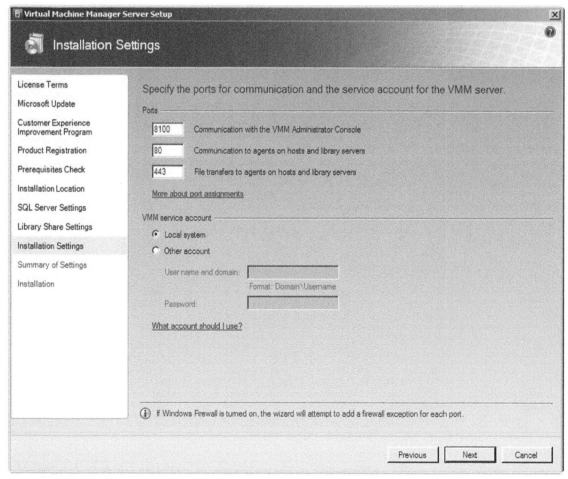

■ **FIGURE 5.14** Installation parameters.

during later installation steps. You can also choose between running the VMM services under the default local system account or an account of your choice. Continue by clicking *Next*.

15. The Summary of Settings Window depicted in Figure 5.15 provides one last chance to confirm all choices you made along the way. If you feel you need to reconsider any of them, click *Previous* until you find the appropriate window. Otherwise, click *Install* when you are satisfied with your choices.

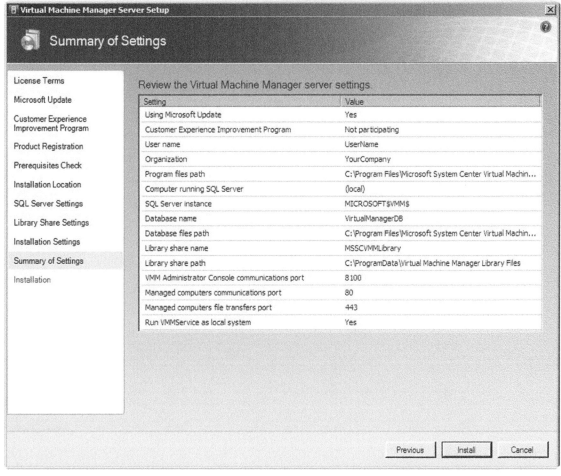

■ **FIGURE 5.15** Final summary of the Installation Settings.

16. Each line item is checked off as it is installed, as shown in Figure 5.16. Once installation is complete, you have the option to automatically look for and install updates for VMM. Keep the default box checked and click *Close*.

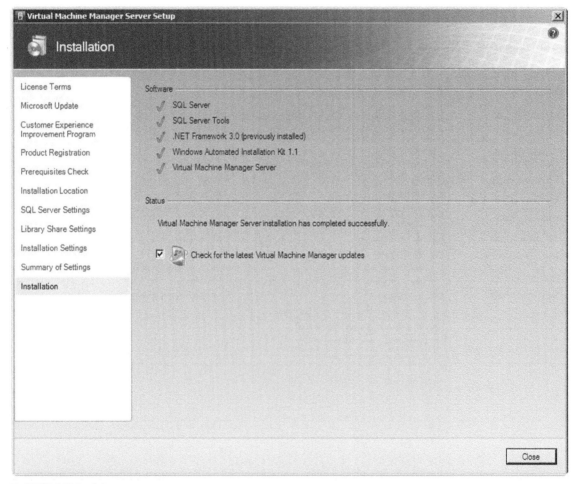

■ **FIGURE 5.16** Installation progress.

17. Let us now move on to the next VMM component. Under *Setup* in Figure 5.17, see *VMM Administrator Console*. Clicking this option starts the installation process for the Admin Console. The Admin Console can be installed locally on the VMM server for convenience when you are standing at the console. You can also install it on a workstation, allowing you to administer your virtual environment right from your desktop. The installation process is the same in either case, and it is advisable to install it in both locations. Since you

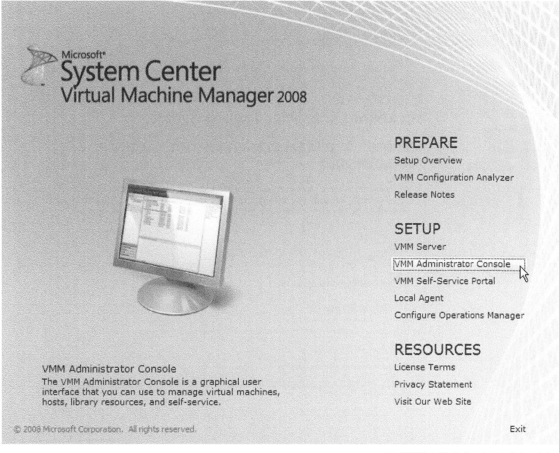

■ **FIGURE 5.17** Starting the installation of the Admin Console.

are already on your VMM server, go ahead and launch the installation of the Admin Console.

18. Step 1, displayed in Figure 5.18, is the usual license agreement acceptance. Select the appropriate radio button and the click *Next*.

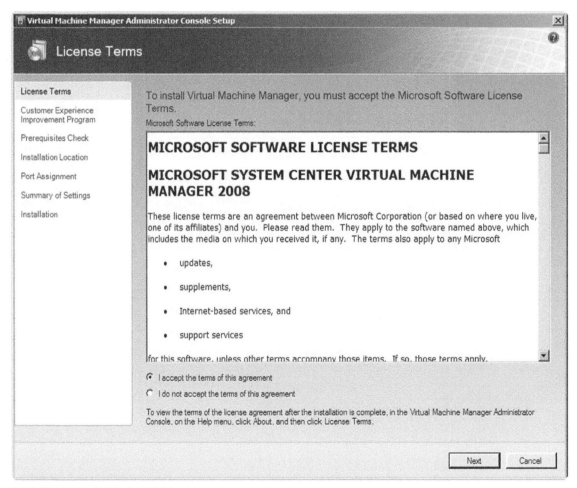

■ **FIGURE 5.18** Accepting the Admin Console Terms.

19. The window displayed now is more or less just a heads-up. As depicted in Figure 5.19, if you plan to point this installation of the Admin Console at a VMM server that is already enrolled in the Customer Experience Improvement Program, the console will automatically participate in the program as well. You can reverse this default behavior after the completion of the setup process. The selection window provides reversal instructions. There are no options to configure in this step, click *Next*.

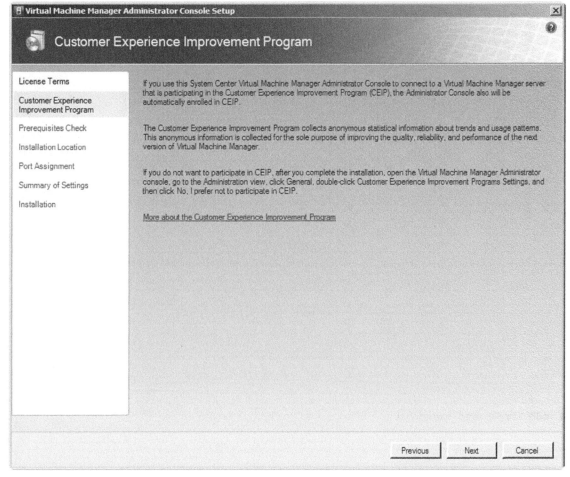

■ **FIGURE 5.19** CEIP.

20. Like during the installation of VMM Server, the Admin Console install will run a prerequisite scan of your machine. If any red checks show up, address them. Once all requirements are met, all green checks as displayed in Figure 5.20, click *Next*.

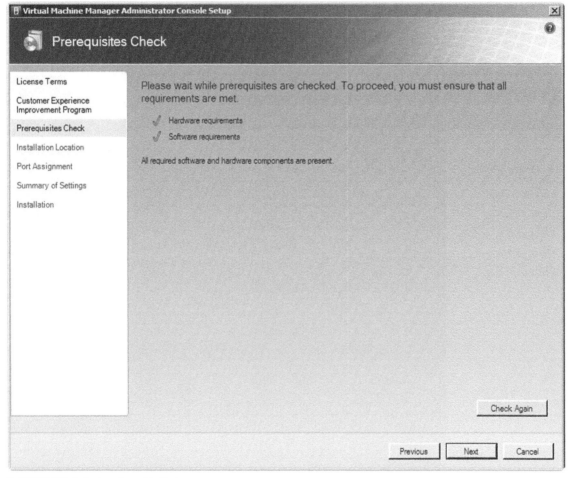

■ **FIGURE 5.20** Performing a Prerequisite Check.

21. See Figure 5.21. The installation path for the Admin Console defaults to your system drive. If you are concerned about performance, redirect it to another location. Once you are satisfied with your install path, click *Next* to continue.

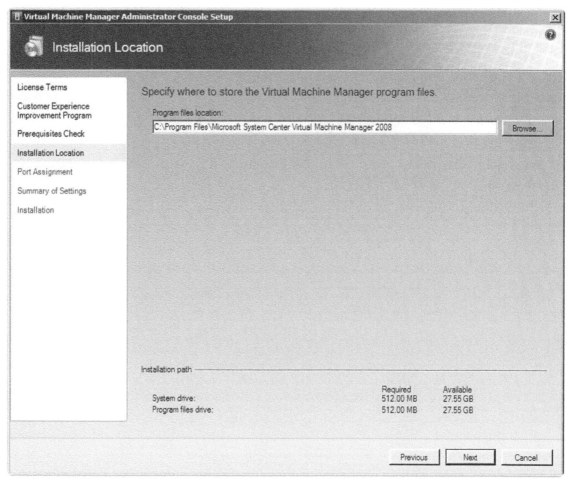

■ FIGURE 5.21 Selecting an Installation Location for the Admin Console.

22. The port number for communication to the VMM Server you
enter in this step must correspond to the port number that you assigned
in Step 14 for communication to the Admin Console. Once you have
entered the correct port number in the field shown in Figure 5.22,
click *Next* to continue.

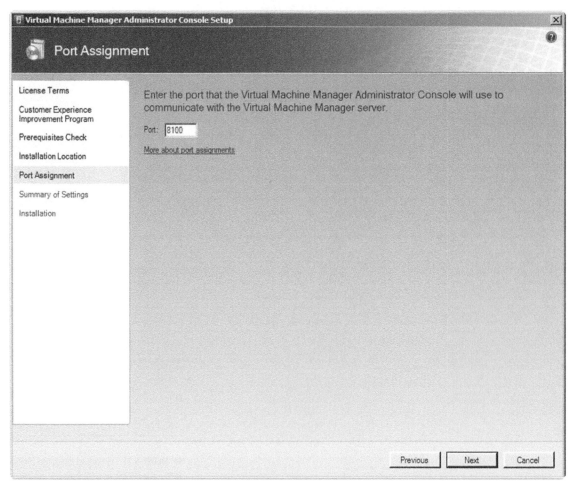

■ **FIGURE 5.22** Assigning the Communication
Port.

23. Using the window shown in Figure 5.23, confirm the installation parameters displayed are correct. If not, click *Previous* until you return to the appropriate window. When all corrections are complete, click *Install* to initiate the process.

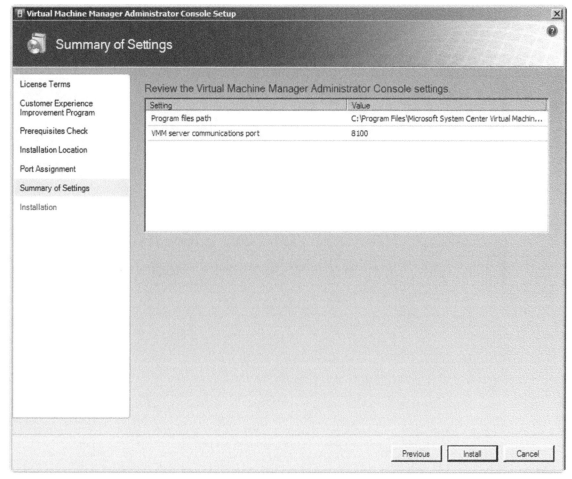

■ **FIGURE 5.23** Admin Console Settings Summary.

24. You can follow installation progress, as shown in Figure 5.24. A green checkmark appears as each component is installed. Again you have the option to look for and install updates to your freshly installed VMM software. You also can choose to place a shortcut to the VMM Admin Console on your desktop. Since our next step is to configure the Admin Console, you will want to check the *Open the VMM Administrator Console when the wizard closes* box. When done, click *Close*.

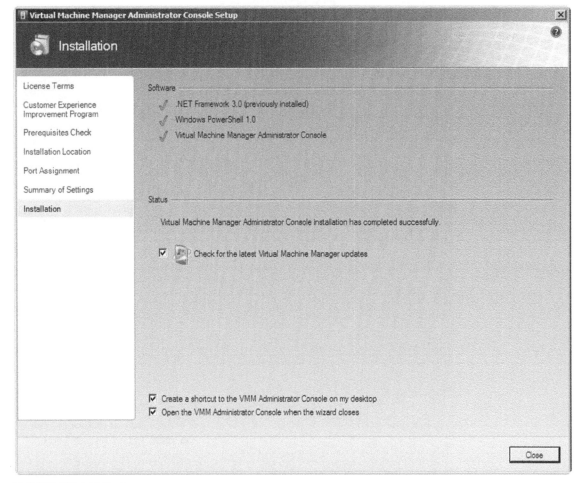

■ **FIGURE 5.24** Installation Progress.

CONFIGURING VMM FOR YOUR ENVIRONMENT

1. Upon completion of the installation of the VMM
   Administrative Console, the *Connect to Server* window opens, as
   displayed in Figure 5.25, and requests confirmation that it is about
   to connect to the correct server. The correct format is
   VMMServerName:port. If you are performing this install on the
   VMM server with the default communication port then the
   correct entry is *localhost:8100.* Otherwise, enter the correct VMM
   server name and port number as you set them in Steps 14 and 22 in
   the preceding section. If you want this configuration to be your
   default or if you simply have only one VMM Server, then check
   the *Make this server my default* box. When all is set properly,
   click *Connect.*

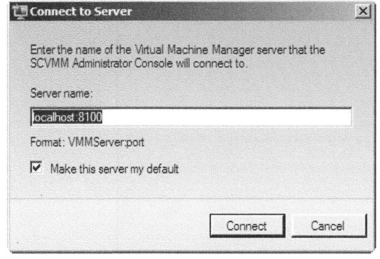

■ **FIGURE 5.25** Entering the VMM Server Name and Comm Port.

2. See Figure 5.26. This is the VMM Administrator Console. It is connected to your VMM Server, but your VMM Server is not yet managing any hosts. On the far right-hand side of this window you will see the Actions menu. Click *Add host* to connect to an existing host server.

3. When adding a host under management by VMM, you must first identify the host's location. For a Windows Server-based host (aka Hyper-V or Virtual Server), it can exist within an Active Directory domain or reside on a perimeter network. You must indicate which of

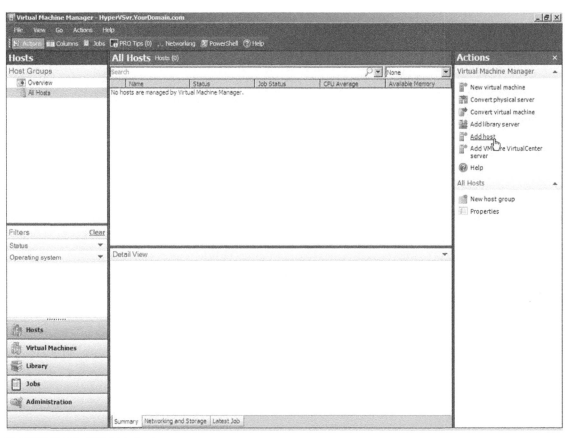

■ **FIGURE 5.26** The VMM Admin Console.

these scenarios applies (see Figure 5.27). If your target host is a VMware ESX server, VMM is not concerned about its location at this point, and you just need to let it know it exists. Select the radio button that is appropriate for your intentions. If you are targeting a host on an AD domain, enter credentials that will grant access to make the connection. If your host's domain and the domain of your VMM server do not have a two-way trust relationship, you must be sure to clear the checkbox *Host is in a trusted domain*. When ready, click *Next*.

Note

The domain credentials you enter must have administrative rights on all of the host servers you intend to add. All of the hosts you select will be part of the same host group and share remote connection ports and VM default paths.

4. Now it is time to search for your host server. Start by confirming that the correct domain name is in the *Domain* field. Optionally, you can enter in the name of the VMM Server before searching. You can also

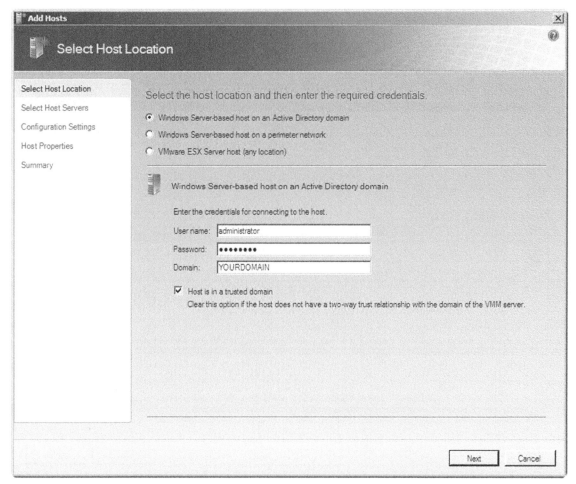

■ **FIGURE 5.27** Selecting the Host Location.

limit the search to machines running Virtual Server and/or Hyper-V. Once you have entered the details you want in the window shown in Figure 5.28, click *Search*. The *Search Results* window lists the servers that meet your search criteria. Highlight the server or servers you want

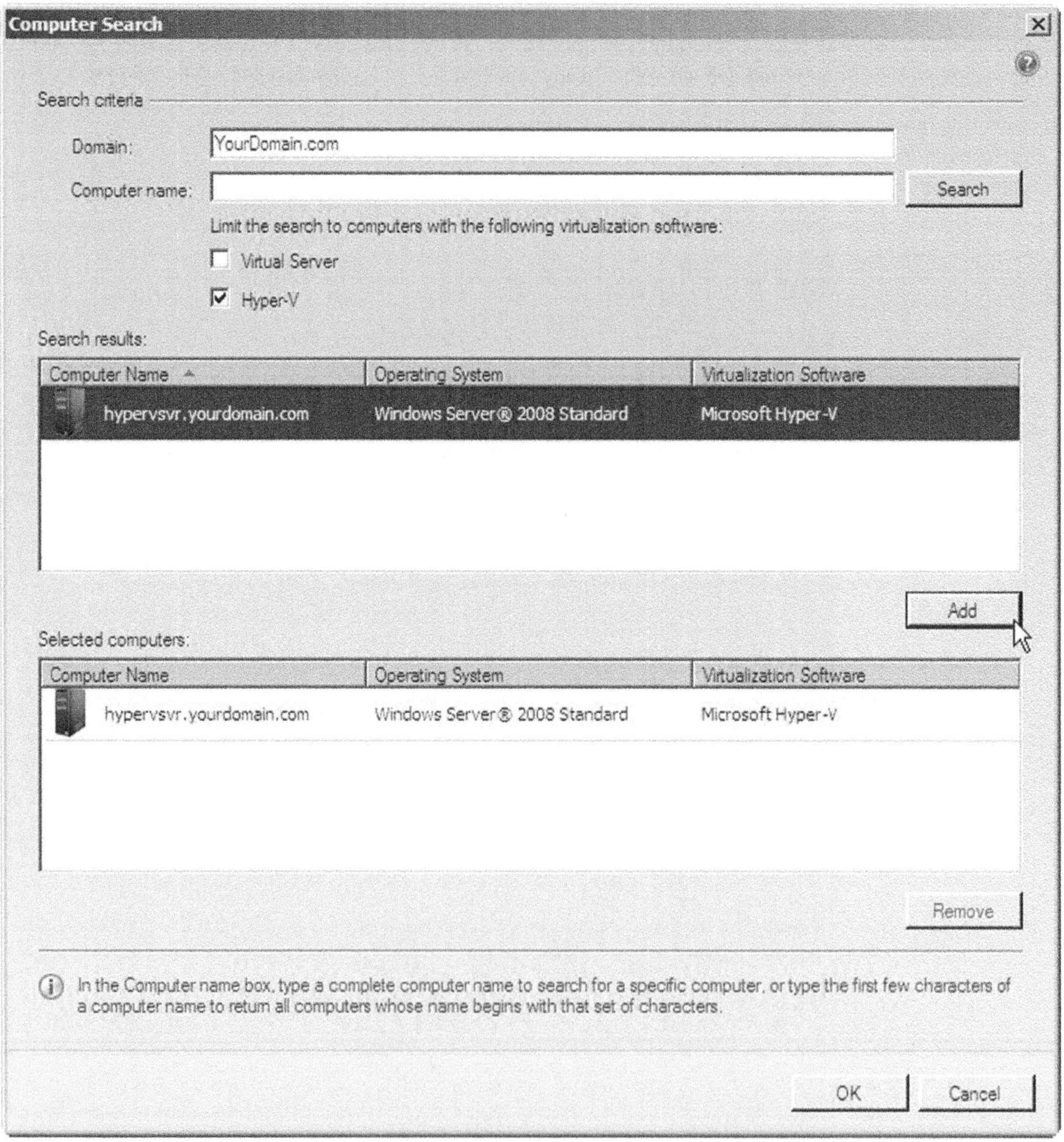

■ **FIGURE 5.28** Performing a Computer Search.

to manage and then click *Add*. The selected machines appear in the *Selected computers* window. Click *OK*.

5. The Select Host Servers window, displayed in Figure 5.29, should already include any servers you added in the previous step. You can also leverage this opportunity to add more hosts or remove any that you do not want to manage. When finished, click *Next*.

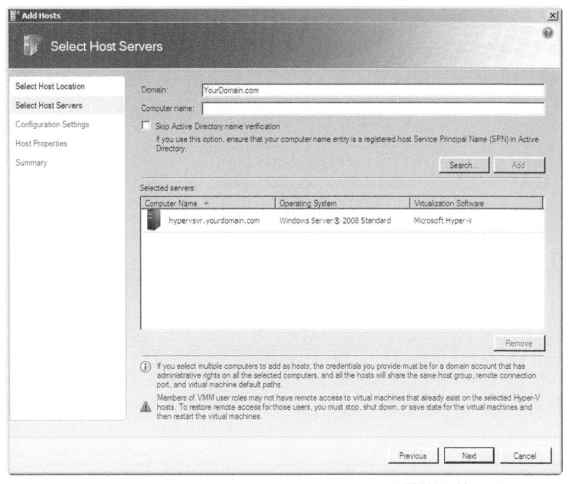

■ **FIGURE 5.29** Selecting a Host.

6. Selecting the host group in which to place your newly added hosts is simply a matter of organization preference. Proceed by using the dropdown list to select the desired group. If any of the hosts that you are adding are already being managed by a different VMM server, you will want to check the *Reassociate host with this Virtual Machine Manager server* box to transfer the management role to your new VMM server, as shown in Figure 5.30. Click *Next*.

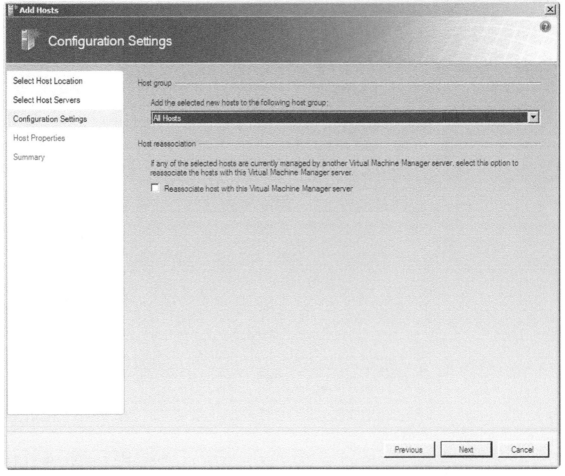

■ **FIGURE 5.30** Configuring your selected Host.

7. There are two parameters you configure in the Host Properties window, Figure 5.31. The first sets one or more default virtual machine paths. VM paths are locations to store files associated with deployed virtual machines. Enter the paths you would like to set by clicking the *Add* button after entering each one. There is also a *Remove* button if you make any mistakes. The second parameter that can be set is the port used for remote connection to your VMs via Virtual Machine Remote Control. You can accept the default port or configure it to meet the security policies at your company. When you are satisfied, click *Next*.

Note

Virtual Machine Remote Control (VMRC) connections are made from within the VMM console by simply right-clicking on the VM of choice and selecting *Connect to virtual machine*. VMRC provides you with remote access very similar to Remote Desktop; however, because it is granted via the host, you can connect to a VM before the guest OS has booted.

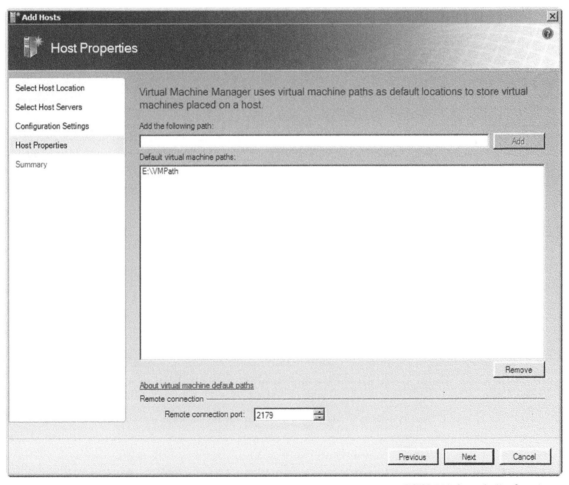

■ **FIGURE 5.31** Setting the Host Properties.

Note
When you configure a default path from within the wizard, it does not automatically create the folder you added within the interface. You must manually create the folder and the path to it if they do not already exist before you save any virtual machines there.

8. Confirm that the Summary window, displayed in Figure 5.32, shows the settings that you intended to make. If not, click *Previous* until you are returned to the proper window to make corrections.
If you would like to see the PowerShell script the wizard is going to execute on your behalf, you can click on the *View Script* button. The script generated by this install is shown in Figure 5.33. Click *Add Hosts*.
9. The Summary tab of the Jobs window, depicted in Figure 5.34, displays the status of the *Add virtual machine host* request you have just made. Your host machine has been added to VMM. If you did not

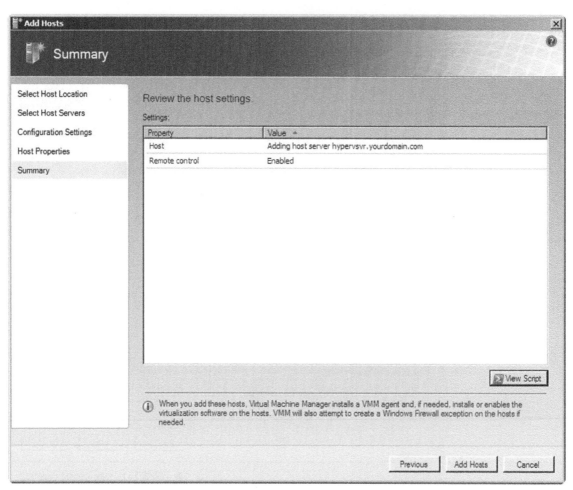

■ **FIGURE 5.32** Host Settings Summary.

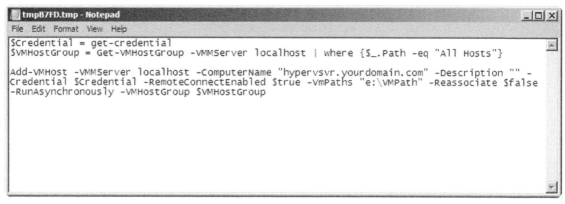

■ **FIGURE 5.33** PowerShell Script.

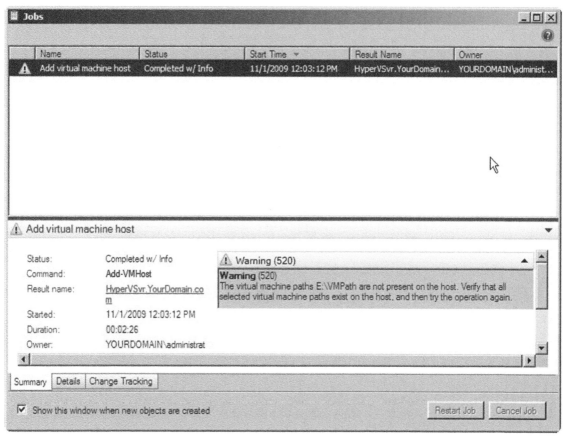

■ **FIGURE 5.34** The Jobs window.

manually create the default path folder, you will be warned that you must complete this task.

The Details tab, as shown in Figure 5.35, lists the status of each task and subtask performed as part of the job request.

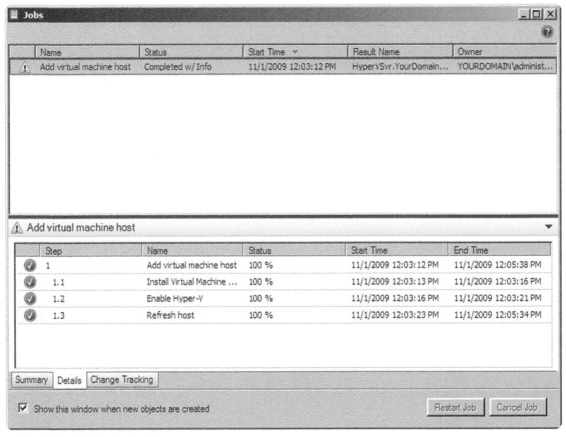

■ **FIGURE 5.35** Job detail.

The Change Tracking tab, depicted in Figure 5.36, illustrates all parameters changed during the process of adding the host machine to VMM. You will see a column for the previous value and one for the new value. Because this was a new add, the previous values should all be 0 or none. When you finish looking things over, you can close this window.

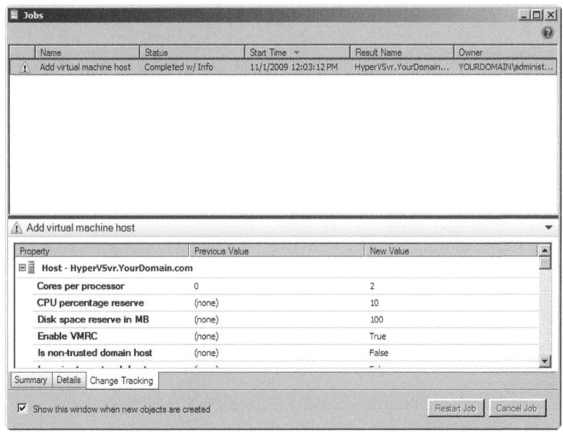

■ **FIGURE 5.36** Change Tracking.

10. Back in the VMM console window, you will see that your host machine is now listed, as shown in Figure 5.37. You may also notice in the "Status" column that it needs your attention. Right click on the host server name and select "Properties" to get more details on its condition.

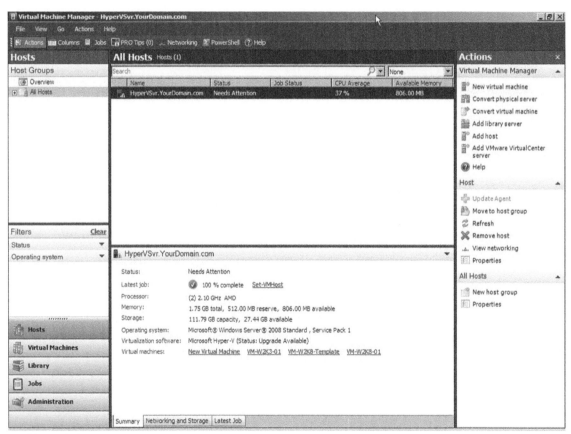

■ **FIGURE 5.37** Your added Host is now displayed.

11. When viewing the properties of a host machine, you are first taken to the Summary tab shown in Figure 5.38. This tab contains the general information pertaining to the host's identification and physical hardware. You may not be terribly interested in this display if you only have a single Hyper-V host in your environment. However, if you have a fleet of such

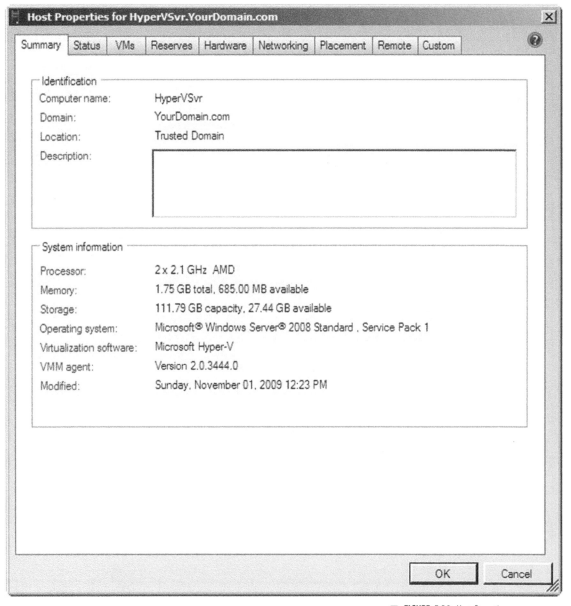

■ **FIGURE 5.38** Host Properties summary.

servers built on a variety of hardware models, this can serve as a quick aid in choosing the right system to support a particular VM.

12. The Status tab, shown in Figure 5.39, displays the status of several host machine components. If any of the items are in a degraded state, this window will inform you what the issue is. Figure 5.39 shows that our

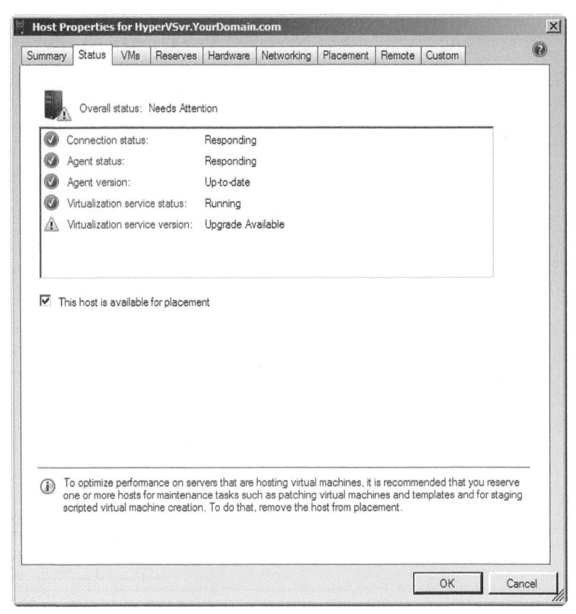

■ FIGURE 5.39 Host Status.

virtualization service version is out of date and an upgrade is available. From this window, you can exclude the host machine from having new virtual machines created or "placed" on it. This is handy if you dedicate this host to maintenance tasks or other special situations.

13. In order for you to manage a virtual machine with VMM, it must first be registered on the VM host. The VMs tab, shown in Figure 5.40, lists

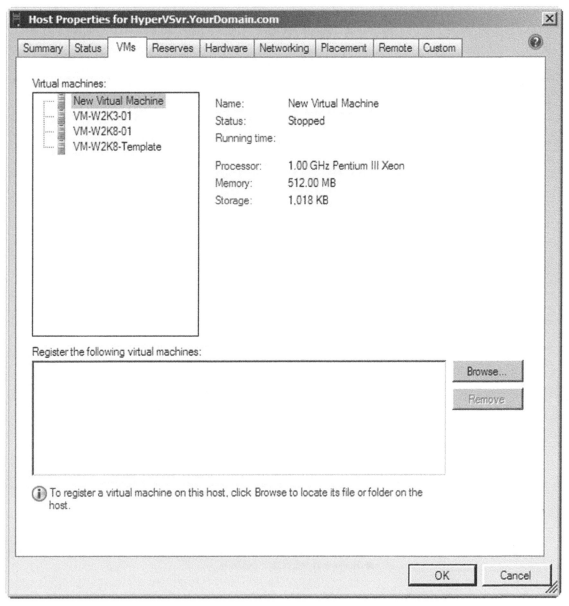

■ **FIGURE 5.40** VMs running on the Host.

all registered virtual machines on the host. Selecting one of the VMs will display its name, status, and what hardware resources are assigned to it. VMs are automatically registered when created, deployed, or migrated to a host. If you have an unregistered VM, you can register it by clicking the *Browse* button and locating the folder that contains the virtual machine's files.

14. To guarantee that a host machine has enough resources available to it for its own needs it is configured to reserve a certain amount of capacity for itself. The Reserves tab depicted in Figure 5.41 allows adjustment of the amount of resources set aside or reserved for the host machine itself. While you can modify the default settings, be careful not to undercut your host. Setting these values too high will limit the number of virtual machines that can be run on the host.

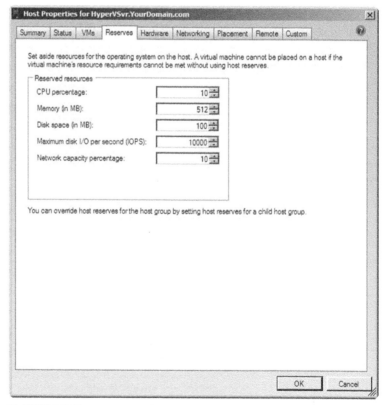

■ **FIGURE 5.41** Host resource reservations.

15. The Hardware tab, shown in Figure 5.42, displays the details of the
host machine's hardware.

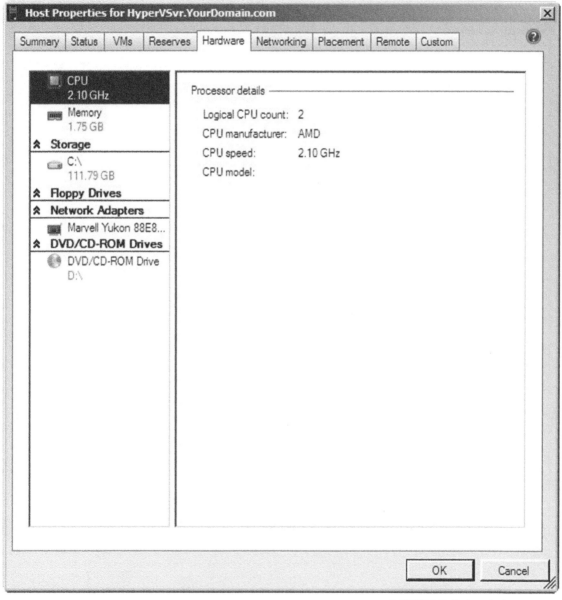

■ FIGURE 5.42 Hardware details.

16. The Networking tab in Figure 5.43 allows modification of the virtual network settings for the host. These are the same as the networks that were set up using the Hyper-V Manager. You can add a network tag for easier identification as well as a description if desired. You can

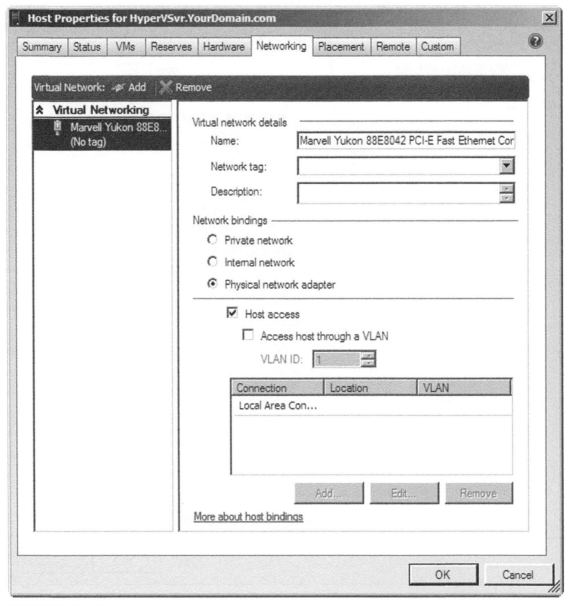

■ **FIGURE 5.43** Networking properties.

also change the network binding selecting from the three types: private network, internal network, or physical network adapter. Private network allows the virtual machines to communicate with each other, but not with the host. Internal network allows the VMs to talk to each other and with the host. You can further require that communication with the host be via a VLAN. Selecting *Physical network adapter* binds the VMs to a physical NIC allowing them to communicate with each other, the host, and other machines on your network. This is the same as the External setting in the Hyper-V Manager. Figure 5.44 illustrates the differences between these options. You can also require communication with the host to leverage a VLAN or block communication with the host altogether by clearing the *Host access* check box.

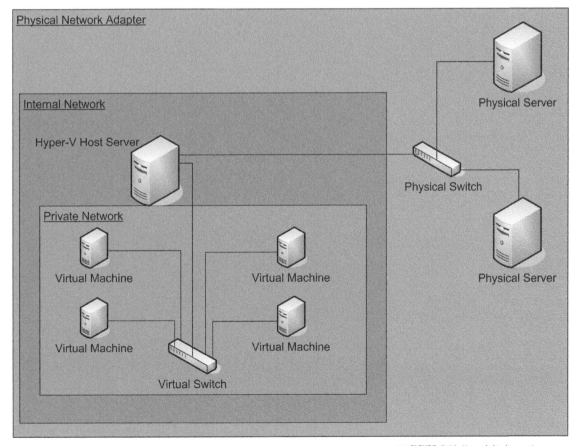

■ **FIGURE 5.44** Network binding options.

17. The Placement tab in Figure 5.45 allows you to add or remove default virtual machine paths.

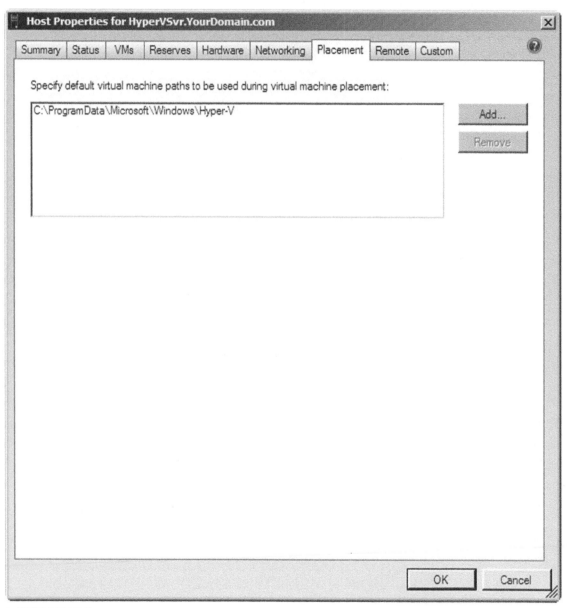

18. The Remote tab in Figure 5.46 allows you to change the remote connection port assignment for the host.

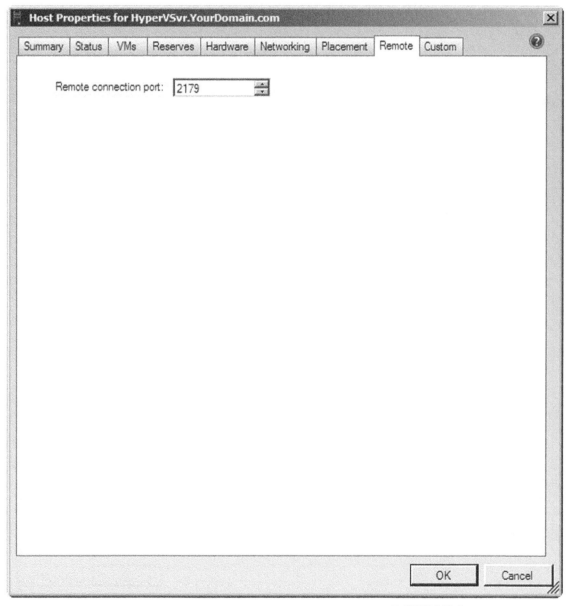

■ **FIGURE 5.46** Remote connection port.

19. If you want to add custom properties to your host that you can later display in the Hosts view in VMM, you can do so up to 10 times from the Custom tab depicted in Figure 5.47. You can leverage this option

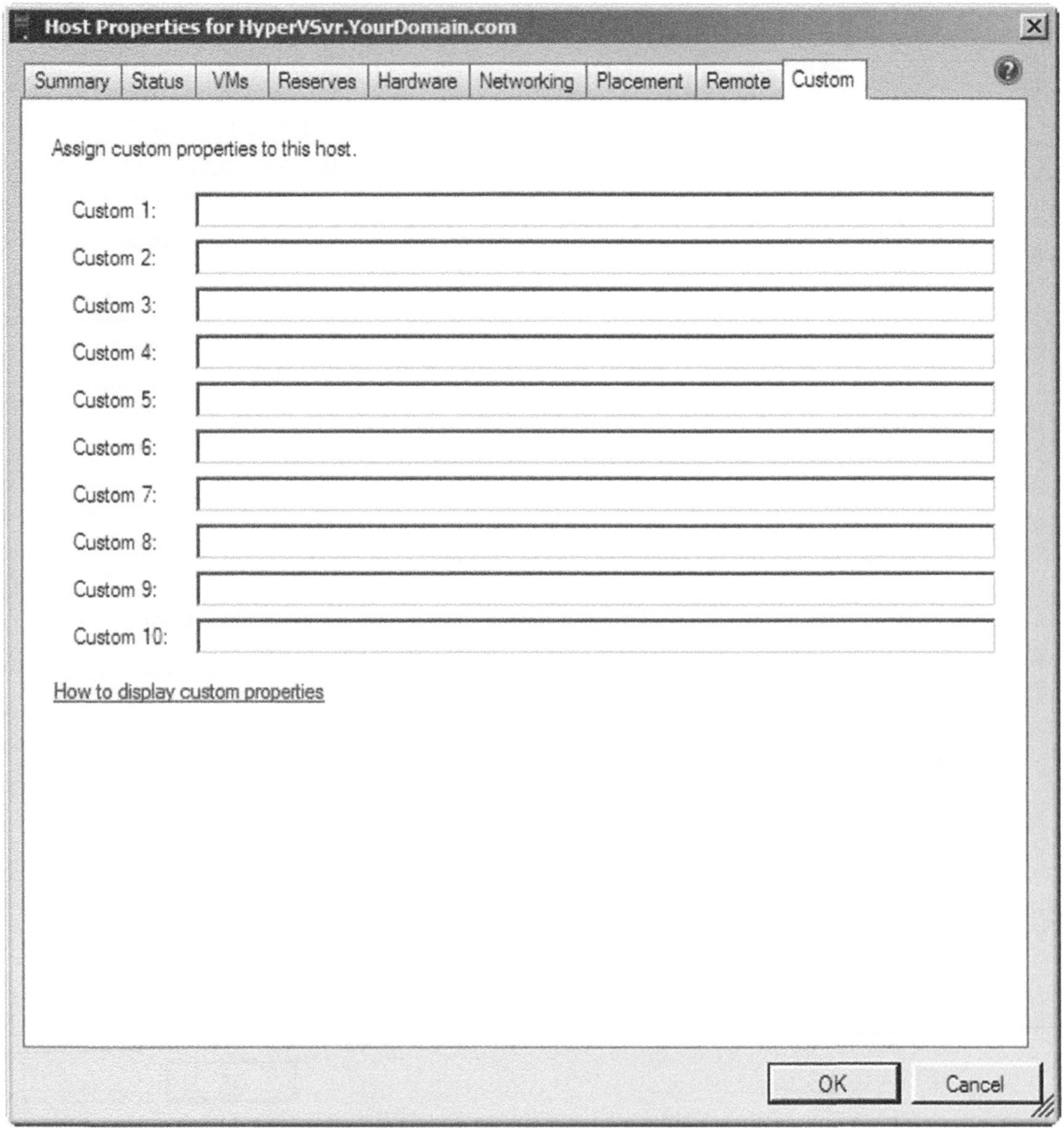

Host Properties for HyperVSvr.YourDomain.com

| Summary | Status | VMs | Reserves | Hardware | Networking | Placement | Remote | Custom |

Assign custom properties to this host.

Custom 1:

Custom 2:

Custom 3:

Custom 4:

Custom 5:

Custom 6:

Custom 7:

Custom 8:

Custom 9:

Custom 10:

How to display custom properties

OK   Cancel

■ **FIGURE 5.47** Adding Custom properties.

to provide details on the host's physical location, the name of the team or individual responsible for maintenance, or various support numbers for easy reference. Basically, any information that will make your life easier and is not included by default can find a home in custom properties.

SUMMARY

It is easy to set up VMs in your datacenter, but it may be difficult to manage them as the numbers of virtual machines and hosts increase. VMM provides the tools necessary to keep your increasingly virtualized environment under control.

As with most configurations in this book, it is a good idea to review all the steps involved before embarking on implementation. There are several configuration parameters you will want to confirm with your LAN/WAN engineers and other server engineers before implementation, including server names, port numbers, database names, etc.

Planning the placement of the VMM Library servers and Administration consoles will be crucial to the implementation and usability of VMM on your network. You should take into consideration any political, geographic, or departmental boundaries that must be accommodated in your design.

Virtual network configurations should conform to an overall virtualization strategy. Do not "wing it." The final configuration of your VMM should reflect the outcome of a thoughtful and well-documented virtualization approach.

Chapter **6**

Hyper-V and high availability

High availability (HA) in a nutshell means making a service available to users with the expectation that they will be able to access that service at all times, usually because some effort has been made to ensure continuous operation. In almost all cases, when someone is discussing HA, they mean some form of server clustering. Server clusters are a collection of two or more servers, usually identical, that are configured and managed as a single resource. Depending on the configuration, a cluster can be either a load-balancing cluster, where physical server resources are utilized based on client need; or a fail-over cluster, where a single cluster member (or "node") is used at a time, reserving the other nodes until the primary one fails.

In this chapter, we will discuss clustering in a Microsoft Windows Server environment, including a brief overview of concepts. We will compare "traditional" host-based clustering with the options that Hyper-V makes available to us, both from a fail-over situation and load balancing. Finally, we will go over some of the unique considerations that Hyper-V brings to building highly available services in your network.

OVERVIEW OF CLUSTERING CONCEPTS

Before we discuss clusters in a Hyper-V environment, it may be useful to go over some of the concepts around clustering, and Microsoft's solutions for providing clustering technology.

Clustering is done by using technology to group two or more servers together into a single functional unit. Traditional clustering techniques require the individual servers, or "nodes," to be physically identical—that is, they need to have the same hardware configuration, memory size, CPU speed, etc. They also need to be identical in software configuration, with the same OS and (ideally) patch levels, and the same applications installed. In addition, all nodes of a cluster must have access to the same data storage, at the same speed; this is typically done with a high-performance SAN.

There are two common types of clusters: fail-over and load-balanced. Fail-over clusters consist of a single node that typically handles all of the client requests, called the Primary node, and one or more nodes that are largely inactive unless the Primary node goes offline; these are called Secondary nodes. In a load-balanced cluster, all of the nodes participate actively in serving client requests. In most cases, a load-balanced cluster can also serve as a fail-over cluster, since one or more nodes of the load-balanced cluster can typically fail without the other nodes being impacted.

In any cluster, two major challenges present themselves: determining the status of a node member (particularly in fail-over clusters), and determining which node of a cluster currently controls a clustered application and its data. The first challenge is met with a heartbeat network, which is typically a physically separate set of network cards that communicate a signal, or heartbeat, to determine the status of each node. Data ownership is tracked by a data partition called the Quorum. The Quorum is a separate partition from the shared data, that also needs to be equally accessible to all nodes in a cluster. The quorum tracks which node is the owner of a given set of applications or data. A simplified diagram can be seen in Figure 6.1.

MICROSOFT FAIL-OVER CLUSTER AND NETWORK LOAD BALANCING

Microsoft has built into Windows Server since 2000 the ability to create a fail-over cluster in their Enterprise and Datacenter editions. The process is greatly simplified in Windows Server 2008, utilizing a wizard-based approach to validation and configuration of the nodes. The validation portion of the setup wizard checks your nodes as well as the available storage and network connections to ensure that the infrastructure will support the cluster, as well as checking the applications to ensure that they can support a clustered environment. It will also confirm that the server hardware is sufficient to support a clustered environment, before performing the steps necessary to set up and configure the cluster.

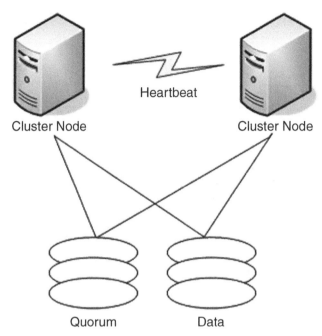

Heartbeat

Cluster Node   Cluster Node

Quorum   Data

■ **FIGURE 6.1** Simplified Cluster diagram.

Microsoft Network Load Balancing (NLB) is a technology that allows multiple network resources to be part of a pool with a common network name. When clients make a request of that network name resource, one of the nodes of the cluster responds. Which server responds is determined by an algorithm that selects servers so that a certain percentage of client requests is processed by each server. This percentage can be configured by the administrator.

DEFINING HA FOR HYPER-V

When we are discussing clustering solutions for Hyper-V, it is important to determine which layer of the virtualization stack is being clustered. Assuming that the physical computer meets the necessary requirements (access to attached storage, a dedicated network interface for heartbeat, etc.), the host can be in a cluster. The virtual machines themselves ("guests") can also be clustered on a single host; using virtual networks for heartbeat and virtual iSCSI for the quorum and other attached storage makes it possible to create guest clusters even if the host hardware would not normally support it. It is also possible to host Hyper-V guests as nodes across multiple physical hosts, provided all of the hosts are capable of being clustered. Figure 6.2 below compares virtual clusters to host clusters.

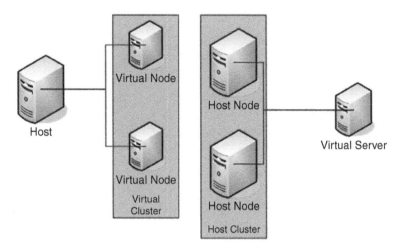

■ **FIGURE 6.2** On the left, a single physical host has a cluster of VMs. On the right, a physical cluster hosts a single VM.

MAKING VIRTUAL MACHINES AVAILABLE

With Hyper-V virtualization, then, you have the opportunity to create extremely robust fail-over solutions. Each physical host can contain multiple virtual machines, each a member node of a fail-over cluster. In addition, physical hosts can also be part of a fail-over cluster. An example of this arrangement can be seen in Figure 6.3.

In this diagram, virtual machines v1a, v2a, and v3a are installed on hosts H1A and H2A as a fail-over cluster; this arrangement is mirrored on the fail-over cluster H2A and H2B, providing nodes v1b, v2b, and v3b. This sort of fail-over clustering solution provides the following options:

- If the physical machine requires upgrades or repairs, the VMs can be activated on another node on the cluster.
- If the physical machine fails, the other nodes will take over for the failed host, bringing up their copies of the VMs automatically.
- If the VM itself fails, it can be restarted on the same host, or another host as appropriate. This is managed by Windows Server Fail-over Cluster, and the changes are done automatically, minimizing downtime.

Note
System Center Virtual Machine Manager 2008 can help in capacity planning and placement by providing calculations for node failure and VM placement for performance.

It is important, therefore, to keep storage and resources in mind when placing virtual machines. Because each VM can be monitored separately, you have the option of spreading your VMs out across the physical nodes of your cluster. This will give you increased performance, but may make it difficult to plan your storage capacity needs.

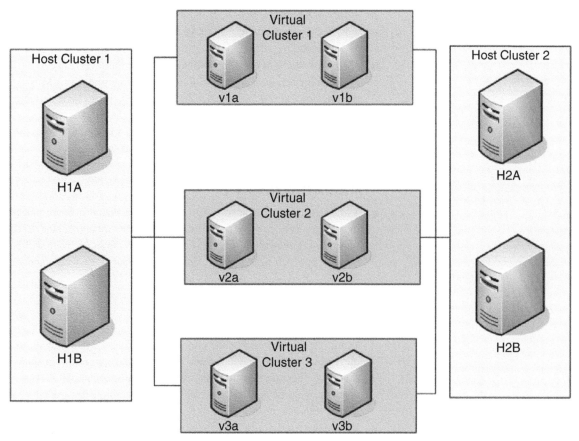

■ **FIGURE 6.3** Basic design of Virtual Clusters hosted by Physical Clusters.

MAKING VIRTUAL MACHINE SERVICES AVAILABLE

Another advantage that NLB clustering VMs provides you is the ability to make your services highly available—NLB can be used within a single host, or across multiple hosts, to provide service availability. In addition to load balancing, NLB allows member nodes to be removed from the cluster for maintenance or in case of failure. VMs that are nodes in a fail-over cluster through the NLB feature gain HA for their work-loads in the following scenario: Virtual machine maintenance. If the virtual machine requires updating or other forms of maintenance, the workload can be transferred to another VM on the host, or on a different host.

- *Host machine maintenance.* If the physical machine requires maintenance or repair, the workload of all of that host's virtual machines can be relocated.
- *Workload health monitoring.* Windows Server Fail-over Cluster can monitor certain resources within the VM to ensure the VM is running correctly. If the resource fails the check, it can be restarted or moved to another VM/host.
- *Host or virtual machine failure.* In the case of a machine failure, the workload can be transferred to VMs on another host.

THINGS TO CONSIDER

- Virtual machines that have VHDs on the same shared disk are placed in the same Service or Application Group. If one virtual machine needs to be moved, then all of the virtual machines in the same group will be moved. You will need to plan your storage capacity to accommodate this.
- Drive volumes can be created with GUIDs instead of drive letters; if such a volume is added to Cluster Management, it will show up under the GUID. When assigning a path to a GUID labeled drive for VHDs, ensure the GUID matches the one shown in Cluster Management, or the virtual machine may not start on other nodes in a fail-over situation. One common situation that can lead to mismatched GUIDs is when the volume is brought online on nodes before being added as a shared resource.
- Drive volumes can also be created with mount points instead of drive letters. If you chose to do so, you must ensure that all of the disks that are part of the same mount point are assigned to the same Application or Service Group. Failing to do so will make it likely that a virtual machine will fail to start up on a fail-over event.

Finally, if you are using Differencing Disks for your VHDs, they also must be stored on shared storage, in the same Application or Services group as the original parent disk. As with the other situations above, failure to do so means the VM will not start up in a fail-over event.

SUMMARY

In this chapter, we touched briefly on the basics of HA. Windows Server Fail-Over Cluster service has been updated for Windows Server 2008, and offers a wizard-based setup for configuring your clusters. Used in conjunction with Hyper-V, Windows Server Fail-Over Cluster gives you the ability to cluster virtual machines and physical machines to create a virtual infrastructure that is highly robust while still maintaining the advantages of virtualizing your server infrastructure.

NLB provides not only service availability, but some fail-over ability as well. You can use NLB and Windows Server Fail-Over Cluster to manage your virtual infrastructure, maintaining user availability in cases when a physical host or virtual machine needs to be updated, repaired, or restarted.

Virtual Hard Drives bring some unique considerations when planning for HA. You must ensure that the VHDs are contained on volumes that are properly labeled and available to the physical cluster to ensure that VMs can restart in the case of a fail-over event.

Chapter 7 will show you how to create virtual machines and templates to automate the creation of new virtual machines.

Creating virtual machines and templates

By this point in the book you should be familiar with the concept of a virtual machine (VM) and are probably getting anxious to create one for yourself. Hyper-V supports a number of guest operating systems including flavors of Windows Server 2008, Windows Server 2003, Microsoft Server 2000, Windows 7, Windows Vista, Windows XP, and Linux. This chapter will walk you through the implementation of a virtual machine and the creation of a virtual machine template. Let us cut short this introduction and get right to it.

CREATING YOUR FIRST VIRTUAL MACHINE

This section will detail out the process to create a virtual machine on your Hyper-V server. This would be a good time to gather the media (CD, DVD, or ISO file) for the operating system that you plan to virtualize.

1. We will start by opening Server Manager. If you are accustomed to earlier OS versions, Server Manager will look a lot different in Windows 2008. To open Server Manager, right-click *Computer* from the Start Menu and select *Manage* or click *Start | All Programs | Administrative Tools | Server Manager*. In the left column, expand the

Note
This chapter assumes you did not skip over Chapter 3 where you learned how to build your Hyper-V server. If you did skip it, please go back and review it now to setup your Hyper-V server before attempting to create your first VM.

Roles tree and highlight *Hyper-V*. Figure 7.1 shows the Server Manager Hyper-V role. You are presented with two useful, quick reference windows for system events and running services. Below those two sections is a third that offers a number of configuration best practices. Highlighting one displays a description below it together with a link to more detail from the Hyper-V help library.

2. Highlight *Hyper-V Manager* under Hyper-V in the left-hand pane. If it does not automatically show your server name below it, click *Connect to Server...* from the right-hand pane. Since you are connecting to the local Hyper-V Server installation, leave the radio button on *Local*

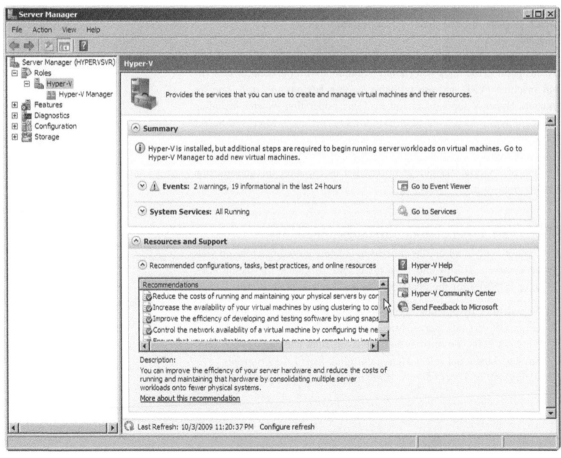

■ **FIGURE 7.1** Server Manager.

■ **FIGURE 7.2** Select your Hyper-V Server.

Computer... and click *OK*, as shown in Figure 7.2. If you have more than one Hyper-V server, you could manage it by entering the server name in the dialog box and clicking *OK* to connect to it.

You should end up with a screen similar to Figure 7.3.

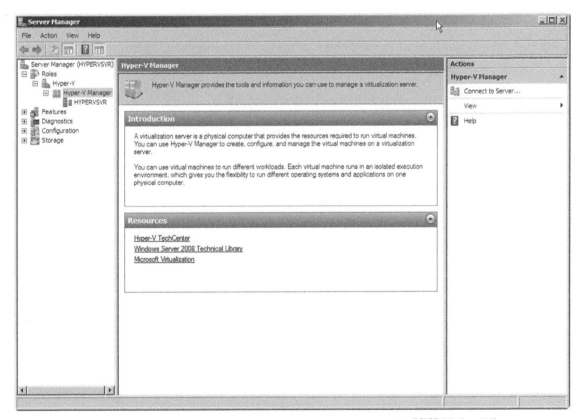

■ **FIGURE 7.3** Hyper-V Manager.

3. Select your Hyper-V server from the left-hand pane and you will be taken to the management console for your server, as shown in Figure 7.4. To begin building a VM, click *New* at the top of the left-hand pane. This displays a menu that allows you to create a virtual machine, hard disk, or floppy disk. Select *Virtual Machine*—to begin creating a VM.

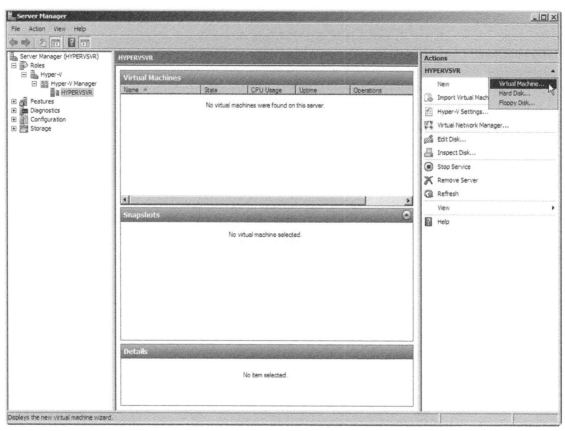

■ **FIGURE 7.4** Begin creating your VM.

4. The New Virtual Machine Wizard is presented, as illustrated in Figure 7.5. At this point, you could just hit the finish button and the Wizard would create a VM with default values, but what fun would that be? Instead, select *Next* to customize your VM.

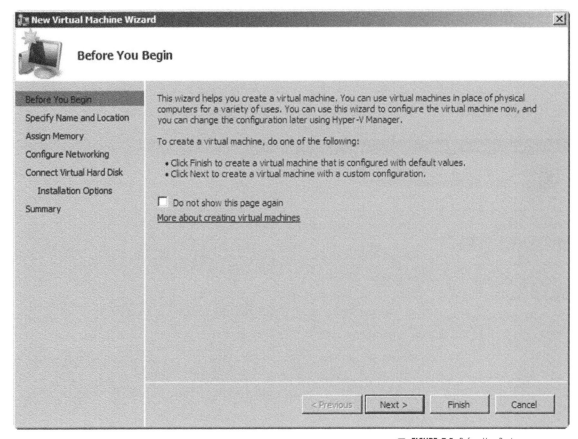

■ **FIGURE 7.5** Before You Begin.

5. As shown in Figure 7.6, name your Virtual Machine VM-01 or whatever name that is unique to your environment and makes sense. From this screen, you can also change the location where the VM files will be stored. If your server has multiple physical drives, it is a good idea not to place your VMs on the one on which the host OS files reside. When ready, click *Next*.

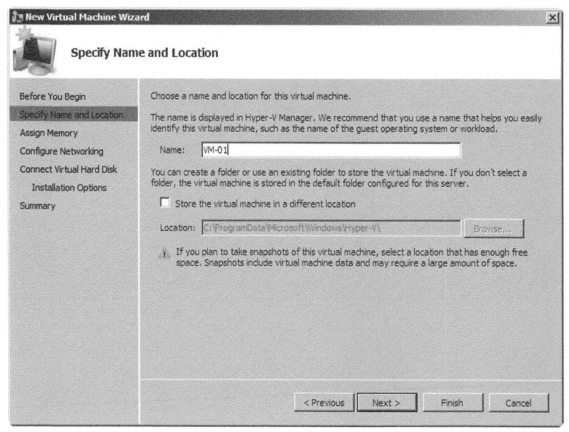

■ **FIGURE 7.6** Specify Name and Location.

6. At this point, you can select the amount of memory you want to dedicate to your VM, as shown in Figure 7.7. Memory requirements for a virtual instance of an operating system are the same as for a physical machine. You can start with the recommended or even the minimum amount and then add more if necessary to meet performance demands. The virtual machine operating system will dictate the maximum amount of memory that can be supported. The total amount of physical system memory is shared by all the virtual machines. Once allocated to a VM, the memory cannot be used by another VM. Set the memory value to whatever you think is appropriate for your particular VM. Click "Next" once you are done.

Note

Hyper-V tracks the sum of allocated RAM to all running VMs. It will not allow a VM to start if there is insufficient memory available.

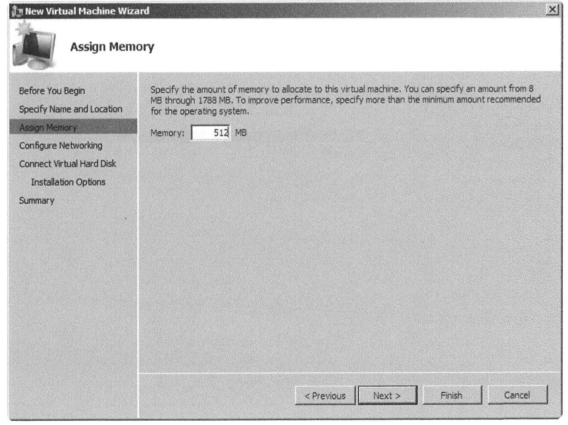

■ **FIGURE 7.7** Assign Memory.

Note

In essence, a physical network adapter becomes a "virtual switch" when it is made available to be assigned to VMs. This enables you to assign the network adapter to multiple VMs at the same time. However, if you are running bandwidth-intensive applications in your virtual environment, you should consider installing multiple network adapters in your server. This gives you multiple virtual switches to assign to your virtual machines to spread out the load.

7. It is time to configure the networking properties of the VM. You will see a dropdown list of the network adapters available for assignment, as shown in Figure 7.8. The Not Connected choice configures your VM in a stand-alone state without the ability to communicate with other machines on your network—virtual or physical. If you intend to install your OS from a server on your network, be sure to select an available network adapter. Select the desired adapter and click *Next*.

8. Every virtual machine is assigned at least one virtual hard disk. A virtual hard disk is simply a file, with a VHD extension, that stores the data associated with the VM just like a physical hard disk. At this point, you can create a new virtual disk or assign an existing one.

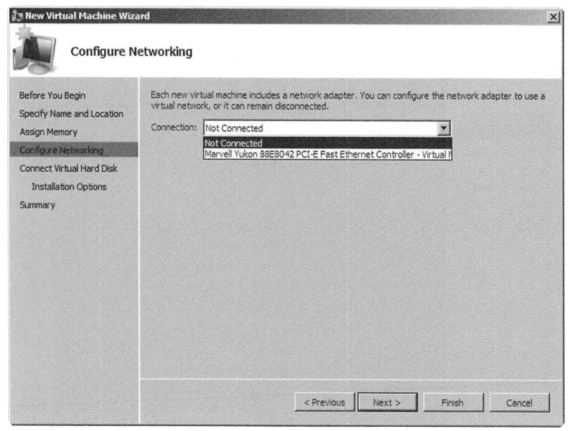

■ **FIGURE 7.8** Configure Networking.

Since we have not created one yet, let us create a new VHD file, as illustrated in Figure 7.9. We will rename the default VM-01.vhd to VM-01-C.vhd to easily identify the virtual disk as the C drive for the VM-01 machine, also as shown in Figure 7.9. You can also change the VHD file's location. You should store it with the other files for your VM. So if you accepted the default earlier, select it again. Otherwise, browse to the location you choose in Step 5. If you are unsure how much disk to allocate, select a size big enough for the operating system with some room for data. The size of the virtual disk can be changed or a second one added later. When you are ready, click *Next*.

Note

Dynamic VHD files start out small and grow up to the limit you assign. Hyper-V will allow you to allocate more virtual disk space than physical space. Exercise caution when oversubscribing your hard disk or you might run out of space at runtime. Oversubscribing the C drive is strongly discouraged for this reason.

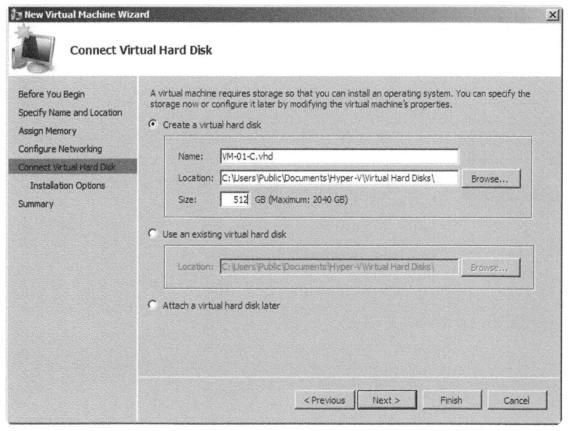

■ **FIGURE 7.9** Connect Virtual Hard Disk.

9. When installing the operating system for your VM, you have a few choices, as shown in Figure 7.10. You can install the OS from CD/DVD, ISO file, boot floppy, or from an installation server. You can also decide to install the operating system later, which will start your virtual machine in the same manner as a physical machine without an OS looking for a boot device. Using network-based PXE boot OS images can be a very convenient way to deploy your virtual operating systems. If you already have a PXE server setup, use it as appropriate. Setting up such a server is out of the scope of this book. However, you can find many useful how-to pages on the Web, including this tutorial on Windows Deployment Services for Windows Server 2008, http://go.microsoft.com/fwlink/?LinkId=81873. For our purposes, we choose to use a CD/DVD or an ISO file. Selecting the radio button for

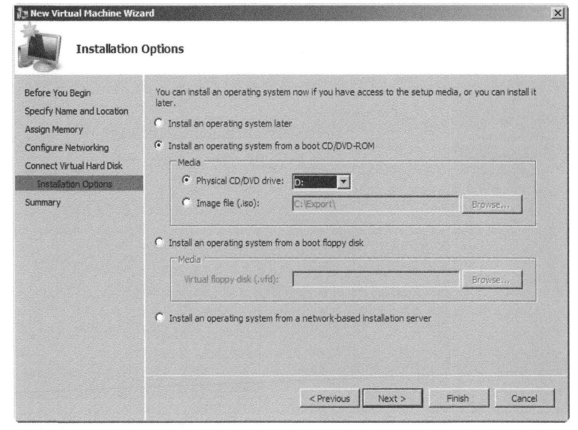

■ **FIGURE 7.10** Installation Options.

Installing an operating system from a boot CD/DVD-ROM will allow you to select a physical optical drive or browse to an ISO file. If you decide on using a CD or DVD be sure to place the disk in the appropriate drive now. Select whichever install option is right for you and then click *Next*.

10. Almost done! Figure 7.11 is the summary information for your virtual machine. Your display may differ from the figure below based on the choices you made during the creation process. The lone option left to you at this point is whether to automatically start the VM after it is created. Go ahead and leave this check box checked and click *Finish*.

Note

Clicking on the VM window may lock your mouse pointer onto the VM itself. If this happens, release the mouse to interact with the host machine again by pressing *CTRL-ALT-LEFT ARROW*. This requirement goes away once Integration Services are installed later in this chapter.

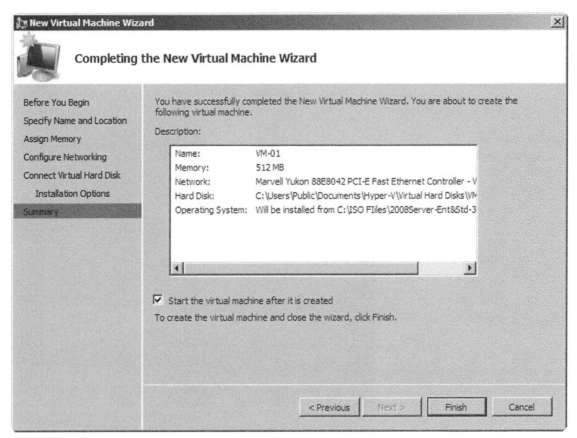

■ **FIGURE 7.11** Completing the Wizard.

Note

If your virtual machine does not automatically launch, you may have missed checking the *Start the virtual machine after it is created* box in the previous step. If so, skip to the next section "Connecting to a Virtual Machine and Basic Hyper-V Commands" and follow the steps to start your VM. Once it is running, return here.

Note

If you receive an error at this point referring to not being able to start the virtual machine, you may not have properly configured virtualization in the BIOS of the machine's motherboard. Consult your manufacturer's documentation for details.

Note

If your VM is running Windows Server 2008, you may be prompted to confirm you want to upgrade a previous version of integration services. Windows Server 2008 was originally built with an integration services version that was compatible with the beta version of Hyper-V. If you see this prompt, click *OK*.

Note

Do not forget that a virtual machine still needs all the same operating system and application patches that a physical machine requires.

11. You are now presented with the initial screen related to the install process for your operating system. Follow the normal install process for the operating system just as if you were installing it on a physical box. Once you complete the installation of the OS, you can proceed. While you are installing the operating system, your mouse may not be usable, and you will need to navigate the setup screen via the keyboard.

12. Congratulations, you just built your first virtual machine! One more step is required to help ensure that everything is functioning. With your VM running and while you are logged in with an administrator (privileged) account, open the *Action* menu of the VM window and select *Insert Integration Services Setup Disk*, as shown in Figure 7.12. This mounts the VMGUEST.ISO file as the virtual machine's DVD drive. Follow the prompts and Integration Services quickly installs. If you choose to implement a virtual machine running Linux, you can download the Linux Integration Components from www.microsoft.com/downloads/details.aspx?FamilyID=c299d675-bb9f-41cf-b5eb-74d0595ccc5c&displaylang=en.

Your first virtual machine is now complete. Go ahead and kick the tires a little. When you are ready, we will be waiting in the next section.

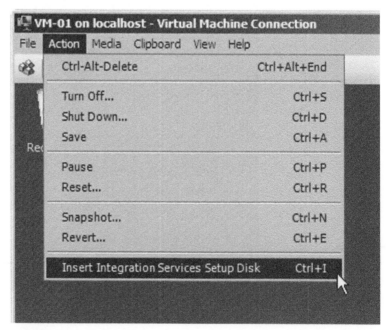

■ **FIGURE 7.12** Loading Integration Services.

CONNECTING TO A VIRTUAL MACHINE AND BASIC HYPER-V COMMANDS

Once you have created a virtual machine you will need to connect to it in order to configure the guest operating system, install applications, and generally take advantage of your efforts. In addition, you will want to begin using some of the basic Hyper-V commands, such as *Start*, *Stop*, *Snapshot*, and others.

1. To connect to a virtual machine you will first need to open Hyper-V Manager by clicking *Start* | *All Programs* | *Administrative Tools* | *Hyper-V Manager*. In the left column of the window, highlight your Hyper-V server name. As shown in Figure 7.13, your virtual machines will be listed in the center of the window. Choose one of your VMs and double click it.

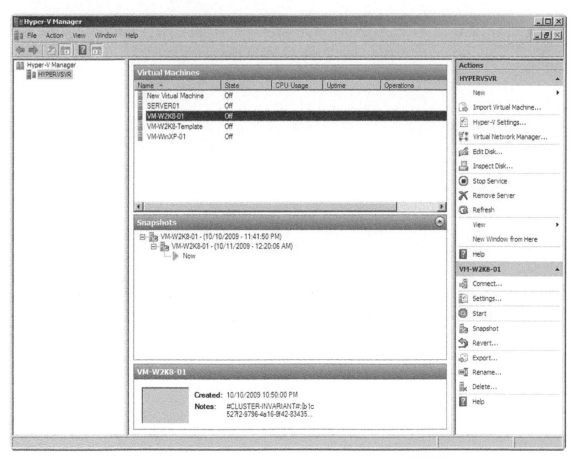

■ **FIGURE 7.13** Choose a Virtual Machine.

2. Figure 7.14 is the virtual machine running in a Virtual Machine Connection window. In our case, the VM is in a stopped state, similar to a powered off physical machine.

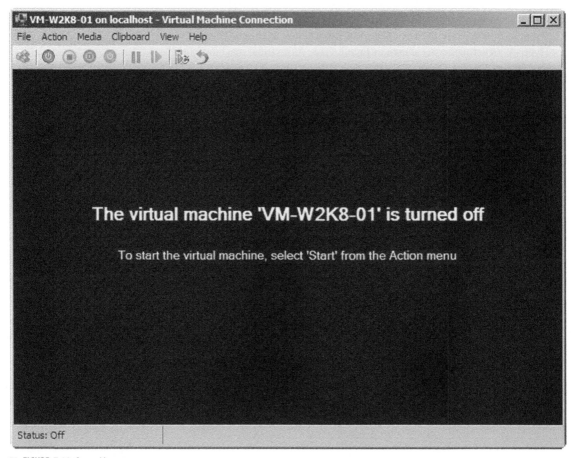

■ **FIGURE 7.14** Server Manager.

3. To "turn on" your virtual machine, click the *Start* button, as shown in Figure 7.15.
4. Your virtual machine will boot up just as a physical server would. Leaving you at the *Press CTRL+Alt+DELETE to log on* screen. As shown in Figure 7.16, click the *Ctrl-Alt-Delete* button at the top of the window to send the keystroke combination to your virtual machine. You can then log on to your VM just as you would do on any other machine to make any desired changes or to install software, etc.
5. A virtual machine can be shut down through the normal methods used to shut down a physical machine or you can click the *Shutdown* button, as shown in Figure 7.17.

Note

A virtual machine can be configured to allow a Remote Desktop connection for administrative access just like its physical counterpart. Once you are logged on to the VM, you can configure Remote Desktop in the same manner as on a traditional server or workstation. This is a valuable option when you want to grant console access to a virtual machine to someone without requiring them to have access to your Hyper-V server.

■ **FIGURE 7.15** Starting a Virtual Machine.

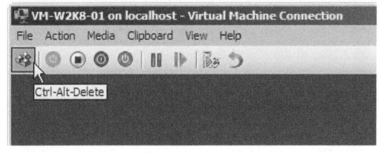

■ **FIGURE 7.16** Logging on to a Virtual Machine.

■ **FIGURE 7.17** Shut down a Virtual Machine.

6. If you want to turn your virtual machine off without performing the recommended shutdown process, you can do so by clicking the *Turn off* button, as in Figure 7.18. This is useful in the event that your VM is locked up or otherwise preventing a proper shutdown.

7. Clicking the *Save* button, as in Figure 7.19, puts the virtual machine into a hibernate-like state that when restarted resumes at the same point that it was prior to entering the saved state.

8. A virtual machine can also be put into a suspended mode by clicking the *Pause* button, as illustrated in Figure 7.20. To release the VM from its suspension, click the *Resume* button, as in Figure 7.21.

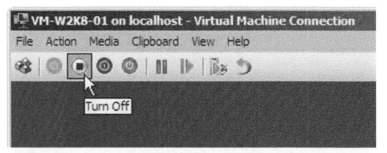

■ **FIGURE 7.18** Turn off a Virtual Machine.

■ **FIGURE 7.19** Saving a Virtual Machine.

■ **FIGURE 7.20** Pausing a Virtual Machine.

■ **FIGURE 7.21** Resuming a Virtual Machine.

9. Clicking the *Reset* button, as shown in Figure 7.22, is the virtual machine equivalent of a cold-reboot. In other words, it is effectively the same as turning the power to the machine off and then back on. Similar to the "turn off" button, this command can be useful when your VM is unresponsive.

10. The *Snapshot* button, shown in Figure 7.23, takes a point in time backup of your virtual machine referred to as a snapshot. This is a very useful feature in any number of situations. For example, a snapshot can be taken before applying operating system or application patches.

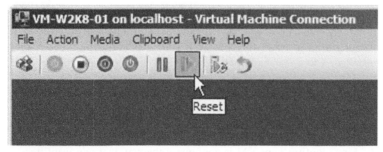

■ **FIGURE 7.22** Resetting a Virtual Machine.

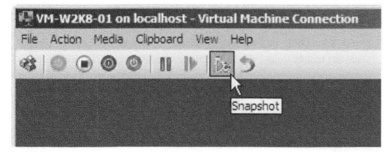

■ **FIGURE 7.23** Taking a Virtual Machine Snapshot.

■ **FIGURE 7.24** Reverting to a Virtual Machine Snapshot.

Then if validation testing fails, you can quickly revert back to the snapshot by clicking the *Revert* button, as shown in Figure 7.24.

WHAT IS A VIRTUAL MACHINE TEMPLATE?

A virtual machine template is an image of a virtual machine you can lever- age to quickly create a new VM without stepping through the entire OS and application installation process. Using templates increases your agility when asked to "standup" a new environment. But perhaps more impor- tantly, it saves *you* time. There are many scenarios where a template can prove valuable. For example, you can create a template of each OS in use in your enterprise, complete with your standard applications already installed. Those standard applications might include your antivirus prod- uct, data backup software, or a monitoring agent.

Warning
Do not forget that a virtual machine is put at risk by vulnerabilities lurking in its operating system just like its physical counterparts.

CREATING YOUR FIRST VIRTUAL MACHINE TEMPLATE

1. First, confirm your VM is configured the way that you want it and you installed the applications you want to include in the template. This is also the time to ensure your VM is fully patched so that you are not starting from square one each time that you build a new VM. Once you are satisfied, take a snapshot backup of your virtual machine just in case something goes amiss. To create the snapshot, simply highlight the desired VM and select *Snapshot* from the right-hand pane. You can monitor the progress of the snapshot creation in the top panel of the middle pane. Once created, it shows up in the center panel, as in Figure 7.25.

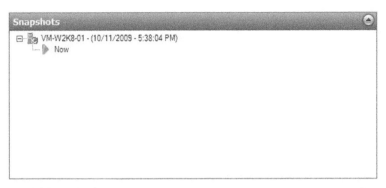

■ FIGURE 7.25 Snapshots.

2. Now you are ready to seal your image with SYSPREP. SYSPREP removes any unique values assigned to the instance of the OS during installation. This process differs somewhat between different OS versions. For instance, SYSPREP is built into Windows Server 2008 while the needed files for Windows Server 2003 are found on the installation CD. Windows 7 and Windows Vista use the Windows Automated Installation Kit. Consult Microsoft's TechNet Web page for the appropriate instructions for your instance. Go to http://technet. microsoft.com and enter in the search window *SYSPREP* followed by the operating system that you have selected to use. You should also try including the service pack you installed in case there is an update specific to it. When SYSPREP finishes, your VM should shutdown and be ready for export.

3. Before exporting your VM, create a folder to house your template. The folder can be located directly on the host machine or on a network share. Returning to the Virtual Machine Manager, highlight the VM and rename it to VM-[OS]-Rename, where OS is the OS of your template. For example, VM-W2K8-Rename. You can either right-click on the VM and select *Rename...*, select rename from the right-hand window pane, or just hit *F2*. When you build a new VM from a template, it takes on the name of the original VM from which the template was created and it goes on the list with all of your other VMs. While this may not be terribly confusing when there is only one or two, when you have many virtual machines, it can be difficult to find the new one. Appending *New* to the template helps to make any new VMs created from it stand out from the others so that you can quickly rename each of them appropriately.

Note
Virtual machine names in the Hyper-V Manager are not tied to the name given to the VM from within its operating system. However, we strongly encourage you to keep these names synchronized to reduce confusion whenever possible. If you are using Virtual Machine Manager, discussed in Chapter 5, you will receive an alert if the names do not match.

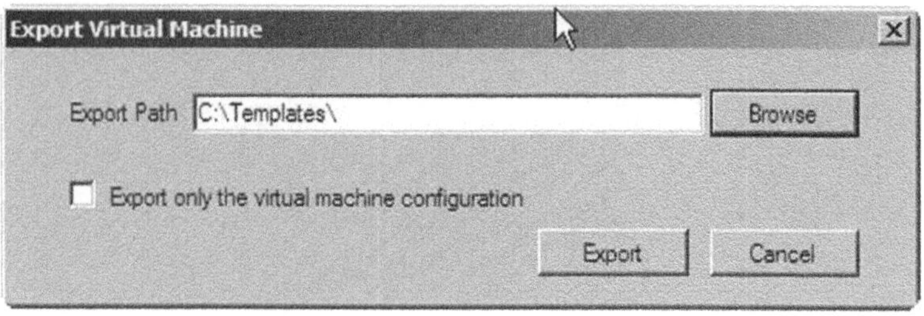

FIGURE 7.26 Export Virtual Machine.

4. Now that our template folder is ready and the VM is named properly, proceed by highlighting the VM and selecting *Export ...* from the right-hand pane. Leaving the *Export only the virtual machine configuration* checkbox empty, browse out to the templates folder you created, as illustrated in Figure 7.26, and click *Export*.

5. When the export process begins, you can monitor the progress by watching the status in the virtual machines operations column in the center pane of the window. When the export process is complete, rename the source VM you used by replacing *New* with *Template*. For example, VM-W2K8-Template. This is simply a good housekeeping step to help keep your VMs straight. As you get more experience with Hyper-V, you will likely develop your own naming conventions. Figure 7.27 is included to help illustrate the proposed naming strategy detailed in this section.

	VM Name Before Export	VM Name After Export
Explanation	Any VM created later from the template that you are making will adopt this name at creation. Including "New" in its name will help it stand out from your other VMs until you can name it appropriately.	After the export has been performed renaming the source VM to include "Template" will help keep you from inadvertly modifying one of your prestine baseline VMs.
Example Name	VM-W2K8-New	VM-W2K8-Template

FIGURE 7.27 Proposed naming convention.

USING A TEMPLATE TO CREATE A NEW VIRTUAL MACHINE

1. When you create a virtual machine from a template, it will use the template's source folder as its destination, and you will not be able to reuse it to create more VMs. Therefore, you will want to first copy the template folder to the folder where you keep your running VMs.
   a. In Windows Explorer, browse to the folder in which you have exported your template.
   b. Copy the entire folder to the directory structure where you want to store your new virtual machine. You can rename the new folder afterward to a name specific to the VM you are creating for easier association. In this example, we have used VM-W2K8-01.
2. Now that you have prepared the files, import them to create a new VM.
   a. Return to the Hyper-V Manager and select *Import Virtual Machine...* from the right-hand pane.
   b. Browse to the folder you created in the previous step and click *OK* to start the import process.
   c. When it finishes you will find a new VM in the Hyper-V Manger, in our case VM-W2K8-Rename, as shown in Figure 7.28.
3. Now is a good time to rename the new VM to reflect the desired name for the new machine. Note that changing the name of the virtual machine in the Hyper-V Manager will not change the computer name within the operating system.
4. Double click your new VM to launch the Virtual Machine Connection window.

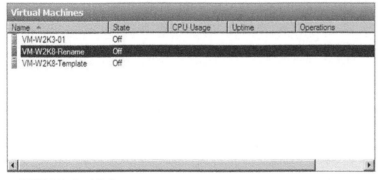

■ **FIGURE 7.28** Virtual Machines.

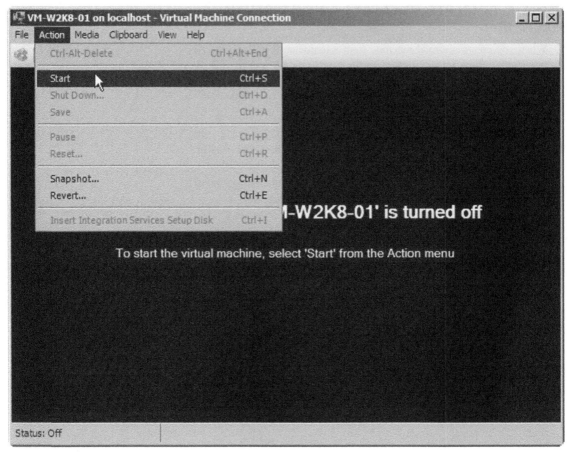

■ **FIGURE 7.29** Starting the VM.

5. Start the VM by selecting *Start* from the *Action* menu, as shown in Figure 7.29.
6. Step through the mini-install process for the operating system. If this is a Linux virtual machine, there may not be a mini-install.
7. That was quick! Unless you elect to leave your new VM as a stand-alone machine, assign it a network adapter.
   a. Right click on your VM and select *Settings...*
   b. Select *Network Adapter* from the hardware list on the left.
   c. Select your adapter from the dropdown list, as shown in Figure 7.30.

You have done it! All you need to do to mass produce production servers with this new image is to repeat the steps in this section.

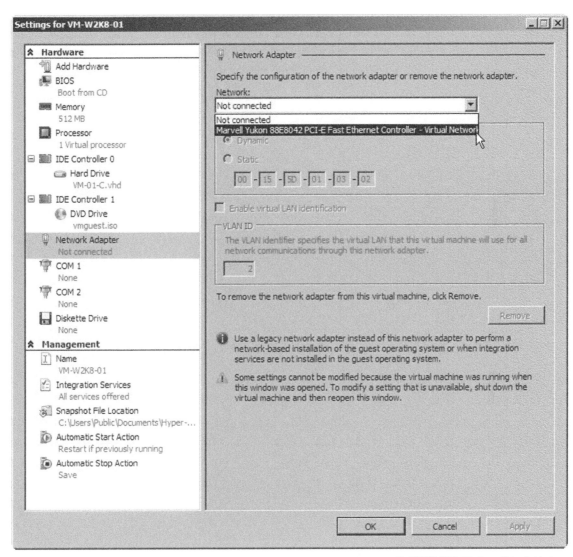

■ **FIGURE 7.30** Selecting a Network Adapter.

SUMMARY

Creating virtual machines for your Hyper-V environment is not difficult. Like everything else in the world of virtualization, planning is key. The hardest decisions you make are how to deploy your target operating systems, naming conventions, and final locations for your images.

As with any technology management process, consistency and control are very important. VM image management can quickly degrade if clear, documented processes are not followed. Poor management will eventually result in image-deployment disconnects. These disconnects can lead to developers unknowingly using wrong images to create new applications or failure to recreate critical systems following a business continuity event.

8

Performing physical-to-virtual and virtual-to-virtual migrations

---

In this chapter, we discuss a function of Hyper-V that will likely become one of the most heavily used in your new "dynamic data center." Whether you perform a migration simply to retire outdated hardware, consolidate workloads, or create mirror-like test environments, you will learn quickly that migrating servers into and among the virtual server farm is something that will be used quite often in the overall migration to your dynamic data center. In this chapter, we will discuss exactly what a migration is, and when to best perform one; benefits are not always gained through a migration from a physical server to a virtual one. We will also step you through actual migrations, both from a physical server to a virtual server and a virtual server to a new virtual server.

HYPER-V MIGRATIONS

Migrating servers is not new; for years, IS professionals have been migrating servers from one piece of hardware to another. Let us face it; we are not quite to the point of hardware life cycles matching up with software life cycles, so there is a really good chance that the brand-new enterprise application you are implementing today will outlive the server platform it is being deployed on; anybody supporting legacy applications knows this well. The introduction of virtualization to the mainstream began to change the rules. Of course, nobody wants to jump right in and be the first to move revenue-generating powerhouse applications to a virtual environment, no matter how hard our inner geek is screaming for us to do so. So starting in the late 1990s, IS professionals began to use virtual environments for testing—not just for applications, but the virtualization technology itself. In its infancy, virtualization technology simply did not allow for migrating existing platforms into the virtual world; as a result, over the years, we all became very fluent at building virtual servers and workstations from scratch. Of course, this process evolved into creating templates or prestaging copies of virtual operating systems that could be implemented within minutes. It was only a matter of time before the technology would catch up to the desire to import an existing physical server platform into the virtual world. We are now on the cusp of flawless migrations of physical server platforms into the virtual world, and doing so seamlessly while the server is in use by end users, without impacting performance.

In the brave new world of using virtualization to support frontline production operations, the upper echelon of management is looking to their own engineers and trusted vendors to provide the confidence and expertise needed to begin moving more toward not only data center virtualization but also a truly dynamic data center environment. You should expect hesitation in the discussions to implement production supporting virtualization; there is a mind-set obstacle that many managers need to overcome when it comes to the use of virtualization. Managers comment on preferring a "real" server over a virtual platform. For some it is as simple as preferring to have a solid object to visualize in their mind, whereas others simply have skepticism about the technology itself. Regardless of the reasoning, your design should be written in a way to accommodate and address all concerns. That said, as mentioned elsewhere in this book, your approach needs to be focused on accomplishing your goals in a feasible, appropriate way. Do not virtualize for the sake of virtualizing.

Microsoft calls out some specific best practices when migrating specialized server platforms. Familiarize yourself with these best practices thoroughly before attempting to migrate any of the specialty servers discussed in the next section.

Microsoft exchange server

Virtualizing Exchange has been a topic of great controversy ever since virtualization first came on the scene. In the early years of virtualization, it was recommended NOT to run Exchange in a virtual environment because of the limitations of the infant technology. Since then, virtualization has matured in a way that has removed many, if not all, of those limitations. Unfortunately, the recommendations of the past have remained as a worry in today's discussions surrounding the partnership of virtualization and Exchange. The truth is Microsoft fully supports the virtualization of Microsoft Exchange today. As with any other environment, you must be sure that you configure your virtual platform to properly support Exchange, but there are no limitations within Microsoft's Hyper-V technology that should cause any concern in your discussions to virtualize Exchange.

There are some key items that Microsoft has called out that IS professionals should be aware of when designing their virtual Exchange environments.

- The software platform should be Windows Server 2008, or any third-party vendor virtualization platform that has been validated by Microsoft's Windows Server Virtualization Validation Program. Located here: www.windowsservercatalog.com/svvp.aspx? svvppage=svvp.htm, the Validation Program includes some of the most well-known vendors of both hardware and software. The site will help you to identify those who have been validated by Microsoft to provide platforms capable of running all flavors of the Microsoft Servers.
- If you are planning to virtualize your Exchange environment, you must use Exchange Server 2007 with Service Pack 1 or later. Earlier, Exchange versions are not fully supported on a virtual platform. The use of the Unified Messaging role is not supported if your Exchange server is running within a virtual platform. It is important to note that the base Exchange 2007 system requirements WITHOUT the use of virtualization is Windows 2003, but the use of this operating system as a host for Exchange 2007 is not supported in the virtualization world. We mention this because some may consider building Exchange 2007 in a nonvirtual environment with the plan to migrate the complete operating system into Hyper-V at a later date. If you plan to do this, you must build your environment using Windows 2008 or later.

Note
Unified Messaging is the ONLY Exchange 2007 server role that is not supported in virtualization, all other server roles are fully supported.

Note

If you plan to use a third-party hypervisor, you should plan to check with the vendor to see what their SCSI, iSCSI, and virtual IDE drive size limitations are prior to designing your new Exchange environment.

- Exchange 2007 on a virtual platform supports all of the most common forms of storage. These include virtual hard drives (VHD), SCSI, and iSCSI storage. If you plan to use SCSI or iSCSI, you must configure it to be presented as block-level storage within the hardware virtualization software, and it must be dedicated to the Exchange guest machine. Exchange 2007 does not support the use of network attached storage, but if the storage is attached at the host level, the guest will see it as local storage. Should you plan to use SCSI or iSCSI in your virtual Exchange environment, Hyper-V only supports VHDs up to 2040 gigabytes (GB) in size, and virtual IDE drives up to 127 GB; plan accordingly.

- Microsoft supports the use of both cluster continuous replication (CCR) and single copy clusters (SCC) within Exchange running in a virtual environment so long as there are no hypervisor-based clustering or migration technologies in use. An example of these technologies would be Quick Migration for Hyper-V and VMotion for VMWare. Likewise, Microsoft does support the use of hypervisor clustering and migration so long as CCR and SCC are not in use within the Exchange environment.

- One of the biggest advantages of virtualization is the ability to take snapshots of your virtual environment as part of a backup or disaster recovery plan. In the Exchange world this can be problematic because this kind of technology is not "application aware." This means the snapshot technology is not capable of taking into account the way the application actually uses and processes its data. Because of the way Exchange processes data, Microsoft does not support the use of any kind of snapshot technology with your virtual Exchange server. However, it should be noted that in the case of Exchange, the other benefits of virtualization tend to outweigh the inability to use snapshot technology.

- When you are configuring the virtual processors for your Exchange host, it is important to understand that Exchange running in a virtual environment does not support a ratio of greater than 2:1. Hypervisors provide the ability to share the logical processors of the host server to the guest machines. For example, a dual processor system using quad core processors contains a total of eight logical processors in the host. You may have some virtual servers that end up using less processor power than another, so the full processor may not be needed by that server. Depending on the virtual servers, this may allow you to have much more than eight virtual servers configured to have two processors each. However, in the Exchange world, Microsoft would not support the allocation of more than 16 virtual processors across all of the guest machines running on the server, or a total of four quad processor Exchange servers.

Microsoft SQL Server

The SQL performance team has published a document related to the use of SQL 2008 in a Hyper-V environment. A few of the key items are listed in this section, but it is strongly suggested that you download and review this document in its entirety prior to implementing SQL in a Hyper-V environment. To download this SQL team's document, go to http://download. microsoft.com/download/d/9/4/d948f981-926e-40fa-a026-5bfcf076d9b9/ SQL2008inHyperV2008.docx.

Use a synthetic network adapter provided by the Hyper-V Integration tools instead of a legacy network adapter when configuring networking for the virtual machine.

Avoid emulated devices for SQL Server deployments when possible. These devices can result in significantly more CPU overhead when compared to synthetic devices.

SQL Server is I/O intensive, so it is recommended that you use the pass-through disk option as opposed to the fixed-size Virtual Hard Disks (VHDs). Dynamic VHDs are not recommended for performance reasons.

In the SQL Team's document, they used locally attached storage on the Hyper-V server. Many virtual hosts are connected to shared storage using Fiber Channel, iSCSI, or NFS. Selecting the proper storage connection will greatly impact the I/O performance of the virtual SQL Server.

Microsoft SharePoint technologies

Microsoft fully supports the use of SharePoint servers and technologies within the Hyper-V environment. A great deal of information can be found at TechNet (http://technet.microsoft.com/en-us/library/cc816955.aspx), but some of the key items are included in the following list.

- Any Hyper-V virtual server must meet the requirements of the physical server (e.g., CPUs, memory, and disk I/O) that you are going to run as a Hyper-V guest. As with all virtual technologies, there is an overhead cost on the host computer for each virtual machine.

- Do not use the Hyper-V snapshot feature on virtual servers that are connected to a SharePoint Products and Technologies server farm. This is because the timer services and the search applications might become unsynchronized during the snapshot process and once the snapshot is finished, errors or inconsistencies can arise. Detach any server from the farm before taking a snapshot of that server.
- Do not use more virtual CPUs than there are physical CPUs on the Hyper-V host computer. Although Hyper-V will allow you to allocate more virtual CPUs than the number of physical CPUs, this causes performance issues because the hypervisor software has to swap out CPU contexts.

Finally, before we jump into some scenarios and examples of how to migrate your servers, there are some key points that MUST be understood by IS professionals in order to establish accurate expectations.

1. Do not expect every migration from physical to virtual to be smooth, or quick. Most migrations will take longer than a vendor may lead you to believe. This is not because you are doing it wrong, it is simply the nature of converting an established server from running on dedicated hardware to running under a virtualized platform.
2. Virtualize properly. Having the capacity to virtualize your entire data center does not mean that you should blindly plan to migrate all of your servers. Do your homework and check twice when creating your design. A proper design will take into account all of the items listed in Chapter 10 of this book.
3. Ease the pain. Discuss with your peers and management the truth and the myths associated with virtualization, if you leave room for skepticism and doubt, both will grow in a negative way.
4. Migrate methodically. Start with a smaller and less critical server and perfect your techniques before tackling the core business application server. Allow time after each round of migration to test and stabilize the environment. Too much change at once can lower client satisfaction and acceptance. Taking the migration in manageable chunks will allow management and other stakeholders to become comfortable with their choice to virtualize.

Migrating into virtualization is a big step for any organization, but it is much safer, and more controllable than a lot of other technologies. The biggest fear about virtualization is typically based on the misunderstanding of the technology. Learn it thoroughly and present it honestly, and you will soon move past the fears and look forward to the benefits. Migrations are nondestructive to the source machine. If the new virtual machine does not work or fails to migrate the source can be turned back on to restore access to the data or services. It is a good practice to power down the migrated server and let it sit in place for at least a day or two before disconnecting and reallocating it.

MIGRATION SCENARIOS

Hyper-V is a great tool for demonstration environments, testing environments, QA environments, and production environments. Many IS professionals have known for years that the use of a virtualization platform on a laptop is a great way to present proposed designs and implementations without the need for a full collection of multiple servers and workstations. There are a growing number of situations where using Hyper-V can be beneficial, but before we jump into some of those scenarios, there are some key considerations of which you should be aware.

Microsoft recommends a minimum of two network adapters on the server or workstation you plan to use as a Hyper-V host. If you plan to use iSCSI, you should bump your minimum network adapter count to three. Common practice would be to use one network adapter for the host, the second network adapter for the iSCSI connection, and the third network adapter exclusively for the hosted environments to communicate with the network. But you can get creative when needed. Here are a few examples of how you can manage your network adapter usage.

1. Four Adapters, no iSCSI—In this example, one adapter is assigned to the host partition, and the remaining three are used for the virtual networking. Storage is either directly attached or provided through fiber. This allows for the creation of three separate virtual switches.
2. Four Adapters, with iSCSI—In this example, one adapter is assigned to the host partition, one adapter is assigned to the iSCSI connection, and the two remaining adapters are used for virtual networking. This setup allows for the testing and use of multiple virtual environments on a single virtual switch.

Server Consolidation is often the first thing to come to mind when people begin to discuss the use of server virtualization. The reduction of 20 hardware servers into a single hardware server is a pretty big incentive. There are still licensing costs associated with the software being used within the virtual servers, but the cost savings related to the reduction in hardware is hard to ignore. Using the advanced Windows Server 2008 licenses will allow different numbers of virtual machines to be run on the same physical host. Using Windows Server 2008 Data Center licenses for a two-processor server to achieve our 20 to 1 consolidation, you can save the

Note

It is important to remember that Hyper-V does NOT provide support for the use of wireless networks. This will rarely be noticed on a true server hardware platform, but as mentioned earlier, a lot of IS professionals prefer to use laptops running full virtual environments for demonstrations, and testing design concepts. Hyper-V also does NOT support the use of "sleep" or "hibernation." Neither should be a problem, but it is something to keep in mind in your configuration steps for the laptop.

cost of about 14 Windows Server licenses. Just remember that in the big picture, server consolidation should be seen as a nice side benefit to using server virtualization, and not the primary focus. Should the focus be to simply reduce the number of hardware servers, chances are key items and considerations will be missed, resulting in future regrets. Done properly server consolidation can result in a much lower total cost of ownership not only for server hardware but also in power consumption and cooling costs. Consolidating servers into a virtual environment also allows for benefits not always initially envisioned, such as infrastructure optimization, more efficient asset utilization, and flexibility.

Business continuity and disaster recovery are issues that a lot of companies are beginning to take a serious look at when it comes to the use of virtualization. The elimination of previous technology limitations is allowing for the use of virtualization in a broad spectrum across the enterprise data center. This is a great plan, but as with anything, it needs to be researched thoroughly for your company. Every company is different in the way it embraces new technology; there is not just the implementation of new technology to consider, but the mindset of those who manage it, and those who must be confident enough to sign off on the cost required.

MIGRATING PHYSICAL TO VIRTUAL

As discussed previously, there are many reasons to migrate a physical server to a virtual platform. In this section, we will walk you through the step-by-step process of migrating a physical server using the System Center Virtual Machine Manager. We will also touch on a new tool called Disk2VHD, that was released by Microsoft while this book was being written, that will allow you to perform a physical migration in alternative ways.

Physical to virtual—System Center Virtual Machine Manager 2008 (VMM2008)

Before performing a physical to virtual migration using the Virtual Machine Manager 2008, be sure the server you plan to migrate is a member of the same domain as your VMM2008 server.

1. Launch the System Center Virtual Machine Manager by browsing
   to *Start | All | Programs | Microsoft System Center | Virtual
   Machine Manager.* Doing so will display the splash screen seen
   in Figure 8.1.

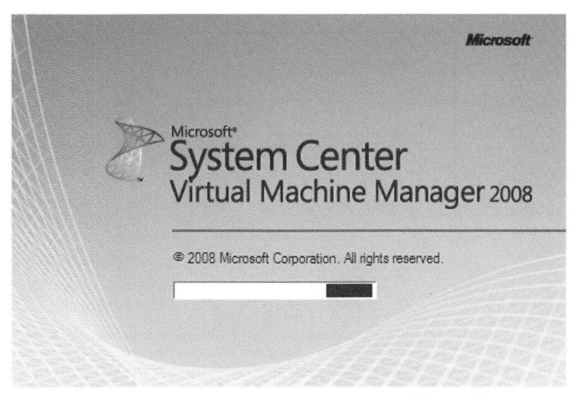

■ **FIGURE 8.1** VMM2008 Splash Screen.

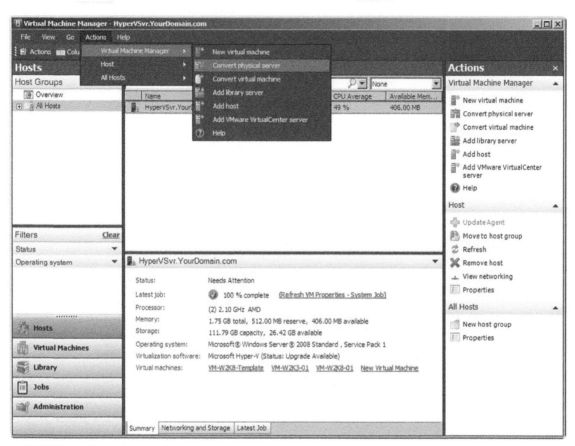

FIGURE 8.2 Launching physical to virtual migration.

2. With the VMM console up and running, browse to *Actions | Virtual Machine Manager | Convert Physical Server* from the toolbar. Figure 8.2 provides an example of this step.

3. The completion of Step 2 will begin the Migration Wizard. All of the steps in this process allow for modification of the default process. Do not make changes you do not fully understand or it could result in a failed migration. The first screen of the wizard is the "Select Source" window, displayed in Figure 8.3.

4. You have a few options. You can enter the hostname of the server, the IP address of the server, or you can browse for the server. For our example, we chose to browse for the server. Clicking the *Browse* button brings up the typical "browse for" wizard used for location computers, users, and user groups. As you can see in Figure 8.4, we entered the hostname of the server we plan to migrate, and then clicked *OK*.

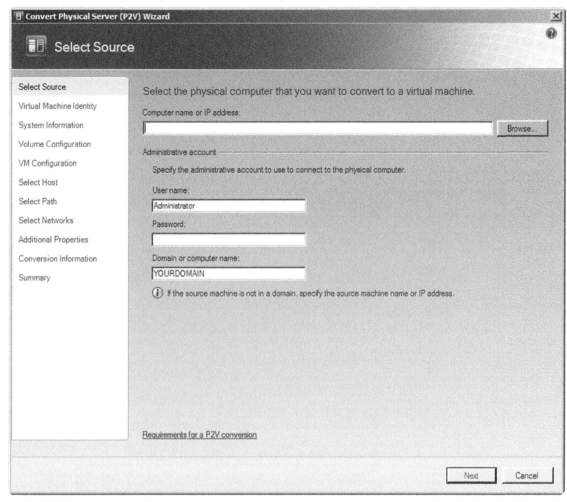

■ **FIGURE 8.3** Select Source.

■ **FIGURE 8.4** Select Computer.

5. Figure 8.5 shows our Select Source window with the server selected. You will need to enter the credentials of an account that has administrative rights on the server to be migrated. Once the credentials have been entered, hit the *Next* button.

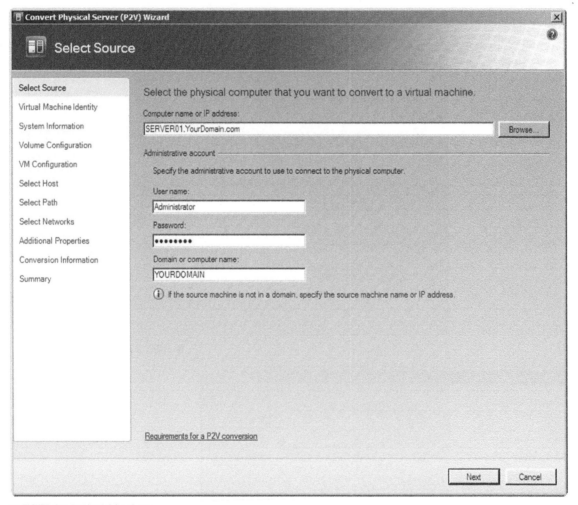

■ **FIGURE 8.5** Populated Select Source.

6. The next window in the Wizard is the Virtual Machine Identity (see Figure 8.6). For our example, we are going to continue to use the same name as the physical server; however, you may want to consider changing server names slightly as they get migrated so that you can more easily manage them, such as adding a "V" to the beginning of the name. With the Virtual Machine name entered, click *Next* to continue.

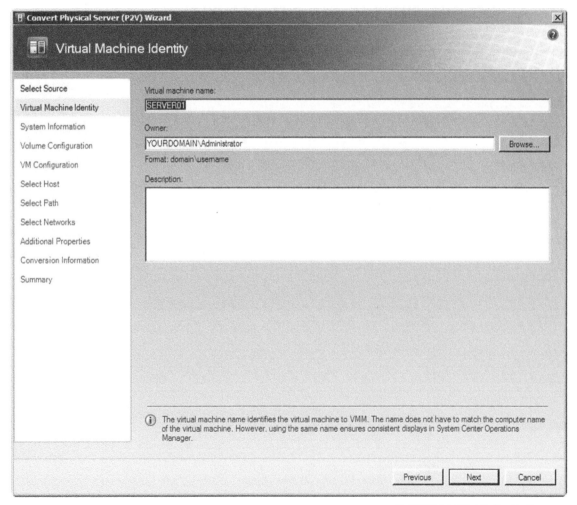

■ **FIGURE 8.6** Virtual Machine Identity.

7. The next window in the Wizard is the System Information window (see Figure 8.7). This step performs a remote scan of the target server in order to validate connectivity, and to gather some of the basic information required to create the virtual framework for the server. Depending on network speed and the attributes of the server being migrated, this step can take a little time. For our example, we migrated a basic Windows 2008 Standard Server on the same local network as our VMM console and it took about 3 min to complete this step. Click *Next* to begin the scan.

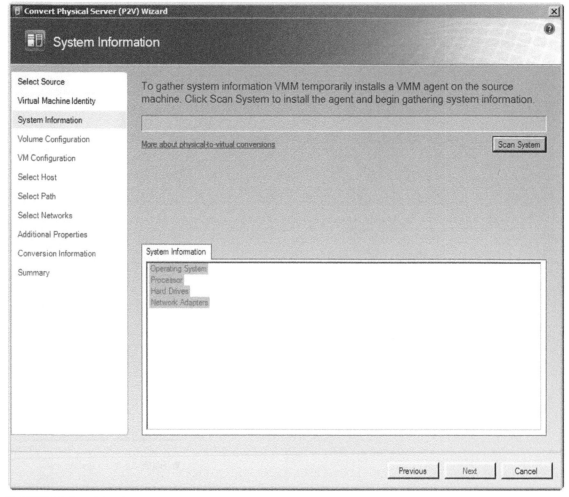

■ **FIGURE 8.7** System Information.

8. When the system scan completes, as you can see in Figure 8.8 that the Wizard will display some of the basic information about the server being migrated. If any of the information displayed is unexpected, verify that you are migrating the proper server before moving forward. Otherwise, click *Next* to continue.

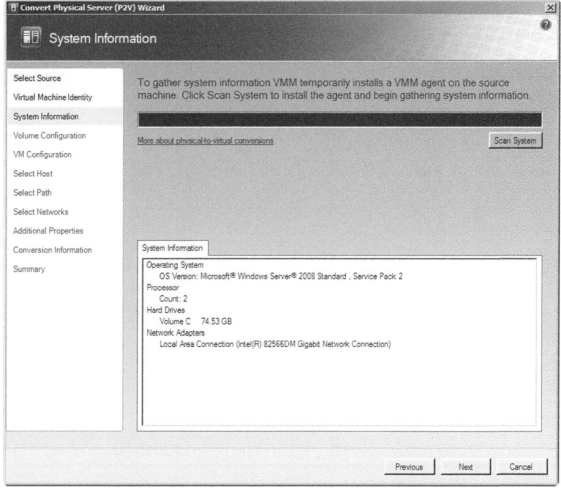

■ **FIGURE 8.8** System Information Scan Complete.

9. The Volume Configuration window of the Wizard will allow you to pick and choose the volumes of the server you wish to migrate (see Figure 8.9). For our example, we had a single volume, but the Wizard will detect as many as you may have, and you can deselect any that you wish NOT to include in the virtual version of your physical server. Verify\Select the volumes to include and click *Next*.

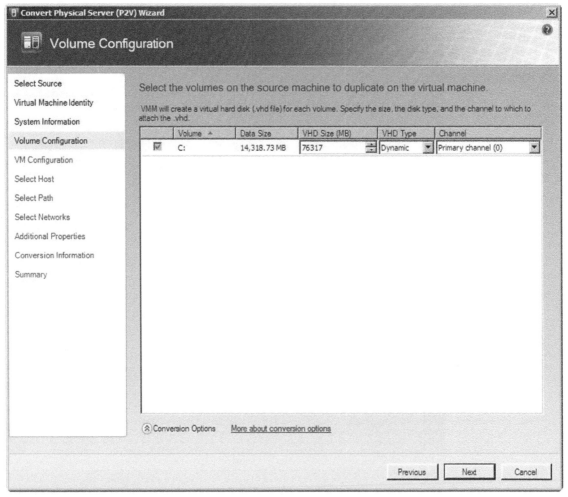

■ **FIGURE 8.9** Volume Configuration.

10. The next window in the Wizard is the Virtual Machine Configuration window (see Figure 8.10). This window will be prepopulated based on the scan of the physical server. It is recommended that these values be used for the creation of your virtual server; however, these values can be modified if needed. Assuming, of course, that your Hyper-V environment has the available resources. Verify\Modify the selections and click *Next* to continue.

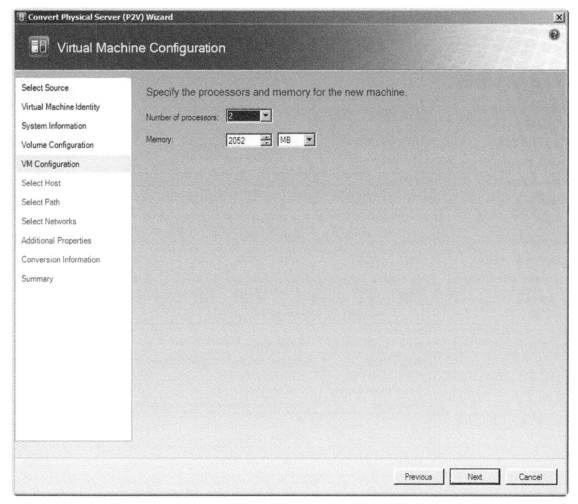

■ **FIGURE 8.10** Virtual Machine Configuration.

11. The Select Host window of the Wizard allows you to choose the Hyper-V host that your virtual server will be added to (see Figure 8.11). For our example, we only have a single host, but most production environments will have multiple Hyper-V hosts for the sake of redundancy. This step also gives you a "rating" based on the available resources of your target host compared to the configurations you just defined for your virtual server. Select your host and click *Next* to continue.

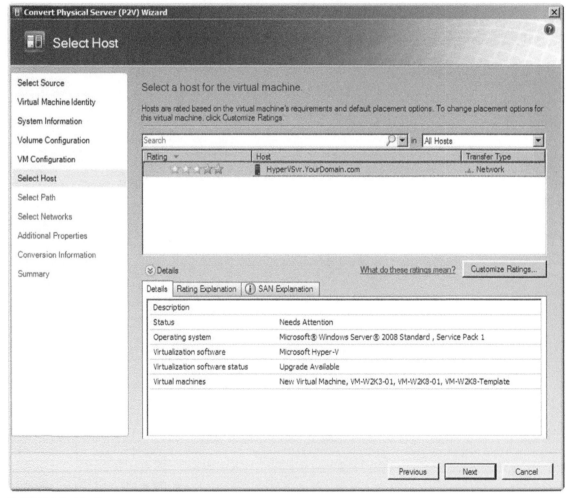

■ **FIGURE 8.11** Select Host.

12. The next step allows you to modify the default path of the VHD file you are about to create. Verify\Modify this selection and click *Next* to continue (see Figure 8.12).

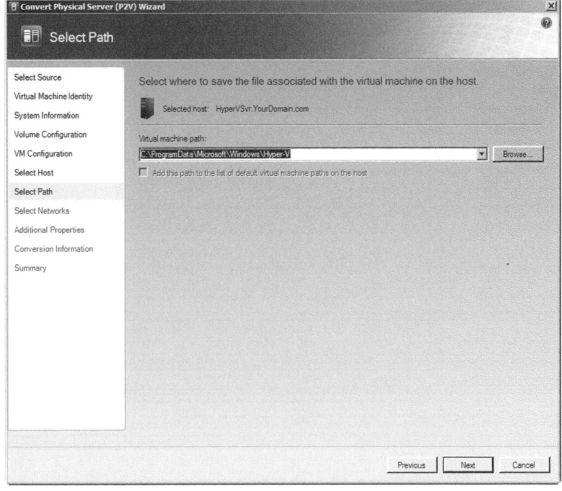

■ **FIGURE 8.12** Select Path.

13. The Select Networks option is the next window in the Wizard (see Figure 8.13). This selection allows you to choose the network adapters or configurations you have availed on the Hyper-V host to create the virtual server on. Select an option and click *Next* to continue.

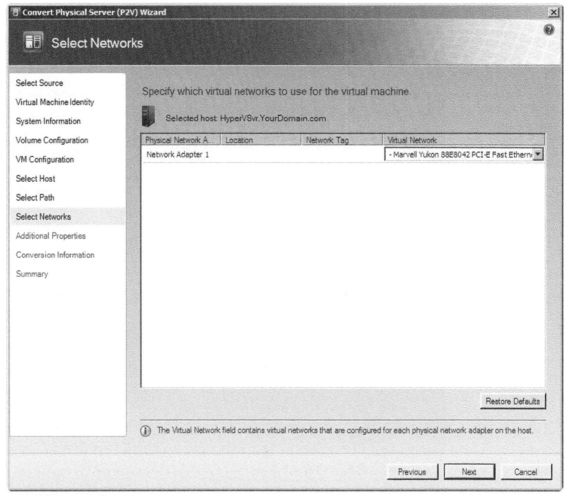

■ **FIGURE 8.13** Select Networks.

14. The Additional Properties window of the Wizard allows you to modify the way Hyper-V manages your new Virtual Server, such as automatically booting the server as soon as the Hyper-V environment is available and how to treat the Virtual Server in the event that the Hyper-V server encounters problems. Choose the selections that best apply to your Virtual Server and click *Next* to continue (see Figure 8.14).

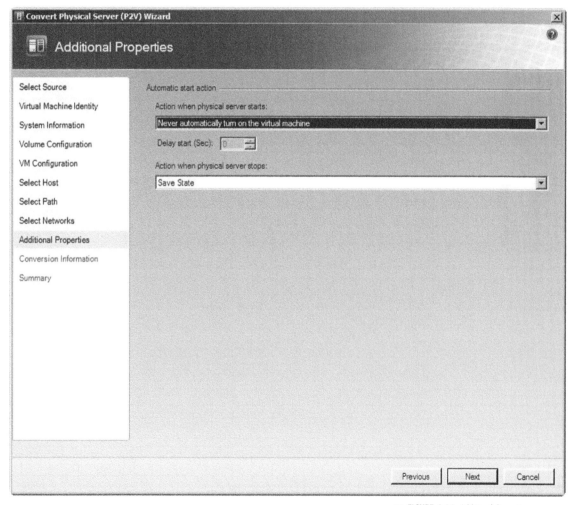

■ **FIGURE 8.14** Additional Properties.

15. At this point you have entered all of the information and configured all of the setting required to migrate your physical server into a virtual server. The next window is the Conversion Information window. This step will inform you of any issues that have been detected and will need to be corrected before continuing. Assuming no issues have been detected, click the *Next* button to continue (see Figure 8.15).

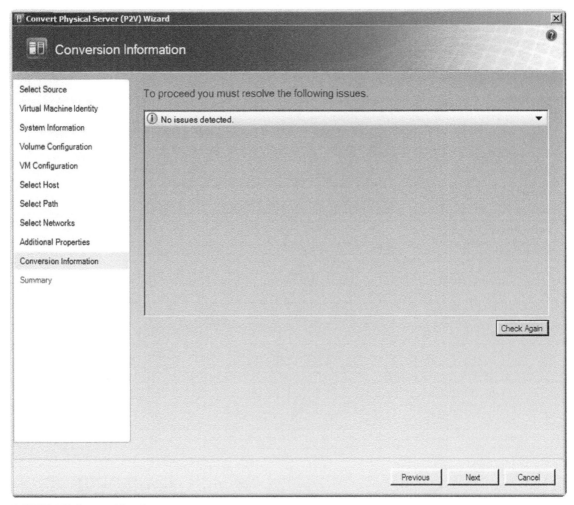

■ **FIGURE 8.15** Conversion Information.

16. The Summary window displays all of the key information related to the migration itself. Review this information and click *Create* to begin the migration (see Figure 8.16).

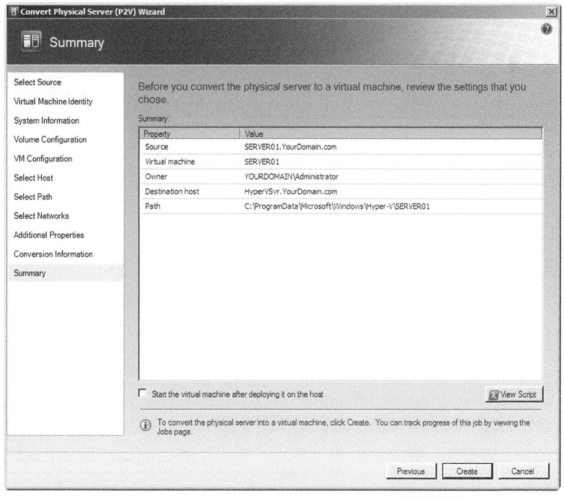

■ **FIGURE 8.16** Summary.

17. Once the *Create* button is clicked in Step 16, the job status window will become active. This window displays a great deal of information related to the migration process (see Figure 8.17). Again, depending on the server you are migrating and your network environment, this step may take a great deal of time. For our example, the migration of a basic 2008 Standard Server took just less than an hour and a half.

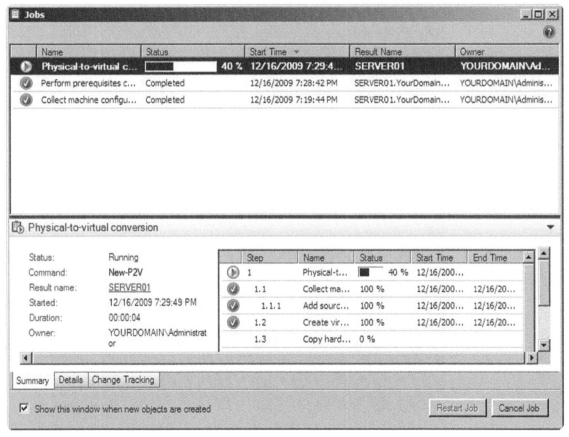

■ **FIGURE 8.17** Job status.

18. Once the migration is complete, the job status will change from a numerical percentage, to the message, Completed. At this time, you can view the logs of the migration on all three tabs at the bottom of the screen: Summary, Details, and Change Tracking. Figures 8.18–8.20 provide an example of the data collected during our server migration.

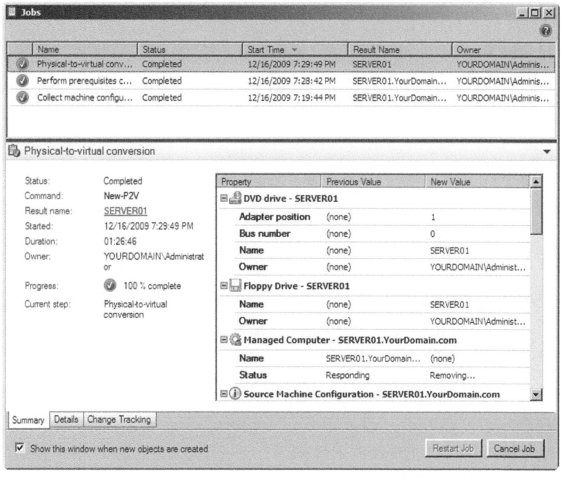

■ **FIGURE 8.18** Completed Status—Summary.

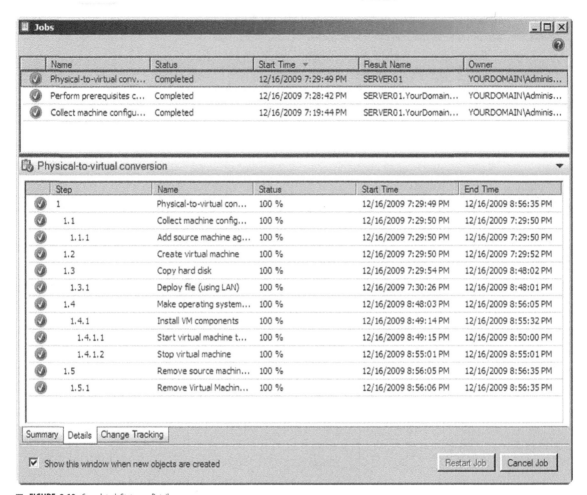

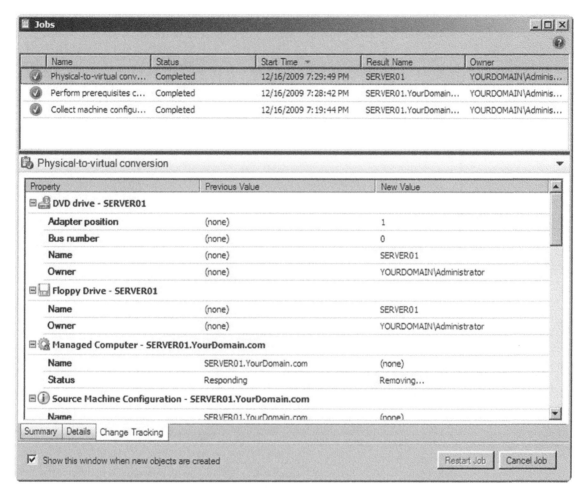

■ **FIGURE 8.20** Completed Status—Change Tracking.

With your new server completely migrated, you will now be able to see it in the Hyper-V console. At this point, the server is completely virtualized and capable of being managed like any other virtual server. Figure 8.21 shows our server fully migrated and running within the Hyper-V console.

Physical to Virtual—Disk2VHD.

As of the writing of this book, Microsoft released a new tool called Disk2VHD (for more information go to http://technet.microsoft.com/en-us/sysinternals/ee656415.aspx). Most IS professionals are familiar with Sysinternals tools. Over the years, we have grown to love the valuable

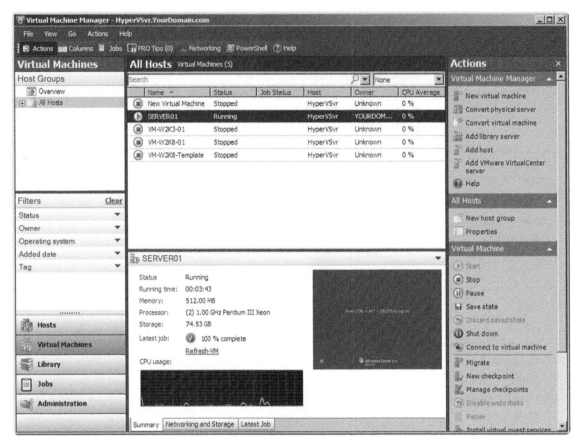

■ **FIGURE 8.21** Virtual Server.

Note

When you are working with Virtual PC, it is very important to remember that Virtual PC supports a maximum virtual disk size of 127 GB. So if you create a VHD larger than this limit, it will not be accessible from Virtual PC.

tools that it includes. Disk2VHD will be no different. A great tool that gets right to point, it will help many IS professional tasked with migrating physical servers to the virtual world. Disk2VHD allows an IS professional to create a VHD of a physical server that you can then take and import into Virtual PC or Hyper-V session.

Once you create the VHD, you can create a new VM with the attributes you prefer and then add the newly created VHD to the VM's configuration as an IDE disk(s). In its current version, Disk2VHD does not make anything other than IDE VHDs. This is an ideal tool to use for legacy servers that may not be a member of the same domain as your SCVMM console or Hyper-V environment. It can also be useful when you have a large number of servers to virtualize, and multiple engineers to assist in the process. Each one can move from server to server and create VHDs independently of the SCVMM console.

Note

Microsoft does not support attaching VHDs to the same system they were created from. So, if you create VHD from the system drive of Server A and then attach it to an instance of Virtual PC running on Server A, it will fail to boot.

As with most of the Sysinternals tools, Disk2VHD includes command-line options to allow for the scripting of VHD creation. Below is the usage syntax and an example:

- Usage: *disk2vhd <[drive: [drive:]...]\[*]> <vhdfile>*
- Example: *disk2vhd * c:\vhd\snapshot.vhd*

We downloaded a copy of Disk2vhd and ran a quick test on my laptop. Here are the screenshots we collected from this test. The test itself was run on a laptop with a Core 2 Duo 2.20Ghz CPU and 4 GB of RAM. The operating system is Windows 7, and the entire process took about 20 min. Obviously, the length of the process will vary depending on the system being used.

In Step 1, we launched a command window and entered the Disk2vhd command (Figure 8.22); for our example, we are creating the VHD file on the root of an external drive mapped to U:\.

Launching the application displays a license agreement prompt (Figure 8.23). Clicking *Agree* allows the process to continue.

Clicking *Agree* opens the Disk2vhd console, it is fairly basic and straightforward, but that is what we liked about it. It is more of a GUI confirmation of the command you entered (Figure 8.24). Clicking the *Create* button will launch the process. The window stays active for as long as the VHD creation is running.

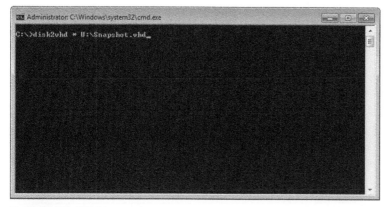

■ **FIGURE 8.22** Disk2vhd command.

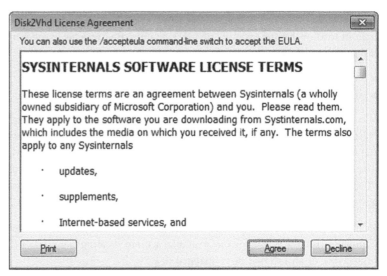

■ **FIGURE 8.23** Disk2vhd License Agreement.

■ **FIGURE 8.24** Disk2vhd Confirmation and Progress Window.

Once the process is complete, the window goes away and you are done. This process turned our 60 GB HDD with 23 GB of used space into a 14 GB VHD file that we can now use to create a VM in Virtual PC or Hyper-V.

MIGRATING VIRTUAL TO VIRTUAL

Some of you may be wondering why this section is even here, migrating virtual to virtual does not seem to make a whole lot of sense? Well for those of you, who are a little confused over this section, think outside of the Microsoft world ... ah yes, it quickly makes sense.

You need to have the ability to migrate your virtual servers between different vendors. For example, you may be a Microsoft shop looking at VMware or vice versa. If you were unable to migrate your huge number of virtual servers from one platform to another, you might choose to stay away from that vendor altogether, so all of the big players in the virtualization world play nicely in this respect. You can migrate your virtual servers between VMware and Hyper-V all day long without issue. This is especially assuring when you begin to look into Disaster Recovery options and alternatives. For example, you may use VMware in your data center, while the facility you need to access for Disaster Recovery services uses Hyper-V. Each of the vendors has their own built-in wizards that allow you to perform a migration from one environment to another. You may want to contact your vendor prior to migrating an especially vital server or an older legacy server just to see if there are any extra steps you should follow, but for standard servers, migrating between vendors is fairly simple.

SUMMARY

In this chapter, we discussed the reasons why and the methods to use when migrating a physical server to a virtual environment. The points mentioned in this chapter must be used as a guideline only. The same server may be a perfect candidate in one data center, and not even a consideration in another. Remember that your data center consists of more than a bunch of hard drives and memory, your data center supports your company, and you must be capable of supporting your data center. Virtualization is no longer in its infancy; it is becoming the method of choice for deploying new servers to the enterprise.

A tool that you may want to consider using in your planning is the Microsoft Assessment and Planning Toolkit. Designed precisely for the purpose of identifying potential virtualization candidates, the toolkit allows you to run a query against your production environment without the need of installing any agent software on your existing devices. The toolkit may also help to identify previously unmanaged devices both virtual and physical.

There are many gains that can come from the use of virtualization, but remember not to virtualize simply for the sake of virtualizing. You must have a solid plan built upon thorough investigation and research in both the technology itself, and how your company in particular might benefit from the use of it.

Design your virtualization plan in a way that includes both short-term and long-term goals. The best short-term plans can easily crumble if they do not take into account future growth.

Chapter **9**

Securing, monitoring, and managing a virtual infrastructure

Working in a virtualized environment does not absolve you of the responsibility of securing the virtual infrastructure. Virtual machines are no less vulnerable to malware, hacking, denial of service, and other attacks than their nonvirtual counterparts. Fortunately, apart from the usual steps taken to secure a nonvirtual infrastructure work in a virtual environment, there are additional steps that can further secure you against mishap. In this chapter, we will discuss the customary methods that are used and how to implement them in a virtual infrastructure. We will also introduce you to the new methods available to you to further secure your virtual systems, and we will offer some design considerations for your virtual network. Finally, we will discuss how to keep your systems up to date, and how monitoring your virtual networks can be accomplished.

SECURING THE HYPER-V HOST

The most efficient step you can take to secure your Hyper-V host and environment is at the beginning, by using Windows Server 2008 Server Core. Server Core installs with a minimal set of features; it does not even

Note

Not all third-party applications will install or run on Server Core edition. The .NET environment in particular is unavailable for Server Core, so anything based on it will not install. We do not recommend running any other applications in conjunction with your Management OS (that is what the virtual machines are for!), but if you choose to do so, keep this restriction in mind.

include a full GUI. It begins with a very small surface of attack. Because it has fewer services running at start, more of the hardware's resources are available for the virtual machines. In addition, Server Core has fewer services installed or running at start, greatly decreasing the attack surface of the underlying OS.

Server Core installation considerations

In Chapter 3, we addressed how to install the Hyper-V role, but in the Standard edition, not Core. Because Core does not have a standard GUI, you will need to perform the steps in a slightly different manner. Any command will need to be typed into the PowerShell window that displays immediately upon logon.

To begin with, patches must be manually downloaded from another machine, transferred to the Core server, and installed via the following command:

msiexec.exe <patchname>.msi

Another option is to enable Windows Update in automatic mode, with the following command:

Cscript c:\windows\system32\scregedit.wsf /au 4

This will enable automatic updates at 3 a.m. If you wish to start an update check immediately, issue the wuauclt /detectnow command to do so.

With the proper patches installed, you next enable the Hyper-V role by typing the following:

Start /w ocsetup Microsoft-Hyper-V

Note that you will not be prompted with the same questions as with the GUI installation. Instead, the defaults you were presented with in Chapter 3 will be chosen, requiring additional configuration once the install has completed.

Once the Hyper-V role is installed, it is worth noting that all of the operating system instances on the physical computer are virtualized, including the one you use to manage the Hyper-V system (called the Management OS). The hardware is accessed by all of the instances through a microkernel that does not allow any third-party code to run within it. Only the Management OS can access the microkernel in any way, allowing the creation and management of additional virtual machines.

The Management OS will still be vulnerable to malware, however, so a business-class malware solution should be a vital part of your security strategy. You will be using this for your Windows-based virtual machines as well, so it will make your life much easier to use a solution that provides a central point of management and updates.

Server Core installs with the built-in firewall at maximum protection, meaning that few outbound or inbound services are enabled through it. You will need to turn on remote management, WMI, and possibly Remote Desktop services before you will be able to efficiently manage the host system. These steps are addressed in Chapter 3, where the installation of the Hyper-V role is discussed in greater detail.

Finally, you will want to ensure that updates are installed on the system on a regular basis. There are several automated systems available for this, the most common one being Windows Server Update Services, available for free from Microsoft.

Network and domain considerations

When you installed Hyper-V, you were given the option of creating a management interface from one of the network cards; a step we recommend. An important step to consider is to determine if you will join the management OS to your domain or not. Because the management OS has no other function beyond managing the virtual machines it hosts, it is not necessary to join it to your domain for full Hyper-V functionality (your virtual machines, of course, will most likely still need to be, depending on their function). However, you trade off losing the significant effort you have put into automating and securing your network resources via AD and related tools for the additional security of isolating the management OS. For instance, if you do not join the management OS to your domain, you will need to configure individual local accounts, security policies, and updates by hand, instead of using the existing infrastructure already in place in your AD. We believe that the ease of management that being an AD member brings to the table offsets the disadvantages of losing the network isolation. If you do join the management OS to your domain, be sure to create a secured OU for the system to reside in, and use Group Policy to ensure that only approved groups have logon access to the Hyper-V hosts.

SECURING THE VIRTUAL MACHINES

Hyper-V is designed to be used primarily with Windows servers and SUSE Enterprise Linux. Because these systems are presented to the network exactly as they would be if installed on physical hardware, you will want to take the typical precautions when securing them, keeping in mind their final function. With Hyper-V, it is much more feasible to have a single instance host a single function, which makes securing the instance much easier. With a single function to concern yourself with, it is much easier to restrict outbound services, for instance, to only those necessary for minimal function and the single service that virtual machine provides. The considerations discussed above when dealing with the host instance hold true with the guest instances as well, including antimalware, updates, and so forth.

There are steps you can take to further secure the virtual machine configuration files and virtual hard disk files. By default, the machine configuration files are kept in *%programdata% | Microsoft | Windows | Hyper-V | directory*. These files are very small, and usually the default location is acceptable. If you choose to move them, be sure that the System account and the Administrators group both have Full Control over the directory and files. Other groups should be allowed only the access required for their function, that is, the service account used for backups, and so forth. Virtual hard drive (VHD) files can vary greatly in size, as they contain the virtual machine OS and data. These are kept by default in the %users% | Public | Documents | Hyper-V| Virtual Hard Disks directory. These files you will most likely want to move, and further secure. You can supply a new location for these files in the Hyper-V manager. The rights listed in Table 9.1 will need to be applied to the directory containing the VHD files.

Note

Table 9.1 lists the default permissions on the default folder for the VHD files. Table 9.2 lists the rights that are required for running the virtual machines and their VHDs. If you were to relocate the default folders you would need to set these rights on those folders.

Table 9.1 VHD File Rights

Names	Permissions	Apply to
Administrators System	Full control	This folder, subfolder, and files
Creator owner	Full control	Subfolder and files only
Interactive	Create files/write data	This folder, subfolder, and files
Service	Create folders/append data	
Batch	Delete	
	Delete subfolders and files	
	Read attributes	
	Read extended attributes	
	Read permissions	
	Write attributes	
	Write extended attributes	

Table 9.2 Default Permissions on the Default Folder for the VHD Files

Location	Account	NTFS rights	Apply to
Configuration location	Administrators	Full control	This folder, subfolders, and files
	System	Full control	This folder, subfolders, and files
VM hard disks location	Administrators	Full control	This folder, subfolders, and files
	System	Full control	This folder, subfolders, and files
	Creator owner	Full control	Subfolders and files only

Bitlocker drive encryption

Windows Encrypted File System, or EFS, was a popular method in previous Microsoft virtualization strategies for encrypting the virtual drive files. With Hyper-V, this is no longer supported for VHD files.

Instead, we recommend placing these files on a separate drive from the management OS, and using Bitlocker to encrypt them, as discussed in Chapter 3. This will provide an additional layer of protection for the data within the virtual machines, with less impact on their performance than if data encryption were performed within the virtual machine. You may also wish to move any Virtual Floppy Disk (VFD) and ISO files to this location, especially if they are used to boot the virtual OS.

Syskey.exe

Syskey is a utility that can be used to encrypt Windows account data, including the SAM on Domain Controllers. On virtual machines, syskey can be challenging to enable in a fashion that actually preserves security; storing the key either on the virtual drive itself, or on a virtual boot floppy, only results in an image that can be taken elsewhere to be cracked at leisure, while a boot password can make automated management and update tools more challenging to use. In addition, a syskey-encrypted SAM is not significantly more difficult for password crackers to manage, as most of them simply obtain the necessary system files to decrypt the SAM at the same time, or use other tools to reset the Administrator password entirely. While syskey does add an additional layer of protection to your passwords, the added difficulty for management makes the trade off debatable.

Windows Firewall

Windows Firewall is a stateful firewall that comes installed with most modern versions of Windows by default. On Windows 2008 Server machines, the firewall is enabled by default, blocking many of the ports that cause so much trouble in otherwise unprotected Windows systems. On virtual servers, the Windows Firewall ensures that only the services necessary for the chosen function are exposed (the firewall will automatically configure itself for new server roles, for instance, and when certain server applications are installed). As members of your domain, the Windows Firewall of your virtual servers can be managed remotely, or through Group Policy.

Auditing

Auditing your server logs is an important way to ensure that nothing has gone awry with your systems. Windows Server 2008 supports event subscriptions, allowing you to send the log files of your virtual servers to a central location for monitoring and management.

You may find it useful, for instance, to have the event subscriptions of your virtual servers to be sent to the computer you use for managing your Hyper-V installation. The logs are also available through the typical remote management options.

Disk and file access can be audited as usual with Windows servers, as well; virtualization does not require you to change your methods there.

Virtualizing your servers does not require you to make significant changes to your auditing strategy. The ability to create separate private networks between virtual servers, however, opens up new opportunities to obtain audit data without impacting the throughput of bandwidth-intensive applications.

DESIGNING YOUR VIRTUAL NETWORK

The introduction to Hyper-V discussed several different types of networks available to a virtual machine. These different networks give us some flexibility in designing our enterprise for security as well as performance.

Remember that when you create a virtual machine, you have the option of creating three different types of virtual networks: External, which connects a virtual machine to the physical network; Internal, which allows virtual machines on the same host to communicate with each other, and with the management OS; and Private, which only allows virtual machines on the same host to communicate with each other. What does this mean to you? Imagine for a moment a typical web store, with purchasing and item data kept on a SQL server, and the Web site itself running on IIS. In a virtual environment, you might set it up similar to Figure 9.1.

By using a combination of private and external networks, you are able to create a site that is much more resistant to attack, by removing the database server from the external network entirely, allowing it to communicate only with the IIS server.

MONITORING AND OTHER CONSIDERATIONS

However, the ability to isolate key functions of your network also creates challenges when it comes to monitoring and maintaining the virtual systems. Systems that do not have an external private network, of course, cannot communicate with your physical network; indeed, unless the virtual machine is part of an internal network, it cannot communicate with the management OS either!

You will want to take this into account when designing your virtual network. In particular, you may have monitoring solutions in place that utilize SNMP, or agent-style probes. These will need to be forwarded to your monitoring server, typically by including some sort of forwarding agent in the private network. In addition, update systems such as WSUS will be unable to communicate with the virtual machines, and enterprise antivirus solutions will be similarly affected. It may be worthwhile to consider using internal virtual networks, instead of private ones, and configure the management OS as an agent for the various monitoring and management systems you have in place. Reserve private virtual networks for those systems that require higher security, and establish a method to monitor and update them either manually, or with an agent system that is included in both the private virtual network and the external one.

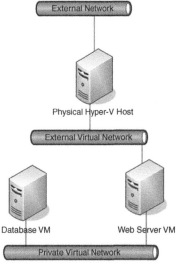

■ **FIGURE 9.1** A Virtual Web site protected by private networks.

Note

The Management OS will always be able to manage a virtual machine instance that it hosts, through the management console.

SUMMARY

We presented an overview of security in the context of a Hyper-V virtual environment. When the Hyper-V role is installed, everything is run in an instance, including the Management OS. This does not mean that your regular duties toward security can be bypassed, however; you still need the usual updates, antimalware, and the like.

The files that are the virtual machine configuration files and VHDs can be relocated, and we presented you with the permissions needed on the folders that contain them. In addition, Bitlocker encryption can provide further security for these files when not in active use.

The three network types available to your virtual machines give you a great deal of flexibility when designing your virtual infrastructure; it is possible to create systems that protect your valuable data by preventing the database servers from communicating on the external network at all. This provides challenges when attempting to maintain and monitor these instances, however.

Chapter 10 will introduce you to the concept of the Dynamic Data Center, and how to use your virtual infrastructure to create and utilize one.

10

Creating a dynamic data center with Microsoft System Center

CHAPTER OUTLINE

In this chapter, we discuss implementing a dynamic data center using Microsoft Virtualization and System Center. The first two chapters in this book defined the overall benefits of virtualization. In this chapter, we dig deeper into each of the key benefits provided by implementing virtualization and discuss how they can be implemented, and how they work in real-world scenarios. But first, what is Microsoft System Center?

Microsoft System Center is a suite of tools that builds upon the five core components listed below:

- *System Center Configuration Manager R2*, also known as ConfigMan, allows data center managers and their engineers to comprehensively assess, deploy, and update servers, client computers, and devices across all physical, virtual, distributed, and mobile environments.
- *System Center Operations Manager* (SCOM) is the end-to-end service-management product that is the best choice for Windows because it

works seamlessly with Microsoft software and applications, helping organizations increase efficiency while enabling greater control of the IT environment.

- *System Center Data Protection Manager* is the new standard for Windows backup and recovery services. It delivers continuous data protection for Microsoft applications and file servers using seamlessly integrated disk and tape media.

- *System Center Virtual Machine Manager 2008* enables customers to configure and deploy new virtual machines and centrally manage physical and virtual infrastructures from a single console. The latest version of VMM allows multivendor virtualization platform support.

- *System Center Essentials* is specifically designed for midsize businesses (*maximum limit of 500 client computers and 30 servers*). It provides a unified management product that enables IT pros in midsize organizations to proactively manage their IT environment with increased efficiency.

In addition to the core components listed above, additional tools exist for Microsoft System Center:

- *System Center Capacity Planner* is used for capacity planning prior to deployment and change management in the postdeployment world. It is especially useful for Exchange Server, Windows SharePoint Services, and Office SharePoint Server deployments.

- *System Center Mobile Device Manager* is a flexible, end-to-end product for the management of applications and corporate data on Windows Mobile devices. It seamlessly provides secure access to sensitive corporate data on Windows Mobile devices.

- *System Center Service Manager*, still in beta as of the writing of this book, promises to meet the needs of the modern IT help desk, providing powerful new capabilities for incident, problem, asset, and change management. It will support organizations as they seek to improve services provided to users.

Note

It is important to understand that workload consolidation is NOT the same thing as hardware consolidation. We will discuss hardware consolidation later in this chapter, but for now just realize that there are some significant differences between the two. You will need this mindset as we go through the discussions in this chapter.

As discussed in Chapter 1, workload consolidation is usually one of the first and most focused upon benefits in the early discussions of a virtualization implementation project. However, as also discussed in Chapter 1, you will quickly learn that full virtualization of an entire data center is often not feasible. So your workload consolidation plan must be thorough, with proper expectation set and presented to the stake holders of the project from the earliest stages.

DATA CENTER WORKLOAD

SearchDataCenter.com defines workload as

> *"...the amount of processing that the computer has been given to do at a given time. Workload consists of some amount of application programming running in the computer and usually some number of users connected to and interacting with the computer's applications."* *[1].*

When you think about workload consolidation, imagine services that your data center is providing to your business. During the initial discussions of workload consolidation, it is common to slip into thinking about power consumption and rack space. While those are certainly key items to consider in your overall virtualization strategy, thinking about them at this point skews the focus you will need for workload planning. So, stop thinking hardware footprint and instead focus on the services your data center delivers to your business. It is these services you want to consolidate in this step.

Workload consolidation is not something that can be implemented in a cookie-cutter fashion across multiple businesses. Even businesses within the same industry vary slightly in the way they perform their tasks. Therefore we are not able to get into the granular details of workload consolidation, but we can discuss it in generalities.

One of the technologies fairly widespread in most industries is published applications. So let us begin our examples there. Publishing an application to remote users consists of a fairly complex and sometimes large infrastructure; this can be even larger depending on the applications published. Common among servers, but even more so among published application environments, is the evolution from its initial design to what it is today. For example, a farm that was initially designed to publish application "X" 5 years ago may now publish application "Z," and not even publish application "X" anymore. Or applications may have been added or removed from the farm altogether. This evolution is inevitable, but it is also a great example of the benefits of workload consolidation.

In our example in Figure 10.1 we have Farm 1. This farm was built 5 years ago to publish a single application to 1200 users. It utilizes 20 application servers, a licensing server, 5 web servers, and an 8-way database server. At the time of its initial design, we used all new hardware based on vendor recommendations and specifications.

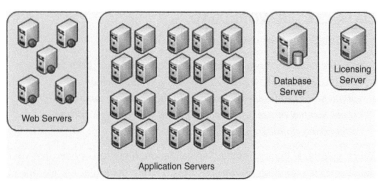

■ **FIGURE 10.1** Server Farm 1.

Farm 1 was built and introduced into the environment based on vendor recommendations for software configuration, hardware specifications, and the number of users that would connect to and use the application being published. Over time, as with many organizations, the true usage of our farm evolved. What was originally 1200 users hitting a single application dropped to about 600 users hitting the original application. An additional application was added to the farm and published to around 200 users. The hardware that was once the latest and greatest has become dated, while the software has continued to get patched, updated, and more efficient. All of these details play into your workload consolidation planning.

The major vendors of application publishing software provide tools and guides that help identify the true usage of your application servers. Using those tools during this phase of your workload consolidation planning is crucial. Keep in mind that even vendor supplied recommendations for their software are based on general usage. The way your users actually use the application being published can only be determined by thorough examination.

The original specifications for Farm 1 called for 20 application servers to support 1200 users. We are now down to 600 users. However, you cannot simply assume that the number of application servers can simply drop by 50%. At this point you will want to contact the vendor supporting the application. You should have collected a matrix of true server usage using the tools provided by that vendor so they can assist you not only in downsizing the size requirements of the farm but also in ensuring that existing support agreements will be maintained through this process. Through a combination of usage statistics and conversations with the vendors, we have discovered we can reduce our make-believe farm from 20 application

Note

In the examination of our make-believe Farm 1 environment, we have discovered that the database of the primary application is no longer accessed nearly as often or as intensely as it once was, this allows us to replace our existing 8-way server with a less powerful server, or even migrate the database to another database server that may have the required specifications in excess. For our scenario, we will migrate the database to another database server.

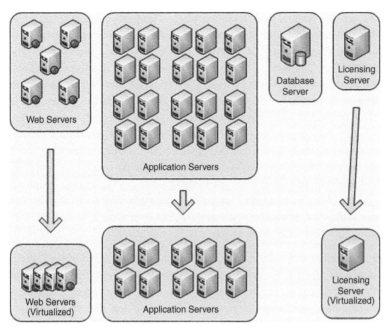

■ **FIGURE 10.2** Consolidating the workload of a published applications environment.

servers to 8. But, as we mentioned earlier, our farm has evolved to include an additional application published to around 200 users. So now we must go through the same steps for this application to determine its true requirements.

With our assessments complete, we have identified the true requirements for the new, consolidated workload of our published applications environment. As you can see in Figure 10.2, we have reduced the number of web servers from five to four, and migrated them into a virtualized environment. The number of application servers has decreased from 20 to 10, our stand-alone database server is removed completely, and the database is migrated to another database server with excess and available resources. Our licensing server is virtualized as well.

HARDWARE OPTIMIZATION

Another topic touched upon earlier in this book is hardware optimization. Before we jump into the data center aspect of this term, it might be easier to grasp the concept if we think about hardware optimization from the perspective of a home user.

Note
Keep in mind during your consolidation planning the possibility for future growth. This may not be as important a topic for environments that are old and slowly growing smaller, but an understanding of your long-term technology road map is essential in gauging proper consolidation.

We all have friends and family members who have a computer at home that they primarily use for sending or receiving e-mail and surfing the Internet. They do not write computer code or over-clock their system processor. They just want to view pictures of their family members online and e-mail their friends. For our example, we consider aunt Betty. Chances are aunt Betty bought her computer from one of the big name vendors, and it came preloaded with antivirus and assorted other tools that promise functionality and longer life of the computer. Aunt Betty is the kind of user who will typically notice her computer getting "slower" over time; more so than the more tech-savvy users who might be constantly installing and uninstalling software and performing other tweaks to their operating systems. Aunt Betty usually has no problem explaining how the computer was really fast when she first bought it, but over time it has gotten very slow; therefore, it must be broken.

So what does this example have to do with hardware optimization? Well, quite a bit actually, but first let us understand what is really happening with aunt Betty's computer. Over time applications generate files they reference as part of regular use and processing, including log files of yesterday's activities or backup files when the application is changed or upgraded. As these files grow in size or number, the application takes longer to reference the files. As more applications are installed on the computer, more files are created and referenced, and so on. Over time this collective "growth" of files causes the computer to respond slower because it is becoming busier doing things behind the scenes. Does this mean the computer is processing slower? No, it simply means that the computer is processing more.

So aunt Betty tells you her computer is slow and needs to be replaced because it is "old." Ok, before you run out and get her a new computer, you need to understand some basics. Computer technology is improving and becoming more powerful. Computers are lasting longer, and chances are aunt Betty does not need a new computer. Unless she has started doing CAD work, or some other processor- or memory-intensive work on her computer she has not done in the past, there is probably no reason to replace her computer quite yet. The best thing you can do to help aunt Betty is to take a good look at her computer, and uninstall software applications that she does not use due to loss of interest, replacement by another application, etc. Then do some basic "housekeeping" to remove temporary files that are not required for the application to continue functioning properly. Many times these files will be identified by the application vendor's website. If not, send an e-mail to their support department and ask them for a list of temporary or log files you can safely delete without impacting the performance of the application.

Again, you may be wondering what any of this has to do with hardware optimization and your efforts to make your data center more efficient and dynamic. Simple, look at your legacy servers the way you looked at aunt Betty's computer.

A lot of people hear hardware optimization and immediately think hardware upgrade or replacement. This is quite simply the worse way to look at it, and typically the exact opposite approach that you should take. Webster's dictionary defines optimize as *"to make as perfect, effective, or functional as possible."* [2]. In the previous section of this chapter we discussed how a published application farm was able to be slimmed down because the number of users who used it declined over the years. This scenario is more common than most realize, and it is not limited to published applications. This is common for database servers as well.

For example, 5 years ago you may have built a brand new database server using the latest and greatest hardware available. Over time this hardware has become dated. It may even be close to EOL (*end of life*), but even that should not keep you from performing a true and unbiased evaluation of the hardware platform in order to determine how to best optimize it. The hardware might have aged, but if the number of users accessing the database has declined, it may be perfectly capable of supporting the database for years to come. Even the cost of extended hardware support may be far less than purchasing a new hardware platform that provides far more performance than you really need. It is really all about understanding what you need and comparing it to what you have.

An important item to remember as you analyze your current servers and their applications is that software applications continue to become more efficient while server hardware continues to become more powerful. You may discover that an older server might need to be replaced with newer hardware in order to keep up with the growing demand of the application it supports. Before you simply throw away the hardware being replaced, however, see if it might be suitable for replacing an even older server. A successful hardware optimization project may not involve buying new equipment at all. It may just be a matter of shuffling applications from their original server platform to a different one.

Warning

Be wary of anybody telling you to replace your server simply because it has reached a certain age. The only people who should be making that kind of call are data center managers and their engineers. They are the only ones who truly understand how the servers are used and maintained and when they should be upgraded or replaced.

LEGACY APPLICATIONS

Often the bane of many a system administrator, legacy applications can be some of the hardest and most frustrating applications to support in any corporate environment. Typically, the longer an application is in use by a company, the more its users grow to rely on the application or its output. This is fine for applications that continue to grow with your business and technology in general; the developer and vendor continue to provide service and support. But there are often applications that become abandoned by their developers and vendors for various reasons. The vendor may become purchased by another company, or it may simply choose to stop supporting the application.

Most companies will continue to provide extended support of an outdated application for a limited time. They do this to allow the customers to either upgrade their applications to a current and supported version or to convert their processes over to another application that can provide the desired functionality. But what happens when you have an application that has fallen out of support, is strongly relied upon by the company, and has no known replacement or upgrade path?

This is one of the things that really make virtualization strategies shine— the ability to preserve and support a legacy application without having to maintain it in its original state. As with the Workload Consolidation section, we use an example to explain this a little easier.

We shall call our legacy application Old App. Old App was originally implemented on a Windows NT server. The server was built using the available and suggested hardware configuration. Old App was implemented in an effort to streamline business process and make it more efficient and less costly. The conversations that surrounded the project during its deployment suggested that the use of Old App would be nothing more than an interim step leading to a larger implementation. The future state vision included more robust software from a larger and better known vendor offering the same solution, but with a higher price tag. So Old App was really more of a "proof of concept" than the final solution.

Once implemented, Old App was quickly accepted by the users, and the business began to see some great benefits. Figure 10.3 gives you a very basic look at the configuration of Old App's infrastructure at the time of implementation.

Old App was implemented the same way the majority of applications were deployed over the last 10 years or so; in most cases, an individual server and its operating system are dedicated to the application.

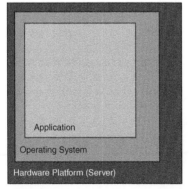

■ **FIGURE 10.3** Old App's infrastructure upon implementation.

So here we are, years after Old App was originally implemented. It is proven to be a solid application, but the underlying components that support Old App are aging. The hardware platform has reached its EOL, and numerous parts have already been replaced. We could simply order a new server, but the operating system Old App requires is a version of Windows no longer supported, not even through extended support.

We attempted to contact the original vendor of Old App to get a newer version that runs on a current version of Windows. However, the vendor is no longer in business, and a comparable replacement application is simply not feasible in the near future. We could certainly buy new hardware and install the outdated version of Windows and be very careful, but that is simply not the best way to handle this task. What are our options?

There are numerous alternatives to consider, and you will need to do your homework before jumping into the best solution for your particular situation. Let us look at two from a fairly high level: operating system virtualization and application streaming.

Operating system virtualization is the more mature of the two options and has been around for years. The concept is relatively simple; you are essentially installing one operating system inside of another. Figure 10.4 gives you an example of how the Old App's infrastructure would look using this strategy.

Think of the host operating system acting as a container for the virtualized operating system. This method still requires you to maintain the legacy operating system, but the benefits you achieve allow you to protect it through the insulation of a host operating system. Two of these benefits are the ability to host the legacy system on newer hardware and the ability to quickly back up and restore the virtual session through the use of snapshots.

In most situations, the conversion of your legacy environment can be done through a physical-to-virtual process that eliminates the need to completely rebuild the legacy server. If the host system is configured properly, and the requirements for the legacy applications allow, you can likely host the new virtualized version of your legacy application alongside other virtual environments on the same host. This helps consolidate hardware and reduce maintenance costs.

The other and less mature option for virtualizing your legacy application is through application streaming. This technology is much newer than operating system virtualization. For some vendors this technology is still in its infancy, but the benefits of this approach may outweigh those of operating system virtualization. Figure 10.5 provides an example of how the Old App's infrastructure would look using this strategy.

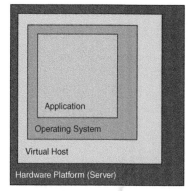

■ **FIGURE 10.4** Old App's infrastructure using a virtualized operating system.

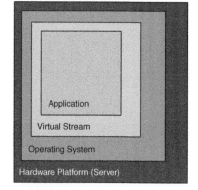

■ **FIGURE 10.5** Old App's infrastructure using application streaming.

With application streaming, you remove the legacy operating system completely and encapsulate the application in its own virtual stream, meeting all requirements once fulfilled by the legacy operating system. Again, this is the less mature technology in the virtualization world, and it may not support all applications. You will need to investigate and test your approach thoroughly. That said, if your application works with this method, you can remove the underlying outdated operating system completely. At that point, you can stream (or present) the application to any currently supported Windows operating system.

This approach has another benefit. It allows you to include the components of applications in the encapsulated stream. This is huge when you consider the traditional limitations of certain applications and their inability to reside on the same operating systems with older or newer versions of themselves. An example of this would be the Java runtime. We recently configured a similar scenario in a test environment where I "streamed" Internet Explorer 6, 7, and 8 all to run on the same operating system. This provided the web developer the ability to test his code on various versions of Internet Explorer all running on the same machine and removed the need for three individual test machines, each running a different version of Internet Explorer.

ISOLATED ENVIRONMENTS

The growing requirements for securing data push data center managers to provide environments that are either partially or completely isolated from the rest of the enterprise environment—while still accessible to certain end users.

Over the years, isolated environments have evolved considerably. There were times not so long ago where an isolated environment was easy to imagine—a locked room containing a server or a collection of servers and workstations that simply could not be accessed unless you entered the room. Technology improvements have allowed the locked room concept to become less and less of a requirement.

Stronger log-in requirements, segmented networks, and firewalls provided the ability for these once segregated environments to be moved back into the data center or reconnected to the general network. However, growing regulatory and common sense security requirements to protect data and audit protection methods are making it more difficult to manage an isolated environment in the general data center. Microsoft System Center includes several components that meet not only the requirements of today's growing data protection needs but also the framework that allows for continued evolution and modification to meet the requirements of tomorrow.

Along with the more heavily discussed virtualization technologies discussed in this book, the System Center provides tools useful for data management and auditing. The Data Protection Manager (DPM) allows for more efficient backup and recovery options that allow everything from full system restores to end user initiated single file restores. The SCOM allows for granular tracking of individual changes all the way through enterprise overviews to track and graph trends. Together with other components of the Microsoft System Center, DPM and SCOM should be considered requirements in the design and implementation of any isolated environment in your enterprise.

We have thrown out a lot of tools and philosophies, but what exactly is an isolated environment? We touched on a very basic example at the beginning of this section, but let us dive a little deeper into understanding the true concept of an isolated environment.

Years ago, one of us consulted for a company that was implementing a new check printing application. It was a smaller office and they wanted this system to be locked away from the common employees. This system was going to be used to print out employee's pay checks, so it certainly makes sense to make it an "isolated environment." This particular environment consisted of nothing more than a computer, a special printer, and special printer paper. These items were all placed in a locked room with no windows and the only person with a key to the room was the accounting manager. The computer was not connected to the Internet or any other network, and the data used to print the checks was taken into the room on disk from another workstation in the common office area. Most isolated environments implemented today rely more on technological barriers than physical ones, but the intended outcome is similar—prevents unauthorized access of protected data through the use of proper security measures, and validates the security through auditing and reporting.

An isolated environment can be as small as a single thumb drive placed in a safe and accessed by only one person, or as large as multiple Active Directory domains accessed by thousands of users around the world. The specific details of an isolated environment will vary greatly, depending on the data being protected and the guidelines defining how that data should be protected and accessed. The number of users who access this data, where they are located physically in relation to the data, and how often they will need to access the data will also come into play when designing your isolated environment. You may also need to consider any regulatory requirements for security and auditing of access to the data.

Note

In designing your new dynamic data center isolated environment, you are going to want to discuss all the requirements of this environment with the information security department, the internal audit personnel, and the legal department. All three of these departments will have their own requirements that they will want to add to functional business requirements. Furthermore, they will know of any other people or departments in your company that may need to be included in the discussions.

Throughout these discussions keep asking yourself and your team how will this design impact the end users who will use or access this system? Often the design of an isolated environment will lose track of the final results and may provide an environment that is simply too restricted or convoluted to use efficiently.

HARDWARE CONSOLIDATION

Earlier in this chapter, we discussed consolidation and how the traditional mindset around it was to simply reduce the number of hardware servers in a data center. Since then we have gotten into the details explaining how consolidation is much more than simply reducing your hardware footprint. Done properly, you should have already gone through workload consolidation and hardware optimization before you even start to think about true hardware consolidation. So, the discussion in this section of the chapter will be based on the assumption that you have already identified those items and considered them for your new dynamic data center.

Sometimes it may be justifiable to pay for extended support of EOL hardware rather than simply replace it with new equipment. This may be a hard concept to understand by some, but others will get it right away. It is really not that hard. You simply need to balance your expectations, costs, and technology to see what combination fits best.

Let us look at an example of a low-impact, development-only server virtualization farm. Here is the concept; a need exists to create a farm of virtual servers that your development staff can use for testing new applications. This farm will not support production users, and it will not be expected to be available and online 24 h a day 7 days a week. Meanwhile you have recently retired a complete blade server chassis due to it reaching EOL. You have already been diligent in crunching the numbers, and your management realizes that the cost of paying for extended support on this blade chassis is far more than the company is willing to pay in exchange for the limited type of support. The plans for this used blade chassis is simply to wipe the drives and pay somebody to haul it away and dispose off it. Believe it or not, this is a fairly common scenario. It is just this kind of situation that can allow you to jump in and provide your company with some additional workspace for little to no additional cost.

As long as you have done workload consolidation and hardware optimization properly, it is almost inevitable that you will end up with a surplus of hardware that has reached its EOL support and in our traditional world would end up on the list of items to be thrown away. However, new technology and ways of thinking can allow you to continue using this hardware to provide a true benefit to your company. So, how do you use an outdated blade chassis and its servers to provide a reliable development platform without paying for extended hardware support? There are a couple of different approaches.

Here is the stage: you have a 14 blade chassis complete with servers, and the requirement for a development platform consisting of multiple servers.

Approach #1: Clustering

In this approach, we are going to take the blade chassis and cluster the server environments across multiple hardware platforms. Figure 10.6 provides a visual look at our example. We are going to build four server operating systems across 12 blade servers; each operating system will be clustered across three server blades, reserving two of the blades to be left offline and labeled as "spares."

This approach allows the operating system to continue running, even if one of its three servers should fail. In this case, one of the two remaining spare blades can be used to replace the failed blade while it is either repaired or replaced. This concept is nothing new; Microsoft clustering improved greatly with Windows Server 2003, and a number of third-party vendors have also been providing clustering solutions for years. It provides the needed workspace while reducing the risk of hardware failure by spreading the risk of a single operating system across multiple hardware platforms.

Approach #2: Clustering with virtualization

Our second theoretical approach builds on the first by adding an additional layer of protection that spans the entire chassis rather than just the three hardware blades used in the first approach. Some may consider this approach to be a little overkill, but it all depends on your available resources, and the faith you have in the hardware you have to work with. If the hardware is extremely old, and the environment you are planning to use it for is extremely important, this approach may quickly change from

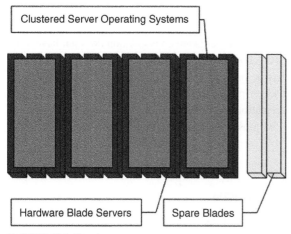

■ **FIGURE 10.6** Clustering.

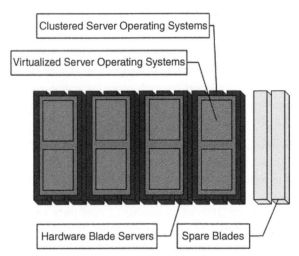

Clustered Server Operating Systems

Virtualized Server Operating Systems

Hardware Blade Servers

Spare Blades

■ **FIGURE 10.7** Clustering with virtualization.

overkill to sufficient. As you can see in Figure 10.7, this added layer of protection can also increase the number of servers from four to eight. Using virtualization, the operating systems can easily be backed up using snapshots and migrated from one cluster to another almost seamlessly.

The two examples listed in Figures 10.6 and 10.7 work well in an environment that requires additional workspace without the desire to continue paying for extended hardware support. Depending on the technology you choose to use, you may or may not have to consider additional licensing costs, but even those additional costs may be feasible if it means the continued use of hardware that might otherwise be thrown away.

Above all else, remember that hardware consolidation does not have to be complex. Whether you choose to build a clustered virtualization farm out of an old blade chassis, or simply provide your development engineers outdated hardware server platforms that provide higher performance than their current desktop platforms, you are consolidating. Sometimes the simplest ideas can be the most fundamental and show the greatest business benefit.

SOFTWARE MIGRATION

Although this is one of the last sections in this chapter, software migration is certainly *not* the least important aspect of creating a dynamic data center. In fact, this is probably one of the most crucial items of consideration in your move to a dynamic data center, so please do not consider its placement in this chapter to be a rating as to how it fits into the entire process.

Up to this point, we have discussed workload consolidation, hardware optimization, continuing the support of legacy applications, working with isolated environments, and hardware consolidation. Assuming you have done your homework with all of these previous items, you are now ready to look at the options that surround software migration.

First, let us look at the obvious. What does it mean to migrate software? At this point you should have identified the best layout for your new dynamic data center. Your design should include everything from the most used and most critical software applications to the best hardware configuration for those applications and your business. You should be left with what most would consider to be the first step of this design—software migration, or simply put, moving the applications to their appropriate place in the data center.

In a perfect world, this step would include a little bit of almost everything from clustering to virtualization to application streaming or hosting. However, if your world is anything like ours, it is far from perfect. So you must work within boundaries, such as available skill sets, limited budgets, and regulatory compliance. Thankfully the broad spectrum of available options should allow you to create a custom layout that not only fits within your budget but also the pool of available skill sets and other limitations that may be in place for your company.

Tip

A lot of these options are capable of performing various tasks that often overlap the functionality of other options. You just need to identify the ones to use, who should manage them, and how to implement them.

There are many, many ways to migrate software. There is the most traditional method which includes, quite simply, freshly installing the software onto a new platform. This is the method used by IT professionals on a daily basis worldwide. If done properly, it works just fine. Chances are you will be using this method for a number of your software applications simply because it will turn out to be the best and most reliable method. But as a data center manager, only you will know when it is best to use this method as opposed to the other options available.

An example of when to use this method may be a software application that installs relatively easily with very few custom options needing to be configured. Here is a good rule of thumb: If the amount of time it would take to perform a fresh install of the application on a new server and make it fully ready for production take less time than it would to implement any of the other options we are about to discuss, it may be your best bet.

Another form of software migration is outsourced, external hosting. Many companies will purchase a rather complex application and choose to host it internally based on the assumption that the application will simply be easier to maintain if managed by their own engineers. Many organizations, however, learn over time that the application needs so much support by the vendor that hosting internally becomes more of a bottleneck than a benefit. When this happens, the option to have the application hosted by the vendor is something that should be reconsidered. Investigation into this approach may result in the same original decision to keep it internal, but at least the investigation is performed. This allows the vendor the opportunity to see what services they may be able to provide better or at a lower cost, and it may provide a more cost-effective change in the future.

"Virtualizing" an application is something relatively new, depending on how you choose to apply that term. For example, some people consider an application published through Citrix to be "virtualized," but that is simply not the case based on how true virtualization and Citrix's published applications work. If that were the case, it could be argued that Citrix has been virtualizing applications in corporate America for years. When we write about virtualizing an application, we are referring to the ability to run an application within a virtual space that can then be managed as its own individual item.

Citrix considers an application "virtualized" because it can be published on more than one server and a user is assigned to the least busy server that offers that application. These applications can be streamed to either the applications server or the client device. The end-user device can be most anything that can run the Citrix client. This allows the end-user device to present the application to the user even if it is not capable of running the application itself.

Virtualization is something you should consider for an application with a relatively small data center footprint that is used by a large number of users. An example of this might be the Microsoft Office Suite. The majority of companies today that use Microsoft Office simply have the suite installed locally on the users' PCs. This works fine until the time comes to apply a large service pack or upgrade to the next version of Office. This often leads to conflicts of how to move such large amounts of data to your remote users, not to mention patching against vulnerabilities in a timely manner.

There are certainly ways to do this without the use of virtualization, but virtualizing your Office Suite provides benefits not always available through other means. Depending on the approach you choose in virtualizing your Office Suite, you can reduce the stress of all other scenarios by providing on-demand patching, background BITS controlled caching, and easier removal or cleanup of older Office Suites.

Software migration does not always have to be done in a complex manner. You may discover through your research that the best option for a specific software application is to simply leave it intact and not migrate it at all. Software migration relies a great deal on how your company manages its applications, users, and data. Once you fully understand each of those, you will be able to fluently decipher the best approach of migrating software within your data center.

EASIER TEST ENVIRONMENTS

One of the best things about creating a dynamic data center with Microsoft System Center is the ease with which you can create test environments. Whether you need nothing more than an application setup to be streamed to a single workstation or an entire Active Directory domain structure that includes all of the functionality of a real-world company, you can do it quicker and easier.

Imagine having the ability to fire up a fully functioning test domain in just a few minutes. Or better yet, have multiple test domains that you can power on and off as needed. Gone are the days of dedicating specific hardware to specific test environments. With the Microsoft System Center suite you can precreate multiple test environments ranging in size from a single application all the way up to multiple domains and simply back them up for later use.

The Microsoft System Center allows you to create complete virtual environments from your existing production environments that can then be used for development or other offline testing of applications, workflows, etc. And the auditing tools included in the System Center suite allow for granular reporting of changes made to the test environment. Imagine a true "Model Office" environment that can tell you proactively the differences between itself and your production or development environments.

A properly designed and implemented virtual environment enables your development team to have access to one test environment one day, and a completely different test environment the very next day, without having to tear down one in order to build the other.

Performing physical to virtual migrations removes the risk of one environment being built slightly different than the other, and reducing the potential of human error in the configuration of the components of the two environments.

SUMMARY

Creating a dynamic data center requires significant planning and a deep understanding of where your organization is today and where it will be tomorrow. Microsoft's virtualization and management tools help make these activities easier and less expensive.

Remember not to virtualize just because you have heard it is a great technology or because senior management is putting on the pressure after reading an article in some business magazine. As the IT professional in the room, it is your job to clearly position virtualization as just one component of an overall plan for designing and managing a robust data center operation.

Finally, virtualization is a great way to repurpose aging servers. Do not be so quick to send them to the shredder, especially if management has been pushing back on development or testing environments because of cost.

REFERENCES

[1] SearchDataCenter.com Definitions . [Web site on the Internet].Techtarget; [Updated 28 January 2006; cited 23 January 2010]. Available from:http://searchdatacenter. techtarget.com/sDefinition/0,,sid80_gci970333,00.html#.

[2] "Optimize." Merriam-Webster Online . [dictionary on the Internet]. Merriam-Webster Incorporated; [cited 23 January 2010]. Available from:http://www.merriam-webster.com/dictionary/optimize.

Chapter

11

Application virtualization (App-V)

In this chapter, we walk you through a sample installation of a simple App-V farm, starting with a functioning Windows 2008 Active Directory setup. We discuss streaming applications and what changes need to be made to your firewalls and proxy servers to allow applications to be streamed to clients outside of your local network, as well as the security implications of doing so. Finally, we discuss the management of the App-V server farm. You will be introduced to the Sequencer in this chapter, but you will explore it in more detail in Chapter 12 when we discuss the creation and deployment of App-V packages.

WHAT IS APPLICATION VIRTUALIZATION?

Microsoft Application Virtualization, also known as App-V, is a component of the Microsoft Desktop Optimization Pack. It allows for easier management and maintenance of the application since it technically resides on a platform separated from the operating system of the client device.

Note
Microsoft created the Microsoft's Optimized Desktop initiative to increase productivity, security, and availability by using the virtualization technologies discussed in this book. More information can be found at *http://tinyurl.com/nct8pg*.

APPLICATION VIRTUALIZATION MANAGEMENT SERVER

The purpose of the App-V Management Server is to deliver prepackaged and configured applications in an "on-demand" fashion to a workstation running the App-V Desktop and Terminal Services clients. The App-V Management Server uses Microsoft SQL Server for its data store. Multiple App-V servers can share a single data store. The App-V server authenticates requests, provides security, metering, monitoring, and data gathering. Active Directory is used to manage users and applications.

App-V includes a Management Console and Management Web Service. Administrators within the App-V infrastructure can use the Management Console to configure one or more Management Servers. They can also add and remove applications, change File Type Associations (FTAs), and assign access permissions and licenses to users and groups. The App-V Management Web Service is the communication conduit between the App-V Management Console and the SQL data store. These components can all be installed on a single server or on one or more other computers, depending on the required system architecture.

APPLICATION VIRTUALIZATION STREAMING SERVER

The Microsoft Application Virtualization Streaming Server provides a source of package content for client computers that are in a remote office away from the Management Server. The package content files are often large, sometimes up to 4 GB in size, so in a production environment they should be placed in a content share that is accessible by the client computers over a high-speed local area network. Streaming very large files across a wide area network (WAN) is not recommended because of the typical bandwidth limitations of WAN links.

The streaming server provides active/package upgrades without the Active Directory or SQL server requirements of the App-V server. Publishing services and licensing, or metering capabilities, must still be performed by the management server. The streaming server is only intended to provide lightweight App-V application delivery to remote offices without the additional overhead of an Active Directory domain controller, or SQL Server in each office. The publishing service of the App-V server is used in conjunction with the streaming server. The management server centrally controls the virtual application publishing, but the local streaming server dynamically delivers the package content from the local network. This includes active/package upgrade without the need for Active Directory or SQL.

Unlike the Management Server, the Streaming Server does not have a publishing service or the ability to meter or assign licensing. When the publishing service of the management server is used in conjunction with the Streaming Server, the management server configures the application and the streaming server delivers it.

APP-V MODES

App-V has two modes: stand-alone and streaming. The stand-alone mode is used primarily for devices that are either offline from the domain or used in remote locations where a streaming server is feasible. The streaming mode is the preferred design and allows for true, real-time centralized management of the applications being managed and deployed by the App-V environment.

Stand-alone mode

The stand-alone mode of App-V uses only the sequencer to package applications into a near full or full installation deployed to client devices. This is very similar to many existing infrastructures that deploy application via Group Policy or SCCM. The primary difference is that you can configure the deployed application to check in with the sequencer occasionally to look for any updates to the application package.

Streaming mode

Streaming mode is the preferred design for the App-V environment, since it allows for minimal caching on the client device and faster management and deployment of application updates and changes. It uses a sequencer and a streaming or management server as the infrastructure. In this scenario a full management server is still not required, but it is suggested. When a management server is not used, permissions are handled via Access Control Lists (ACLs) in place of the SQL database that a full management server implementation provides.

SYSTEM REQUIREMENTS

The system requirements for an App-V deployment are minimal. These are, of course, recommended minimum requirements. Larger deployments may require more powerful systems for both the clients and the servers.

Some of these requirements may appear overwhelming at first, but a closer look shows that most of them easy to achieve are already in place in most organizations.

- App-V Management and Streaming Servers
  - Processor—Intel Pentium III, 1 GHz
  - RAM—512 MB
  - Disk space—200 MB available hard disk space (*not including content directory*)

- Operating system—Windows Server 2003 Standard (SP1 or higher), Windows Server 2003 Enterprise (SP1 or higher), or Windows Server 2008

- Data Store (*this is required for the management server only and is not required for the streaming server*)
  - Processor—Intel Pentium III, 850 MHz
  - RAM—512 MB
  - Disk space—200 MB available hard disk space
  - Operating system—Windows Server 2003 Standard (SP1 or higher), Windows Server 2003 Enterprise (SP1 or higher), or Windows Server 2008
  - Database—SQL Server 2000 (SP3a or SP4), SQL Server 2005 (SP1 or SP2), or SQL Server 2008
  - Microsoft Data Access Components—MDAC 2.7 or higher
  - Domain controller—Active Directory Domain Services or NT 4 PDC (*central authentication authority*)

- Management Web Service
  - Processor—Intel Pentium III, 800 MHz
  - RAM—256 MB
  - Disk space—50 MB available hard disk space
  - Operating system—Windows Server 2003 Standard (SP1 or higher), or Windows Server 2003 Enterprise (SP1 or higher), or Windows Server 2008
  - Internet Information Services—Internet Information Services 6.0 (IIS configured with ASP.NET
  - .NET Framework—.NET 2.0 or higher

- Management Console
  - Processor—Intel Pentium III, 450 MHz
  - RAM—256 MB
  - Disk space—200 MB available hard disk space
  - Operating system—Windows XP (SP2 or SP3), Windows Vista Business (no SP or SP1), Enterprise (no SP or SP1), and Home (no SP or SP1), Windows Server 2003 Standard (SP1 or higher), or Windows Server 2003 Enterprise (SP1 or higher), or Windows Server 2008
  - Microsoft Management Console—MMC 3.0 or higher
  - .NET Framework—.NET 2.0 or higher

INSTALLATION

For this book, we created a clean 2008 Active Directory environment running in Native Mode. Prior to continuing, you will want to make sure that you have a security group already created in Active Directory for App-V administrators. Depending on your security infrastructure you may choose to use Domain Admins, but we created a group called App-V Admins. You will want to do the same for App-V Users; App-V Users are authorized to log in to the App-V management console without having full access to the console. We created a group called App-V Users for this role. We will begin the setup of our App-V environment on a server named APP01. Before you can begin installing App-V, you will need the .NET Framework, a Microsoft SQL database, and IIS configured properly. We installed App-V and its components while logged in as the domain administrator.

Note
You can install App-V to run using a SQLExpress database for testing, training, etc. However, the use of a SQLExpress database in a production implementation of App-V is NOT supported by Microsoft.

Installing the .NET framework

Open the Server Manager and click the *Features* option in the left-hand pane (see Figure 11.1). This displays the Features control panel in the right-hand pane.

■ **FIGURE 11.1** Choosing the Features option in the Server Manager.

1. Click *Add Features* to open the list of available features for Windows 2008 (see Figure 11.2).

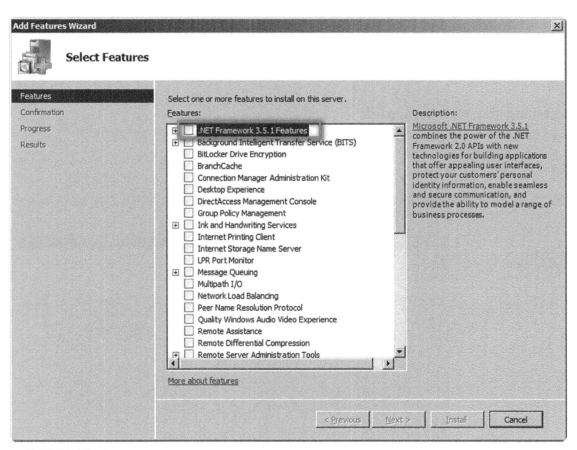

■ FIGURE 11.2 Adding Features.

2. Clicking the *.NET Framework 3.5.1. Features* checkbox displays a
   message telling you there are several dependent features also required,
   which you can select here. Click *Add Required Role Services* to
   continue (see Figure 11.3).

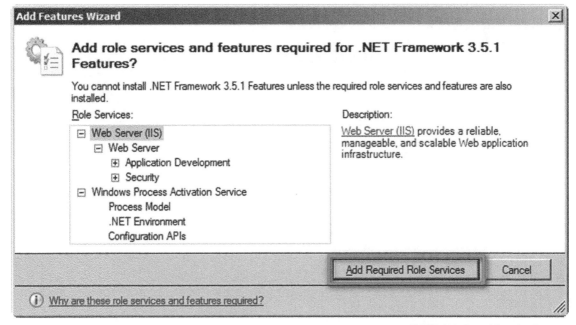

■ **FIGURE 11.3** Required Dependent Features.

3. You now see the Add Features Wizard. Click *Next* (see Figure 11.4).

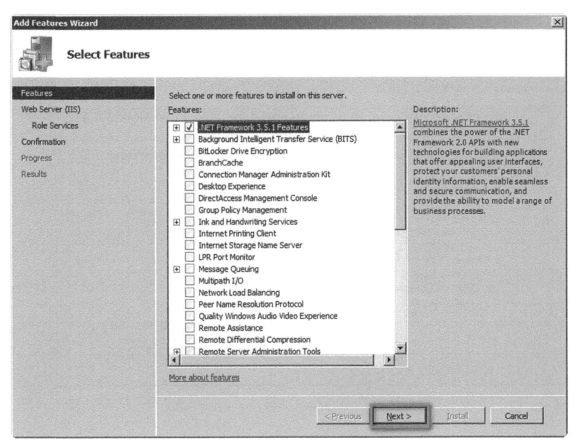

■ FIGURE 11.4 The Add Features Wizard.

4. The next window, Introduction to Web Server (IIS), provides general
   information on the Windows Web Server. Click *Next* (see
   Figure 11.5).

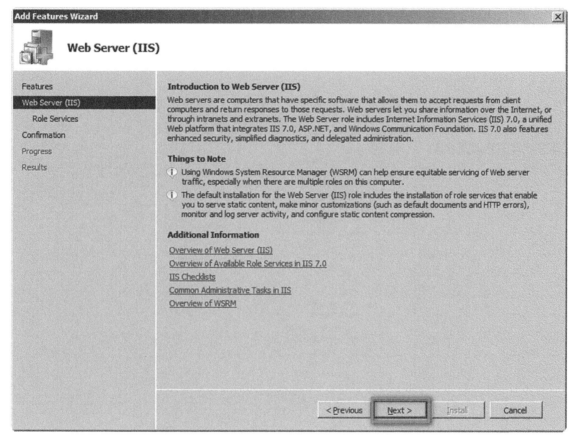

■ FIGURE 11.5 The Introduction to Web Server Window.

5. The Web Server Role Services window provides the option to include additional roles. Since this was initiated by the .NET framework install, all required dependencies are already selected. So there is no reason to add anything at this time. Click *Next* (see Figure 11.6).

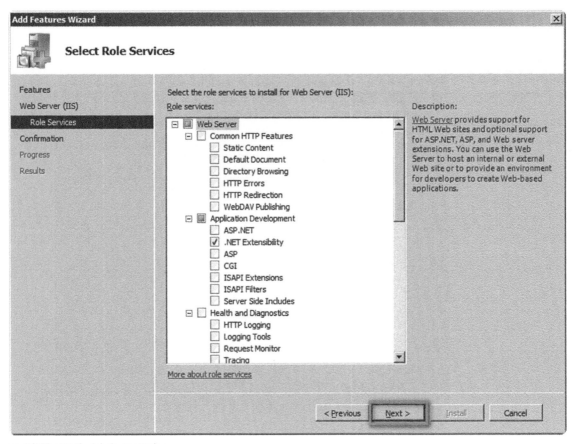

■ **FIGURE 11.6** The Role Services Window.

6. The final screen you see prior to the installation starting is the validation screen, which explains how the install process will work and what to expect in terms of restarts, etc. Click *Install* to begin (see Figure 11.7).

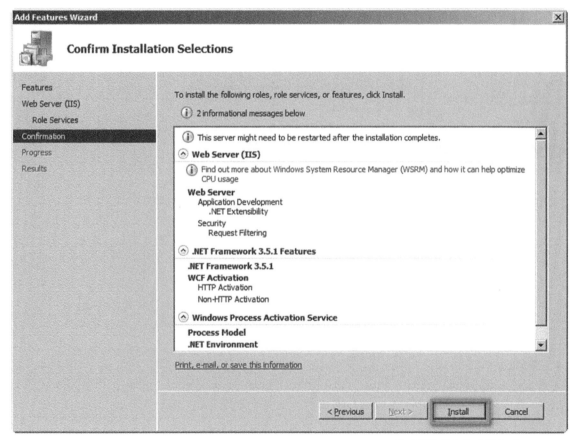

■ **FIGURE 11.7** The Validation Screen.

7. The install process begins, installing the Web Server (IIS) feature, the .NET Framework feature, and the Windows Process Activation Service (see Figure 11.8).

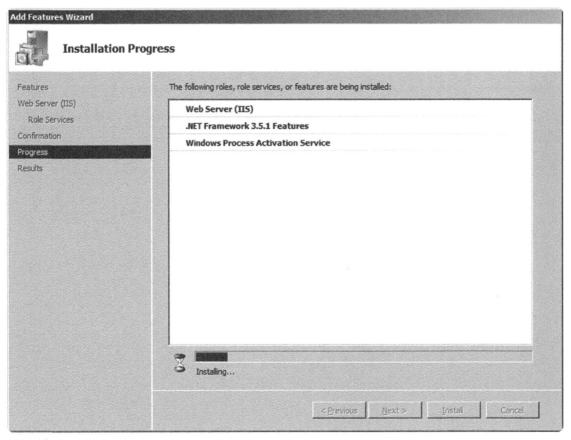

■ **FIGURE 11.8** Starting the Installation process.

8. Once the install is complete, an Installation Results window is displayed. Click *Close* and then close out of the Server Manager console as well (see Figure 11.9).

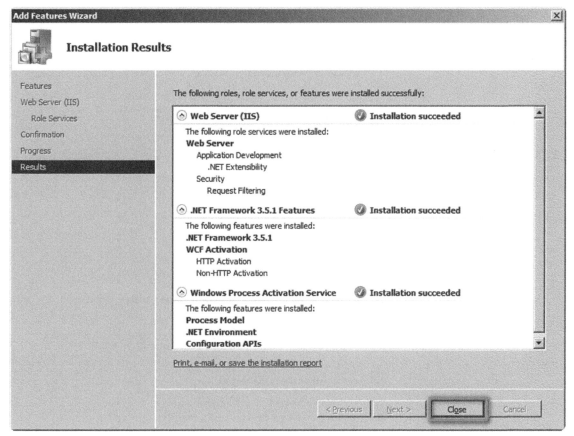

Installing SQL 2008

From the root of the SQL 2008 install disk, double-click *setup.exe*.

1. You will see a small processing box pop up while the SQL install process begins. Once this is done, you will be brought to the main SQL Installation Center window. Click the *Installation* link (see Figures 11.10 and 11.11).

SQL Server 2008

Please wait while SQL Server 2008 Setup processes the current operation.

■ **FIGURE 11.10** The SQL Server 2008 processing box.

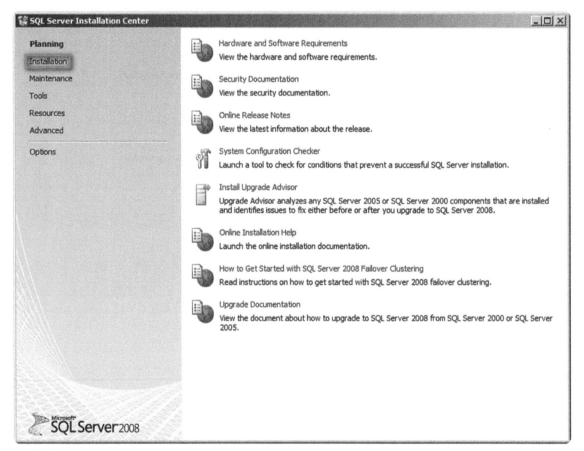

■ **FIGURE 11.11** The SQL Server 2008 Installation Center.

2. In the next window, click on the top link to install a fresh stand-alone instance of SQL Server 2008 (see Figure 11.12).

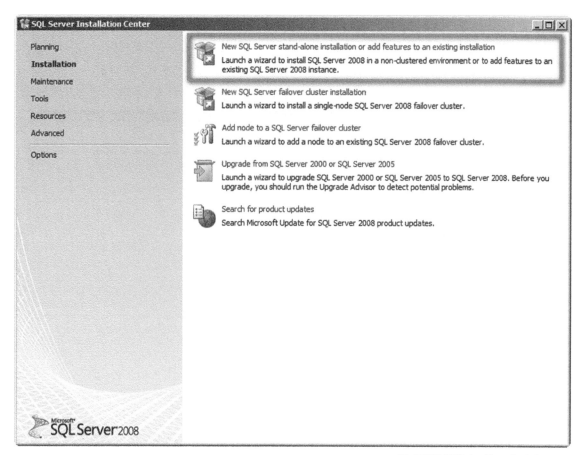

■ **FIGURE 11.12** Installing a Stand-alone instance of SQL Server 2008.

3. The Setup Support Rules window appears next. This step of the install process checks your server to ensure all proper roles required for SQL to install are defined on the server. Click *Ok* to continue (see Figure 11.13).

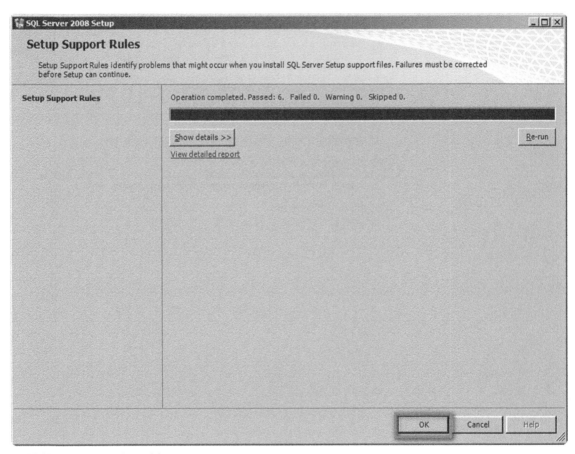

■ **FIGURE 11.13** Setting up Support Rules.

4. Next is the Product Key window, enter your key if needed and click
Next (see Figure 11.14).

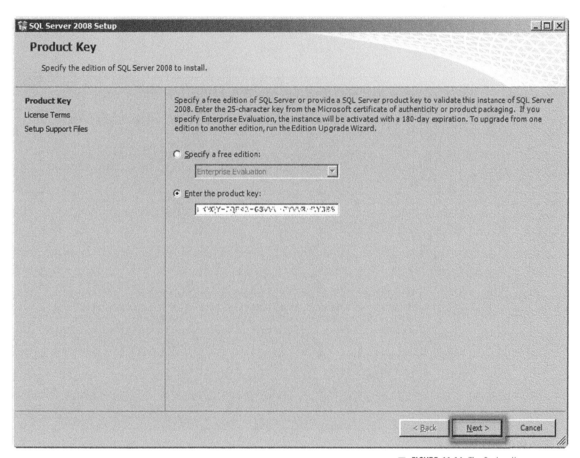

■ **FIGURE 11.14** The Product Key.

5. Read and accept the license terms. Click *Next* (see Figure 11.15).

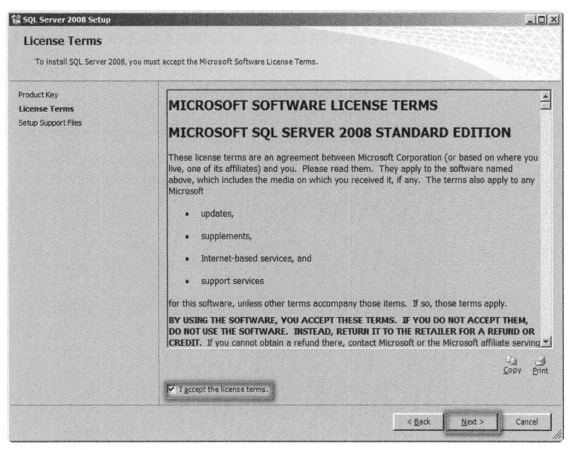

■ **FIGURE 11.15** The License Terms.

6. The Setup Support Files window is next. These files are required for a
SQL installation. Click *Install* to continue (see Figure 11.16).

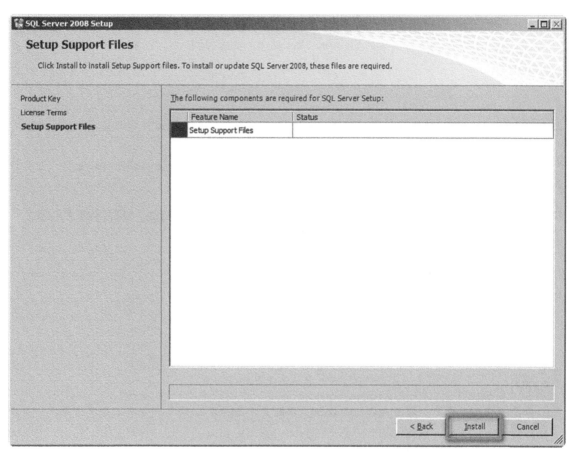

■ **FIGURE 11.16** Setting up Support Files.

7. Once the Setup Support Files install is complete, you are presented with a completion status window listing every dependent rule and its rating (see Figure 11.17). Should you receive more than a warning on any one item, you will need to correct that item before continuing. Depending on the item, it may be a matter of improper configuration of your server operating system, or a missing prerequisite. Assuming all of the roles passed, click *Next*.

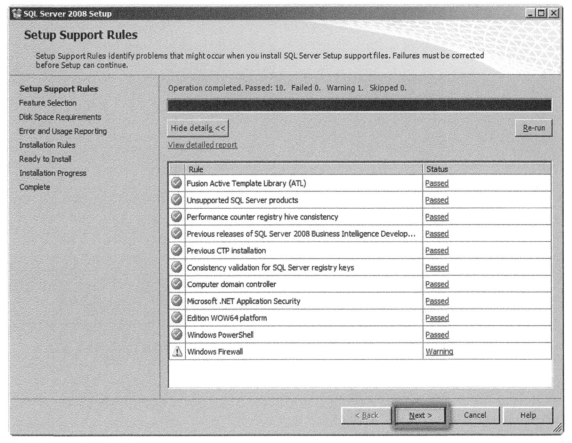

■ **FIGURE 11.17** Dependent Rules.

8. The Feature Selection screen is displayed (see Figure 11.18). The only items required for App-V are the database engine and the management tools. Additional features may be added at a later time should you use the SQL database for additional tasks that require additional features. Click *Next*.

Note

Depending on your specific infrastructure and firewall requirements, you may or may not need to create firewall exceptions for SQL to communicate properly within the App-V environment.

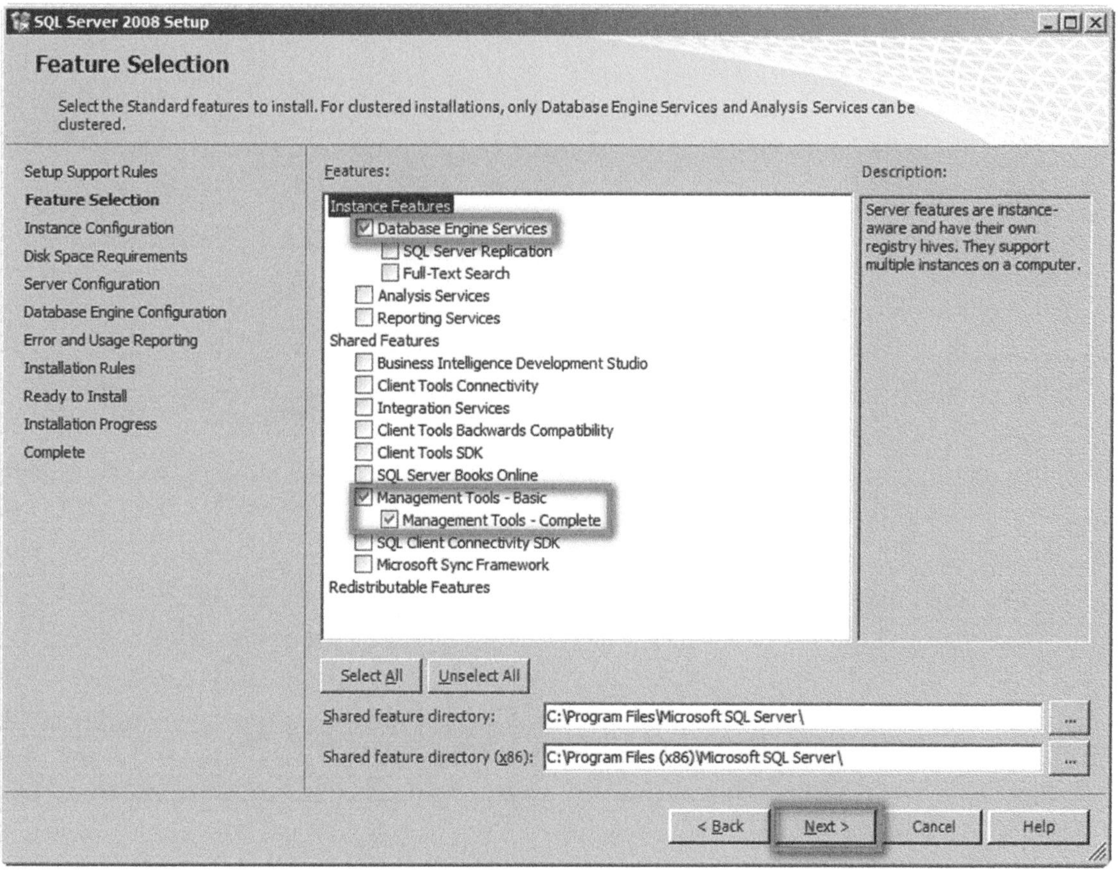

■ **FIGURE 11.18** The Feature Selection screen.

9. The Instance Configuration screen is next (see Figure 11.19). Since this is a fresh install and nothing other than App-V will be using this database, we left it at Default Instance and clicked *Next*. Should you plan to use this SQL server for more than just App-V, you may want to create an instance with a name more meaningful, one that conforms to your existing naming convention.

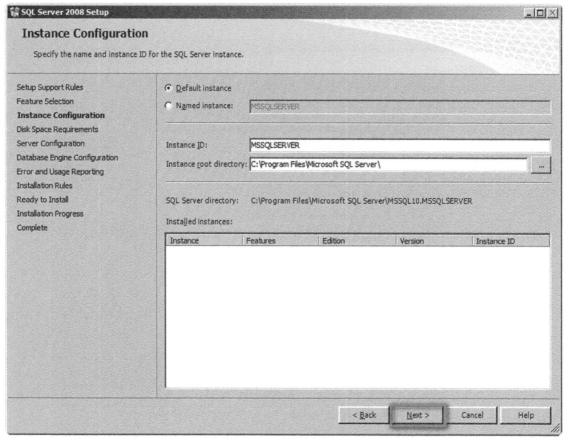

■ **FIGURE 11.19** The Instance Configuration screen.

10. The Disk Space Requirements window appears (see Figure 11.20). If
this screen does not have a green check mark, you will need to cancel
out of the install, review the system requirements for SQL and either
increase the amount of disk space required or locate new hardware that
does have the proper disk space. Assuming all is green, click *Next*.

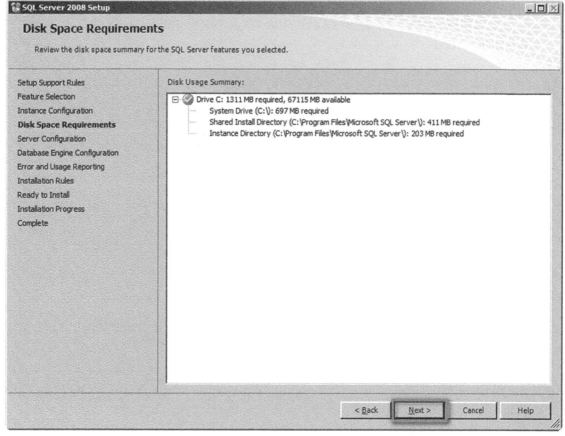

■ **FIGURE 11.20** The Disk Space Requirements
Window.

11. In the Server Configuration screen, you set up the account authentication types. Based on Microsoft Best Practices, we used NT Authority\System and left the collation at its default. If you use an alternate server configuration, be sure to verify with Microsoft or any third-party application vendor that your choices will not conflict with the installation of App-V or any other applications that may use this SQL instance. Click *Next* (see Figure 11.21).

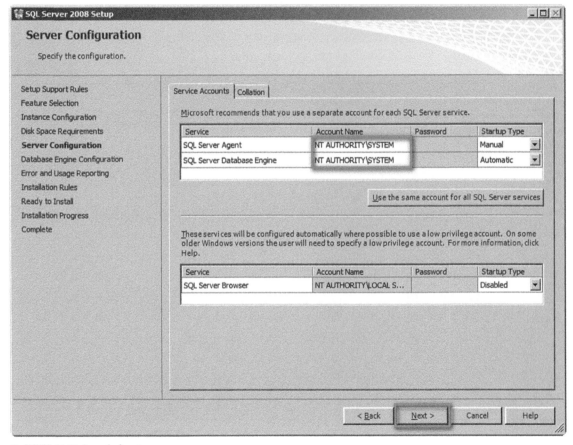

■ **FIGURE 11.21** Server Configuration.

12. The next window is the Database Engine Configuration. We created a SQL service account for this install called SQLSvc and added it to the list of SQL Server Administrators. For our testing, we left the two remaining tabs at their default state. Note that your Database Administrator will likely prefer to modify these settings for your environment. Click *Next* (see Figure 11.22).

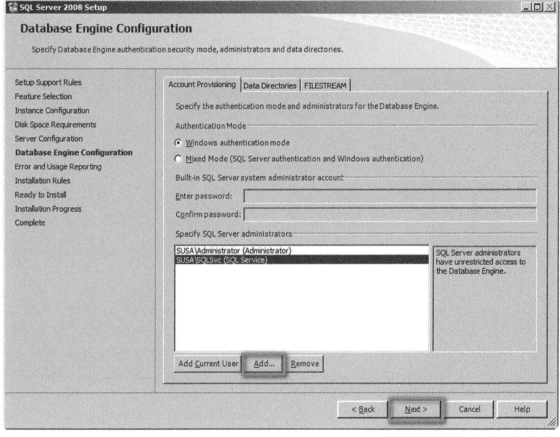

■ **FIGURE 11.22** Database Engine Configuration.

13. The Error and Usage Reporting screen allows you to enable the reporting of errors and feature usage directly to Microsoft. Choose your preference and click *Next* (see Figure 11.23).

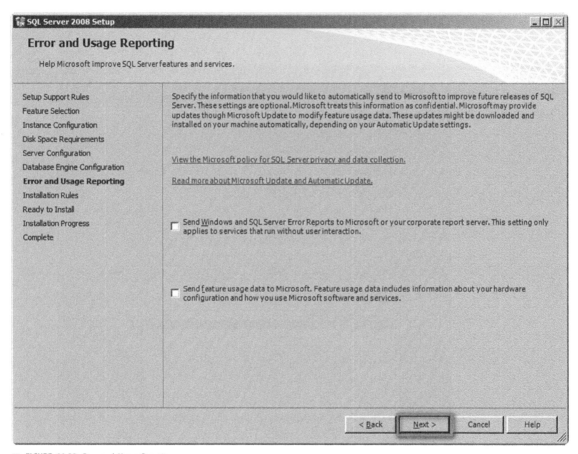

■ **FIGURE 11.23** Error and Usage Reporting.

14. The Installation Rules window runs a series of tests to determine any potential reasons why the installation might fail. If it detects issues, it provides problem details and gives you the opportunity to correct them. If all goes well, click *Next* (see Figure 11.24).

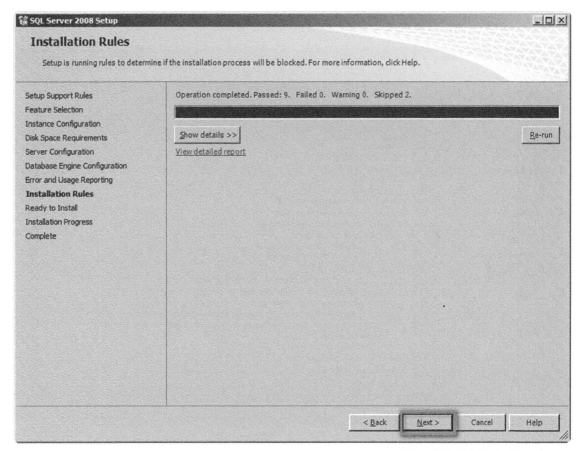

■ **FIGURE 11.24** Installation Rules.

15. The Ready to Install screen displays an overview of the selections and options you have chosen for your install. Review and click *Install* (see Figure 11.25).

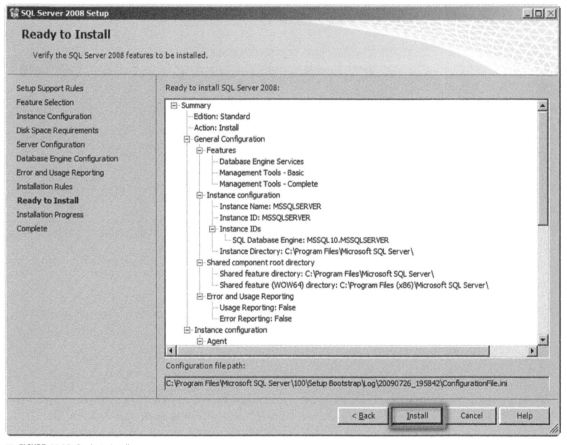

■ **FIGURE 11.25** Ready to Install.

16. The Installation Progress screen displays the progress of the SQL
server install (see Figure 11.26). Depending on the options selected
and your hardware, this may take some time to complete. This took

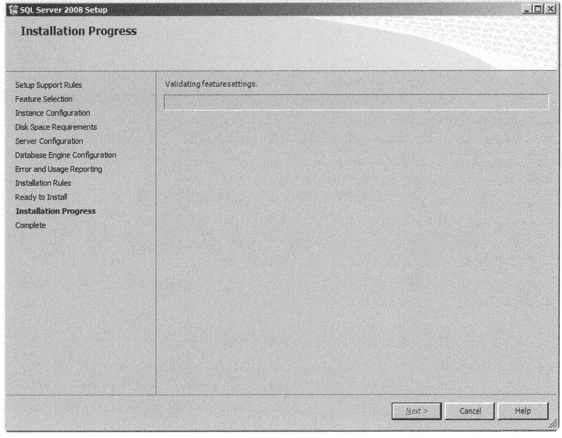

■ **FIGURE 11.26** SQL Server Installation
Progress.

approximately 20 min on our test network. Once finished, all options you chose for your installation will be listed as successful. Click *Next* (see Figure 11.27).

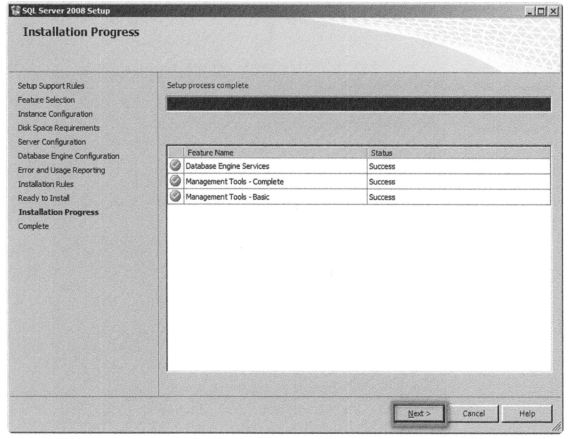

■ **FIGURE 11.27** SQL Server Setup process complete.

17. The Complete screen confirms that the installation was successful. You can click *Close* to exit out of the SQL installation (see Figure 11.28).

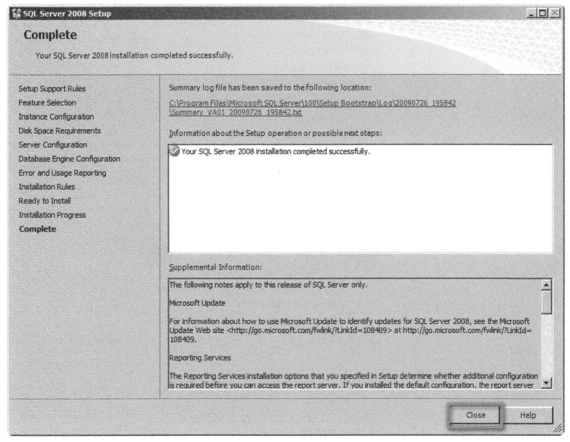

■ **FIGURE 11.28** SQL Server Installation Complete.

18. App-V requires you to configure SQL 2008 to allow TCP/IP network access. This is done by default. To verify, browse to *Start | All Programs | Microsoft SQL Server 2008 | Configuration Tools | SQL Server Configuration Manager* (see Figure 11.29). When the

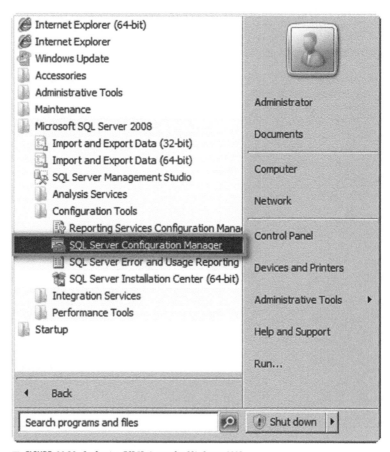

■ **FIGURE 11.29** Configuring TCP/IP Access for SQL Server 2008.

configuration manager console opens, browse in the left-hand
pane to *SQL Server Network Configuration | Protocols for
MSSQLServer* and make sure that TCP/IP is set to enabled in the
right-hand pane (see Figure 11.30).

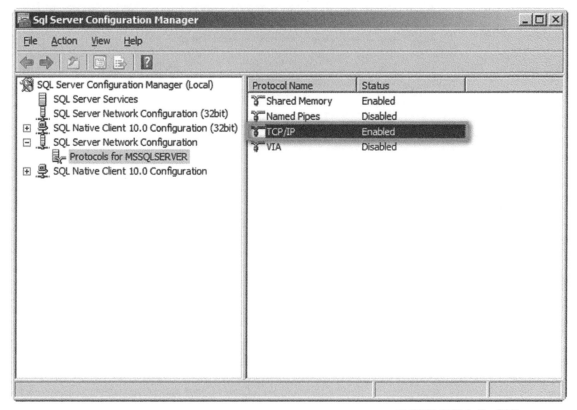

■ **FIGURE 11.30** Enabling TCP/IP.

Configuring IIS 7

Open the Server Manager and expand the *Roles* option to show Web Server (IIS). Click *Web Server (IIS)* and scroll down in the right-hand pane to locate Add Role Services in the upper right corner of the pane. Click *Add Role Services* (see Figure 11.31).

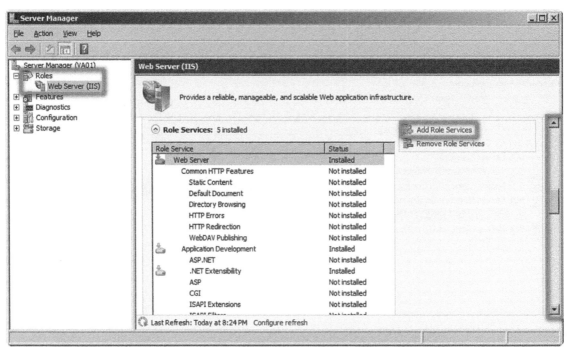

■ **FIGURE 11.31** Adding Role Services.

1. Add the *Static Content, Default Document, Directory Browsing*, and *HTTP Errors* from the Web Server | Common HTTP Features section. Add *ASP.NET, .NET Extensibility, ISAPI Extensions*, and *ISAPI Filters* from the Web Server | Application Development section. Add *HTTP Logging* and *Request Monitor* from the Web Server | Health and Diagnostics section. Add *Windows Authentication* and *Request Filtering* from the Web Server | Security section. Add *Static Content Compression* from the Web Server | Performance section. Add *IIS Management Console, IIS Management Scripts and Tools*, and *IIS 6 Management Compatibility* from the Management Tools section (Figure 11.32).

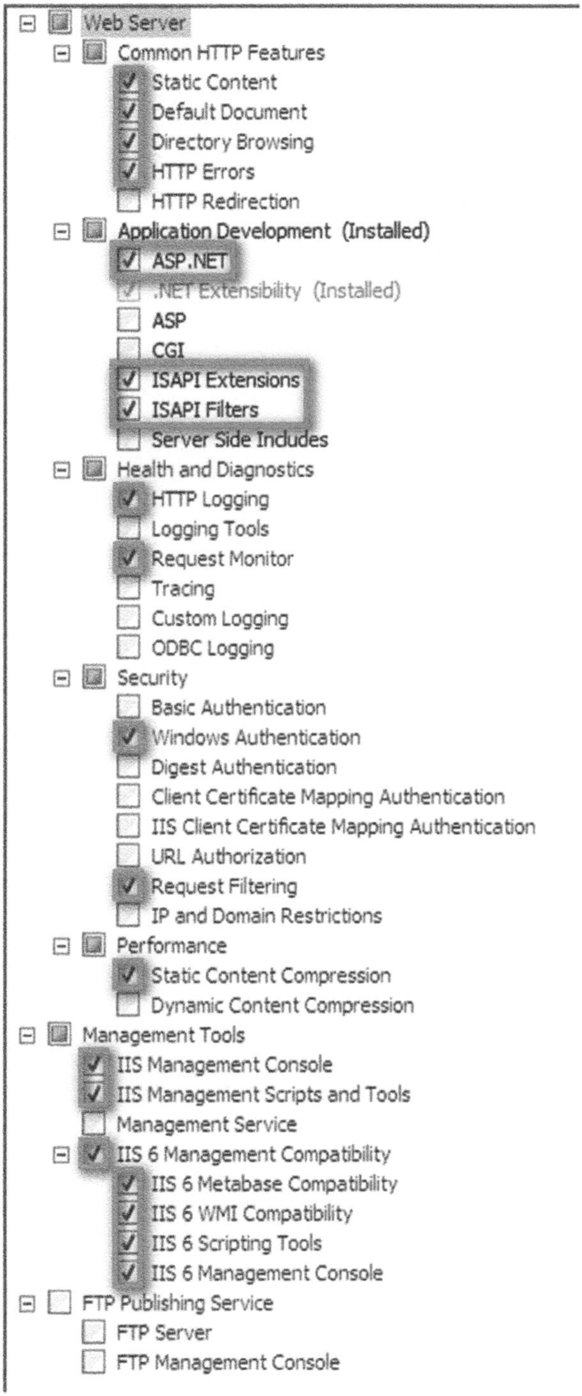

FIGURE 11.32 Select items.

2. Once all items are selected, click *Next*.
3. The Confirm Installation Selection screen provides an overview of the items you selected to install. Once you review this screen, click *Install* (Figure 11.33).

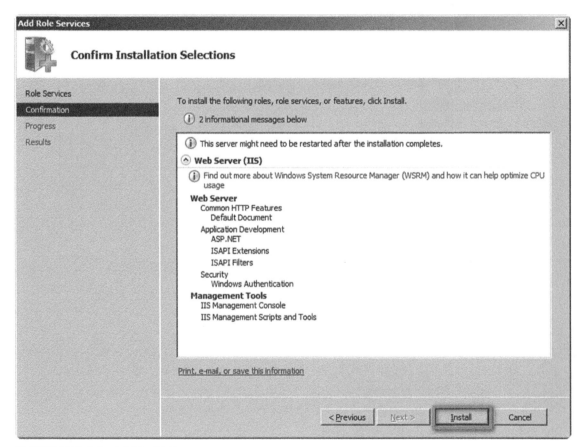

■ **FIGURE 11.33** Confirm Installation Selections.

4. The Installation Progress window displays as selected services are being installed (Figure 11.34).

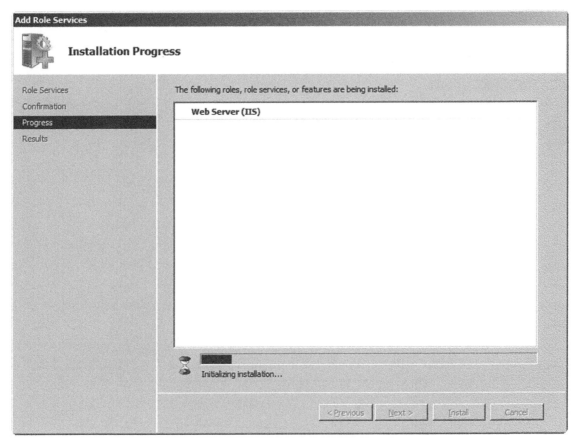

■ **FIGURE 11.34** Installation Progress.

5. Once the installation is complete, you will see the Installation Results window. Click *Close* (Figure 11.35).

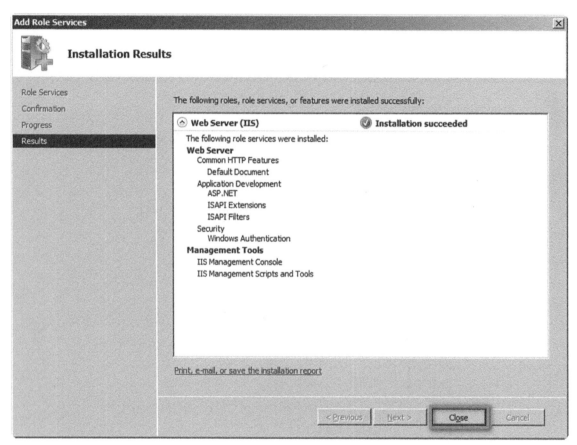

■ **FIGURE 11.35** Installation Results.

Installing the App-V Management Server

At this point, we have installed all of the necessary prerequisites for an App-V Management Server.

All components for the App-V server environment are available through the Microsoft Volume Licensing Site (MVLS). The link is called Application Virtualization Hosting for Desktops 4.5 and can be found

under the Windows section. Once downloaded, extract the files or burn
the ISO to a CD.

1. Browse to *App-V | Installers | Server | Management* and click *Setup.
   exe*.
2. At the Welcome Screen, click *Next* (Figure 11.36).

■ **FIGURE 11.36** Welcome to the InstallShield
Wizard for the Microsoft System Center Application
Virtualization Management Server.

3. In the License Agreement window, accept the agreement and click *Next* (Figure 11.37).

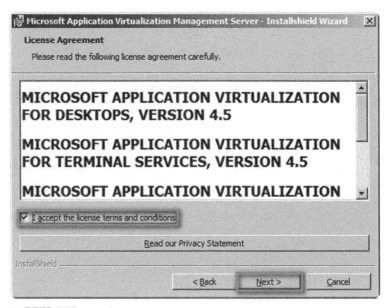

■ **FIGURE 11.37** License Agreement.

4. Enter or validate the correct registration information in the
Registration Information window and click *Next* (Figure 11.38).

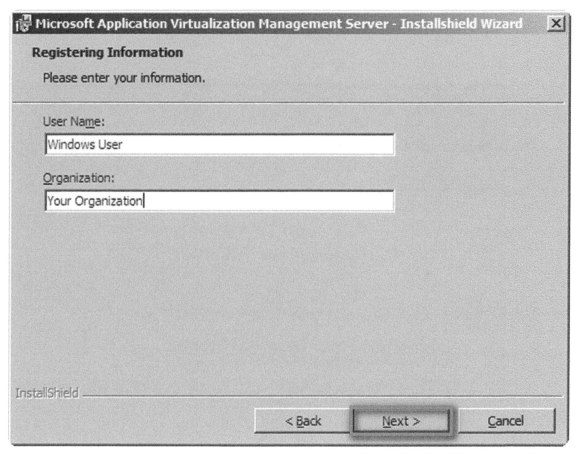

■ **FIGURE 11.38** Registration Information.

5. In the Setup Type window select *Custom* and click *Next* (Figure 11.39).

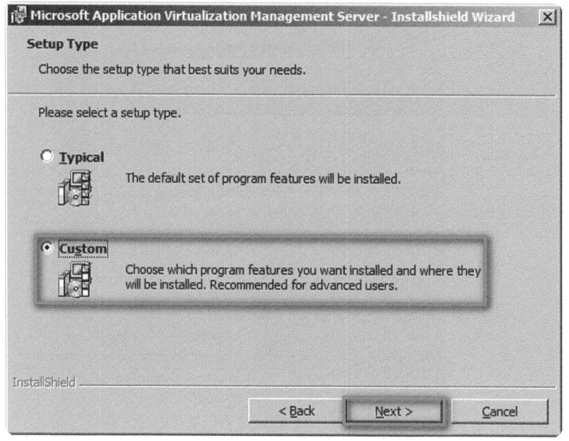

■ **FIGURE 11.39** Setup Type.

6. In the Custom Setup window you can choose various options (for this example we are leaving the selected items in their default states), but it is here where you can change the install path if needed. There are no known issues related to choosing an alternate path. Make your choices and click *Next* (Figure 11.40).

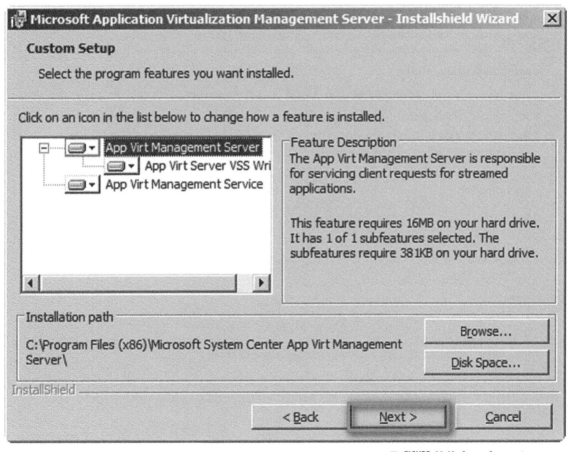

7. The next screen is the Database Configuration screen. This is where you specify the database server you plan to use. For this example, we installed the database on the same server as the Management Server. The name of the server is VA01, and we have left the default port of 1433 configured. Check the *Use the following hostname to access the database server* box, enter your server name and appropriate port, and click *Next* (Figure 11.41).

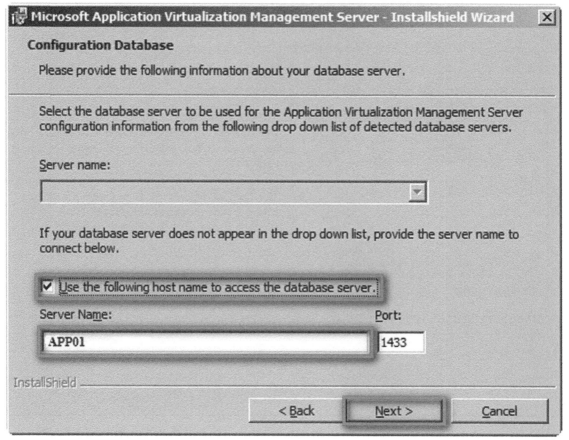

■ **FIGURE 11.41** Configuration Database—
Server Configuration.

8. In the Configuration Database window you can either use the existing default database or choose a new one. We elected to create one with the default name provided by the installer. Set your choices and click *Next* (Figure 11.42).

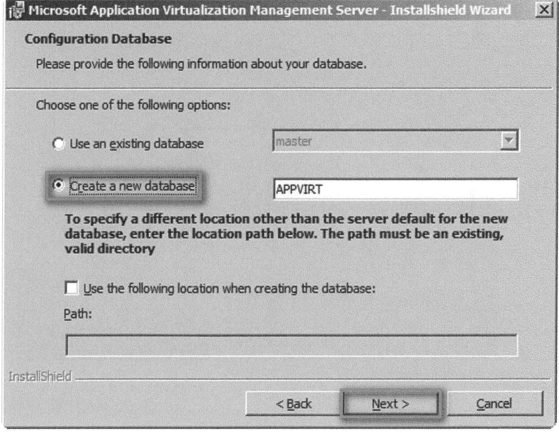

■ **FIGURE 11.42** Configuration Database—Database Configuration.

9. Unless you have a public key infrastructure (PKI) in place, the next window will be grayed out only allowing you to click *Next* (Figure 11.43).

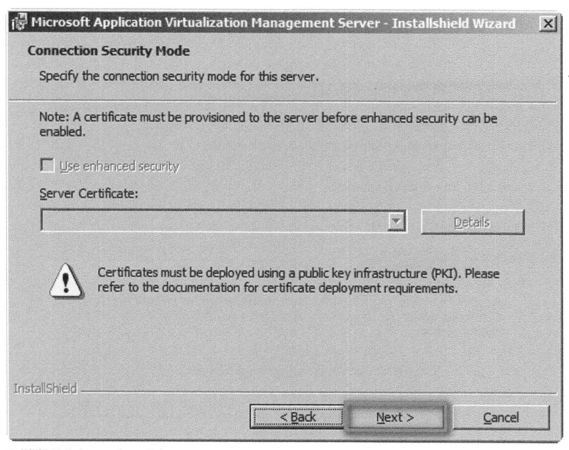

■ **FIGURE 11.43** Connection Security Mode.

10. For this example, we used the default TCP port for App-V. But this
window allows you to change this to a different port. Click *Next*
(Figure 11.44).

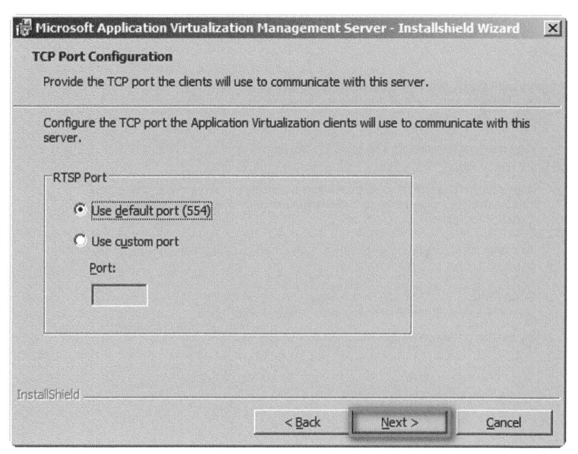

11. The Administrator Group window allows you to specify the Active Directory administrative security group for the App-V server. As discussed earlier in this document, we created a new security group called App-V Admins prior to beginning the install of the App-V Management Console. Enter the name of the group you created for this task and click *Next* (Figure 11.45).

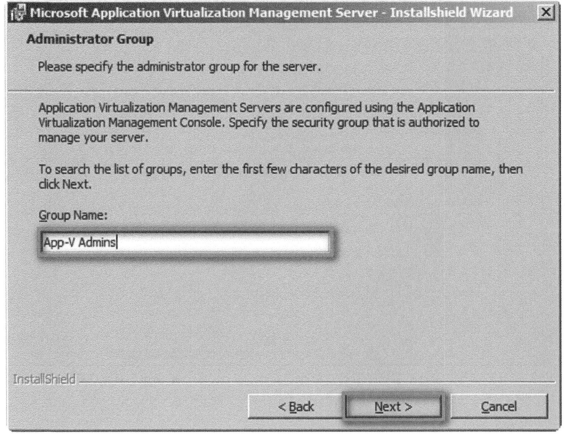

■ **FIGURE 11.45** Administrator Group.

12. The Default Provider Group window allows you to specify the Active
Directory security group listing users who will be able to use the
App-V Management Server. As discussed earlier in this document, we
created a new security group called App-V Users prior to beginning
the install of the App-V Management Console. Enter the name of the
group you created for this task and click *Next* (Figure 11.46).

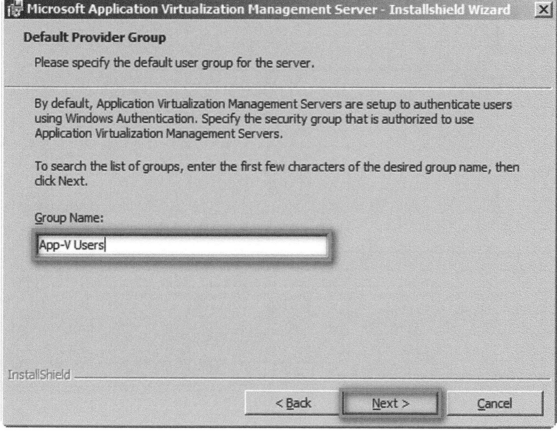

■ **FIGURE 11.46** Default Provider Group.

13. In the Content Path window, you have the option to modify the default path where content is stored. For this example we used the default path. Click *Next* (Figure 11.47).

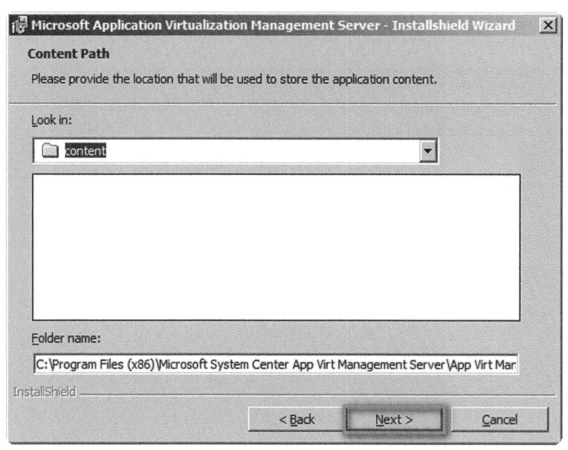

■ **FIGURE 11.47** Content Path.

14. In the Ready to Install the Program window click *Install*; please note
that this step may take some time depending on the options you
selected and your hardware. On our equipment, this step took 12 min
(Figures 11.48 and 11.49).

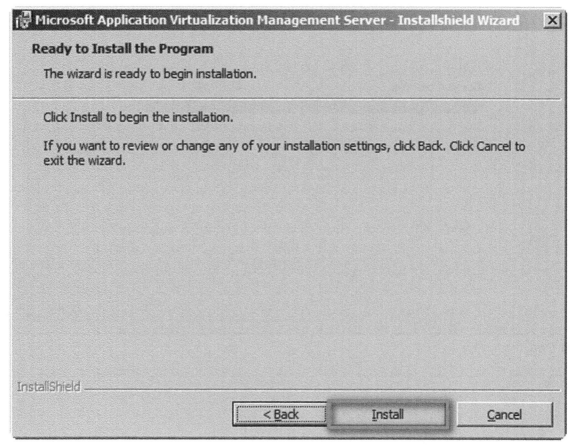

■ **FIGURE 11.48** Ready to Install.

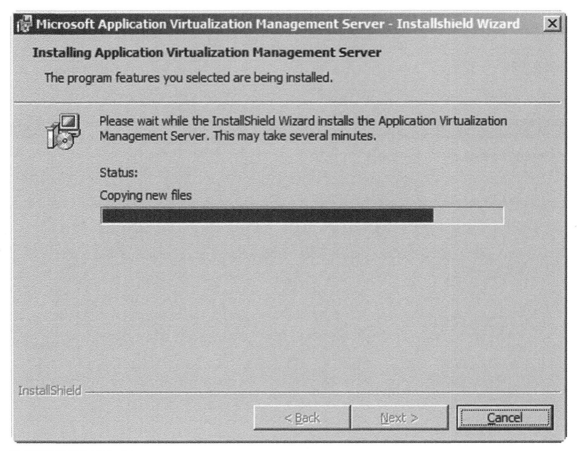

■ **FIGURE 11.49** Installation Status.

15. Once the install is complete, you will see the *InstallShield Wizard Completed* screen. Click *Finish* and reboot your server (Figure 11.50).

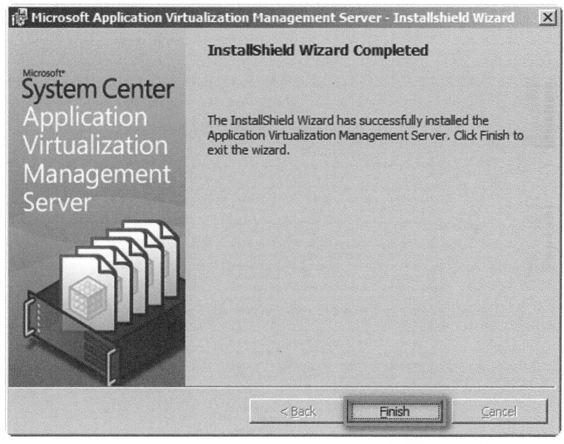

■ **FIGURE 11.50** Installation Complete.

16. With the App-V Management Server installed and the server rebooted, we need to configure the Windows Firewall to allow exceptions for this application. You can add these exceptions via a Group Policy Object (GPO) or locally. For this example, we added them locally through the Windows Firewall console. Browse to *Start | Administrative Tools | Windows Firewall with Advanced Security*.

17. Within the Firewall console select *Inbound Rules*. Right-click this item and choose *New Rule* (Figure 11.51).

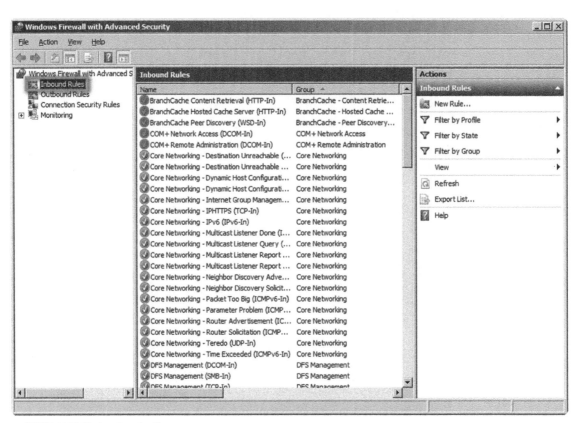

■ **FIGURE 11.51** Windows Firewall with Advanced Security.

18. Select the *Program* radio button and click *Next* (Figure 11.52).

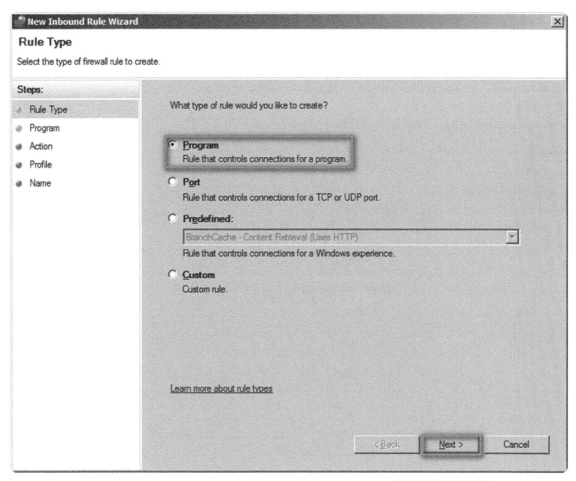

■ **FIGURE 11.52** Rule Type.

19. We will now add the paths of two different executables to the firewall rules. You will need to perform Steps 20-24 twice in order to apply both paths. The paths to enter are:

   a. Path 1—*%ProgramFiles%(x86)\Microsoft System Center App Virt Management Server\App Virt Management Server\bin\sghwdsptr.exe*

   b. Path 2—*%ProgramFiles%(x86)\Microsoft System Center App Virt Management Server\App Virt Management Server\bin\sghwsvr.exe*

20. In this window, you will see the option to add *All programs* or specify a *This program path:*. We are going to specify a path, so click that radio button.

21. Enter the full path and click *Next* (Figure 11.53).

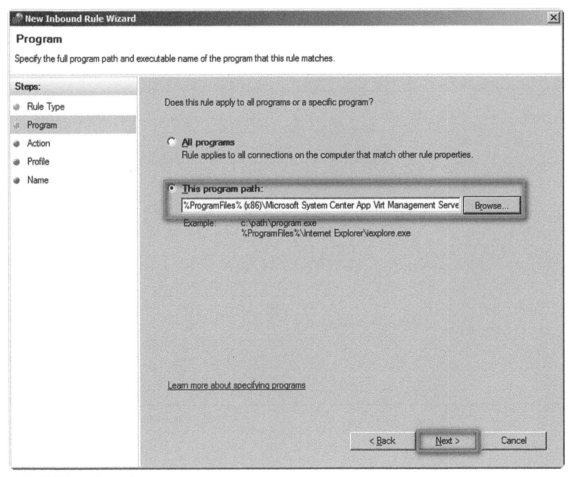

■ **FIGURE 11.53** Rule Program Path.

22. In the Action window choose *Allow the Connection* and click *Next*
(Figure 11.54).

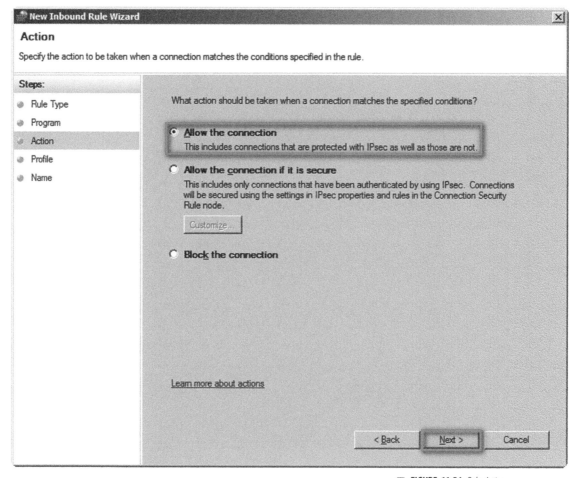

23. In the *Profile* window choose all three profiles (Domain, Private, Public) and click *Next* (Figure 11.55).

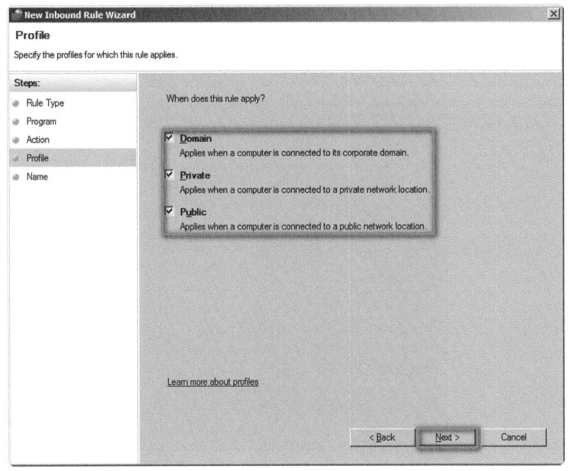

■ **FIGURE 11.55** Rule Profile.

24. The Name window allows you to add a simple name and explanation for this rule. This comes in handy for future administrators who analyze what exceptions have been enabled and why. Enter an appropriate name and description and click *Finish*. If you have just entered the first path (Path—1), go back to Step 20 and enter the second path (Path—2); otherwise, continue with Step 25 (Figure 11.56).

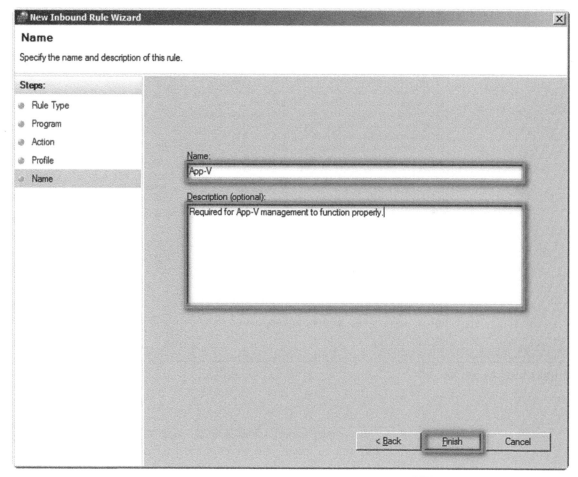

■ **FIGURE 11.56** Rule Name.

25. With your firewall exceptions complete, you can verify them by checking the firewall console (Figure 11.57).

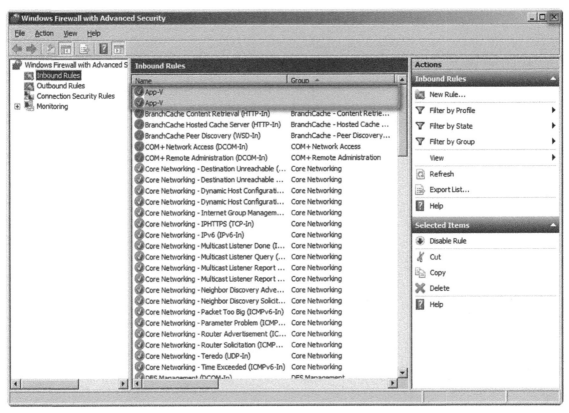

■ **FIGURE 11.57** Verify New Rules.

This completes the installation of the App-V Management Server. You will want to reboot your server in order for all of your changes to take effect. Once you reboot, you can access the App-V Management Console by opening Internet Explorer and browsing to http://localhost.

Installing the App-V Streaming Server

1. From the root of the MDOP download, browse to *App-V | Installers | Server | Streaming* and click *Setup.exe*.
2. At the Welcome Screen, click *Next* (Figure 11.58).

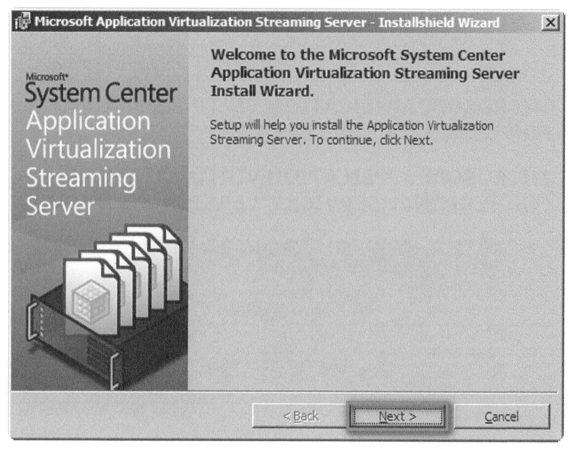

■ **FIGURE 11.58** Welcome to the Microsoft System Center Application Virtualization Streaming Server Install Wizard.

3. Accept the terms of the licensing agreement and then click *Next* (Figure 11.59).

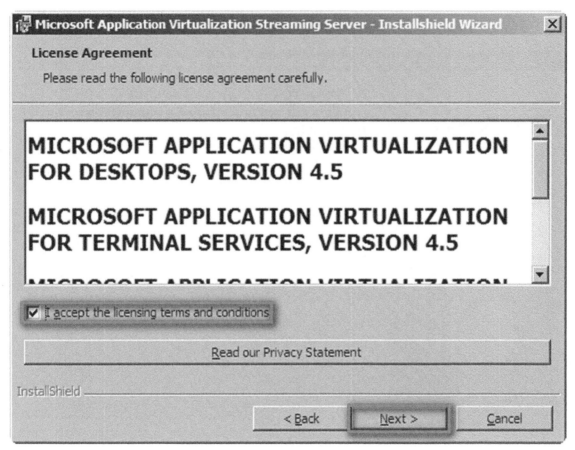

FIGURE 11.59 License Agreement.

4. Enter the proper customer information and click *Next* (Figure 11.60).

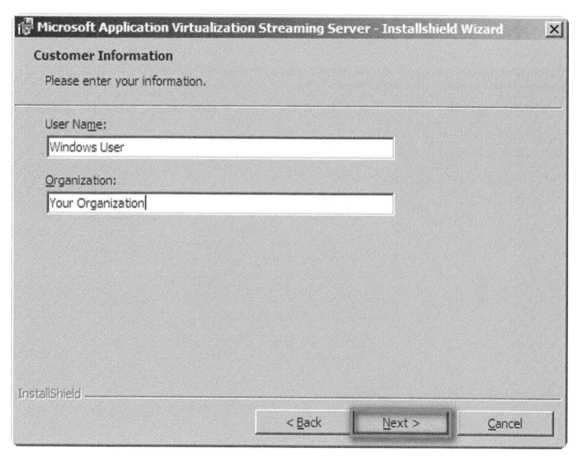

■ **FIGURE 11.60** Registration Information.

5. Review the installation path, change if necessary, and click *Next* (Figure 11.61).

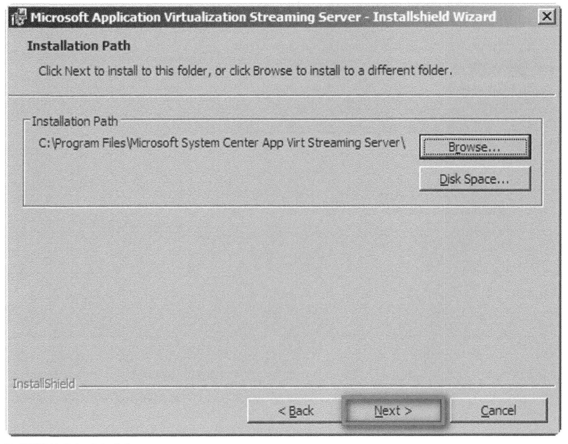

■ FIGURE 11.61 Installation Path.

6. The connection security mode screen allows you the option of adding security certificates to your Streaming configuration. This will only be available if you have certificates previously configured, click *Next* (Figure 11.62).

Note
Although we did not use certificates in our examples, we recommend you seriously consider them for your production implementations. PKI is a significant project on its own, and it is far outside the scope of this book.

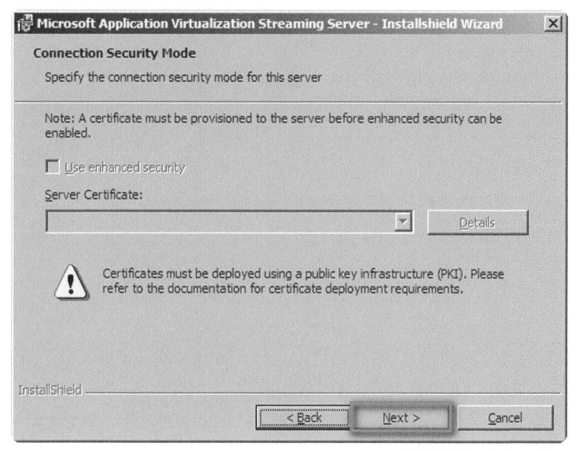

■ **FIGURE 11.62** Connection Security Mode.

7. The TCP Port configuration screen allows you to modify the port clients will use to communicate with the Streaming server. Please note that this port may need to be configured on your firewall depending on your firewall configuration. Review this port, change if necessary, and click *Next* (Figure 11.63).

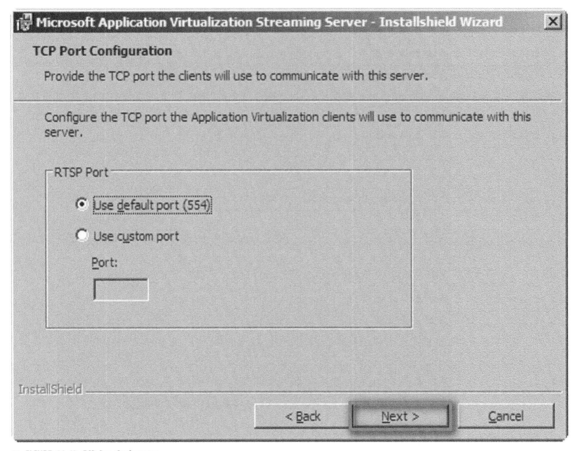

■ **FIGURE 11.63** TCP Port Configuration.

8. Review the content root path and click *Next*. Unless you have disk space constraints that would not allow it, it is suggested that this path be left to the default (Figure 11.64).

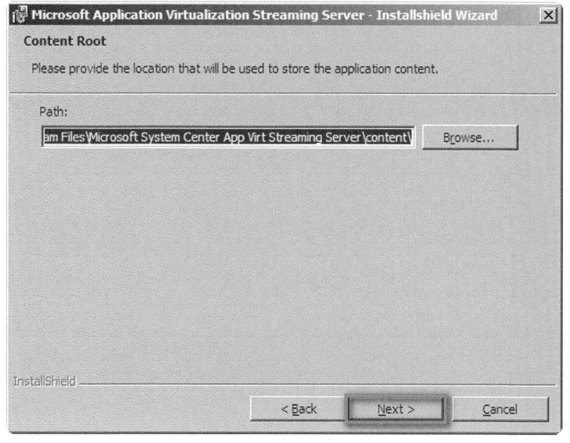

■ **FIGURE 11.64** Content Root.

9. The Advanced Settings screen allows you to modify the way clients connect to the Streaming server. The recommendation is to leave these settings at their default values. Click *Next* (Figure 11.65).

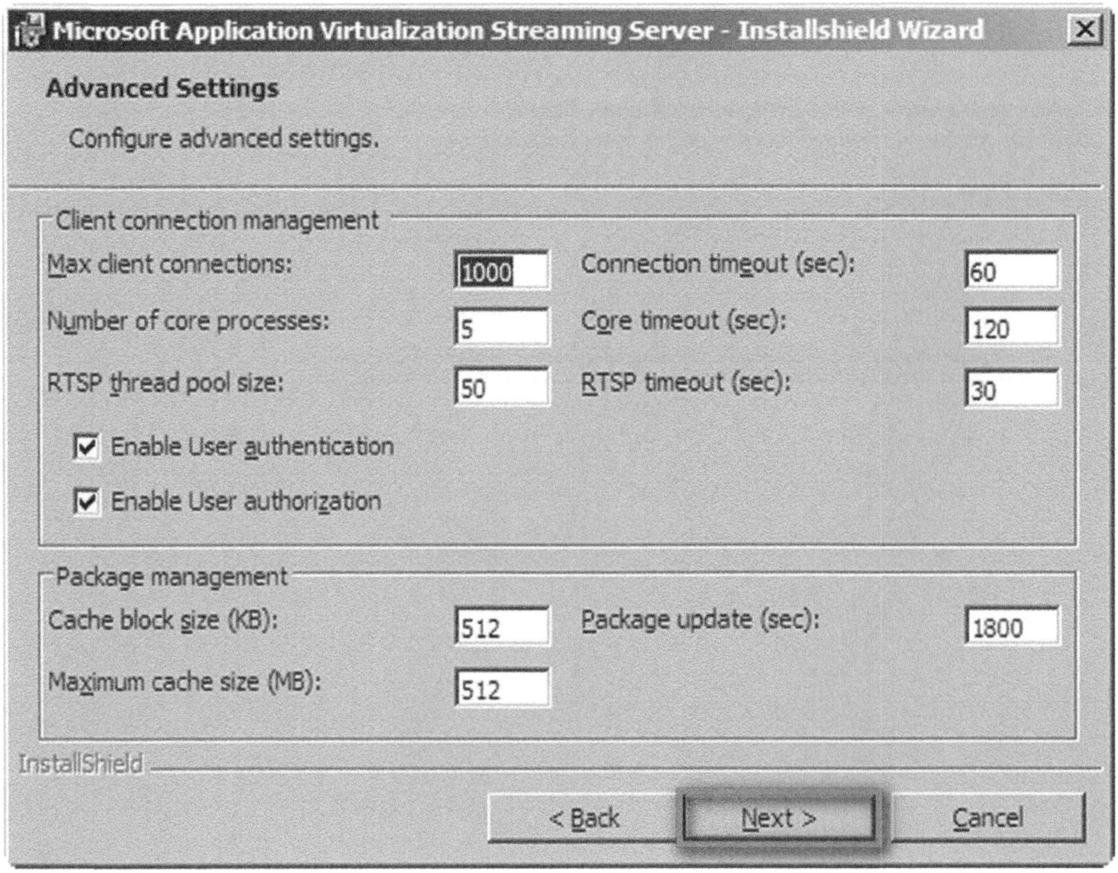

■ FIGURE 11.65 Advanced Settings.

10. Click *Install* (Figure 11.66).

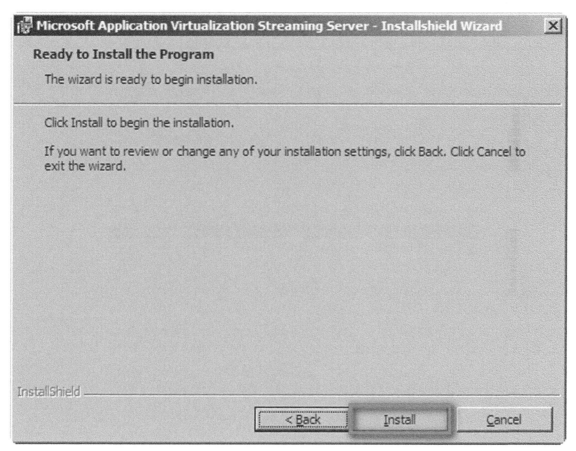

11. The install progress will be displayed, and may take several minutes depending on the server hardware and location that you are installing to\from (Figure 11.67).

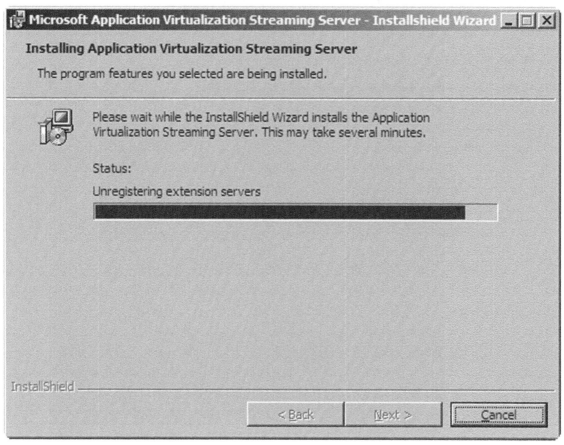

■ **FIGURE 11.67** Installation Status.

12. When the installation completes, click the *Finish* button. You will be
prompted to reboot. Reboot before you make any further changes to
the server (Figure 11.68).

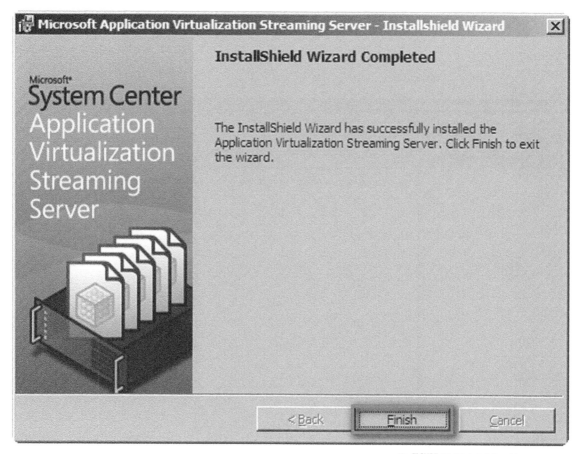

■ **FIGURE 11.68** Install Complete.

With the server environments installed, you can now access the App-V environment by browsing to *Application Virtualization Management Console* located in Administrator Tools within the Control Panel. The Application Virtualization Management Console will launch. At this point you will still need to connect to the environment itself. To do this, click the *Connect to Application Virtualization...* link in the upper right-hand corner of the console (Figure 11.69).

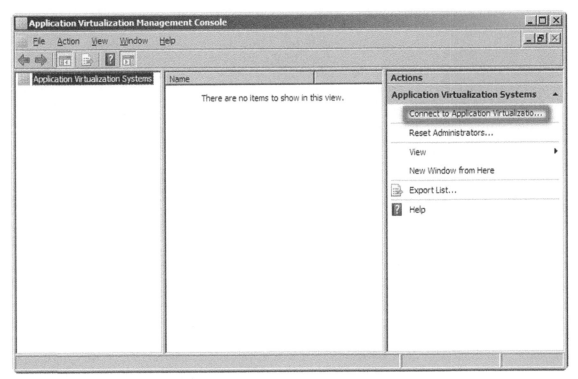

■ **FIGURE 11.69** Application Virtualization Management Console.

You will receive the dialog box shown in Figure 11.70. By default, this dialog box has the Use Secure Connection option enabled. If you have configured your App-V and IIS environments to utilize secure connections, this can remain selected. If you have not configured secure

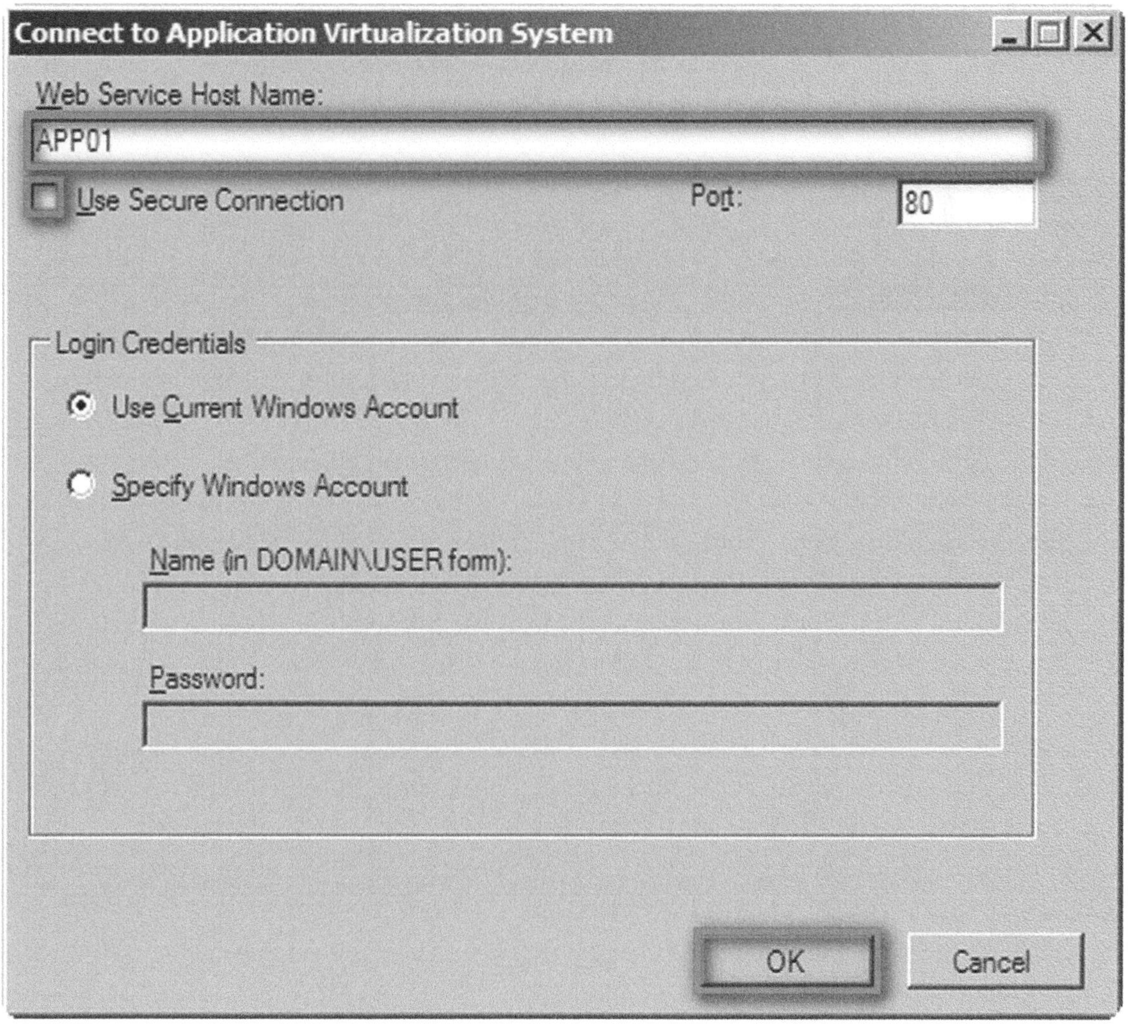

Connect to Application Virtualization System

Web Service Host Name:

APP01

☐ Use Secure Connection   Port: 80

Login Credentials

○ Use Current Windows Account

○ Specify Windows Account

Name (in DOMAIN\USER form):

Password:

OK   Cancel

■ **FIGURE 11.70** Configure Connection.

connections, you will need to unselect this option before clicking *Ok*. If the user account you use to launch the console connection is not a member of the App-V Administrators group created during the install of App-V, you will also need to click the radio button labeled *Specify Windows Account* and enter the correct credentials. Otherwise, click *Ok* to connect to the App-V environment.

Once connected, you will see your console populate with information similar to the screenshot shown in Figure 11.71.

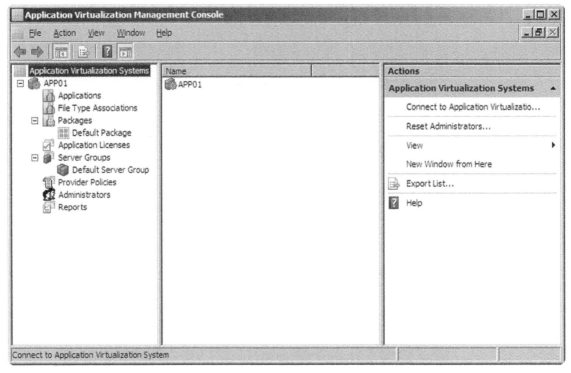

■ **FIGURE 11.71** Application Virtualization Management Console—Logged In.

SUMMARY

In this chapter, we introduced you to Microsoft's application virtualization platform, called App-V. We discussed the system requirements and the installation procedure, as well as the changes you will need to make in your network to allow external access to streamed applications. Finally, we discussed the management of the App-V server farm. In the next chapter, we will walk you through the creation and deployment of virtualized applications.

The key to a successful implementation of these components is planning. Understand all the prerequisites before clicking the first setup application. In other words, read through this chapter BEFORE starting your implementation—read the instructions first—to make sure you do not run into any roadblocks along the way.

Once completed, the applications and services configured here form the foundation for creating sequenced applications and streaming services for your end-user devices. If you are ready to move on to actually using what you have done in Chapter 11, turn the page and jump into Chapter 12.

Chapter

12

Deploying App-V packages

In this chapter, we specify system requirements and network considerations of both the App-V Sequencer and the App-V Desktop Client. We step through the installation of the Sequencer and the Desktop Client. Finally, we will create an App-V package using the Sequencer.

WHAT IS AN APP-V PACKAGE?

An App-V package is the next generation of an application installation. Apart from some specialized scenarios, most applications prior to the introduction of App-V were simply "installed" on a user's workstation and the state of the installation remains largely static unless the user or their network administrator choose to force the application to upgrade, update, etc. An App-V package is much more dynamic in that it can be custom designed to

- Reside completely on a user's workstation
- Partially on a user's workstation and partially on a server
- Completely on a server only allowing access to the application from the user's workstation
- And many variances in-between.

This approach allows you to efficiently maintain an App-V package. For example, an App-V package can be designed to install completely on a user's workstation and still regularly "check-in" to the App-V infrastructure to look for updates, and then apply those updates in the background without impacting the user's experience of the application.

Isolating an application addresses application compatibilities that otherwise would make it impossible to run two applications on the same workstation. An example of this is two different applications, each requiring a different version of the Java runtime. Prior to App-V, installing both applications on the same desktop caused pain and frustration. App-V allows you to package an application together with its prerequisites, and then stream the collective package to a workstation without the need to actually "install" anything on the user's workstation. You can do this for any or all applications, including two different versions of the same program.

Application Virtualization Sequencer

The Sequencer is a wizard-based tool; App-V administrators will come to use and appreciate more than any other function in the App-V world. The Sequencer is used to create App-V sequenced applications and produce an application "package." A package consists of several files, including

- A sequenced application (.sft) file
- Open Software Description (.osd) "link" files
- Icon (.ico) files
- A manifest xml file that can be used to distribute sequenced applications with electronic software delivery (ESD) systems
- A project (.sprj) file

The Sequencer can also be used to build Windows Installer files (.msi) for deployment to clients configured for stand-alone operation. The .sft, .osd, and .ico files are stored in a shared content folder on the Management Server and are used by the App-V client to access and run sequenced applications.

Application Virtualization Client

The App-V Client is required on endpoint devices receiving applications from the App-V environment. It allows for management of package streaming on the client device; such as how much local cache is to be used by the application. It also manages how often the application checks in for any changes, and any user-specific configuration settings.

SYSTEM REQUIREMENTS

You will notice the system requirements for the App-V Sequencer and Client are very similar to a typical end-user workstation.

- App-V Sequencer Requirements
  - Processor—Intel® Pentium® III, 850 MHz or faster. The sequencing process is a single-threaded process; it does not take advantage of dual processors.
  - Memory—256 MB RAM or greater. A 500 MB page file is recommended.
  - Hard drive—Two physical drives, 20-GB minimum each. (Install the operating system and local applications on one drive, and use the second drive as the target for your virtual applications.) It is recommended your disk drives should be at least three times as large as the largest application you will sequence. If you have only one hard drive, you must use at least two NTFS volumes to partition it.
  - Operating system (*this must be the same as the clients*)—The Sequencer runs on the following operating systems:
    - Windows XP Professional (*SP2 or SP3*)
    - Windows Server 2003
    - Windows Vista
    - Windows Server 2008 with Terminal Services
    - Windows 7

Note

The sequencing process is very system resource intensive. We strongly suggest that your sequencing workstation have plenty of memory, a fast processor, and a fast hard drive (*a fast disk speed decreases sequencing time*). The amount of additional memory and processing power is determined by the types of applications you plan to sequence, and the type of package you plan to create for those applications. We recommend you validate your configuration with Microsoft. Other than the memory and processor requirements, the sequencer workstation should have the same hardware and software configuration as the target App-V clients.

Note

Software installed on the sequencer should match the software installed on the target clients as closely as possible. For example, if Microsoft Outlook is installed locally on each client, it should also be installed on the sequencer. This is because the Sequencer takes into account all available system files that may already exist on a workstation to make the App-V package as efficient as possible.

App-V Client requirements

Now we will discuss two App-V client requirements: App-V Desktop Client and App-V Terminal Services Client.

App-V Desktop Client

- Processor—See recommended system requirements for the operating system you are using.
- RAM—See recommended system requirements for the operating system you are using.

- Disk—30 MB for installation and 4096 MB for cache.
- Windows XP Professional (SP2 or SP3) 32-bit
- Windows Vista RTM/SP1 (Business, Enterprise, or Ultimate) 32-bit
- Windows 7

The following software prerequisites are installed automatically if the setup.exe method is used. For setup.msi install program, these must be installed first. Microsoft recommends using setup.exe.

- Microsoft Visual C++ 2005 SP1 Redistributable Package (×86)—For more information about installing Microsoft Visual C++ 2005 SP1 Redistributable Package (×86), see http://go.microsoft.com/fwlink/? LinkId=119961.
- Microsoft Core XML Services (MSXML) 6.0 SP1 (×86)—For more information about installing Microsoft Core XML Services (MSXML) 6.0 SP1 (×86), see http://go.microsoft.com/fwlink/?LinkId=63266.
- Microsoft Application Error Reporting—The install program for this software is included in the Support\Watson folder in the self-extracting archive file.

App-V Terminal Services Client

- Processor—See recommended system requirements for the operating system you are using
- RAM—See recommended system requirements for the operating system you are using (also depends on the number of users and applications)
- Disk—30 MB for installation and 2 GB for cache
- Windows Server 2003 (Standard, Enterprise, or Datacenter, SP1 or later) 32-bit
- Windows Server 2008 (Standard, Enterprise, Datacenter) 32-bit
- Windows 7

INSTALLING THE APP-V SEQUENCER

Before installing the Sequencer on a workstation or server, there are some items that you must be aware of, and may want to configure in advance. Microsoft's support requirement since version 4.2 of App-V has been to sequence and publish on "like" operating systems. This means that creating a sequenced package on Windows XP and then publishing that package to Vista, and vice versa is not supported. You should plan to have a sequencer workstation or server for every operating system you plan to publish applications to. For example, to publish to a Server 2003 operating system, you must create the package on a Server 2003 operating system, including service pack and hot fix level. Although you may be able to sequence on one operating system and publish to another, the practice is not supported.

In addition to operating system, service pack, and hot fix level, you will also want to include any applications that are a part of your base image. For example, if Adobe Reader is a part of your base image, you should include it in the building of your sequencer workstation. This is especially important if you include the Microsoft Office suite on your base image. Some applications install differently if they see that Microsoft Office is already installed.

If you plan to package applications that include ODBC DSN settings, you will want to create one on the sequencer workstation prior to sequencing a package. The registry key associated with the ODBC setting will become virtualized and prohibit the packaged application from seeing any ODBC DSN settings on the base client machine.

The following locations can be checked to determine ODBC information was captured:

- Search for odbc.ini: It will be located in the VFS\% CSIDL_WINDOWS% folder
- HKLM\Software\ODBC\ODBC.INI\ODBC Data Sources
- HKCU\%SFT_SID%\Software\ODBC\ODBC.INI

You will want to include a printer as part of the Sequencer base image as well. Printer configurations are handled like ODBC settings. So it is necessary to include a printer device in the sequencer PC image.

You will need to set up your sequencer machine with at least two primary partitions. The first partition, C:, should have the operating system installed; format it as NTFS. The second partition, Q:, is used as the destination path for the application installation. It should also be formatted as NTFS.

The sequencer uses %TMP%, %TEMP%, and its own scratch directory for temporary files. These locations should be large enough to accommodate the full installation size of the application being packaged. The sequencer uses the scratch directory to temporarily store the files generated during the sequencing process. The location of the scratch directory can be seen by launching the sequencer and browsing to *Options / Tools* and then clicking the *Paths* tab. You can improve performance by configuring the temp directories and the scratch directory to reside on different physical hard drives.

Before you begin to sequence an application, you will want to shutdown other programs that may be running. Ensure no scheduled tasks are running, or will begin running, during the sequencing process. Disable the following programs before starting a sequencing job:

- Windows Defender
- Antivirus Software
- Disk defragmentation software
- Windows Search
- Microsoft update
- Any open Windows Explorer session

All components for the App-V Sequencer are available through the Microsoft Volume Licensing Site (https://licensing.Microsoft.com). The link is called "Application Virtualization Hosting for Desktops 4.5" and can be found under the Windows section. Once downloaded, extract the files or burn the ISO to a CD.

1. Using the media you just downloaded in the previous step, browse to... / *App-V / Installers / Sequencer* and click *Setup.exe.*
2. The setup wizard prompts you to install the Microsoft C++ Redistributable Package, Microsoft MSXML, and Microsoft Application Error Reporting if they are not already installed. Click *Install.*
3. Once the prerequisites have been installed (or if they were already installed), you are taken to the Welcome page for the Application Virtualization Sequencer. On the Welcome page click *Next.*
4. Read and accept the license agreement, and then click *Next.* Doing so takes you to the Setup Page. Leave the installation path at its default setting and click *Next.*
5. Click *Install* to begin the installation of the App-V Sequencer.
6. When the installation completes, click *Finish.* The Sequencer will now start.

INSTALLING THE APP-V DESKTOP CLIENT

In this section, we will walk you through the installation of the App-V Desktop Client. Depending on the operating system, you may see visual differences from the examples below.

The following steps are to be done while logged in to the workstation with local administrator rights. All components for the App-V Desktop Client are available through the Microsoft Volume Licensing Site (https:// licensing.Microsoft.com). The link is called "Application Virtualization

Hosting for Desktops 4.5" and can be found under the Windows section. Once downloaded, extract the files or burn the ISO to a CD.

1. Using the media you just downloaded in the previous step, browse to… / *App-V* / *Installers* / *Client* and click *Setup.exe*.
2. The setup wizard prompts you to install the Microsoft C++ Redistributable Package, Microsoft MSXML, and Microsoft Application Error Reporting if they are not already installed. Click *Install*. See Figure 12.1.

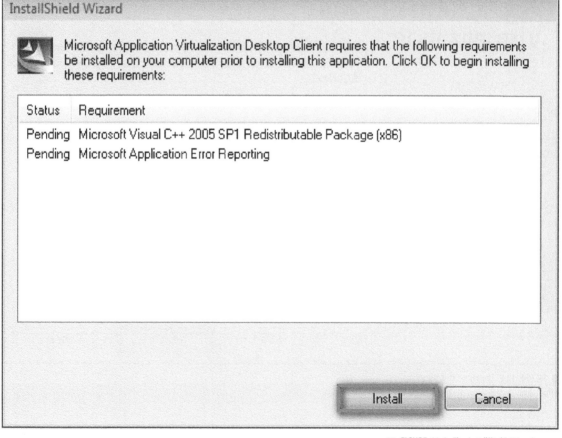

■ **FIGURE 12.1** The InstallShield Wizard.

3. Once the prerequisites are installed (or if they were already installed), you are taken to the Welcome page for the Application Virtualization Desktop Client. On the Welcome page click *Next*. See Figure 12.2

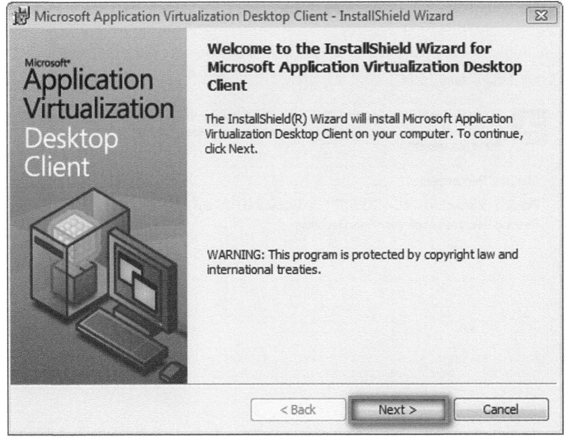

■ **FIGURE 12.2** The Microsoft Application Virtualization Desktop Client Welcome page.

4. Read and accept the license agreement, and then click *Next*. Doing so takes you to the Setup Page (see Figure 12.3). Select the *Custom* radio button and click *Next*.
5. On the Destination Folder page leave all items to their default value and click *Next*.
6. On the Application Virtualization Data Location page leave all items at their default value and click *Next*.

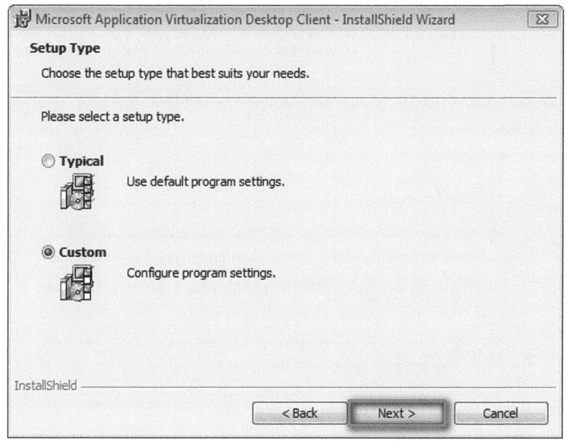

■ FIGURE 12.3 The Microsoft Application Virtualization Desktop Client Setup page.

Note

The option to "Automatically contact this server to upgrade settings when a user logs in" is essential to keep the client current with the latest version of the package. This setting is managed either through the App-V group policy templates or through the creation of the package. The only reason you would ever *not* want to select this check box is if you plan to deploy a package and never maintain it with updates.

7. On the Cache Size Settings page leave all items at their default value and click *Next*.
8. On the Runtime Package Policy Configuration page leave all items at their default value and click *Next*.
9. On the Publishing Server page select the check box to *Set up a Publishing Server now*. In the Display Name field enter the name of the App-V server—based on our examples, this is APP01. In the Host Name box, type the fully qualified domain name (FQDN) of the App-V Management Server. In the Type drop-down list, select *Application Virtualization Server*. In the Port box, ensure that *port 554* is selected. Leave the *Automatically contact this server to update settings when a user logs in* check box selected, and then click *Next* (see Figure 12.4).

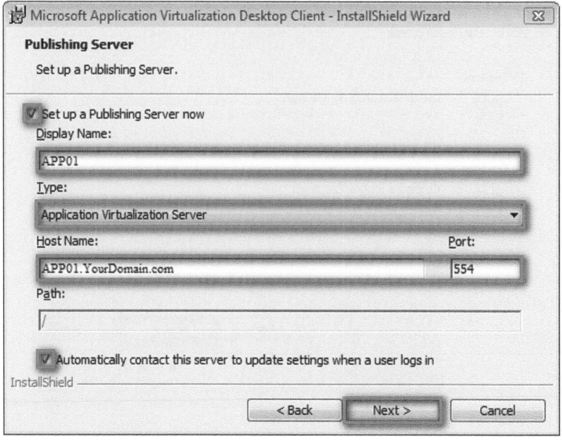

■ **FIGURE 12.4** The Microsoft Application Virtualization Desktop Client Publishing Server page.

10. Click *Install* to begin the installation of the App-V Desktop Client.

11. When the installation is complete, click *Finish*. You can now log off of the workstation.

CREATING AN APP-V PACKAGE

In this section, we explain Microsoft's best practices for sequencing applications, walk you through the steps of creating an App-V package, and explain the various options for publishing that application.

Before sequencing, familiarize yourself with installation and use of the target application. Failure to fully understand the configuration and functionality of the application prior to sequencing may lead to an inefficiently sequenced package; one that may not work all. Specifically,

- What are all of the application components needed to complete the installation of the application?
- What updates such as adding new files to the package will need to be performed while sequencing?
- What postinstallation configuration steps need to take place while sequencing?
- How is the application commonly used by its target users?

When sequencing on Windows Vista or Windows 7, configure the User Account Control (UAC) as it will exist on the target desktops. Disable the UAC if it is disabled on your target client machines.

Always use the Comments field in the sequencer to include details about the package you may want to reference in the future. This allows the sequencer to maintain a log of your actions.

Always sequence to a unique, 8.3 directory name. This applies to both the Asset and Installation directories. ('Q:\MYAPP' and 'Q:\MYAPP.001' are correct, 'Q:\My Application' is incorrect.)

Sequence to a folder in the root of the drive, not to a subdirectory ('Q:\MYAPP' is correct; 'Q:\' is incorrect; 'Q:\Temp_Junk\MYAPP' is incorrect). If the suite has multiple parts, install each application in a subdirectory of the Asset Directory. For example, if a package contains a primary application with the Java Client, use Q:\AppSuite as the Asset Directory; sequence the application to Q:\AppSuite\APP; and sequence the Java Client to Q:\AppSuite\JavaClient.

Use globally unique paths and Package names across the set of application sequencings. For example, place multiple Microsoft Office sequencings in the same Asset Directory name. Use a standardized naming scheme that can be incremented, for example, Q:\OFFXP.v1 or Q:\OFFXP.001.

Launch, configure, and test the application during the installation phase. Often this requires performing several manual steps that are not part of the application installation process, such as configuring database connections, copying updated files, etc. Launch and use the application multiple times in order to ensure that all of the most common features are utilized and captured properly by the sequencer. For example, run the application to get past any registration or initial pop-up dialog boxes. Some applications perform different tasks on first launch, second launch, and sometimes subsequent launches. Multiple launches ensure relevant application code makes it into Feature Block 1 during the execution phase.

Use the Application Wizard to launch each executable in a suite of applications; do not just browse to their location under All Programs. Doing so may result in the sequencer failing to grab the proper first launch data for the primary feature block.

Some applications have the option to Install on First Use for certain components. *Do not* sequence applications with this option selected.

Disable any Auto Update features. Some applications have the ability to check a Web site or a server for the latest application updates. Leaving this feature enabled will not break the application, but it may affect version integrity should the application ever be resequenced to apply updates.

There are applications that cannot or should not be sequenced, and there are limitations within App-V. The following list of applications that SHOULD NOT be sequenced is provided by Microsoft:

- Applications (*when sequenced*) that are over 4 GB in size. If the application is too large the sequencer will not save the application. It will attempt to compress the file.
- Applications that start services at boot time. App-V requires a logged in user initiate the launch of an application.
- Applications that require device drivers. App-V cannot virtualize drivers, but it may be possible to bypass this issue and install the driver locally on the target computer, outside of the App-V package.

- Applications required by several applications for information or access. For example, a program that launches another program. Normally you want to include both programs in the same suite. However, this is not always possible. This is especially true if one of the reasons you are deploying App-V is to avoid application conflicts. Remember that the virtual "bubble" can see the OS and what is installed on it but the OS can neither see the "bubble" nor interact with it.
- Applications that are a part of the operating system, such as Internet Explorer.
- Applications that use COM+. COM+ is dynamic and initiates at runtime. The sequencer cannot capture this information.

To demonstrate how sequencing works, we used Microsoft Office Word Viewer 2003.

The first portion of the process is performed on the workstation\server on which you installed the App-V Sequencer.

1. Download the Microsoft Office Word Viewer 2003 installation package and copy it to a temporary directory on the App-V Sequencer workstation\server. It does not matter where you do this, the path will only be used in a manual fashion by the package builder, and can be deleted once the package is created.
2. Open Windows Explorer and browse to the Q:\ drive. Create a folder called *wdviewer.2k3*. There is no hardcoded naming convention for these folders, so name them something that is easy for you to remember\manage.
3. Create a folder on the App-V Sequencer desktop called *WordViewer2003*; output from the Sequencer will be saved here. This is only a temporary location that is easy to access. Once the package is complete, you can move this to another location of your choice, or you can use the permanent location from the start.
4. From the Start Menu, go to All Programs\Microsoft Application Virtualization\Microsoft Application Virtualization Sequencer and launch the Application Virtualization Sequencer (see Figure 12.5).

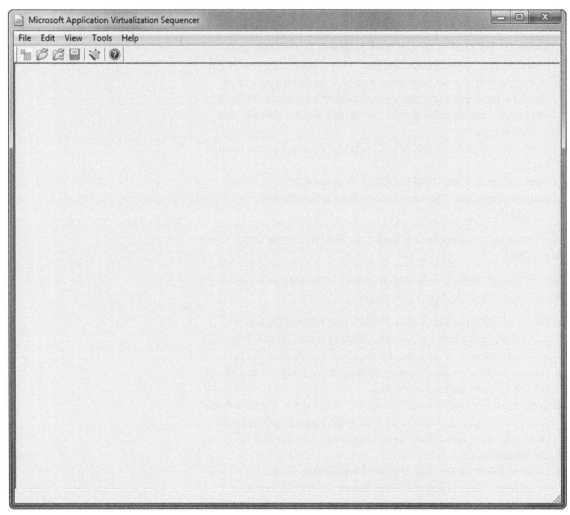

■ FIGURE 12.5 Launching the Microsoft Application Virtualization Sequencer.

Note

The Package Name must be unique, but can be whatever makes sense to you. As an example, Microsoft uses the following naming convention: <Appname>_<AppVendor>_<Version>_<MNT | VFS>, where MNT indicates the application was installed to Q: and VFS indicates the application was installed to C:.

5. Click File\New Package. This launches the Sequencing Wizard (see Figure 12.6). On the Package Information page enter *Word Viewer 2003* as the Package Name; the package name is a common label. Use the Comments field to record any relevant information you feel would be beneficial to others who might access this console. This could be the name of the user who created the package, and the date. This information is recorded in the ABSTRACT element of the OSD file, but does not affect the functionality of the package in any way. Once you have entered this information click *Next*.

6. On the Monitor Installation page click *Begin Monitoring* (see Figure 12.7).

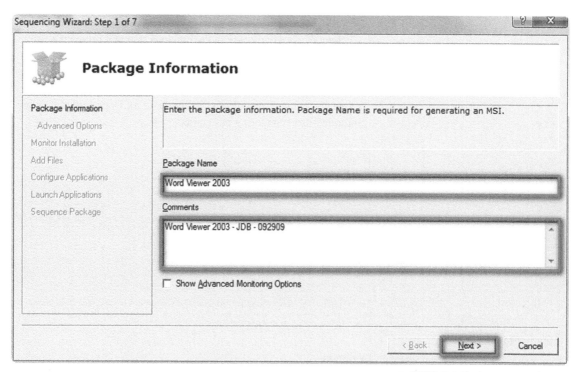

■ **FIGURE 12.6** The Sequencing Wizard.

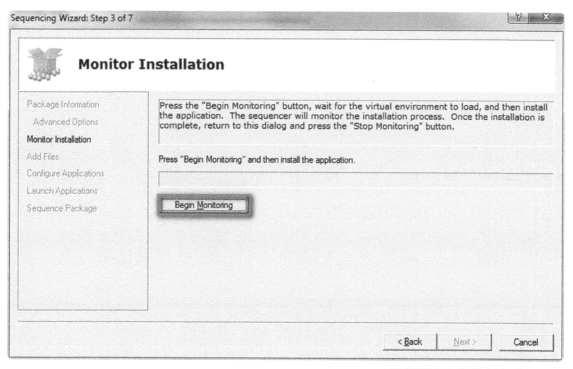

■ **FIGURE 12.7** The Monitor Installation page.

7. Clicking *Begin Monitoring* in the previous step will bring up a Browse for Folder prompt. Browse to Q:\wdviewer.2k3, and click *Ok*.

8. At this point the monitor loads a virtual environment it uses to install the application without actually installing it. It takes a couple of minutes for this to complete (see Figure 12.8). Once loaded, you are informed that monitoring has started.

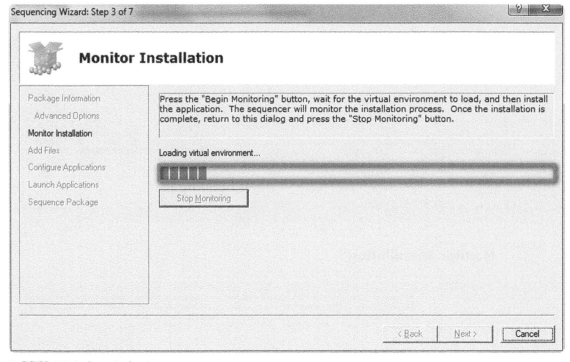

■ FIGURE 12.8 Loading a virtual environment.

9. Once monitoring has started, the virtual environment is running (see Figure 12.9). Browse to the folder that contains the wdviewer.exe installer, and launch the install.

Note
You will initiate an install that will not perform a true install in the sense of the term. This process is comparable to a "snapshot" session used in MSI and other application development.

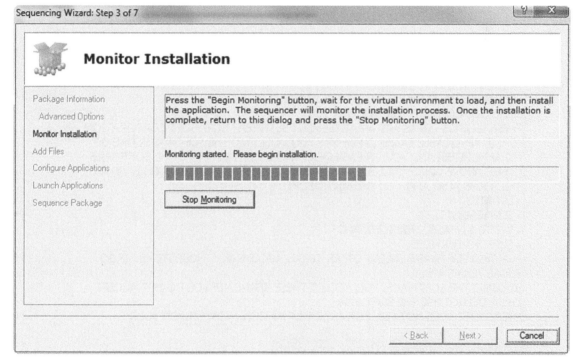

■ FIGURE 12.9 Starting to monitor a virtual environment.

10. Accept the terms of the end-user license agreement (EULA), and click *Next* (see Figure 12.10).

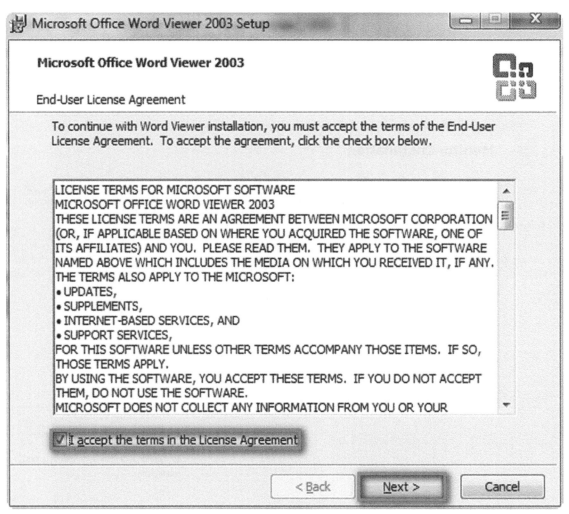

■ **FIGURE 12.10** Microsoft Office Word Viewer EULA.

11. Click *Browse* and go to *Q:\wdviewer.2k3* (see Figure 12.11). Click the
New Folder button and create the *Microsoft Office* folder. Click the
Microsoft Office folder and then click *Ok*. Now, click *Install*.

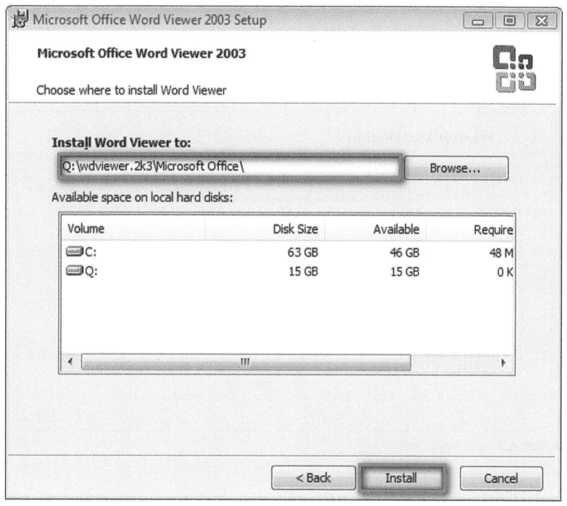

■ **FIGURE 12.11** Choosing where to install
Word Viewer.

12. When the install is complete, you will see the Success dialog box. Click *Ok* to close the dialog box. Browse to Q:\wdviewer.2k3 \Microsoft Office\OFFICE11 and double-click WORDVIEW.EXE to confirm that the install has completed successfully, and then close the viewer.

13. With the install of the viewer complete and tested, go back to the Sequencing Wizard and click *Stop Monitoring* (see Figure 12.12). It may take a few moments to stop.

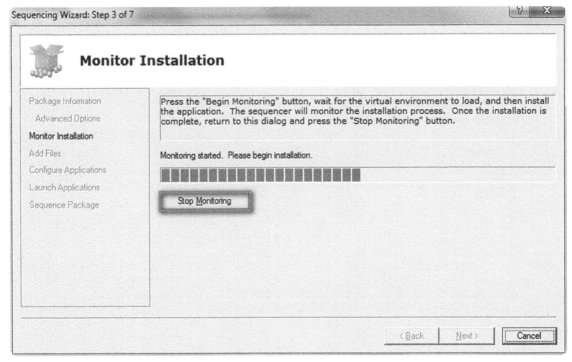

■ **FIGURE 12.12** Stopping monitoring.

14. Once it is finished, click *Next* (see Figure 12.13).

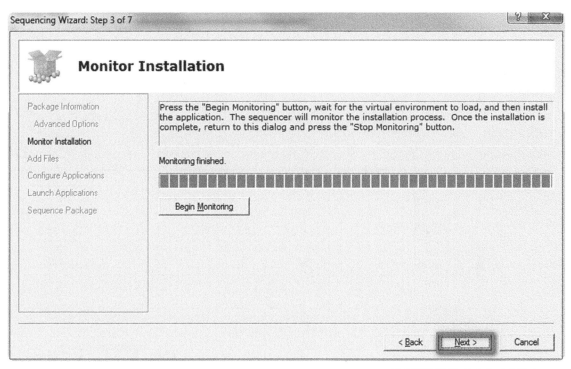

■ **FIGURE 12.13** Monitoring is finished.

15. In the Add Files to Virtual File System window, click *Next*. (see Figure 12.14).

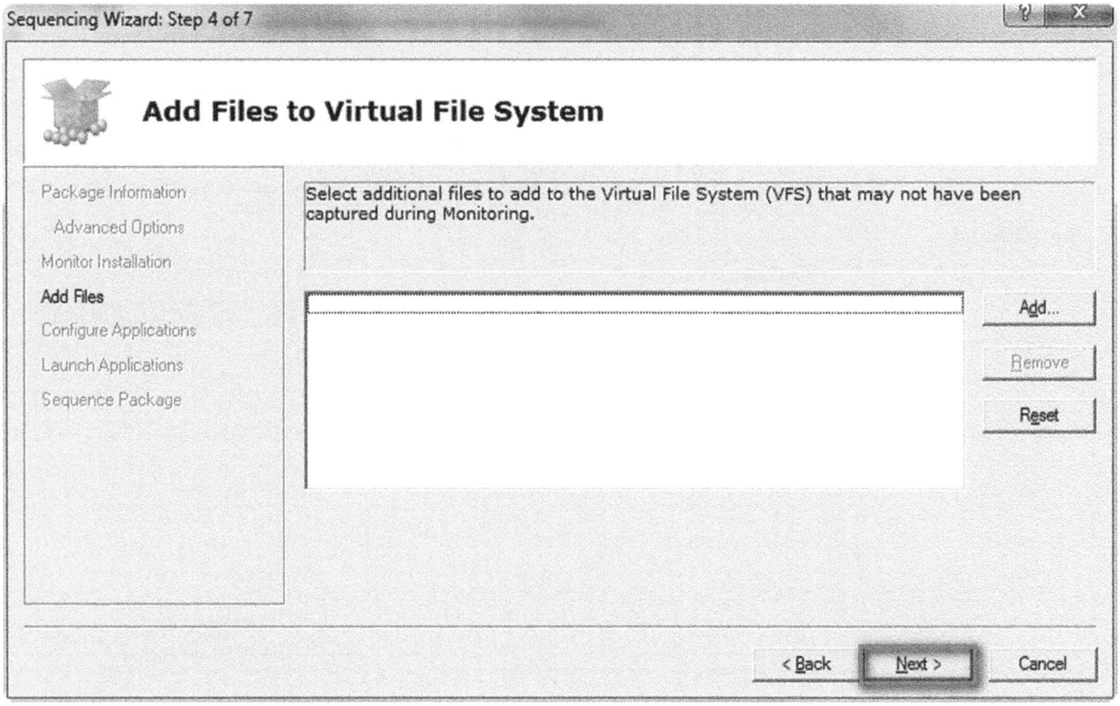

■ FIGURE 12.14 The Add Files to Virtual Files System window.

16. In the Configure Applications window, click *Applications* (see
Figure 12.15).

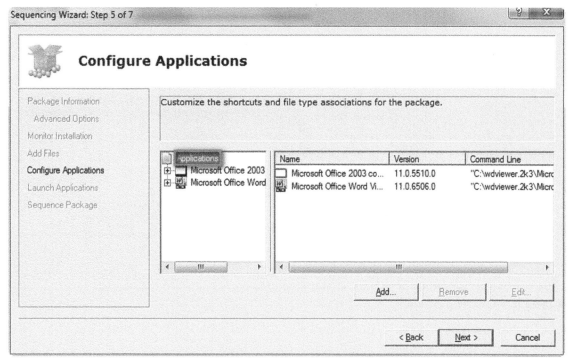

■ **FIGURE 12.15** The Configure Applications
window.

17. In the details pane, click *Microsoft Office 2003 component*, click *Remove*, and then click *Ok* (see Figures 12.16 and 12.17).

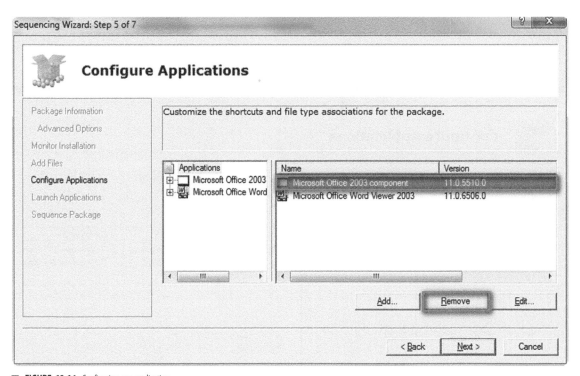

■ **FIGURE 12.16** Configuring an application.

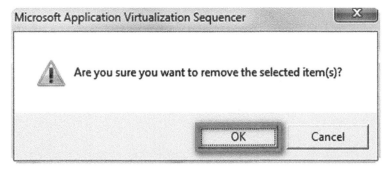

■ **FIGURE 12.17** Removing a selected item.

18. In the details pane, click *Microsoft Office Word Viewer 2003* and click *Edit* (see Figure 12.18).

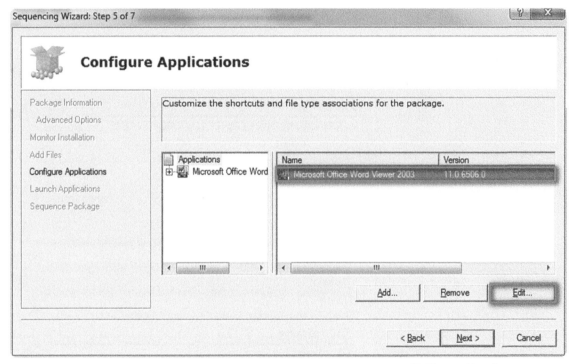

■ **FIGURE 12.18** Editing file type associations and shortcuts.

19. In the Edit Application dialog box, set the following .osd file properties and then click *Save* (see Figure 12.19). The information in
   these fields is informative for App-V engineers. It helps identify the
   associated components of a sequenced package.
   a. Name: Word Viewer
   b. Version: 2003
   c. OSD Filename: WordViewer2003.osd

■ **FIGURE 12.19** The Edit Application dialog box.

20. Under Applications, expand Word Viewer and click *File Type Associations* to view the FTAs the Sequencer has recorded. Select *Shortcuts* to view where the shortcuts for this application will be located on the App-V Desktop Client and then click *Next* (see Figure 12.20).

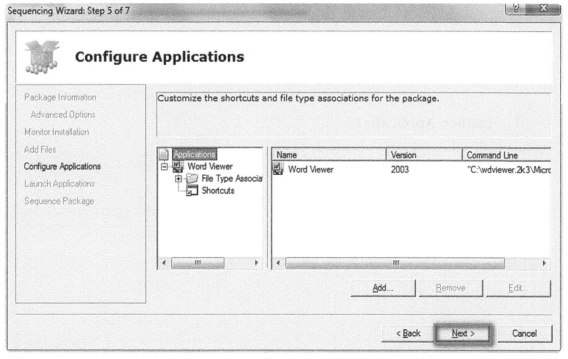

■ **FIGURE 12.20** Selecting a file type association.

Note

There are two feature "blocks" in App-V Sequencing. The primary feature block consists of the minimum content necessary for an application to run. It is identified during the application phase of sequencing and includes the content of the application features used most. The secondary feature block is quite literally the rest of the application content that is not included in the primary feature block. This is the content that will stream to the client as relevant features are used.

21. In the Launch Applications window, click *Word Viewer* and then click *Launch* (see Figure 12.21).

The Launch Applications window allows you to start the applications associated with the shortcuts App-V created. Doing so determines the primary feature block which contains the portion of the application required to launch the application on the App-V Desktop Client. During this phase, be sure to launch the application and run any functionality or features that you feel your targeted users will use the most. This allows the primary feature block to include all of the most needed features.

22. The Word Viewer will open a file browse window allowing you to browse for a file to open. There is no reason to open a file for Word Viewer, so click *Cancel* and exit out of the Word Viewer.

23. You will now see a checkmark next to your application. This means the Sequencer has created the primary feature block. Clicking *Next*

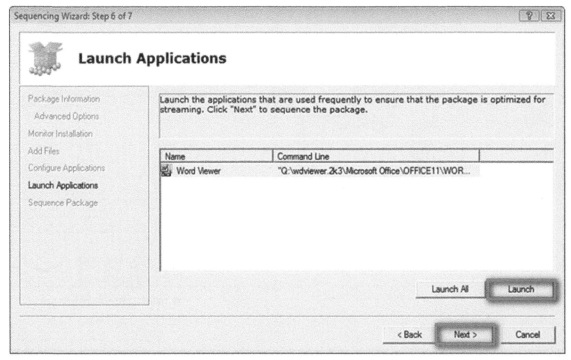

■ **FIGURE 12.21** The Launch Applications windows.

will perform the actual sequencing of the application. For Word Viewer this process is very fast, but you should expect this step to take longer depending on the complexity of the application you are sequencing. When sequencing has completed, click *Finish* (see Figure 12.22).

24. In the Sequencer summary window, click the *Deployment* tab. In this step you can supply several configuration options. The *Protocol* field allows you to choose from RTSP, RTSPS, HTTP, HTTPS, and FILE. It allows you to specify how to send the application to the target workstation. The Hostname option is the name of your App-V server. The Port option is the port that App-V will use to publish the application to the target workstations. The Path option is the relative path of the package content of the App-V server. The Operating Systems option allows you to select the operating systems on which the application will run. (Although this option exists, the recommendation to sequence only within the target OS still stands.) The Enforce Security

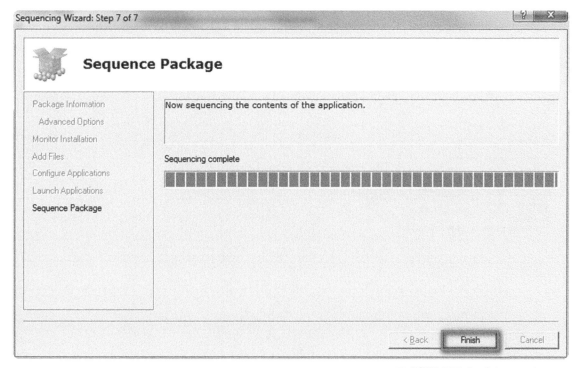

■ **FIGURE 12.22** Completing sequencing.

Descriptors option allows the sequencer to capture the security descriptors at packaging time. The client enforces them on the file system drive at runtime. The Generate MSI Package option allows you to create a MSI package for stand-alone deployment of the package. The Compression Algorithm option allows you to compress the size of the package. Once the package is streamed to the target workstation, however, it expands back to normal size. We selected the following properties for the package (see Figure 12.23):

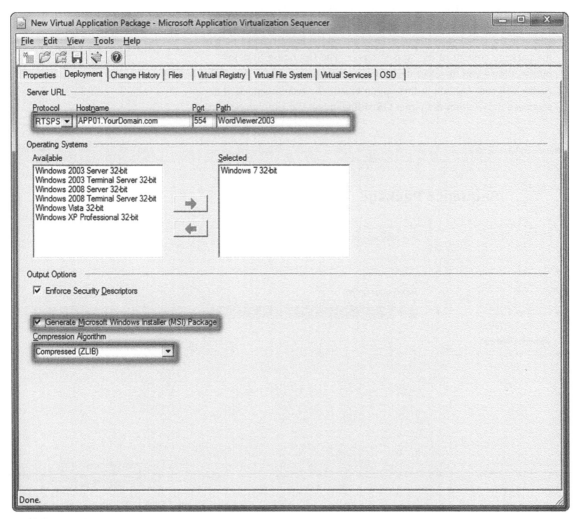

■ **FIGURE 12.23** The Sequencer summary window.

    a. Protocol: RTSP

    b. Hostname: APP01.YourDomain.com

    c. Path: WordViewer2003

    d. Generate Microsoft Windows Installer (MSI) Package: Enabled

    e. Compression Algorithm: Compressed (ZLIB)

    f. Operating Systems: Check that the operating system displayed is the same as that used on your client computer.

25. Click File\Save. Go to the folder WordViewer2003 you created on the desktop and save your work as WordViewer2003.sprj (see Figure 12.24).

26. Close the Sequencer and copy WordViewer2003 folder to the content share on the App-V Management Server.

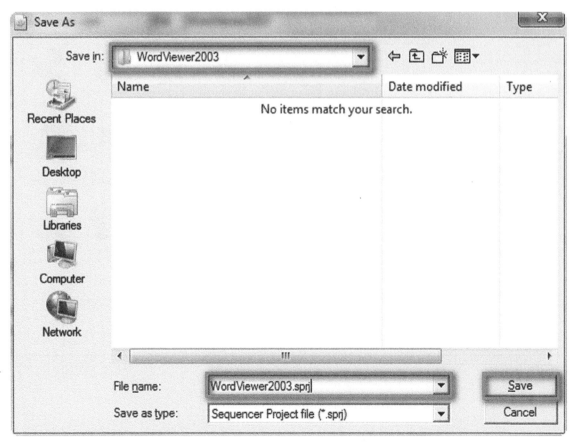

■ **FIGURE 12.24** Saving a file.

PUBLISHING THE APP-V PACKAGE

In the previous section we created a package, and moved that package to the content share of the Application Management Server. The package is now ready to be delivered, but there are many ways to deliver a package to a workstation, as defined later in this chapter. The following steps are performed on the App-V Management Server.

1. Launch the App-V Management Server by browsing to *Administrative Tools* and clicking *Application Virtualization Management Console* (see Figure 12.25).

■ **FIGURE 12.25** Launching the App-V Management Server.

2. Expand the server node and click *Applications*.
3. Right-click *Applications* and choose *Import Applications...* (see Figure 12.26).
4. Navigate to \\<server name>\content, and open the *WordViewer2003* folder.
5. Click the *WordViewer2003.sprj file* and choose *Open*. The New Application Wizard will launch.

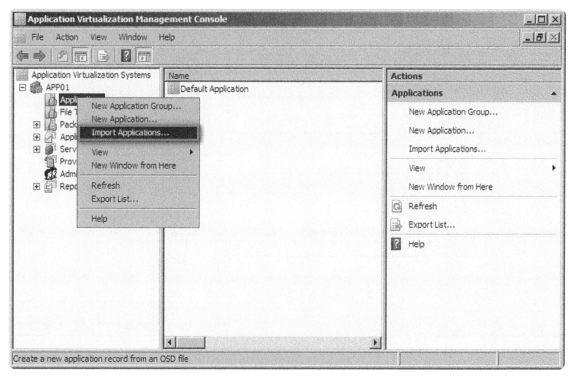

■ **FIGURE 12.26** Importing applications.

6. In the General Information window, verify that values for the OSD Path and Icon Path are in UNC format (e.g., \\server\content \WordViewer2003\WordViewer2003.osd) and that the Enabled check box is selected, click *Next* (see Figure 12.27).

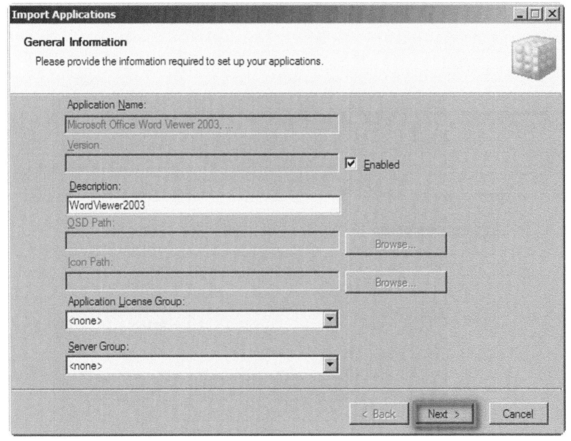

■ **FIGURE 12.27** The General Information window.

7. In the Published Shortcuts window, select the appropriate shortcut location checkboxes and click *Next* (see Figure 12.28).

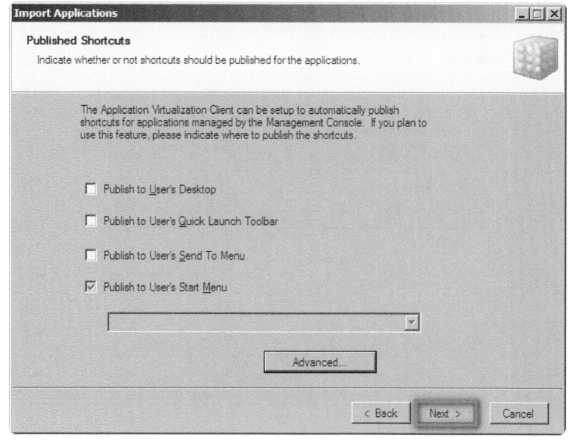

■ **FIGURE 12.28** The Published Shortcuts window.

8. Click *Next* in the File Associations window, and *Add* in the Access Permissions window. In the Add/Edit User Group dialog, navigate to the appropriate user group to access the application (*App-V Users*), click *OK*, and then *Next* (see Figure 12.29).

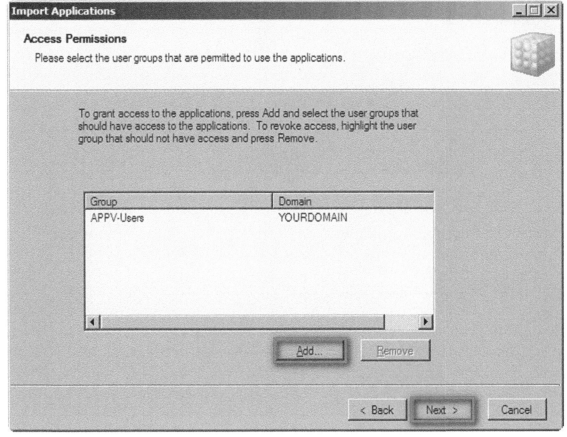

■ **FIGURE 12.29** The Access Permissions window.

9. On the Summary page, click *Finish* (see Figure 12.30).

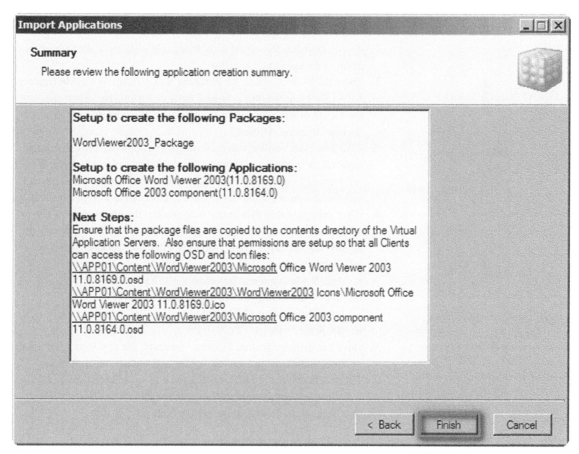

STREAMING THE APP-V PACKAGE

Once the application is published, there will be a period when the application is initially launched. During this process, the package that contains the application features will have to be loaded, unless the autoload features have been enabled to preload packages for published applications. In App-V, several options are available for loading the application initially.

Application streaming with Management Servers

1. A user launches the application by double-clicking a shortcut or by opening an associated file type.
2. The App-V client sends the initiating user's ticket to the Management Server for authorization to launch the application. The client also sends the GUID of the application to verify that the current version of the package is being delivered.
3. After successful authorization, the client verifies available cache space required for primary and secondary feature blocks of the package. If there is not enough cache space, the App-V client will remove packages to make space, increase the size of the cache, or fail to load the application.
4. After verifying that disk space is available, the client streams the primary feature block of the package (SFT file) from a server with the appropriate package. App-V supports streaming package files from the following locations:
   a. App-V Management Server using RTSP or RTSPS
   b. App-V Streaming Server using RTSP or RTSPS
   c. File Server using SMB/CIFS
   d. IIS Server using HTTP/HTTPS
5. Once the primary feature block is streamed, the application's virtual environment is created and the client will launch the application.
6. The secondary feature block is streamed to the client when a user uses features on a block-by-block basis called an "Out of Sequence" process, unless autoload settings are enabled.

Note

The registry value ApplicationSourceRoot can be configured during setup, using the App-V ADM Template, or through the registry. This value overrides all HREF elements in all OSD files on an App-V client. Using SFTMIME ADD or CONFIGURE PACKAGE with the /OVERRIDEURL switch allows an administrator to change the Streaming Server for an individual package.

NEW FEATURES IN APP-V 4.5

AutoLoad packages

One of the new features in Version 4.5 of App-V is the AutoLoad settings in the registry. These settings are created during the client installation and can be adjusted. By default, when a user logs on, the client attempts to load all previously used applications in cache. This ensures all features for are available locally on the computer. For mobile users, this option enables them to leave the network and still be able to use any application that has previously launched. However, this does not give them access to published applications that have not launched before. The AutoLoad options can be modified to download all applications published for a user and can also be triggered by a background publishing refresh.

Application streaming with Streaming Servers

Another new component in Version 4.5 is the Streaming Server. The Streaming Server does not provide the publishing refresh process. It relies on another resource to perform this operation. The publishing refresh process is achieved by implementing a Management Server to handle the publishing refresh and using the Application Source Root (ASR) setting on the client to point to the Streaming Server. You can also use the manifest.xml file created during sequencing to script the package publishing using SFTMIME. These options provide flexibility in remote office scenarios. Streaming Servers implement authorization via NTFS permissions.

Application streaming with File Servers

A file server can deliver packages in an App-V infrastructure, but like the Streaming Server, it cannot provide the publishing refresh process to the clients. As previously noted, this is accomplished by providing a Management Server for the publishing refresh process. This file server could be an actual server or a powerful desktop. File servers implement authorization by using NTFS permissions.

Application streaming with IIS

IIS can also be used for streaming. However, like the Streaming Server and the File server, it cannot provide the publishing refresh process to the clients. The client supports a publishing refresh over an HTTP/HTTPS connection. However, App-V currently has no Web-based publishing refresh service. So the IIS streaming option would require a Management Server to publish applications. IIS Servers implement authorization by using NTFS permissions.

Stand-alone mode with MSI

The App-V Sequencer supports creation of an MSI during the sequencing process. The stand-alone option does not have a formal publishing or streaming procedure. The MSI contains the ICO, OSD, and Manifest.xml files that are necessary for publishing the application on the machine and importing the SFT file into the App-V client cache. However, the package file (SFT) is not created as part of the MSI. It should be placed in the same directory as the MSI to successfully complete. You can place SFT files on a file server. In this scenario, the administrator uses the SFTPATH parameter to specify an alternate location of the SFT file. This removes the requirement that the SFT file to be in the same directory as the MSI. In Stand-alone mode the package will be published and the SFT file contents will be loaded into the client cache completely.

Streaming mode with MSI

Another option is to use MSI packages and choose to stream the SFT file from an alternate location. In this configuration the package is published, but the SFT file is streamed to the App-V client cache. The process of streaming the SFT file is done by default as part of the installation of the MSI, but could optionally be configured to happen when the user launches the application the first time. This mode enables the features of streaming, such as Active Upgrade. The following registry key value must be set on the client to enable Streaming Mode supporting MSI deployment:

HKLM\SOFTWARE\Microsoft\Softgrid\4.5\Client

- Configuration\AllowIndependentFileStreaming = 1

SUMMARY

With Application Virtualization (App-V), Microsoft has taken the tried and true method of application packaging to the next level by,

- Allowing more flexibility
- Improving application compatibility
- Improving the user experience
- Granular patch management and application maintenance for system administrators.

Applications can be deployed in real-time to any client from the App-V infrastructure, completely removing the need for local installation for many applications. Because the deployed applications reside in their own "virtual bubble" on the client, incompatibilities with other applications already installed on the client workstation are eliminated. This same functionality also allows multiple versions of the same application to be deployed to the *for* testing or compatibility reasons.

Thanks to the numerous options available in streaming an application, the end-user experience becomes more enjoyable because the user can begin using the application immediately without having to wait for every feature to be installed. The same functionality allows a system administrator to patch or upgrade an application in a single location and be confident the upgraded version of the application will be published to all clients authorized to run it. The license compliance feature of App-V enables system administrators to effectively control the usage of a license controlled application and withdraw the application if needed, simply by modifying the list of authorized users.

Chapter

13

Presentation virtualization (Terminal Services)

Presentation virtualization is a buzz phrase that refers to the features and functionality delivered by Windows Server 2008 version of Terminal Services (TS). With TS you can publish an entire Windows desktop just as in previous versions of TS. This enables your users to make a Remote Desktop connection to a terminal server accessing a fully functional desktop environment. In addition, by leveraging a subcomponent of TS called TS RemoteApp, you can publish individual applications that appear to be running locally on the desktop, but are actually running in your data center on a terminal server. RemoteApp will be discussed in more detail in Chapter 14.

INTRODUCTION TO PRESENTATION VIRTUALIZATION

The value of the TS approach to application deployment is realized in multiple areas. In an enterprise with remote locations utilizing slow links back to a centralized data center, this technology can substantially reduce the bandwidth used across slow Wide Area Network (WAN) circuits. This is because only the keyboard and mouse input along with display information is transmitted keeping the data flow between the TS server and the data source exclusively over the data center Local Area Network (LAN), as illustrated in Figure 13.1.

TS can enable you to extend the useful life of client computers by moving the heavy processing off of the aging client equipment and onto your terminal servers. This allows you to implement newer more intensive applications without having to perform an expensive and time-consuming enterprisewide PC upgrade project. Along a similar line, performing an upgrade of a TS deployed application is accomplished from your centralized data center location. This can eliminate the need to visit all of the client computers in your enterprise to upgrade a locally installed program. Depending on the circumstances (numbers of computers and

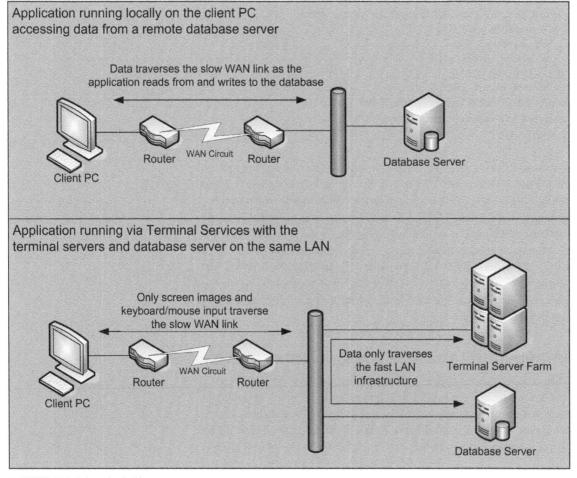

■ FIGURE 13.1 Reducing bandwidth use.

remote locations, etc.) this can save your company a considerable amount of money and you a considerable amount of time.

THE FIVE WINDOWS SERVER 2008 TERMINAL SERVICES ROLE SERVICES

The TS role is split into five parts called role services. Each role service performs its own unique function and each is explained in this section.

Terminal Server

A server with the Terminal Server role service installed is referred to as a terminal server. It hosts the Remote Desktop sessions and the Windows-based applications that are made available to your users.

TS Licensing

Each connection to a terminal server requires a TS client access license also known as a TS CAL. There are two types of TS CALs: TS Per Device CALs and TS Per User CALs. If Per Device licensing is chosen, you will need to purchase a CAL for each device in your enterprise that may be used to access your TS infrastructure. This can be a more economical choice if you have more users than computers in your enterprise. Per User licensing requires you to purchase a CAL for each user that may access your TS deployed applications or desktops. This is often the choice made by companies whose employees need to make a TS connection from a variety of different machines. It is highly recommended that you consult with a Microsoft licensing specialist when deciding which path is right for you.

Note

A TS Licensing server will deduct an available license when it permanently assigns a Per Device CAL to a computer. However, if you choose to use Per User CALs it is your responsibility, as a TS administrator, to ensure that you have enough licenses to cover each of your TS users. This is because, unlike Per Device CALS, the TS Licensing server will not track available Per User CALs for you. Oversubscribing your CALs is a violation of the licensing terms.

TS CALs are managed by a TS Licensing server, and you are required to have at least one in any TS infrastructure. If you implement a large TS environment with multiple terminal servers, it is recommended that you install TS Licensing on a separate server. However, if you are implementing a TS environment with a small footprint or just for testing you can install TS Licensing on a server running the Terminal Server role. For more detailed information on the installation and configuration of TS Licensing you can go to http://go.microsoft.com/fwlink/?linkid=85873.

Note

Terminal Services grants you a 120-day temporary license before requiring you to establish a licensing server. This is convenient if you install Terminal Services for a short duration educational or testing purpose.

TS Session Broker

The TS Session Broker serves two purposes in a TS environment with a farm of terminal servers. The first is TS Session Broker Load Balancing. When this feature is enabled, the TS Session Broker monitors the number of TS sessions open to each terminal server and directs new session requests to the server with the fewest open sessions. This allows for an even distribution of sessions across all servers in a farm.

The second function provided is the ability to ensure a TS user is automatically reconnected to their active session, if one exists. TS Session Broker tracks information on all open sessions within the farm, recording which user sessions reside on which terminal server. This allows a user to pick up where they left off if their session is unexpectedly disconnected. More detailed information on the installation and configuration of TS Session Broker can be found at http://go.microsoft.com/fwlink/?linkid=92670.

TS Gateway

By leveraging TS Gateway, a TS environment and computer with Remote Desktop enabled can be configured to be accessible by authorized users over the public Internet without the need for an additional secure method to access your internal network such as a Virtual Private Network (VPN) connection. This is done by establishing an RDP over HTTPS connection from an Internet connected computer over port 443 versus the standard RDP port 3389. Security settings for this access are configured via TS Gateway Manager and include the ability to define several parameters, such as authorized Active Directory user and computer groups, accessible network resources, device and disk redirection, and acceptable authentication methods like passwords or smart cards. For TS Gateway installation information and a step-by-step installation guide, you can go to http://go.microsoft.com/fwlink/?linkid=85872.

TS Web Access

TS Web Access makes available from a web browser the applications you publish with the traditional TS methods, such as RemoteApp programs and virtual desktops. You can choose to limit the access to the TS Web Access Web site to your local intranet or use it with TS Gateway as another way to enable your users to access TS applications from across the public Internet. TS Web Access will be discussed in more detail in Chapter 14.

INSTALLING THE TERMINAL SERVICES TERMINAL SERVER ROLE

The TS server role can be quickly installed by following these instructions:

1. The first step in adding a server role is to open the "Server Manager" window, selecting "Roles" in the left-hand pane, and then clicking on "Add Roles" in the right-hand pane as illustrated in Figure 13.2.

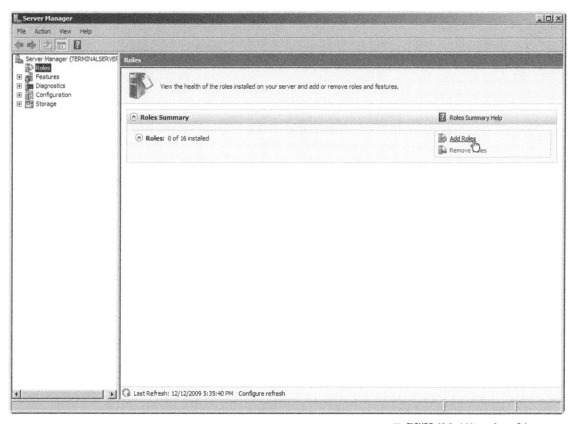

■ **FIGURE 13.2** Adding a Server Role.

2. The initial screen of the roles wizard, shown in Figure 13.3, displays some general tips you should read before adding a role to a server. Read over the list displayed and address any issues. When ready, proceed by clicking *Next*.

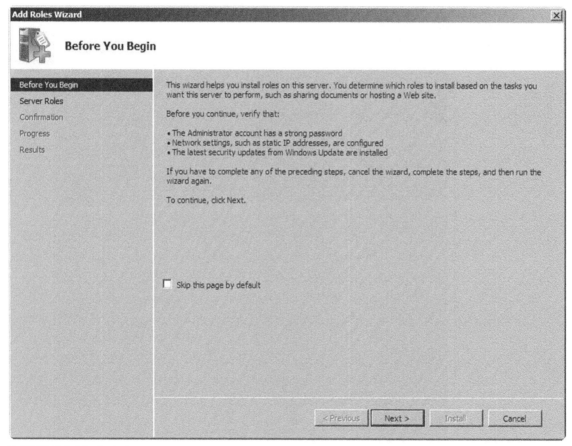

■ **FIGURE 13.3** Before You Begin.

3. The next window displayed is Select Server Roles. Select the
check box next to *Terminal Services*, as illustrated in Figure 13.4.
Click *Next* to proceed.

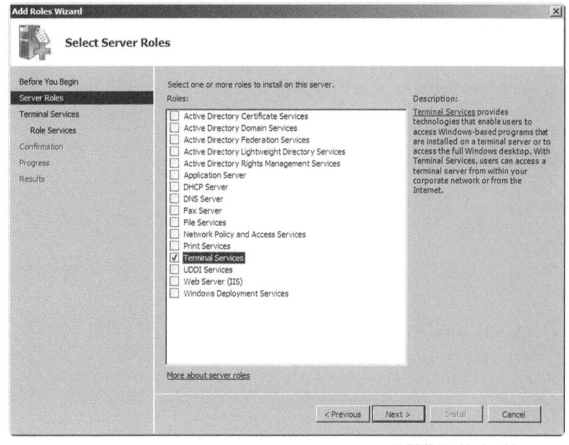

■ **FIGURE 13.4** Select Server Roles.

4. The next screen, shown in Figure 13.5, is meant as an introduction to TS. It explains how TS enables you to provide users with access to programs or full desktops running on a terminal server. One additional item of note is a reminder that installing TS is not required if all you need to do is provide Remote Desktop access to a server for administrative purposes. This function simply needs to be enabled within Windows. There is also a shortcut link to an overview of TS. When ready, click *Next*.

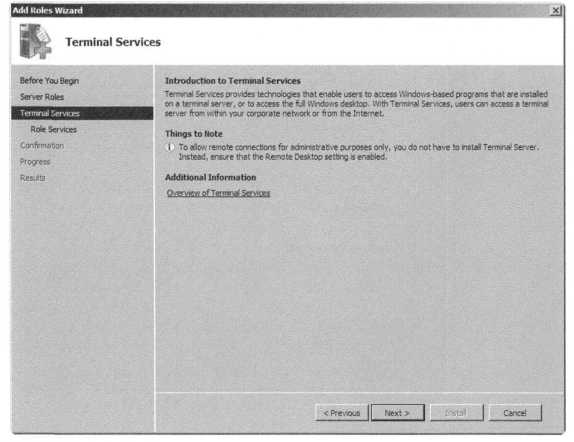

■ **FIGURE 13.5** Introduction to Terminal Services.

5. As illustrated in Figure 13.6, the Select Role Services window
allows you to choose from any or all of the five TS components.
For this walk through, we will select and install the Terminal Server
component, but we will revisit this window later in this chapter and
in the next. Once you have checked the *Terminal Server* box click
Next.
6. It is a strongly suggested practice that you install the Terminal Server
role on your machine before you install any of the applications you
want to publish or share with your users. While this does not always
cause an issue, it can, and it is far easier to just avoid the risk

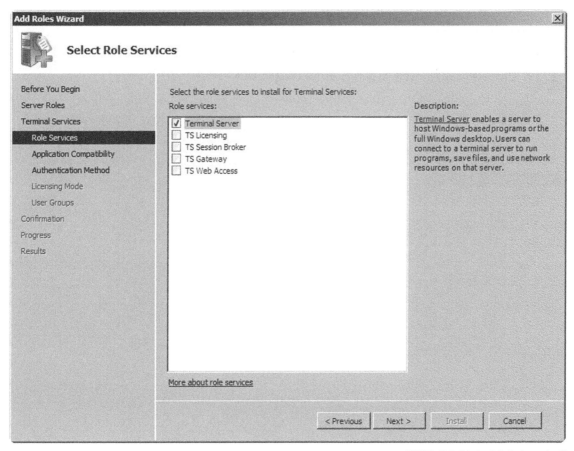

■ **FIGURE 13.6** Selecting Role Services to install.

altogether. The window in Figure 13.7 reminds you of this best practice. Once you have finished reading this informational window, click *Next*.

7. Network-level authentication is a new feature available to you in Windows 2008 TS. It is a more secure authentication method that occurs prior to establishing a Remote Desktop connection and reduces the risk of denial-of-service attacks. This risk reduction is based on the fact that fewer resources on the server are required during the authentication process as it does not need to initiate a full Remote Desktop session. The full session is not established until after

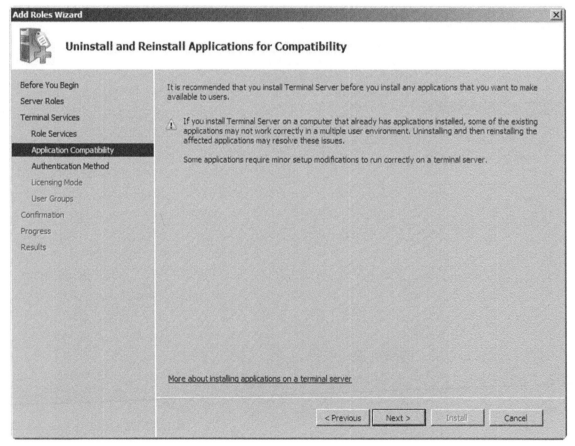

■ **FIGURE 13.7** Uninstall and Reinstall Applications for Compatibility.

successful authentication has occurred. This new method, however, comes with certain requirements that your environment may not be able to meet. Your client machines will need to use Remote Desktop Connection 6.0 and support the Credential Security Support Provider (CredSSP) protocol. CredSSP is part of Windows Vista and Windows 7, but not earlier Windows operating systems. If your target client base is running Windows XP or older OSs, you will not be able to take advantage of Network-level authentication. Select the option that is preferred and supported by your environment, as shown in Figure 13.8, and click *Next*.

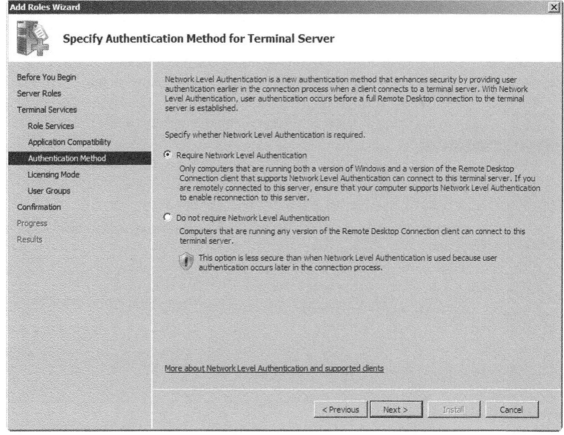

■ **FIGURE 13.8** Specify Authentication Method for Terminal Server.

Note

Later, once you have decided on a licensing mode and have built your licensing server it is easy to update your licensing setting on your terminal server by opening the *Terminal Services Configuration* interface from the TS menu. The TS menu can be found under the Administrative Tools menu. Once you have opened the TS configuration interface, just double click *License server discovery mode* and make the appropriate change, as shown in Figure 13.10.

8. Your selection of a TS licensing mode must correspond to the method that your eventual license server is configured to hand out. As mentioned earlier you can learn more about setting up a licensing server at the following link, http://go.microsoft.com/fwlink/?linkid=85873. For now we will take advantage of the 120-day grace period that is offered. Select *Configure later*, as shown in Figure 13.9, and click *Next*.

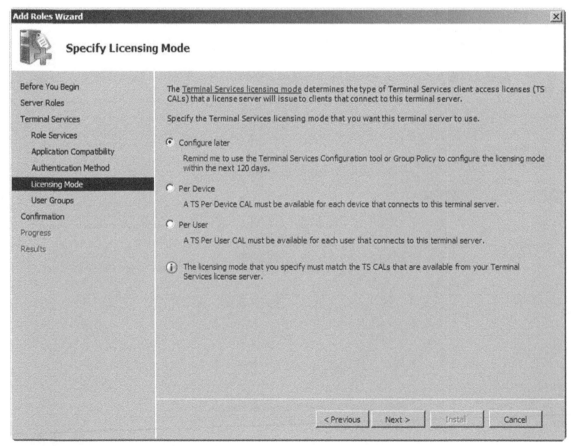

■ **FIGURE 13.9** Selecting the Terminal Service Licensing Mode.

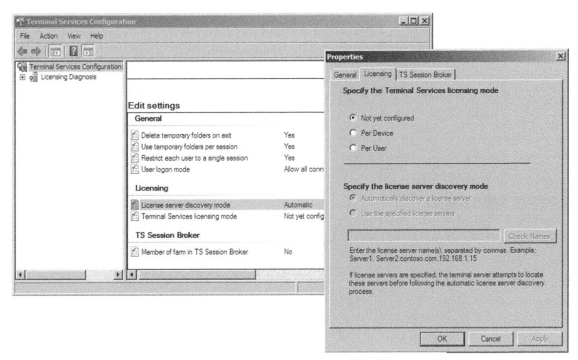

■ **FIGURE 13.10** Updating the Terminal Service Licensing mode.

9. Figure 13.11 displays the user access configuration window. From this interface you can assign users and/or groups of users permitted to connect to your terminal server. The Add... button is used to make your selections and is shown in Figure 13.12. After you have finished making your desired selections, click *Next*.

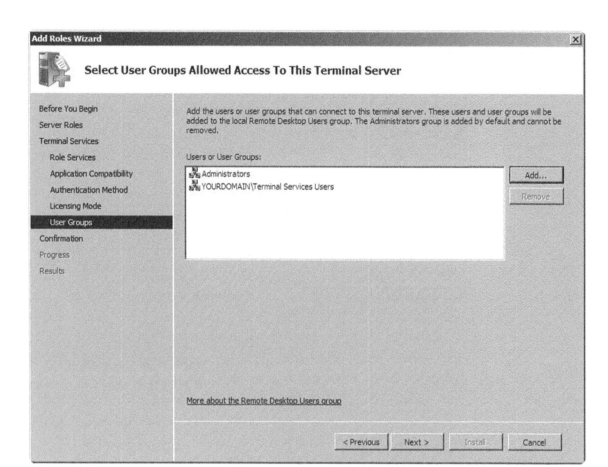

■ **FIGURE 13.11** Configuring User Access.

■ **FIGURE 13.12** Adding a User or Group.

10. You are now presented with a summary of the configuration options you selected through the installation thus far. If you see anything that you would like to change, now is your chance to use the "Back" button to return to the appropriate window. In our example, shown in Figure 13.13, there is a warning message reminding you that if we plan to share any applications that are already installed, we may need to reinstall them. Once you are satisfied that you have made the correct configuration choices, click *Install*.

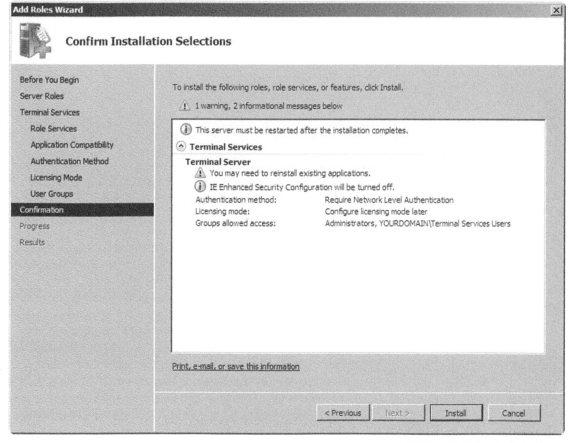

■ **FIGURE 13.13** Configuration Confirmation.

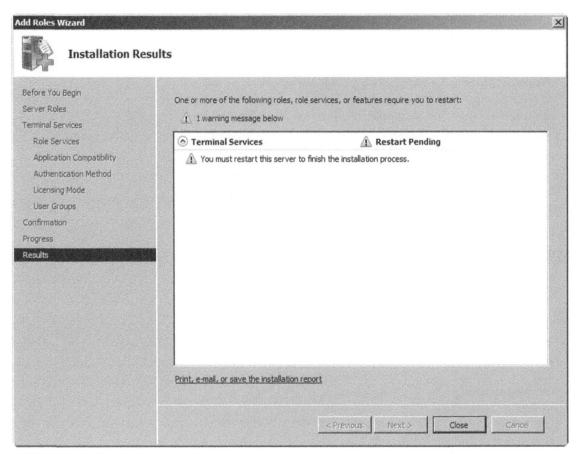

■ **FIGURE 13.14** Installation Results.

11. The installation results, shown in Figure 13.14, let you know the status of your installation. Click *Close* and then click *Yes* when prompted to restart your system and complete the installation process.

12. After rebooting, your system will automatically resume the installation process. Once it is complete, you will be shown an installation results window similar to the one in the previous step and illustrated in Figure 13.15. Notice that this screen has two links to information on helpful utilities you can leverage to improve overall user experience. First is Windows System Resource Manager (WSRM). When WSRM is leveraged with TS, it allows you to monitor and balance the use of server system resources with regard to users and their TS sessions. WSRM is installed via Server Manager and to learn more about it you should see the Windows Server 2008 Windows System Resource

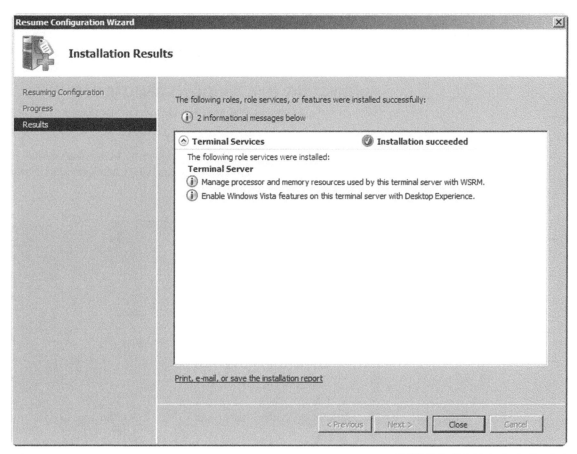

■ **FIGURE 13.15** Installation Results after reboot.

Manager Help and the following Web page, http://technet.microsoft. com/en-us/library/cc771218(WS.10).aspx. The second utility is called Desktop Experience. This tool provides the end user of Remote Desktop Connection with a desktop session that more closely resembles the look and feel of a traditional Vista desktop. Windows Calendar, Defender, and Media Player are some of the features made available to the end user if you choose to install Desktop Experience. Like WSRM, this utility is also available for installation via Server Manager's Add features option. While these features may immediately seem like a good idea to include, you will want to consider the performance impact of all your users listening to music via Media Player or other potential pitfalls.

13. Now that you have completed the installation of your first Terminal Server, you should install any Windows-based applications you want to get published on Windows desktops.

CONNECTING TO A WINDOWS REMOTE DESKTOP

Now let us make Remote Desktop connection and see the fruits of your labor.

1. From any Windows client machine on your network launch *Remote Desktop Connection* from the Start menu, under Accessories, as shown in Figure 13.16.

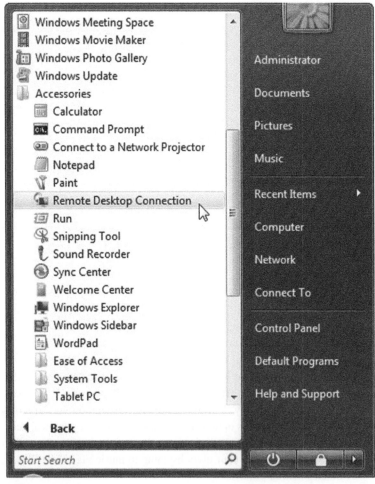

■ **FIGURE 13.16** Launch Remote Desktop.

2. Enter in the name of your terminal server in the Remote Desktop Connection window, as demonstrated in Figure 13.17, and click *Connect*.
3. As shown in Figure 13.18, enter in the credentials of an account in the AD user group you granted permission to connect to your terminal server in Step 9 of the previous section, "Installing the Terminal Services Terminal Server Role," and click *OK*.

■ **FIGURE 13.17** Select Your Terminal Server.

■ **FIGURE 13.18** Enter your credentials to connect.

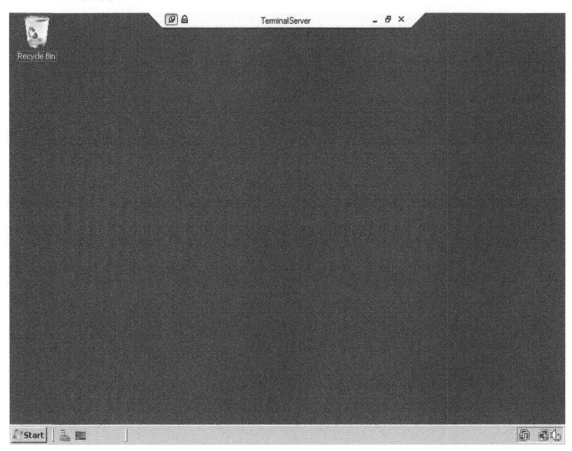

■ **FIGURE 13.19** Launch Remote Desktop.

4. What now opens, as shown in Figure 13.19, is a Remote Desktop session presented from your terminal server and including the Windows-based applications you installed in Step 13 of "Installing the Terminal Services Terminal Server Role."

SUMMARY

TS has changed for the better, with several tools and functions which allow faster performance and enhanced security. Together, they provide a centralized environment with low maintenance costs and quick recovery after a business continuity event.

Remember that not all workstations can take full advantage of these new features. In general, any desktop running a Windows OS prior to Vista is affected. Windows Vista or Windows 7 desktops can take full advantage of the TS features.

Finally, be sure to properly design your TS environment. If you need a server for each server role, it is better to figure that out before your users, and their managers, start beating on your door because performance is inadequate or access is intermittent.

Integrating application and presentation virtualization (Terminal Services)

In Chapter 13, we learned about Terminal Services and publishing an entire remote desktop. In this chapter, we focus on how to publish individual applications that will run on your terminal server, but appear to your users to be running locally on their PCs. Terminal Services RemoteApp is the key to accomplishing this. RemoteApp programs can be distributed via installable .msi files or self-contained executable .rdp files. You can go even further by combining TS RemoteApp with the TS Web Access role service to give your users access to their published applications via a Web page.

CONFIGURING TS REMOTEAPP

Unlike most of the other TS elements, TS RemoteApp is not installed as a separate role service; it is part of the Terminal Services role. The steps to configure it and publish a couple of applications follow:

1. Log on to the terminal server you built in Chapter 13 using an account with administrative level access, go to *Start / Administrative Tools / Terminal Services*. Select *TS RemoteApp Manager*, as shown in Figure 14.1.

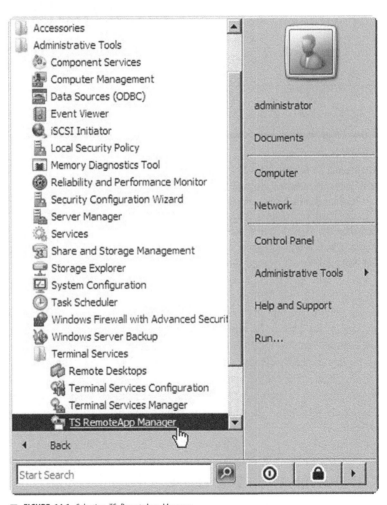

■ **FIGURE 14.1** Selecting TS RemoteApp Manager.

2. The TS RemoteApp Manager window is intuitive. As illustrated in Figure 14.2, there are three subwindows covering an overview of the current setting and status, a list of the programs published via RemoteApp, and the menu of actions you can perform. Let us start by adding a couple of applications in the RemoteApp programs list. Under the Actions menu on the right-hand side, click *Add RemoteApp Programs.*

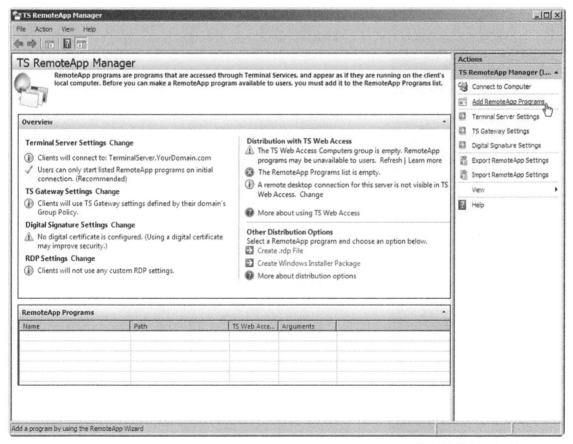

■ **FIGURE 14.2** TS RemoteApp Manager.

3. The RemoteApp wizard walks you through the application selection process. Be sure to be logged in with an account with administrator privileges for your terminal server. Click *Next* to continue, as shown in Figure 14.3.

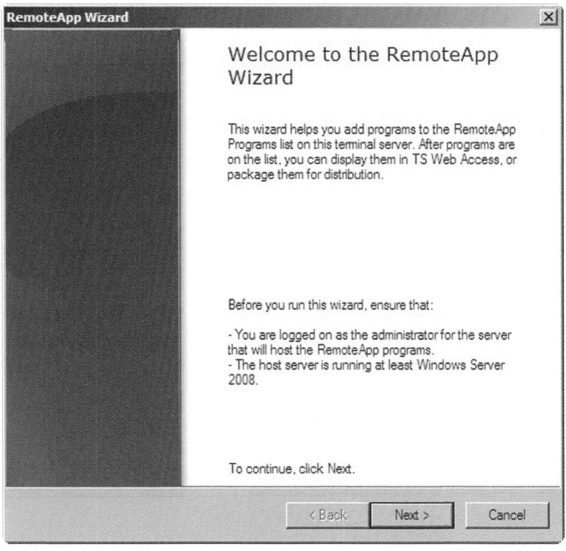

■ **FIGURE 14.3** RemoteApp Wizard.

4. The screenshot in Figure 14.4 may differ from what you see displayed on your screen, depending on the applications you have previously installed on your terminal server as only installed programs will show up on the list. For this example, we selected *Microsoft Office Excel 2007* and *Microsoft Office Word 2007* as the programs we want to publish with TS RemoteApp.

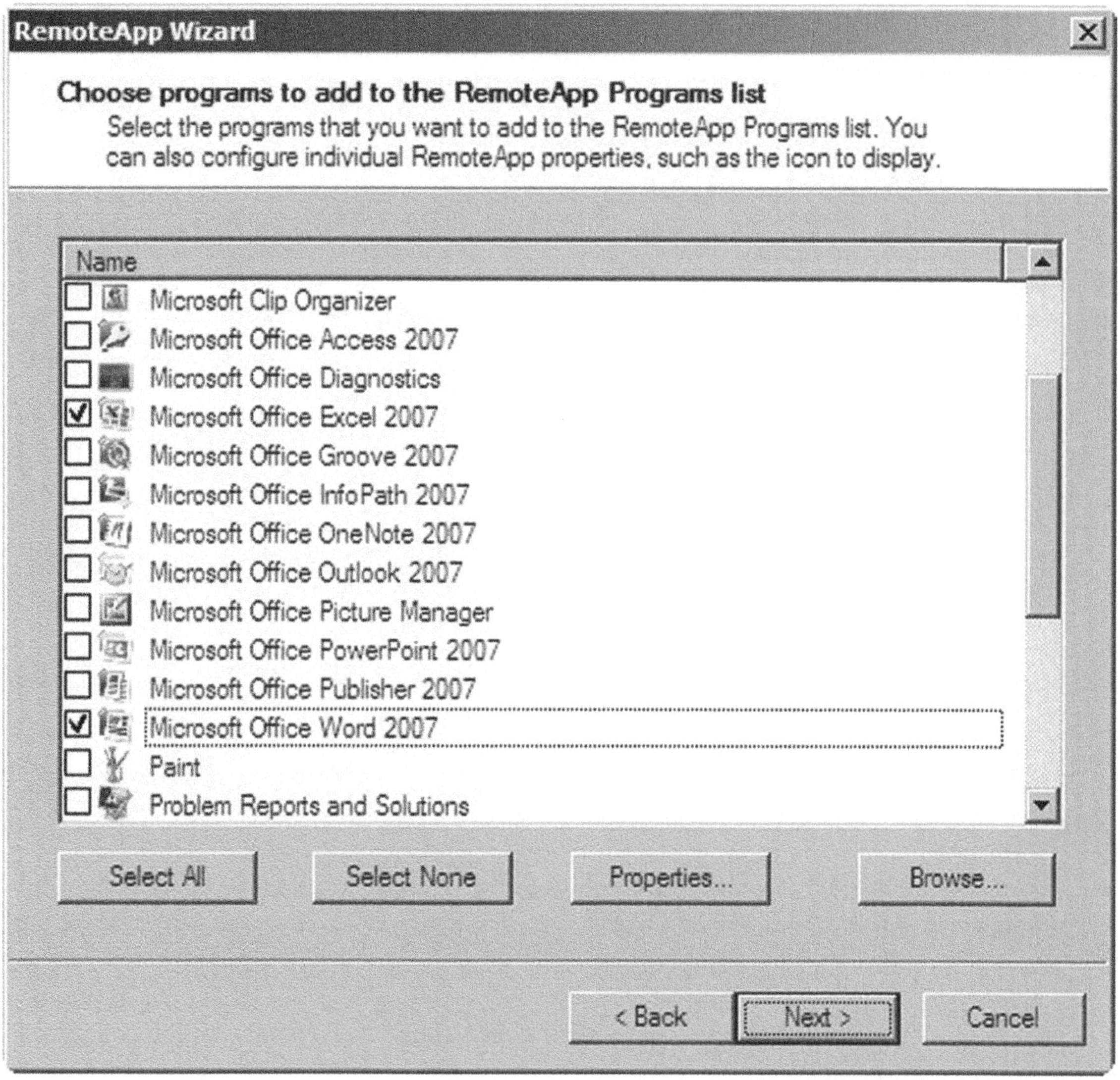

FIGURE 14.4 RemoteApp Program list.

You can also set parameters for each application. Highlight one of the programs you selected and click the *Properties* button. The example in Figure 14.5 shows the settings relevant to Microsoft Word. You can modify the RemoteApp program name as it will be displayed to your users. This is helpful if you prefer to identify the program instance as

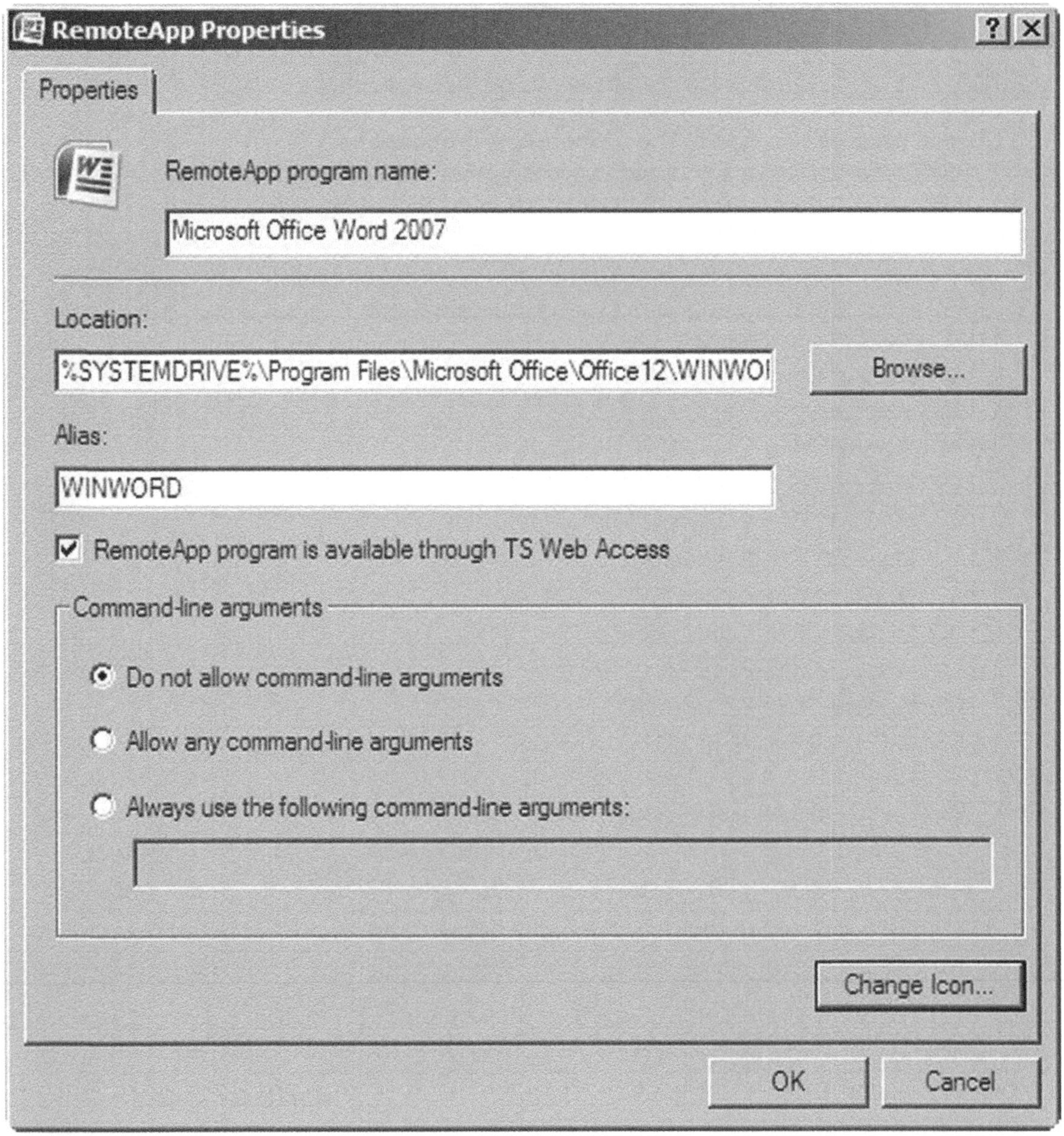

■ **FIGURE 14.5** RemoteApp Properties.

virtualized instead of running locally. This is also useful if you are publishing an Internet Explorer instance to a Web-based application. Your users will know the application name and do not need to know that Internet Explorer is the core application. You can change the program file location where the program is installed on the terminal server. However, it is unlikely you will ever need to change this. The wizard automatically pulls this information in for you. You can create a new alias for the remote application which is a unique identifier Windows translates into the program's executable file name. It is recommended that you do not change this setting. If you plan to use TS Web Access—which we will be covering shortly—and you do not want this program to be presented on the Web Access page, you can unselect *RemoteApp program is available through TS Web Access*. Allowing access through TS Web Access is the default setting. Near the bottom of the window is a section of options about the use of command-line arguments. It is unlikely you will want your users running their RemoteApp programs from a command-line. So the default is set to not allow the use of command-line arguments at all. You may need to preconfigure a particular program to always run with the same arguments, and you can enter those into the appropriate field in this window. As in the preceding example or Internet Explorer, this is where you would configure those command arguments. Lastly you can click the change the application icon assigning a nonstandard icon to the RemoteApp program. Again, this is useful if you want to identify an application as running remotely. This is also useful if you have several similar applications such as a set of Web-based applications all using Internet Explorer. Using a different icon for each will help your users find and use the correct RemoteApp. It is best to have different icons for all published applications. Many applications have several alternate icons to choose from. Click the *Change Icon...* button to see the choices for your selected application. Click *OK* to save any changes made and close the window.

After you select the applications you want, click *Next* in the RemoteApp program list window to continue.

5. Presented on your screen, and illustrated in Figure 14.6, is a summary of the programs and settings you chose in the last few steps. If anything looks incorrect, you can use the Back button to return to the appropriate screen and make changes. Click *Finish* to close the wizard.

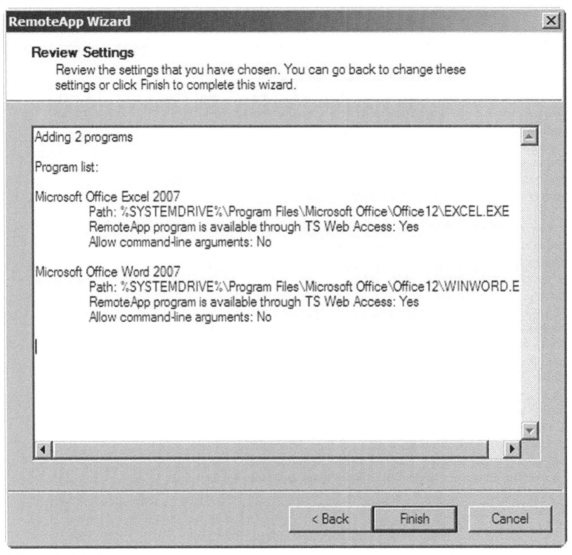

FIGURE 14.6 Review Setting.

6. As you are returned to the TS RemoteApp Manager, you will find the programs you just added the list near the bottom of the window, as shown in Figure 14.7. Proceed now to the next section to learn how to distribute your RemoteApp applications.

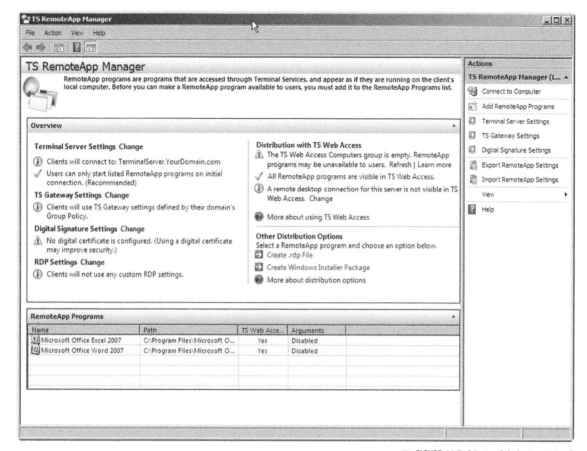

■ **FIGURE 14.7** Selecting Role Services to Install.

DISTRIBUTING REMOTEAPP PROGRAM FILES

There are two file-based methods for distributing RemoteApp programs to your users. The first is to create a Windows Installer package file (.msi) which can then be distributed and installed just like traditional locally installed programs. The second is to create a Remote Desktop Protocol file (.rdp) that launches the remote application without the need to perform an install. The following two sections will provide more detail into each method as well as step-by-step instructions to create both file types.

Creating and distributing a Windows Installer package

Terminal Services allows for the easy creation of a Windows Installer package file, commonly referred to as an .msi file. This method installs the RemoteApp to appear like a conventional local installation. If you

Note

To use RemoteApp programs via .msi or .rdp files your clients must be running remote Desktop Connection (RDC) 6.0 or greater. If you plan to use TS Web Access, client machines are required to be running RDC 6.1. RDC 6.0 is included with Windows Vista and is available via download from http://support.microsoft.com/?kbid=925876 for Windows XP Service Pack 2 and Windows Server 2003. RDC 6.1 is included with Windows 7, Windows Vista Service Pack 1, and Windows XP Service Pack 3. RDC 6.1 can be downloaded for Windows XP Service Pack 2 from http://support.microsoft.com/?kbid=952155.

want to make the virtualization aspect of the RemoteApp program nearly invisible to end users, this is the method you will want to choose. Once the .msi file is created, you can distribute it to your enterprise via your existing distribution methods, such as Microsoft System Center Configuration Manager or through an Active Directory Group Policy Object. You can also place the .msi file on a file share and instruct your users to execute it. The steps to create the .msi file are

1. First make sure that you are logged on the terminal server with an account that has administrative privileges. This is a requirement for creating the RemoteApp package. From TS RemoteApp Manager, and within the RemoteApp Programs window, highlight one of the applications you previously added to RemoteApp. You should now see a menu in the Actions window specific to the program that you selected. As shown in Figure 14.8, click *Create Windows Installer Package* within this menu to start the creation process.

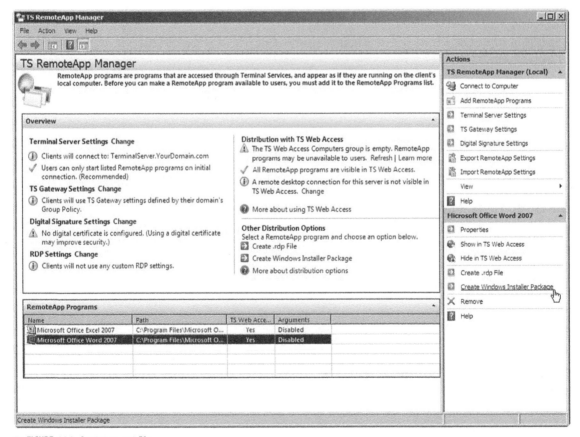

■ **FIGURE 14.8** Creating an .msi File.

2. Again you are reminded, as shown in Figure 14.9, that you need
   to be logged in with administrative level access to the terminal
   server before beginning. Click *Next* to continue.

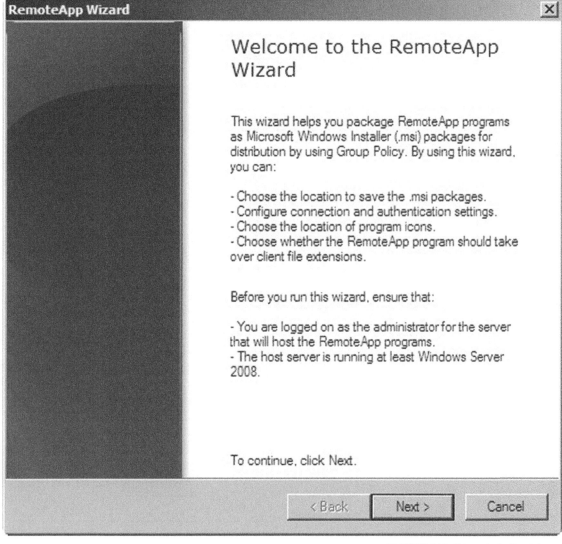

RemoteApp Wizard   ☒

Welcome to the RemoteApp Wizard

This wizard helps you package RemoteApp programs
as Microsoft Windows Installer (.msi) packages for
distribution by using Group Policy. By using this wizard,
you can:

- Choose the location to save the .msi packages.
- Configure connection and authentication settings.
- Choose the location of program icons.
- Choose whether the RemoteApp program should take
over client file extensions.

Before you run this wizard, ensure that:

- You are logged on as the administrator for the server
that will host the RemoteApp programs.
- The host server is running at least Windows Server
2008.

To continue, click Next.

< Back | Next > | Cancel

■ **FIGURE 14.9** Welcome to the RemoteApp
.msi File Wizard.

3. You are able to set several configuration options when building your .msi file, as illustrated in Figure 14.10. First, decide where to save your packages. Use the browse button if you prefer to change the default setting of C:\Program Files\Packaged Programs.

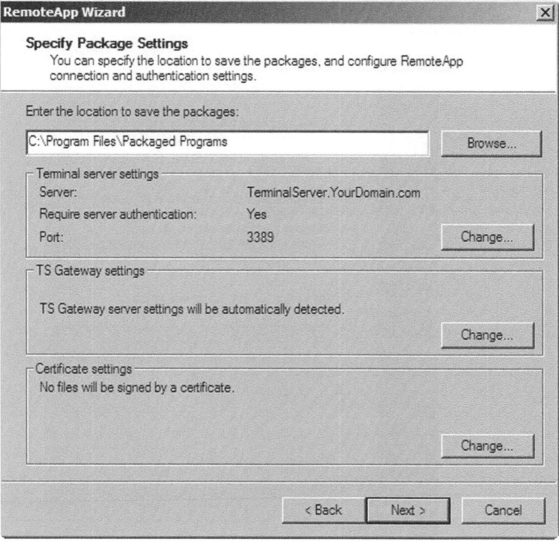

FIGURE 14.10 Specify Package Settings.

Clicking *Change...* in the *Terminal server settings* box allows you to modify three settings, as shown in Figure 14.11. The *Server name* field should be populated with the fully qualified DNS name of your terminal server. Port 3389 is the standard RDP port number. Unless you changed it during TS configuration, leave it as displayed. The third option presented is *Require server authentication*. Since we set up our terminal server with it set, you should leave the checkbox checked. Press *OK* to close the terminal server settings window.

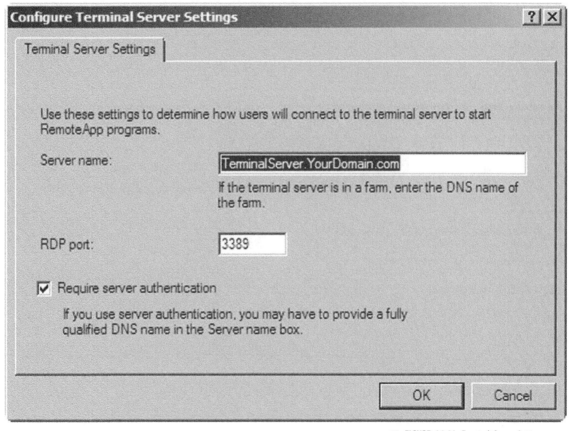

■ **FIGURE 14.11** Terminal Server Settings.

By default, an install package automatically detects the TS Gateway settings via Group Policy Object (GPO), as exhibited by Figure 14.12. If you are certain that you will not be leveraging a TS Gateway server you can select *Do not use a TS Gateway server*; otherwise, chances are that configuring your TS Gateway setting with a GPO and leaving the default autodetection is your best choice. However, if you would like to learn more about TS Gateway and determine if you want to configure specific server settings within the .msi file you can visit http://go.microsoft.com/fwlink/?linkid=85872. Press *OK* to close the TS Gateway settings window.

Certificate settings is the last box on the Specify Package Setting window. If your enterprise is using certificates you can click *Change...* to select an appropriate cert; otherwise, click *Next* to continue.

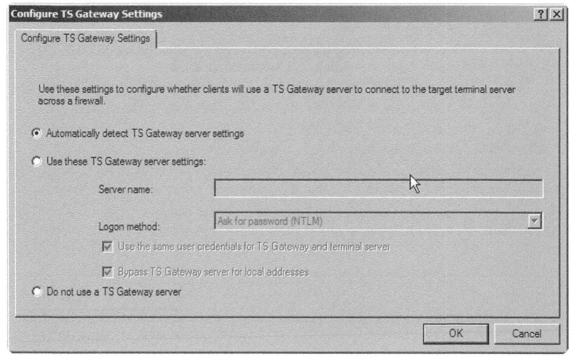

■ **FIGURE 14.12** TS Gateway Settings.

4. The next set of options control the end-user experience. Figure 14.13 shows two option boxes. First, in *Shortcut icons*, you must decide where on the user desktop to place the program icon. You can check one or both checkboxes to place it directly on the desktop or in a Start

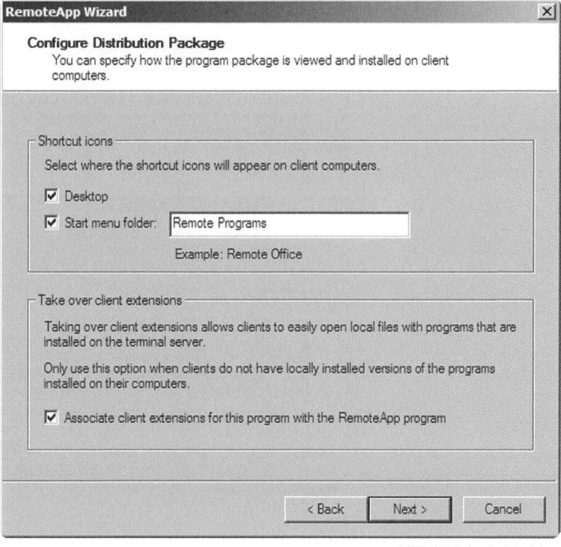

■ **FIGURE 14.13** Configure Distribution Package.

menu program group. The second option block in this window, *Take over client extensions*, is concerned with the file extension associations on your end-user PCs. This option requires a little more thought. If your end users have earlier versions of an application installed locally, you should leave the check box in this section blank. However, if your virtualized program does not have a local counterpart to open the applicable file types with, then check the box to associate the RemoteApp program with the matching file extension. In our example, by checking this box all file types associated with Word, such as .doc/.docx and .dot/.dotx, will be opened with the RemoteApp version of Word. Double clicking a Word file will automatically launch the Word RemoteApp just as it was loaded locally. Click *Next* to continue.

5. As shown in Figure 14.14, the final window for this wizard offers the opportunity to review the options you selected before committing them. If you want to change anything, use the Back button. Once satisfied with your selections, click *Finish*.

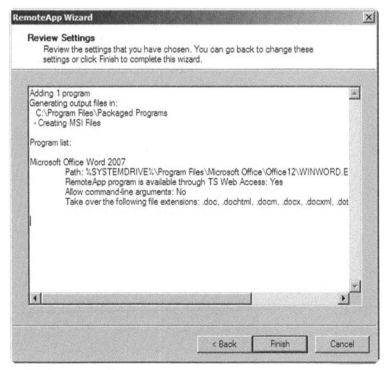

■ **FIGURE 14.14** Review Settings.

6. A Windows Explorer window now opens showing you the .msi file you just created, as depicted in Figure 14.15. You can now distribute it to your users.

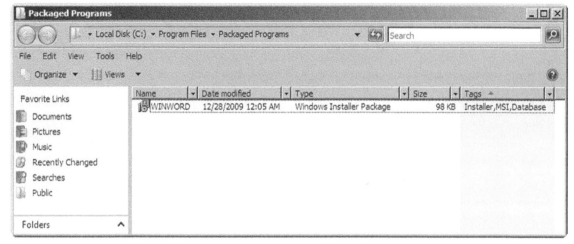

■ **FIGURE 14.15** Packaged Programs.

Creating and distributing a Remote Desktop Protocol File

Terminal Services has its own file type for running a RemoteApp program that Windows recognizes and treats appropriately. The file type is .rdp, which stands for Remote Desktop Protocol. Unlike an .msi that installs on a PC when launched, this is a standalone executable that can be accessed from a simple file share or dropped on a client PC. While this method is less transparent to the end user than the installed .msi method it makes updating the RemoteApp program easier since you can simply overwrite the .rdp file with a new version when needed. This is made even simpler if the .rdp file is in a file share versus deployed to each workstation. To create a RemoteApp .rdp file:

1. While still logged on with administrative level access, go to the TS RemoteApp Manager and within the RemoteApp Programs window highlight one of the applications you added to RemoteApp previously. You should see a menu in the Actions window specific to the program you selected. As shown in Figure 14.16, click *Create .rdp File* within this menu to start the creation process.

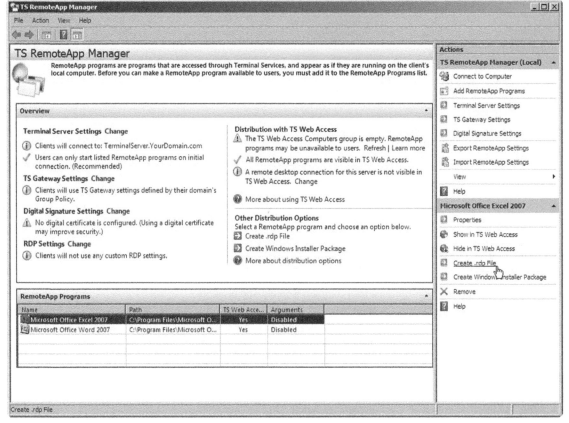

■ **FIGURE 14.16** Creating an .rdp File.

2. Once again, as reminded in Figure 14.17, you need to be logged in with administrative level access to the terminal server to proceed. Click *Next* to continue.

■ **FIGURE 14.17** Welcome to the RemoteApp .rdp File Wizard.

3. This screen is identical to the one encountered when building an .msi file. You can set the same configuration options when building your .rdp file, as illustrated in Figure 14.18. First, decide where to save your packages. If necessary, use the browse button to change the default setting of C:\Program Files\Packaged Programs.

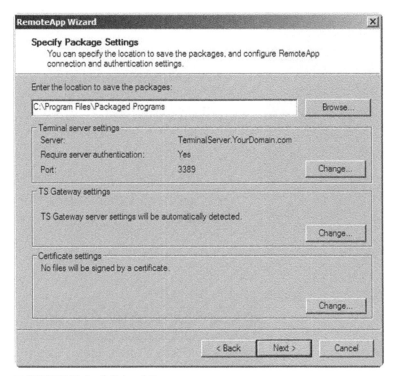

■ **FIGURE 14.18** Specify Package Settings.

Clicking *Change...* in the Terminal server settings box allows you to modify three settings, as shown in Figure 14.19. The Server name field should be populated with the fully qualified DNS name of your terminal server. Port 3389 is the standard RDP port number and, unless you changed it within the TS configuration on your own, you should leave it as displayed. The third option presented is *Require server authentication.* Since we set up our terminal server with it set, you should leave it checked. Press *OK* to close the terminal server settings window.

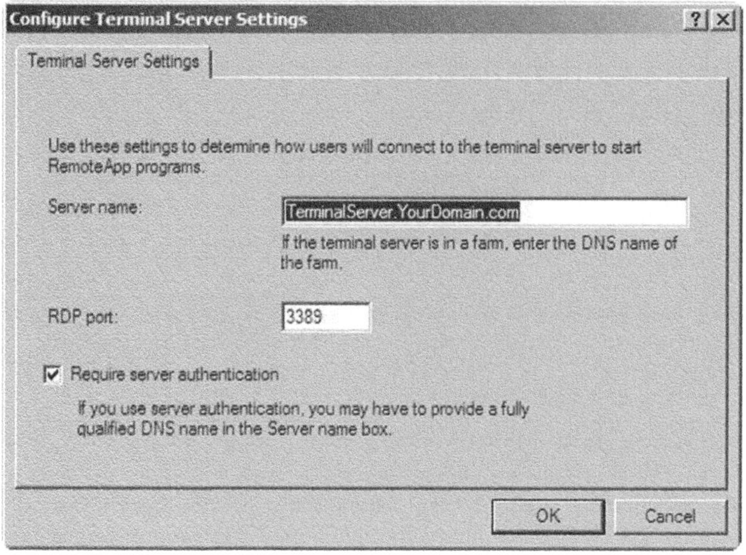

■ FIGURE 14.19 Terminal Server Settings.

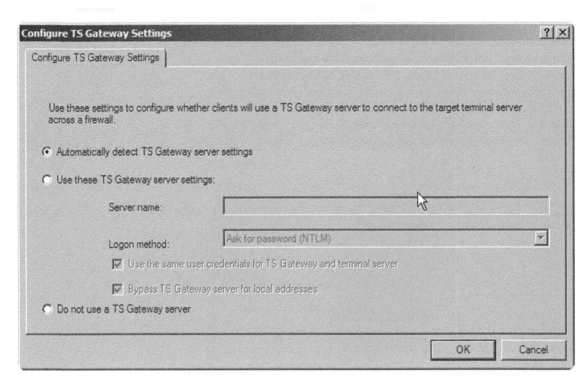

■ **FIGURE 14.20** TS Gateway Settings.

By default, an install package automatically detects the TS Gateway settings via GPO, as exhibited by Figure 14.20. If you are certain that you will not be leveraging a TS Gateway server you can select *Do not use a TS Gateway server*; otherwise, chances are that configuring your TS Gateway setting with a GPO and leaving the default autodetection is your best choice. However, if you would like to learn more about TS Gateway and determine if you want to configure specific server settings within the .rdp file you can visit http://go.microsoft.com/fwlink/?linkid=85872. Press *OK* to close the TS Gateway settings window.

Certificate settings is the last box on the Specify Package Setting window. If your enterprise is using certificates, click *Change...* to select an appropriate cert; otherwise, click *Next* to continue.

4. As shown in Figure 14.21, the final window for this wizard provides the opportunity to review the options selected before committing them. If you want to change anything, use the Back button. If you are satisfied with your selections click *Finish*.

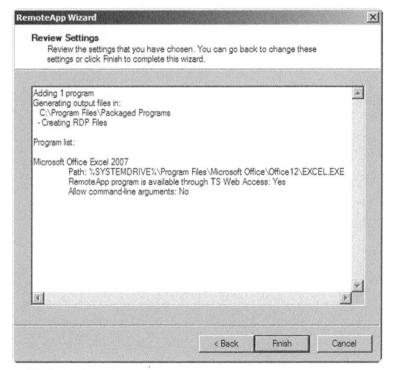

■ **FIGURE 14.21** Review Settings.

5. A Windows Explorer window, shown in Figure 14.22, now opens up showing the .rdp file you created along with the .msi file you created earlier. The file can now be distributed to your end users.

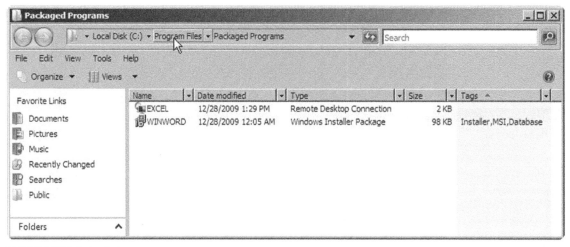

■ **FIGURE 14.22** Review Settings.

INSTALLING THE TS WEB ACCESS ROLE SERVICE

The TS Web Access role service installs quickly from the Server Manager console by following these instructions:

1. As shown in Figure 14.23, the first step in adding a role service is to open the *Server Manager* window. In the left-hand pane, expand *Roles* and then *Terminal Services*. The main window now contains all the information detailing your Terminal Services installation. You may need to scroll the window down, but you will find a section titled Role Services. Within this section click *Add Role Services*.

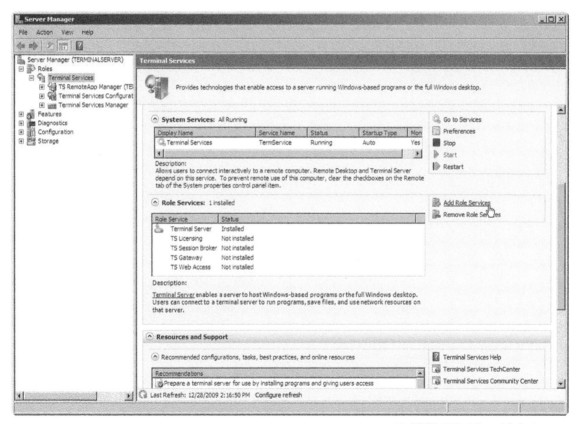

■ **FIGURE 14.23** Adding a Role Service.

2. Your list of role services should be similar to that shown in Figure 14.24. Select the *TS Web Access* checkbox and a new window pops up detailing the additional role services you must

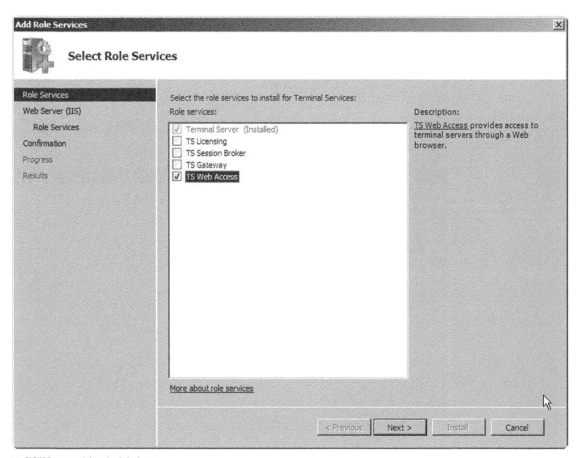

■ **FIGURE 14.24** Select the Role Service.

install to support TS Web Access. As shown in Figure 14.25, these additional components include the IIS Web Server and Windows Process Activation Service. IIS provides the Web application infrastructure to present your RemoteApp programs to your users. The Windows Process Activation Service enables IIS to provide all the functionality you need to host your applications, without the need for HTTP. For more detail, highlighting each of the role services and subservices displays immediately to the right of the list an explanation of what each item does. Click the *Add Required Role Services* button to automatically queue up the required components to be installed at the end of the wizard. When ready proceed by clicking *Next*.

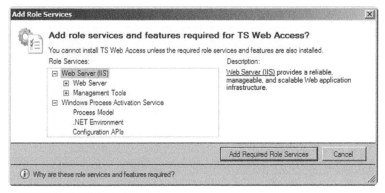

■ **FIGURE 14.25** Add Required Role Services.

3. The next window, illustrated in Figure 14.26, provides a short introduction as to what the IIS Web Server is and provides. Windows System Resource Manger (WSRM) is also discussed again and, as mentioned in Chapter 13, you can learn more about it at http://technet. microsoft.com/en-us/library/cc771218(WS.10).aspx. When you are done reviewing the information displayed and browsing the links to additional information, click *Next* to continue.

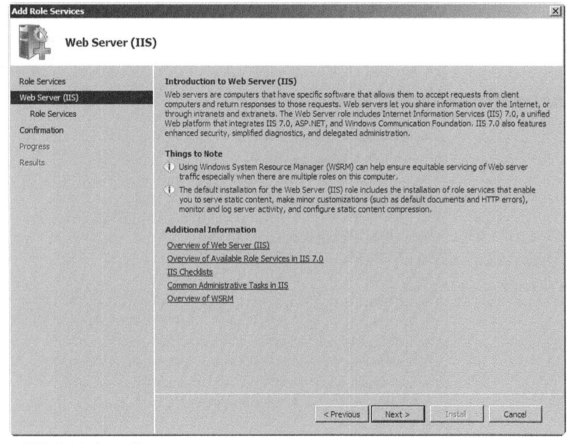

■ **FIGURE 14.26** Introduction to IIS.

4. A display of all of the Web Server and management tool components needed to support TS Web Access is indicated in the current window and shown in Figure 14.27. All of the needed components are checked by default. It is recommended that you do not alter what is already checked unless you are experienced with IIS and the management tools; in other words, you know what you are doing. Review the list to familiarize yourself with what will be installed and then click *Next* to continue.

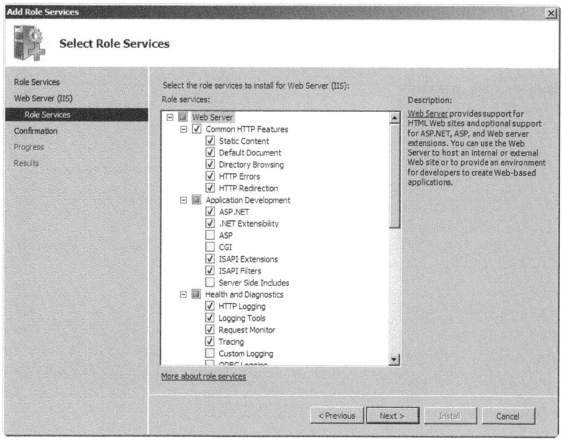

■ **FIGURE 14.27** Role Services for IIS.

5. Review the list of the options you selected as you went through the wizard, as shown in Figure 14.28. Use the Previous button to step back through the process and make necessary changes. When you are ready, click *Install*.

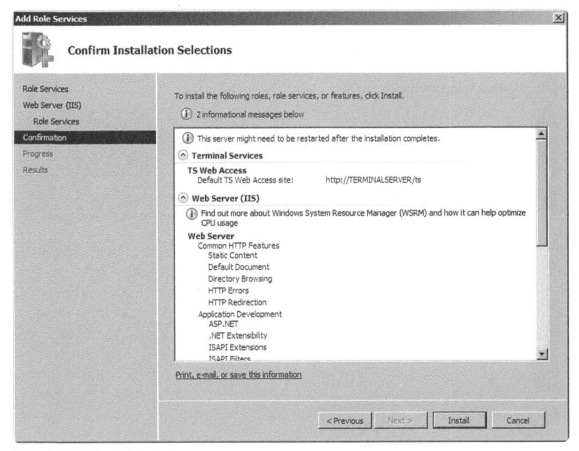

Add Role Services

Confirm Installation Selections

Role Services
Web Server (IIS)
  Role Services
Confirmation
Progress
Results

To install the following roles, role services, or features, click Install.

(i) 2 informational messages below

  (i) This server might need to be restarted after the installation completes.

(^) **Terminal Services**
   TS Web Access
    Default TS Web Access site: http://TERMINALSERVER/ts

(^) **Web Server (IIS)**
  (i) Find out more about Windows System Resource Manager (WSRM) and how it can help optimize CPU usage
   Web Server
    Common HTTP Features
     Static Content
     Default Document
     Directory Browsing
     HTTP Errors
     HTTP Redirection
    Application Development
     ASP.NET
     .NET Extensibility
     ISAPI Extensions
     ISAPI Filters

Print, e-mail, or save this information

< Previous   Next >   Install   Cancel

■ **FIGURE 14.28** Confirm Installation Selections.

6. The install results screen, shown in Figure 14.29, details all the role services installed during the process of adding TS Web Access. Click *Close* to close the window.

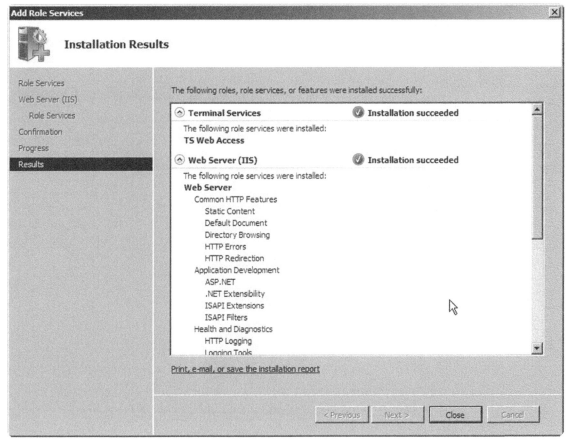

■ **FIGURE 14.29** Installation Results.

7. If you look in Server Manager now, as shown in Figure 14.30, you will see that IIS Admin Service and the World Wide Web Publishing Service are now installed and running. You should also see that TS Web Access is installed.

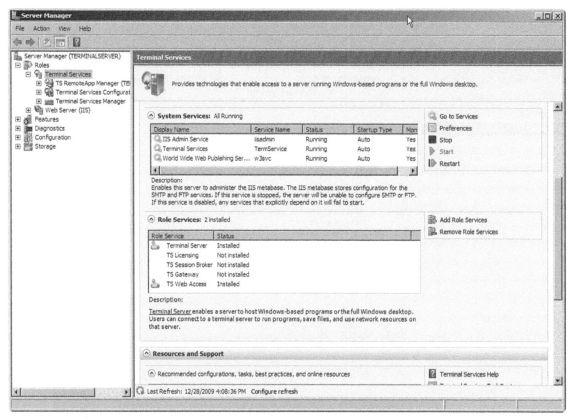

■ **FIGURE 14.30** Confirming that the Services were installed.

ACCESS A WEB PUBLISHED REMOTE APPLICATION

Now that you have configured both TS RemoteApp and TS Web Access, it is time to access the applications. The steps that follow will detail the simple process:

1. The default URL for the TS Web Access page is http://<Your Terminal Server Name>/TS. Open your Internet Explorer Web browser and enter the URL for your terminal server. Figure 14.31 shows the two applications we set up within RemoteApp. Your window should show the applications you configured. Launch one of your RemoteApp programs by clicking it.

■ **FIGURE 14.31** The TS Web Access page.

2. In our example we are not using certificates to identify ourselves as a trusted publisher, so the window shown in Figure 14.32 is displayed. If you encounter this same window, accept the defaults and click *Connect* to continue.

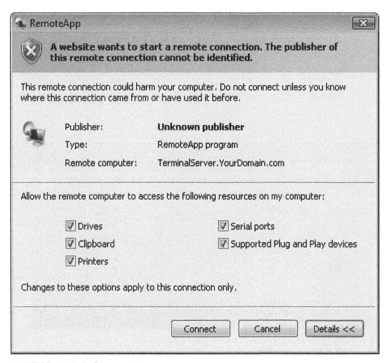

■ **FIGURE 14.32** Confirm access to resources.

3. When prompted for credentials, enter in an appropriate username and password of an account for which you granted access to Terminal Services applications, as in the example in Figure 14.33. Do not forget to include the correct domain name if needed. While not recommended due to security concerns, if you prefer not to get prompted for credentials the next time you access your RemoteApp program, select the checkbox to *Remember my credentials*. Click *OK* to access your program at last.

■ **FIGURE 14.33** Enter your credentials.

4. Your program should now be open and appear like it was installed locally, that is, no browser window. Our example in Figure 14.34 shows Microsoft Excel 2007 running from our terminal server.

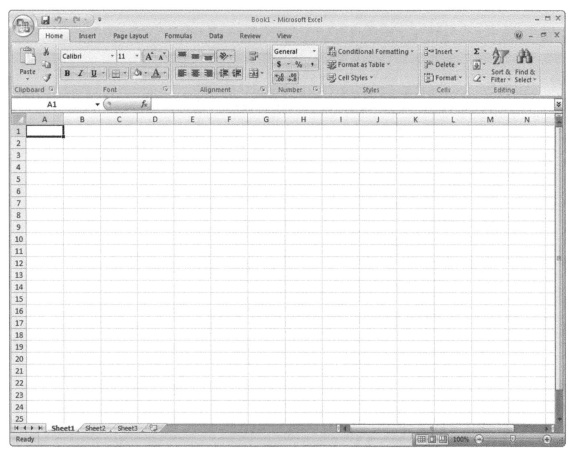

■ FIGURE 14.34 Microsoft Excel 2007 Running via RemoteApp.

SUMMARY

RemoteApp takes application virtualization with Terminal Services one step closer to seamlessness from the user's point of view. Leveraging Active Directory, System Center Configuration Manager, or other distribution methods you can deploy your remote programs just like you do traditional ones. Coupling this technology with TS Web Access allows you to present your client applications via a Web page avoiding time-consuming and sometimes costly conventional deployments.

Just like with straight up Terminal Services you must remember that not all workstations can take full advantage of these new features. To take full advantage or RemoteApp with TS Web Access your clients need to be running RDP 6.1. If you are only running RDP 6.0 you will have to forgo TS Web Access.

As you deploy more RemoteApp programs and extend them to more users, be sure to keep an eye on the performance of your Terminal Server(s). Good resource monitoring and management, with a tool like Windows Resource Manager, and having a defined plan such as creating or expanding a Terminal Server farm will help to keep you out of the dog house. Make sure that you communicate your plan to management ahead of time, so that when you need to add more hardware the costs do not come as a surprise.

Chapter 15

Desktop virtualization

Microsoft's enterprise desktop virtualization solution consists of two parts: Virtual PC and Microsoft Enterprise Desktop Virtualization (MED-V). In this chapter, we install and configure Virtual PC and something new for Windows 7 called XP Mode. We also show the installation of the MED-V server and client, including their initial configuration options. We will show you how to set up Virtual Machines using the Virtual Machine Wizard, as well as some of the configuration options available to you. Finally, we demonstrate how to use MED-V to manage Virtual PC images for your enterprise.

VIRTUAL PC AND XP MODE

Technology demands you keep up with new desktop operating system versions, but software does not always keep pace. Fortunately, there is a solution that has been around for a couple of years called Microsoft Virtual PC 2007 and its new cousin, Windows Virtual PC. The latter is the solution for use with Microsoft's latest desktop OS, Windows 7.

Note
In order to avoid negatively impacting the performance of your virtual machines, it is recommended that you exclude the following file types from both your antivirus and backup solutions on your host operating system: *.VHD, *.VUD, *. VSV, *.CKM, *.VMC, *.INDEX.

Note
Licensing virtual machines is no different from licensing their conventional physical counterparts. While the Virtual PC software is free, you need to have a license and a license key to implement a virtual operating system. XP Mode is free to licensed users of Windows 7 Professional, Ultimate, and Enterprise editions; however, your machine must support hardware-assisted virtualization and have it enabled in its BIOS. Intel chipsets must include Intel VT or AMD's AMD-V. To learn how to determine if your machine is compatible, visit www.microsoft.com/windows/virtual-pc/support/configure-bios.aspx.

The offering for Windows 7 also includes a new feature called XP Mode. XP Mode allows you to run legacy applications, in a Windows XP virtual workspace, from the Windows 7 desktop as if it were a conventionally installed application. While IT types might embrace running applications in a separate window emulating a virtual version of an older OS, the average user will appreciate the seamlessness of running in XP Mode.

The recommended system requirements, shown in Figure 15.1, for both incarnations of Virtual PC are fairly modest. However, more RAM and a beefier CPU will not hurt performance any. If you have to make a choice between the two, go with more RAM.

The guest operating systems supported by the two versions of Virtual PC are shown in Figure 15.2.

Component	Processor	Memory	Operating System
Microsoft Virtual PC 2007 SP1	AMD (Athlon, Duron), Intel (Celeron, P II, P III, P 4, Core Duo, Core2 Duo)	Sum of the RAM requirements for the host OS and all guest OS instantances	Windows Server 2003 (Standard, Standard x64), Windows XP SP3 (Professional, Professional x64), Windows XP Tablet PC Edition), Windows Vista SP1 (Enterprise, Business, Ultimate)
Windows Virtual PC	1 GHz 32 or 64 bit	2 GB	Windows 7 (Enterprise, Professional, Home Basic, Home Premium, Ultimate)
Windows XP Mode	As above	As above	Windows 7 (Enterprise, Professional, Ultimate)

■ **FIGURE 15.1** Virtual PC requirements.

Supported Guest Operating Systems	
Microsoft Virtual PC 2007 SP1	Windows Virtual PC
Windows 98	Windows XP Professional (SP3)
Windows NT Workstation	Windows Vista Enterprise & Ultimate
Windows 2000	Windows 7 Enterprise & Ultimate
Windows XP	
OS/2	
Windows Vista	
Windows NT Server	
Windows 2000 Server	
Windows Server 2003	
Windows Server 2008	

■ **FIGURE 15.2** Supported Guest Operating Systems.

INSTALLING AND USING MICROSOFT VIRTUAL PC 2007 SP1

Remember that Virtual PC 2007 is the desktop virtualization platform for pre-Windows 7 machines. The Windows 7 solution is included later in this chapter, so if you are planning to only use Windows 7, feel free to skip this section of the chapter.

1. In order to install Virtual PC 2007 SP1, you must first download it from the Microsoft Web site: www.microsoft.com/downloads/details. aspx?FamilyID=28C97D22–6EB8–4A09-A7F7- F6C7A1F000B5&displaylang=en#top. Then download the hot fixes for Virtual PC 2007 SP1. At the time of this writing, they are available at http://support.microsoft.com/kb/958162.
2. A quick double click on the freshly downloaded file starts the installation process. When you are presented with the wizard welcome screen click *Next*. You will now see the license agreement dialog, as shown in Figure 15.3. Go ahead and select *I agree...*, after carefully reading it over of course, and click *Next*.

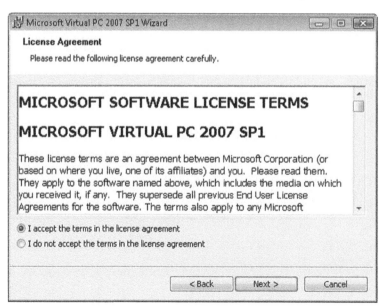

■ **FIGURE 15.3** License Agreement.

3. As illustrated in Figure 15.4, enter your name and company and decide if you are to be the only user of Virtual PC on this machine or if you want to open it up to allow any user of the machine to use the application.

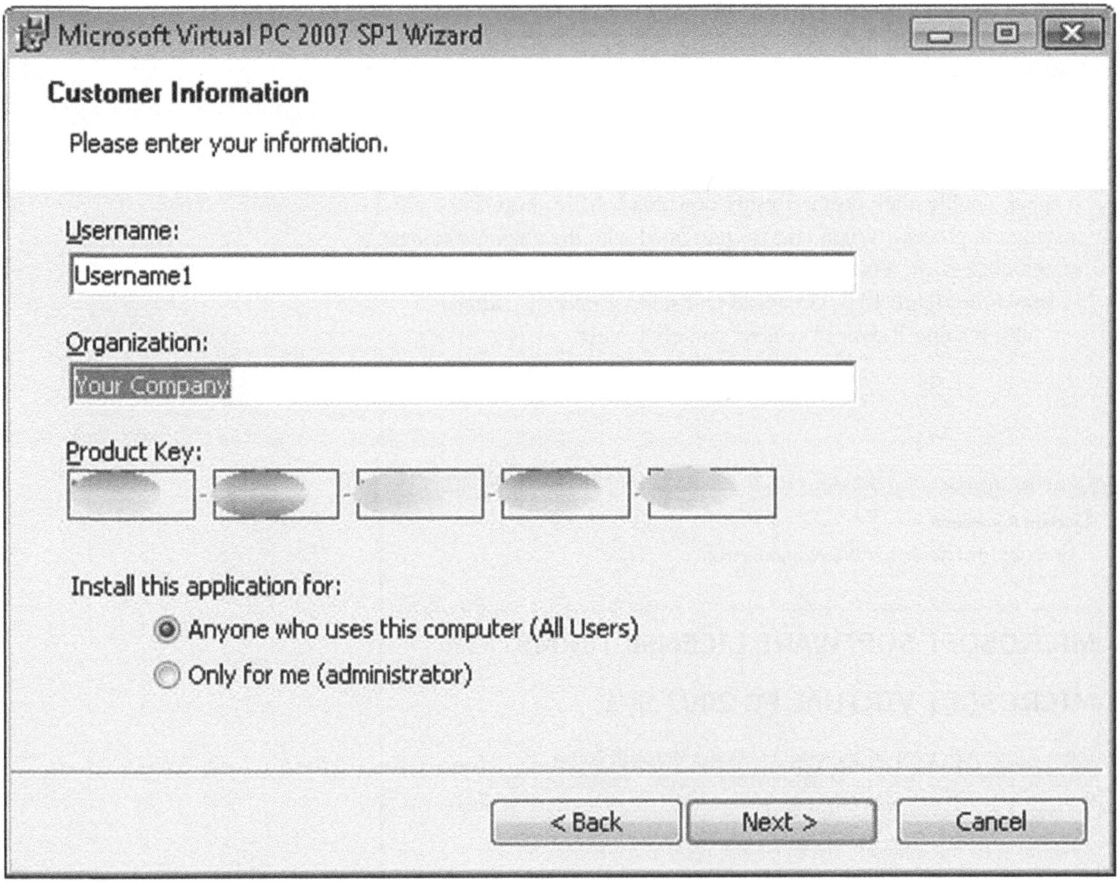

■ **FIGURE 15.4** Customer Information.

4. If you need to change the installation path from the default, now is your chance. Just click the *Change* button and select the desired location, as shown in Figure 15.5.

5. Click *Next* one last time in the Installation Completed window and reboot if you are prompted to do so. You should now apply the hot fixes for Virtual PC 2007 SP1 that you downloaded in Step 1. The process is quick and simple. Just accept the license agreement and go.

Creating a virtual machine in Virtual PC 2007

Since having Virtual PC installed is not much use without a virtual machine, let us set one up.

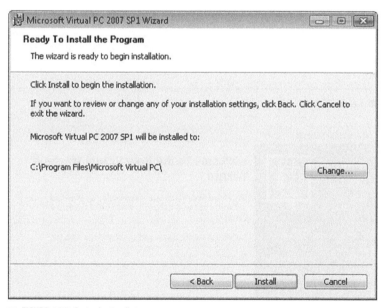

■ **FIGURE 15.5** Begin the installation.

Note

The Remove button in the Virtual PC Console allows you to remove a VM from the active list. This action does not delete the VM from the physical disk, so it can be added back later.

1. When you install Virtual PC the console, shown in Figure 15.6, and the New Machine Wizard, shown in Figure 15.7, will automatically launch. Alternatively, you can launch the console from your program menu and click the *New...* button.

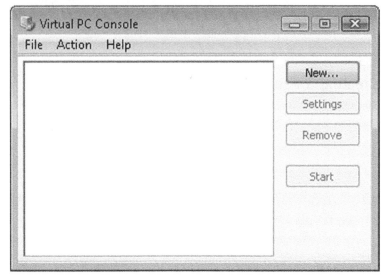

■ **FIGURE 15.6** Virtual PC Console.

■ **FIGURE 15.7** New Virtual Machine Wizard.

2. After clicking *Next* on the welcome screen you are presented with your options as shown in Figure 15.8. You can create a new virtual machine from scratch, create one based on default settings, or add a virtual machine that you have already created or acquired from another source. For this walk-through select *Create a Virtual Machine* and click *Next*.

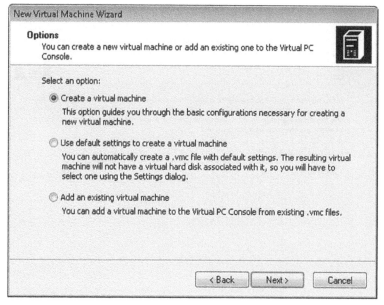

■ **FIGURE 15.8** Options.

3. Now go ahead and name your new creation, as shown in Figure 15.9. You can also, via the Browse... button, change the location where the VM will be saved or just stick with the default My Virtual Machines folder located under your Documents folder. When you are ready, proceed by clicking *Next*.

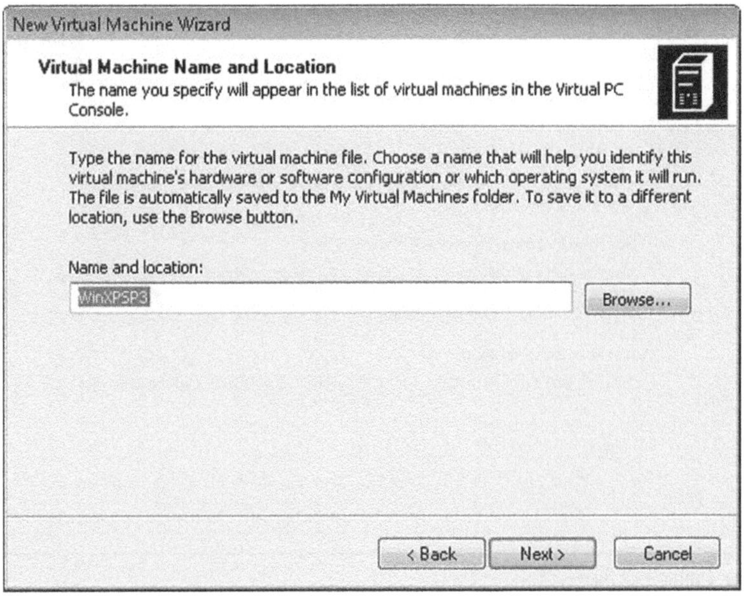

■ **FIGURE 15.9** Name and Location.

4. The default OS for a VM is Windows XP, but as shown in Figure 15.10, by clicking the button under *Operating system* a list of choices is presented. The wizard uses your selection to fill-in the applicable set of default options as you continue through the creation process. You still need the media for the OS (CD, DVD, or ISO file) and, of course, a license key. For this walk-through we will select Windows XP and click *Next*.

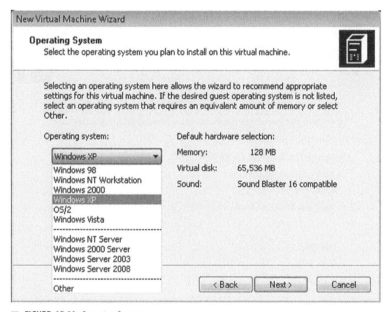

■ **FIGURE 15.10** Operating System.

5. In the case of Windows XP, the default RAM allocation is 128 MB, depending on the operating system that you selected the recommended value will vary. By clicking the appropriately named *Adjusting the RAM* radio button, shown in Figure 15.11, a slider bar appears to enable adding or subtracting memory. You can also just type the value that you want in the box. Set the RAM to what you want and click *Next*.

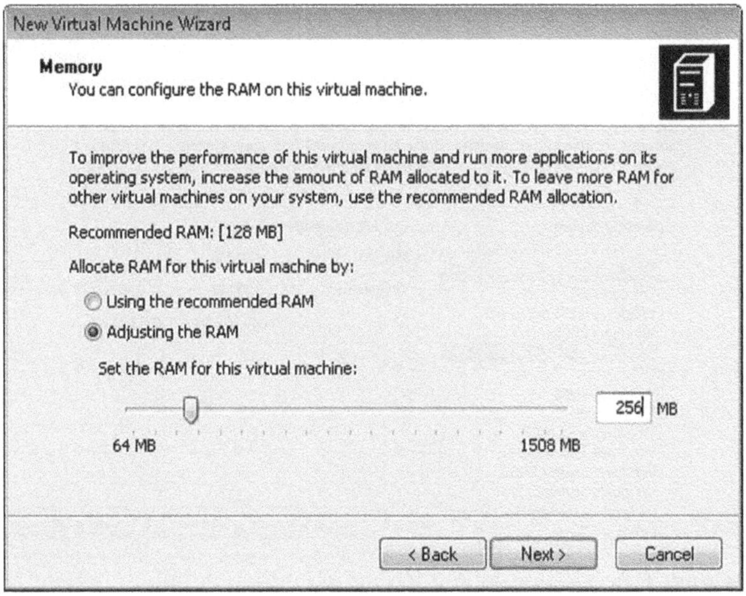

■ **FIGURE 15.11** Memory.

6. A virtual hard disk is simply a .VHD file created on your physical host system's drive. It is then presented to a VM and used to store everything related to the VM that would normally be stored on a conventional drive, such as the operating system, installed programs, or data files. In other words, it represents a complete computing environment. Let us go through the creation of a new virtual disk, as illustrated in Figure 15.12. Select the new disk option and click *Next*.

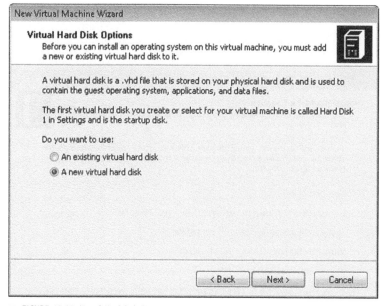

■ **FIGURE 15.12** Virtual Hard Disk Options.

7. The default location for the .VHD file is the folder created earlier to house your VM's files, as shown in Figure 15.13. Since that seems logical, let us leave it there. The file can, however, be placed anywhere on your physical system. By default, you are creating a dynamic disk. So the .VHD file grows as more data is placed on your VM's virtual drive. We show you how to change this later in the chapter. At this point in the process, you must decide the maximum to which the disk can grow. Since the file starts out small and grows over time, it is possible to oversubscribe your physical drive and run out of space. So, exercise caution. You can always add an additional virtual drive (up to three drives total) to your VM later if needed. For now, let us set the size to 10,240 MB, aka 10 GB, and click *Next*.

Note

A .VHD file does not shrink on its own after data has been deleted from a virtual disk. You will need to shut down the VM and compact it manually via the Virtual PC Console. This is illustrated later in this chapter.

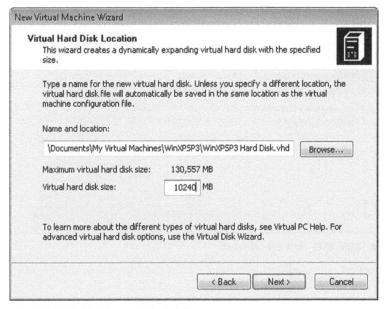

■ **FIGURE 15.13** Default location for the .VHD file.

8. That is it for the wizard! Figure 15.14 shows a short summary
of what was just created, if it looks good click *Next* and
then *Finish*.

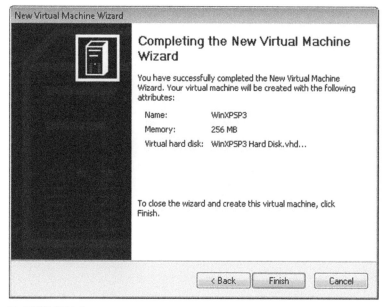

■ **FIGURE 15.14** Summary.

9. The *Settings* button in the Virtual PC Console allows you to configure a wide variety of configuration options for your VM. The majority of the settings require the target VM to be in a Not running state. Since your new VM has not been started yet, click the *Settings* button, as shown in Figure 15.15, and take a look.

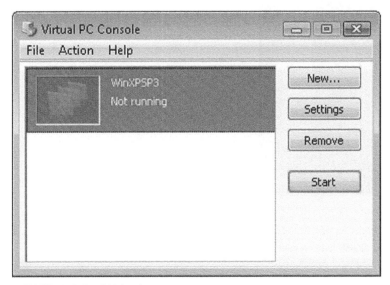

■ **FIGURE 15.15** Virtual PC Console.

10. We will not go into every option available, but you can see in
Figure 15.16 that pretty much anything that you can configure on
a physical machine can also be configured on a virtual machine
and more. Highlight *Memory* and you will see a familiar window
display on the right. You can adjust the amount of RAM
assigned to the VM with the same slider bar interface as in the
creation process.

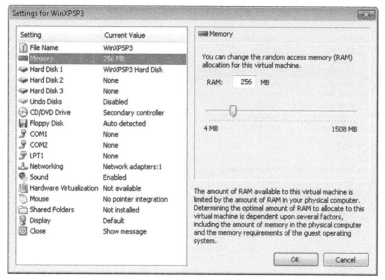

■ **FIGURE 15.16** Settings.

11. Let us check out one more option. As shown in Figure 15.17, highlight *Hard Disk 1*. From the interface on the right you can now remove the virtual disk, change it, create a new disk, or edit an existing one.

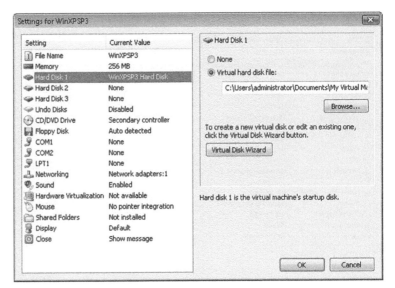

■ FIGURE 15.17 Hard Disk settings.

12. Go ahead and click the *Virtual Disk Wizard* button. Click *Next* to get past the welcome screen and you will see the Disk Options window shown in Figure 15.18. From here you can create a new disk. But since you already know how to do that, select *Edit an existing virtual disk* and click *Next*.

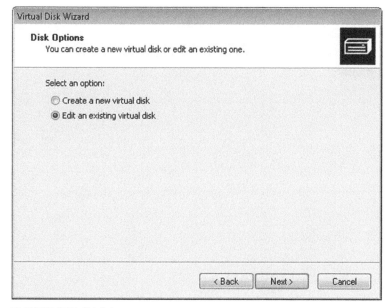

■ **FIGURE 15.18** Disk Options.

13. Click *Browse...* and select the disk that you created earlier. If you kept the default settings, you will find the folder for your VM in *Documents / My Virtual Machines*. Once there open the folder for your VM and select the virtual disk that you want to modify, as shown in Figure 15.19, click *Open* and then *Next*.

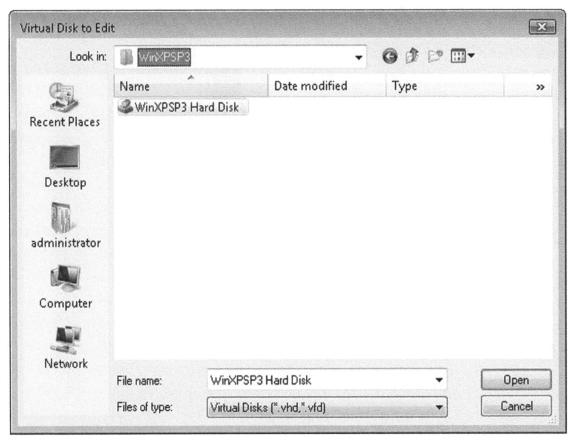

■ **FIGURE 15.19** Modifying a Virtual Disk.

14. Shown in Figure 15.20, you are now faced with two options. You can compact the file to remove "white space" caused by deleting data from the virtual disk. This is handy if you need to reclaim physical disk space on your host machine. The other option is to convert the dynamic virtual disk to one with a fixed size. With this option the resultant .VHD file will be expanded to the full maximum size that you specified when you created it. This is helpful if you are concerned about oversubscribing your physical disk. Select *Compact it* and click *Next*.

Warning

Converting a disk from dynamic to fixed-size is a one-way trip. You cannot convert it back.

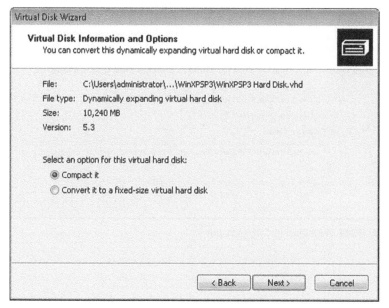

■ **FIGURE 15.20** Virtual Disk Information and Options.

15. Both the disk compaction and conversion processes give you the option to overwrite the existing .VHD file or to save the new file with a different name or location as shown in Figure 15.21. Unless you do not have enough free disk space, we would strongly encourage you not to overwrite the existing file in case the file is corrupted. Select *Saving the file as:* then hit the *Browse...* button. Give the new file a name and location. When you are ready click *Next*.

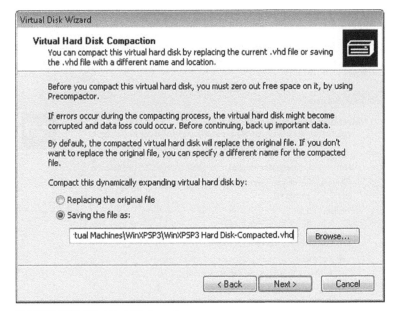

■ **FIGURE 15.21** Virtual Hard Disk Compaction.

16. The act of compacting or converting a virtual disk can take a very long time. Since our file is new and will not contain any white space, it will be very quick. Click *Finish* and the process will begin, as shown in Figure 15.22.

■ **FIGURE 15.22** Completing the Virtual Disk Wizard.

17. Now you can close any open windows until you are taken back to the Virtual PC Console, as shown in Figure 15.23. If you have physical media, CD or DVD, for the operating system you are virtualizing, place it in your drive now. If you are planning to use an .ISO file, place it on the physical drive of your host computer. Select your new VM in the Virtual PC Console window and click the *Start* button. This will launch your VM in a new window. If you are using a CD or DVD, the setup of the OS should automatically begin within the virtual machine window. At this point you do not need to take any actions until Step

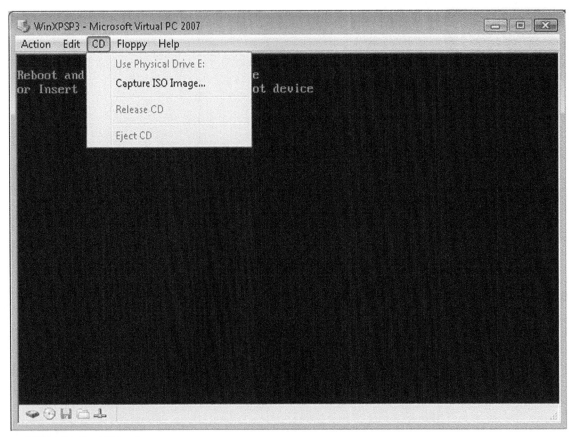

■ **FIGURE 15.23** Virtual PC Console.

20, but you should keep reading and familiarize yourself with using. ISO files as you may want to install software in this manner. If you elected to use an .ISO file to install the OS click *CD* in the menu bar of the virtual machine window and select *Capture ISO Image ...*

18. Browse to and select the .ISO file that you wish to use, as shown in Figure 15.24, and it will be presented to your VM just as if it were a CD/DVD in your drive. Click *Open*.

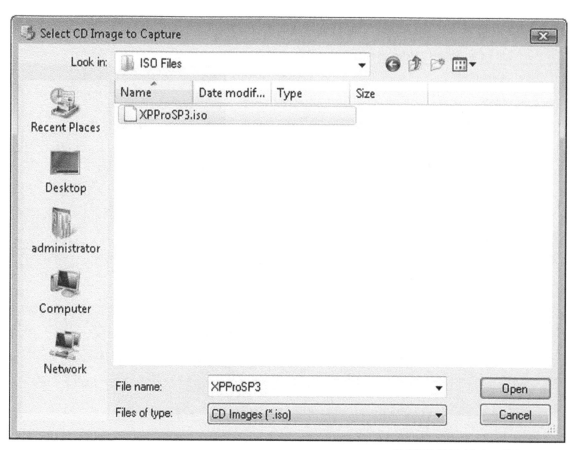

■ **FIGURE 15.24** Selecting a CD Image.

19. Now that the .ISO file is mounted, click *Action* on the menu bar and select *Reset*, as in Figure 15.25. Confirm you do want to reset the virtual machine and that you do not care about losing your changes, since you did not make any. The VM will reboot and the OS setup will begin.

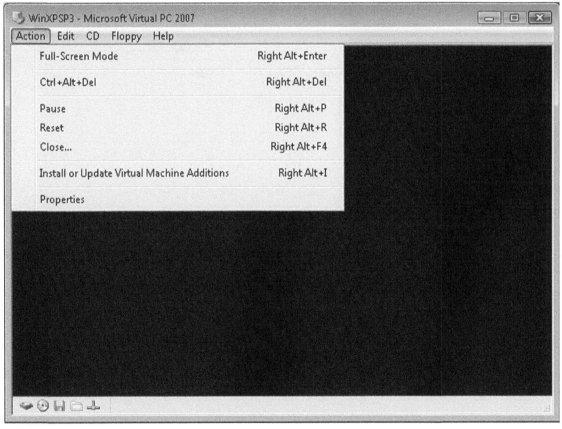

■ **FIGURE 15.25** Resetting the Virtual Machine.

20. Proceed with installing the OS as if it were a conventional deployment. You will likely notice that using the mouse is extremely frustrating as the pointer will be erratic as you attempt to move it. We cannot address this until after you have completed installing the OS, so try to leverage the keyboard as much as possible until then. Once the OS is up and running, return to the *Action* menu from the menu bar, as shown in Figure 15.26. This time select *Install or Update Virtual Machine Additions.*

Note

During the OS setup process you can remove focus from a virtual machine window so that you can interact with the host desktop, by pressing the *Alt* key on the right side of your keyboard. This is not necessary once you install the VM Additions. Install additions by opening the *Action* menu and clicking *Install or Update Virtual Machine Additions.*

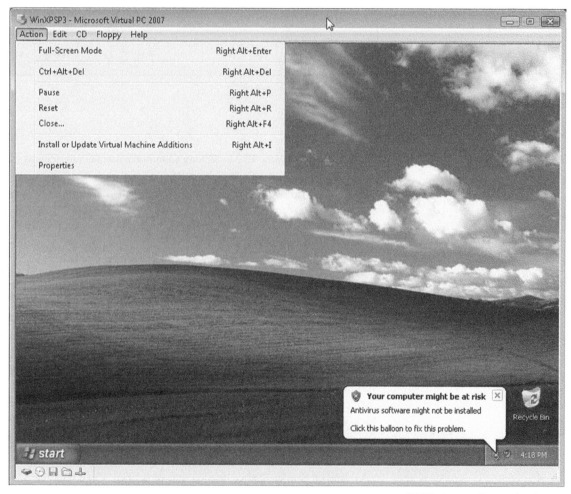

■ **FIGURE 15.26** Installing Virtual Machine Additions.

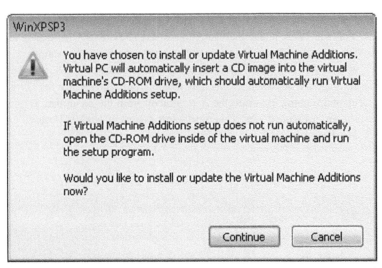

WinXPSP3

⚠ You have chosen to install or update Virtual Machine Additions. Virtual PC will automatically insert a CD image into the virtual machine's CD-ROM drive, which should automatically run Virtual Machine Additions setup.

If Virtual Machine Additions setup does not run automatically, open the CD-ROM drive inside of the virtual machine and run the setup program.

Would you like to install or update the Virtual Machine Additions now?

[Continue] [Cancel]

■ **FIGURE 15.27** Confirm Install.

21. As shown in Figure 15.27, clicking *Continue* automatically mounts an .ISO file and launches the installation.
22. This is a very simple install, just click *Next* to get past the welcome screen, click *Finish* when it is done, and then click *Yes* if you want to reboot. When the VM restarts you will notice that the mouse is back under your control and that the VM window now behaves like an ordinary windowed application with regards to the pointer.

Warning
A virtual machine is just as vulnerable to malware as is a conventional PC. Be sure to keep your VMs patched and install an antivirus package.

You are done! You have created your first virtual machine and it is ready for installing applications and getting to work.

INSTALLING WINDOWS VIRTUAL PC AND XP MODE

Windows Virtual PC is to Windows 7 as Virtual PC 2007 is to Vista. If you have no immediate intentions to introduce Windows 7 to your environment you can take a pass on reading this section, but remember to refer back when you decide to take the plunge.

1. The first thing you need to do is download the installation files from the Microsoft Web site. You can find what you need at www. microsoft.com/windows/virtual-pc/download.aspx. Grab both the

Windows Virtual PC install file as well as Windows XP Mode. Be certain to take note if you need 32- or 64-bit code. Both are available.

2. Start the installation process by executing the Virtual PC.MSU file. When prompted, read and accept the license terms and restart your machine.

3. From your start menu select *Manage virtual machines* from the Windows Virtual PC group. This will open the Virtual Machines folder where you manage your VMs. Now click on *Create virtual machine* on the menu bar, as shown in Figure 15.28.

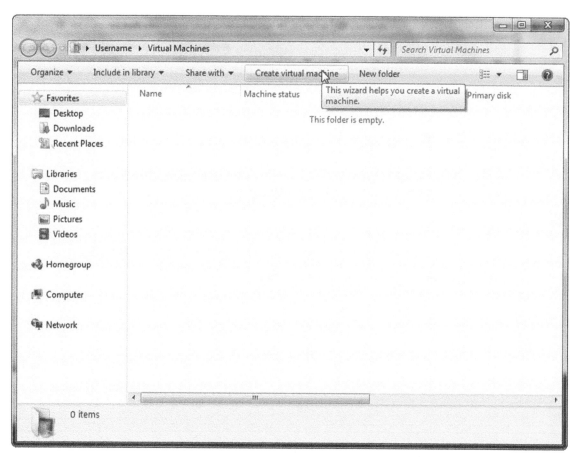

■ **FIGURE 15.28** Create virtual machine.

Note
Although there is no Back button in the setup
wizard, you can return to the previous screen by
pressing *Alt-Left Arrow*.

4. Type in a name for your virtual machine that reflects its purpose
or OS, as in Figure 15.29. You can also change the folder that
your VM will be stored in if you wish. Click *Next* when you
are ready.

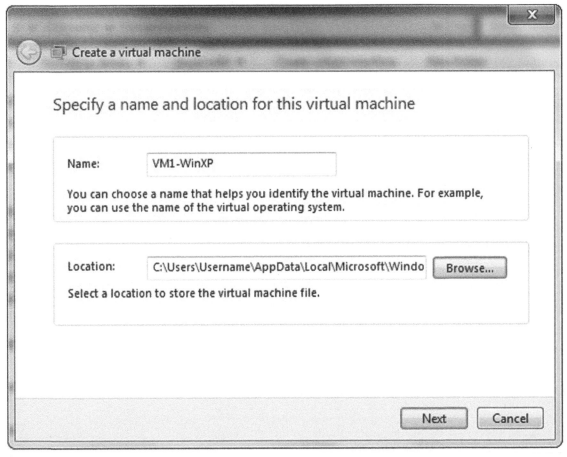

■ **FIGURE 15.29** Name and location.

5. As shown in Figure 15.30, select the amount of RAM to assign to this VM. This number is changeable later, so do not over-think it. If it does not run as well as you would like, you can increase its memory allocation at any time.

6. Now it is time to create a virtual hard disk. You can create three different types. The differences between the types are centered on the manner in which physical disk space is consumed. As in Virtual PC 2007, the .VHD of a Dynamic disk starts small and grows with usage. Fixed-size disks consume an amount of physical disk equal to their maximum size upon creation and never change. The newest disk type, Differencing, starts out small and stays that way. All changes made to this type of disk are stored in separate files thus preserving the original state of the disk. You can use this technique to manage multiple states of a virtual machine, but all of the differencing disk will still refer back to the parent for their base OS and application files.

Warning

The single biggest problem noticed about running OS/Apps in a VM is NOT ENOUGH MEMORY. Just because you are running it a VM does not mean you can give it LESS than you normally would a physical box. In order to start a virtual machine, the host must have at least as much memory available as is assigned to the VM. If you plan to run multiple VMs simultaneously, there must be sufficient memory available to meet or exceed the sum total of the memory specified for all of the VMs.

Note

It is recommended that you write protect the original parent disk of a Differencing disk type in order to maintain its integrity. If some other process were to modify this file, the virtual disk would become useless. While the odds of this happening may be slim, the impact would be devastating. Any differencing disk associated with the parent would be rendered useless and all of your data would be lost.

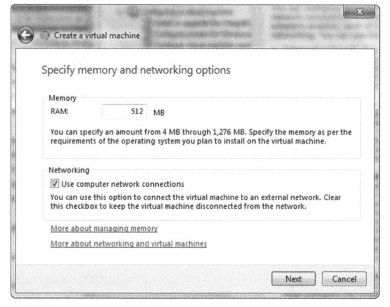

■ **FIGURE 15.30** Memory and network options.

Note

There are many advantages to Undo Disks including the ability to roll back the latest OS patches if they negatively affect your applications. However, keep in mind that discarding an Undo Disk removes all changes including all data files or applications recently installed. It is crucial to remember to commit your Undo Disks regularly to minimize the negative impact of rolling back.

You also have the option to enable Undo Disks. Undo Disks apply to all of the virtual disks assigned to a VM. When enabled, they store any changes made to them in a separate .VUD file. Changes can consist of applied patches, software being installed, data files created, and so forth. While this sounds similar to the behavior of a Differencing disk, Undo Disks can be committed to the virtual machine making the changes permanent or discarded, thus returning the VM to the state that it was in the last time its .VUD file was applied.

For this walk-though let us select *Create a dynamically expanding virtual disk drive* and not enable Undo Disks, as shown in Figure 15.31. Click *Create* when ready.

7. You now have a VM without an operating system. Let us fix that. If you are installing the OS for the VM from physical media, insert it now. If you want to use an .ISO image as the source for your

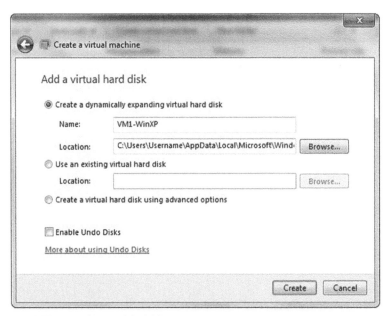

■ **FIGURE 15.31** Add a virtual hard disk.

installation, proceed as follows. As shown in Figure 15.32, return to the Virtual Machines management window, highlight your new VM, right click it, and select *Settings*. The window that opens shows all of the features of your VM that can be modified. Select the CD or DVD Drive, click the *Open an ISO image* radio button that appears on the right, and the browse to and select your .ISO file. Click *OK* to mount the .ISO file.

8. Now just double click your VM in the Virtual Machines management window and follow the normal process as if you were installing the OS on a physical machine. Once complete, you are ready to leverage your VM as if it were a physical machine.

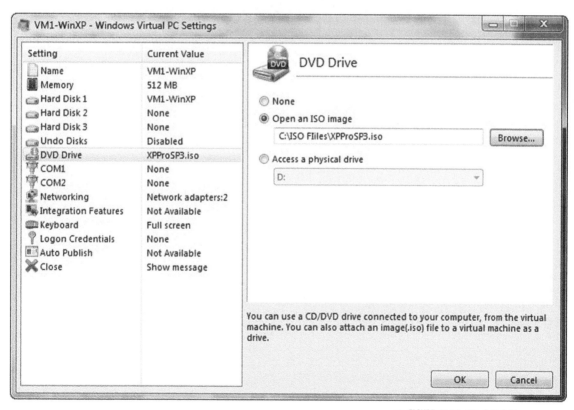

■ **FIGURE 15.32** Virtual PC Settings.

Warning
Windows XP Mode is a 32-bit version of Windows XP with Service Pack 3 installed. Keep this in mind when determining if this is an option for you. The installer comes in 32-bit and 64-bit versions, to match the version of Windows Virtual PC. In both cases, however, the resulting Windows XP image is 32-bit.

Note
Window XP Mode requires 1.6 GB of disk space to install.

The integrated Virtual PC Help is an excellent tool in assisting you to get the most out of your virtual work space, so do not shy away from using it.

Installation and configuration of XP mode

1. It is time to launch the Windows XP Mode install file that you downloaded earlier. Go ahead and click *Next* to get past the welcome screen. At this point you can select where you would like XP Mode to be installed or simply accept the default path, as shown in Figure 15.33. Once done click *Next*.

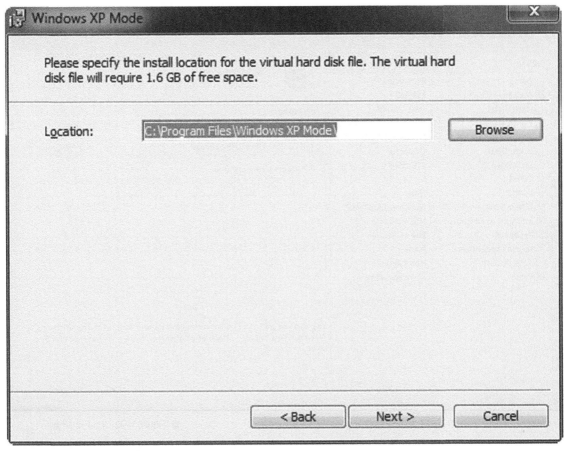

■ **FIGURE 15.33** Windows XP Mode Location.

2. That is it! Leave the *Launch Windows XP Mode* box checked, click *Finish*, and let us check it out.
3. At the first launch, you are asked to accept the license agreement and then to select an installation folder and to set a password for the XPMUser account, as illustrated in Figure 15.34. XP Mode and the applications installed in the virtual Window XP instance all run under the XPMUser account created by the install wizard.

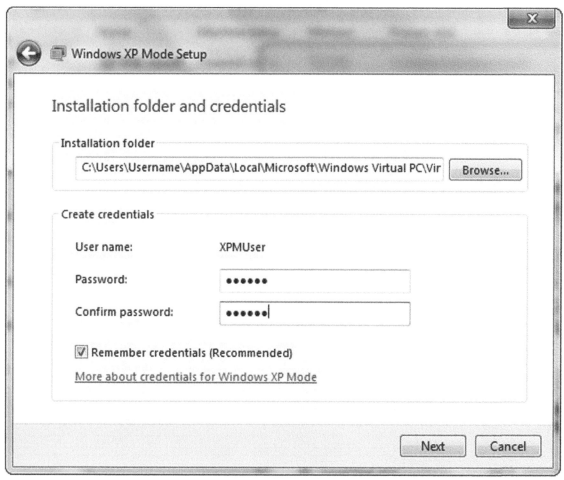

■ **FIGURE 15.34** Installation folder and credentials.

4. Since Window XP Mode is a virtual instance of Windows XP SP3, it needs to be patched and maintained in the same manner. Whether you choose to leverage Automatic Updates or not, patch levels should be kept as current as possible to help ensure the integrity of the operating system and your data. Similar consideration should be given to antimalware software. As shown in Figure 15.35, make your choice and click *Start Setup*.

■ **FIGURE 15.35** Automatic Updates.

5. That completes the setup of Windows XP Mode, but the real value of it will not be seen until you virtualize an application. From within the XP Mode's Virtual PC instance you can access the virtual drive of the VM as well as the physical drives of the host machine. Therefore, you install software on the VM from files on your host or from a CD/DVD. Figure 15.36 shows the My Computer window from the VM you have just created.

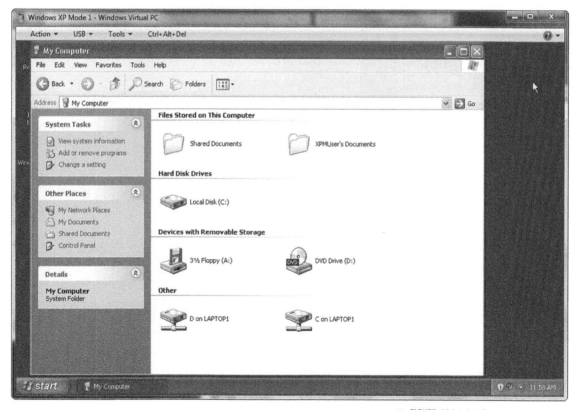

■ **FIGURE 15.36** My Computer.

6. Proceed with installing an application that you would like to virtualize. For our example we chose Microsoft Access 2000, as shown in Figure 15.37. As you can see in the following two images, Access is installed and functional in the VM window and is

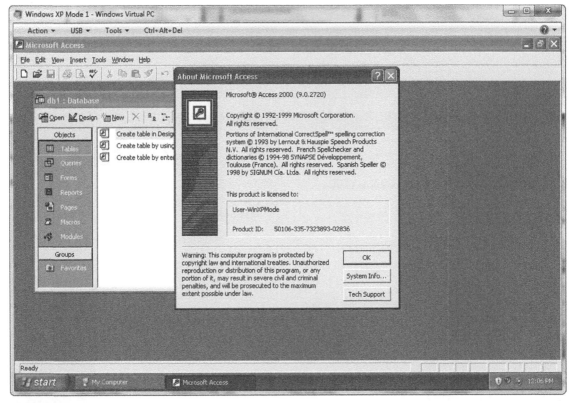

■ **FIGURE 15.37** Installing an application.

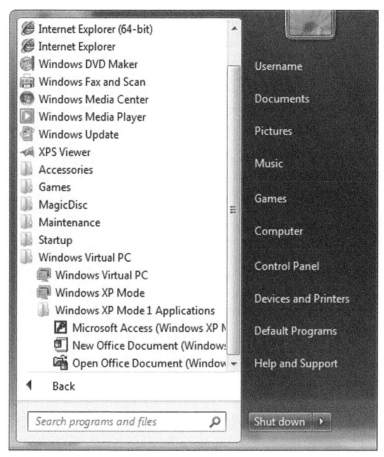

■ **FIGURE 15.38** Start menu.

now an available application on the host machine start menu within a folder named Windows XP Mode 1 Applications, as shown in Figure 15.38.

INTRODUCTION TO MED-V

MED-V is the engine behind the management of an enterprise virtual desktop environment. It empowers an administrator to control the deployment and management of Virtual PC images. You must be a Microsoft Software Assurance customer to take advantage of this functionality as it is part of the Microsoft Desktop Optimization Pack (MDOP).

Note
For applications to show up on your Windows 7 start menu, the application must install shortcuts to the All Users Start Menu folder on the XP VM. If it does not, you can create shortcuts manually.

Note
Clicking the X in the corner of the Windows XP Mode's Virtual PC instance puts the VM into a hibernation state and closes the window. However, you must first logout from within the running virtual OS instance and then click the X to completely close the window before you can launch a virtualized application directly from your host machine.

Note
MED-V requires an Active Directory infrastructure to allow for the provisioning of Virtual PC images via AD users and groups.

There are several components that comprise the MED-V solution architecture.

- *Management server and console*—Distributes the Virtual PC images to the appropriate users and governs them according to the defined policies and permissions. The interface for configuring the management server is the management console which can be installed locally on the management server, on a separate server, or a desktop.
- *Virtual PC images and repository*—Virtual PC images are defined by a systems administrator to reflect all components that would be part of a conventional desktop deployment. These include the operating system, applications, and any required data. The collection of images for an enterprise is stored in a web server hosted image repository. The repository in turn allows for the downloading and updating of images as well as version management of the images.
- *Desktop client*—This is where the magic happens. The client performs the presentation of the virtualized desktop via the users start menu as if it were a conventionally installed application. The client is also responsible for managing the general operation of the virtual desktop and carrying out any image lifecycle policies defined by the system administrator.

The system requirements to operate MED-V and its components are illustrated in Figures 15.39 and 15.40.

Component	Processor	Memory	Operating System
MED-V Management Server	Dual Processor 2.8 GHz	4 GB	Windows Server 2008 Standard or Enterprise Edition
MED-V Client	No processor requirement beyond that of the operating system	Win XP: 1 GB Vista: 2 GB	Windows XP SP2/3 32 bit (Professional or Home Edition), Vista SP1 32 bit (Enterprise, Business, Home Basic, Home Premium, Ultimate)

■ **FIGURE 15.39** MED-V system requirements.

Optional Components	Requirments
Image Repository	Microsoft IIS based web server(s)
Reporting Database	MS SQL Server (2005 SP2 Enterprise or 2008 Express/Standard/Enterprise)

■ **FIGURE 15.40** MED-V Optional Components.

MED-V server installation

The longest step in the MED-V install process is the prep work. Get started by building your Windows 2008 sever with IIS enabled. You will then need to log in to the Microsoft Volume License Services Web site (https://www.microsoft.com/licensing/servicecenter/), download the MDOP 2009 ISO file, and create an installation DVD.

Note
If you do not enable IIS on your MED-V server during the initial build process you will not be able to access the MED-V management interface until you do so.

Now that you have the installation media, let us get started:

1. Put the DVD in your server's drive and let autorun load the installation interface, shown in Figure 15.41, or launch it manually from Windows Explorer.

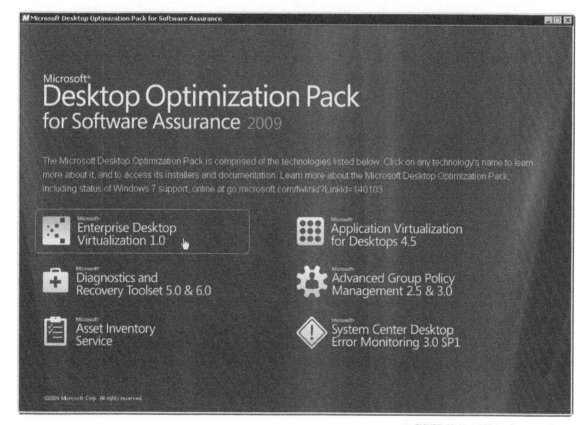

■ **FIGURE 15.41** MDOP installation interface.

2. Click *Enterprise Desktop Virtualization 1.0* to access the MED-V installation menu, shown in Figure 15.42.
3. Select the *Server component* appropriate for your architecture (32- or 64-bit).
4. After accepting the licensing terms and installation path, installation begins. When completed, choose the option to launch the Server Configuration Manager.

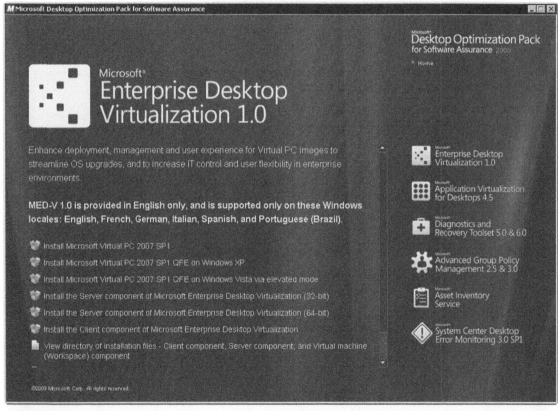

■ FIGURE 15.42 Med-V menu.

5. You must now choose whether to protect your sessions, as shown in Figure 15.43. Leveraging unencrypted HTTP sessions leaves you open to packet interceptions. You may feel comfortable over your internal network allowing unencrypted transmissions, but if you will be extending MED-V outside of your enterprise we strongly recommend you enable encrypted connections. If you desire a layer of obscurity, you may change the ports used for communication from the defaults to any available port that you are not already using. However, this does not replace encryption.

Note

If you do enable HTTPS connections, you must bind the required certificate to the proper port. The wizard gives an example of the *netsh* command to use. You can learn more about how to do this at http://msdn.microsoft.com/en-us/library/ms733791.aspx.

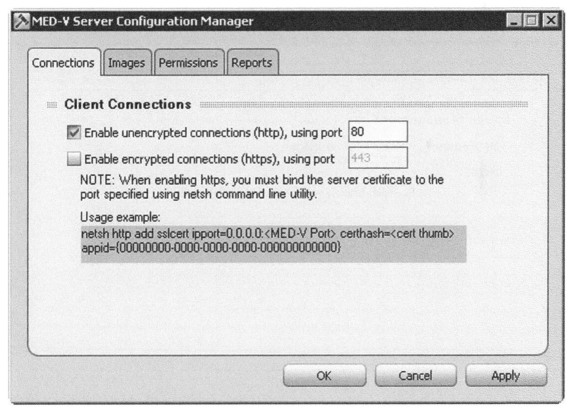

■ **FIGURE 15.43** Connections.

6. Next click the *Images* tab, shown in Figure 15.44. You have to determine if the default directory for the VMs meets your needs or if you prefer to locate them somewhere else. You can also configure a URL to point to an optional image download server. While the creation and management of an image repository is outside the scope of this book, you will find additional resources to assist you in fully rounding out your implementation of MED-V at http://technet .microsoft.com/en-us/library/ff433567.aspx. If you do set up an image repository later, you may return to this screen to enter its address.

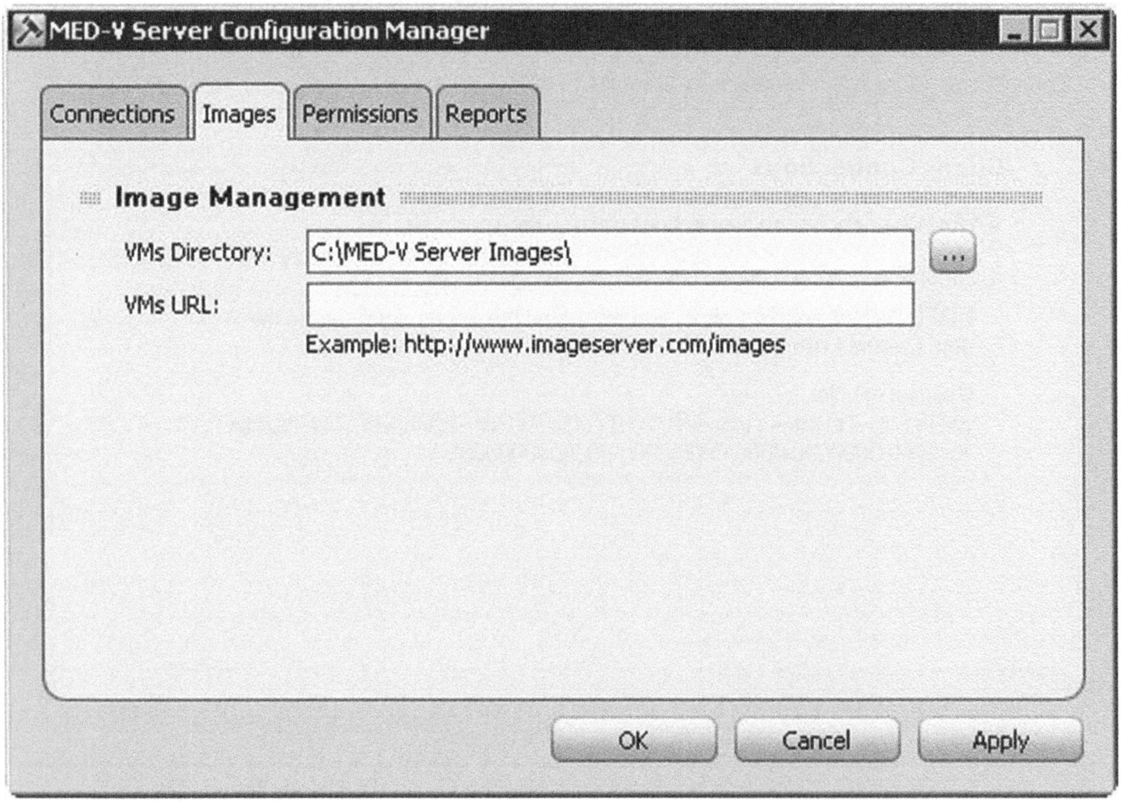

■ **FIGURE 15.44** Images.

7. Next click the *Permissions* tab, shown in Figure 15.45. You can
now establish the AD users and groups, which need to access the VMs
and what level of access they will have. You will most likely want to
use the buttons on the interface to remove the Everyone group and add
an administrator group. Clearing the *Changes Allowed* checkbox
applies read-only permissions to the associated user or group.

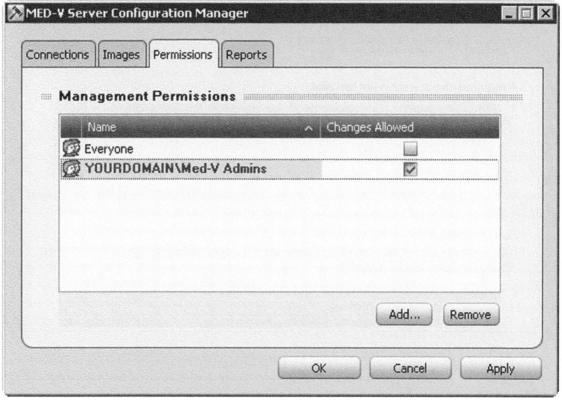

■ **FIGURE 15.45** Permissions.

8. Click the *Reports* tab, shown in Figure 15.46. The final screen allows you to set up usage and access reports for your MED-V environment. Note that this will require access to either a Microsoft SQL Server 2005 or SQL Server 2008 as described in Figure 15.40. MS SQL can be installed locally on the MED-V server or on another server on your network. If you do have access to an appropriate database server and you want to enable reporting you will also need to load a few components on your MED-V server. Links to information on downloading the required software are presented if they are not already installed.

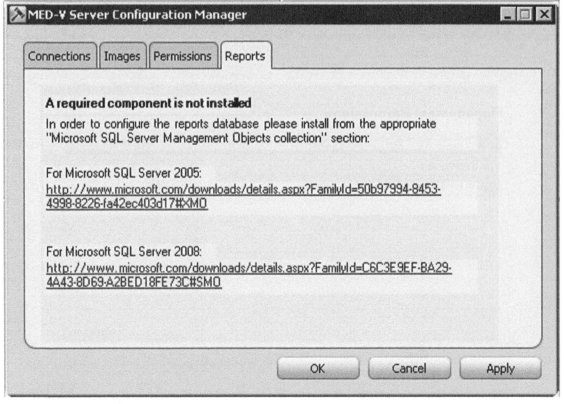

■ **FIGURE 15.46** Reports.

9. If you decide that you want to enable reporting and you have all of the required software components installed, check the *Enable reports* box and enter your server connection string. After which you can test your connection and create your database by clicking the appropriate buttons, shown in Figure 15.47.

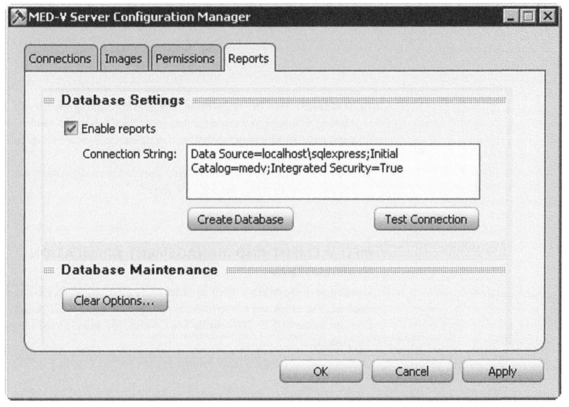

■ **FIGURE 15.47** Creating a Database and Testing Connections.

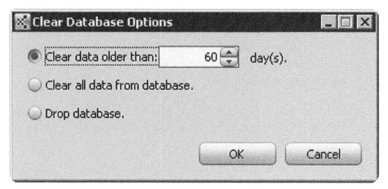

■ **FIGURE 15.48** Clearing Database Options.

10. This same screen can be revisited later, and by clicking the *Clear Options...* button, you can clear data older than a specified number of days, clear all data from the database, or delete the database altogether, as shown in Figure 15.48.
11. That is it! When you have completed your initial configuration, you are prompted to restart the MED-V server.

MED-V CLIENT AND MANAGEMENT APPLICATION INSTALLATION

Installation of the MED-V client requires local admin rights on the target machine. The client and management application for MED-V are installed from the same MDOP 2009 media from which you installed the server components.

1. Select the Enterprise Desktop Virtualization 1.0 group of applications, as shown in Figure 15.49.

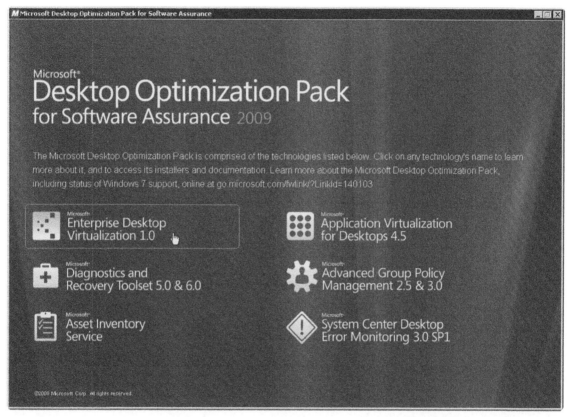

■ **FIGURE 15.49** MDOP installation interface.

Note

Take note that at the time of this writing the MED-V client will not install on a 64-bit platform and it is not compatible with Windows 7. The pending release of MED-V 2.0 addresses this.

2. Select Install the Client component of MED-V, as shown in Figure 15.50.
3. Proceed with accepting the licensing terms and modifying or confirming the installation path.

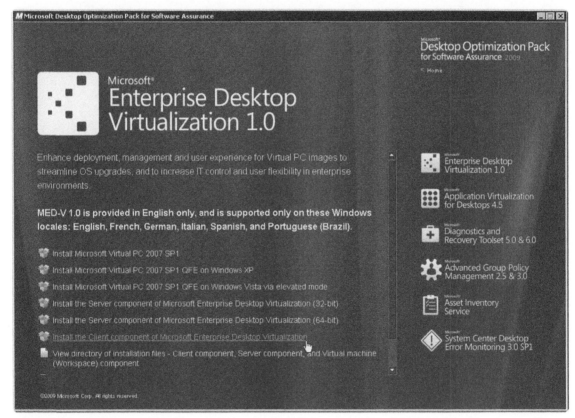

■ **FIGURE 15.50** Installing the client component of Med-V.

4. As shown in Figure 15.51, if you are installing the client on a machine you intend to use for managing your MED-V environment, check the box to include the management application. If you elect to have the virtual workspace automatically launch on Windows startup, you want to check the *Load MED-V when Windows starts* box. Adding a desktop icon for MED-V is a matter of taste, so check it if you like. In the Server address field enter the DNS name of your MED-V server and then enter the port number if you elected to change it from the default of 80. In addition, if you choose to require an encrypted connection for added security, click the *Server requires encrypted connections* check box. You may also choose to change the default path for your local copy on the Virtual Machine Image files by clicking the *Change...* button.

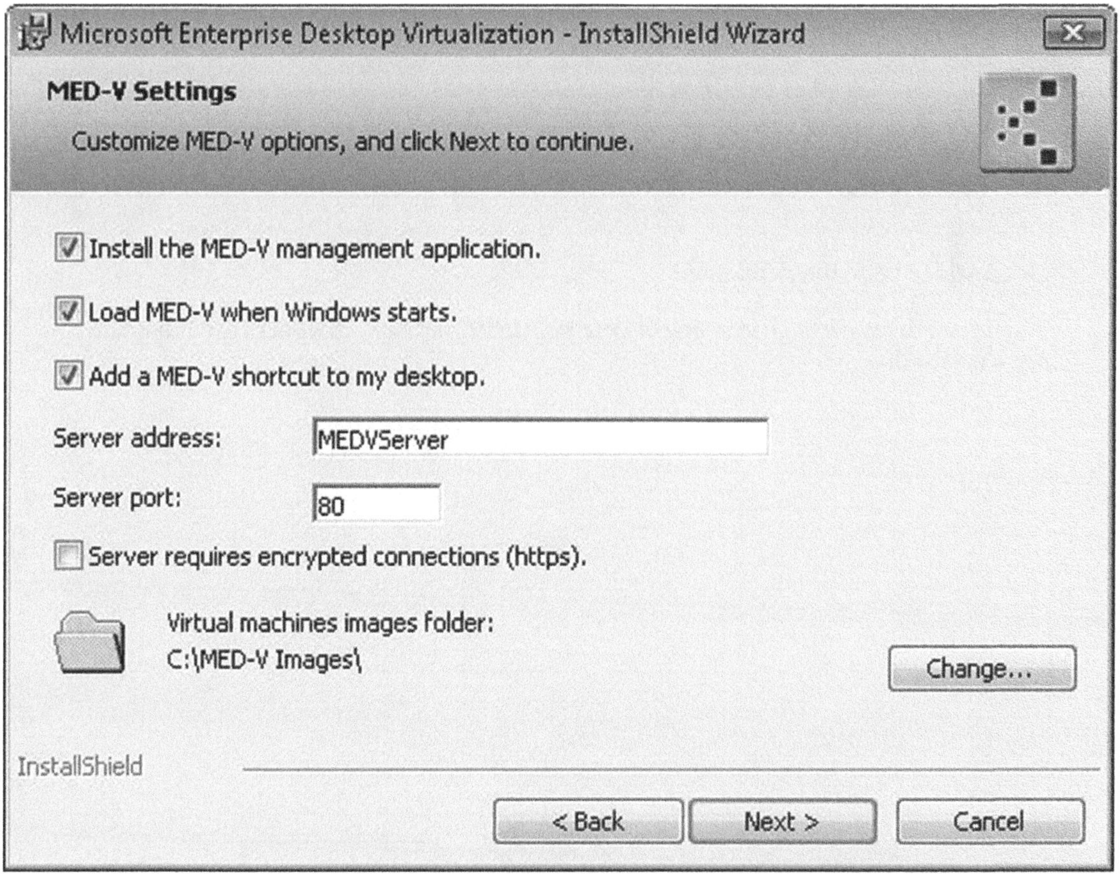

■ **FIGURE 15.51** MED-V Settings.

5. One last chance to go back and change any of the available options. If you are ready, click *Install*, as shown in Figure 15.52.

6. When you have completed your initial configuration, you are presented with the completed installation screen. You may be prompted to restart the machine.

CREATING A VIRTUAL MACHINE IMAGE

A Virtual Machine Image is a fully configured virtual machine used to create a MED-V image for deployment to your enterprise. Let us step through creating one based on the Virtual PC 2007 VM that we made earlier in this chapter. In order to not unnecessarily burden the PCs in your environment, the VM image should be optimized so that it meets your needs while not running any extra services. Since it is not possible

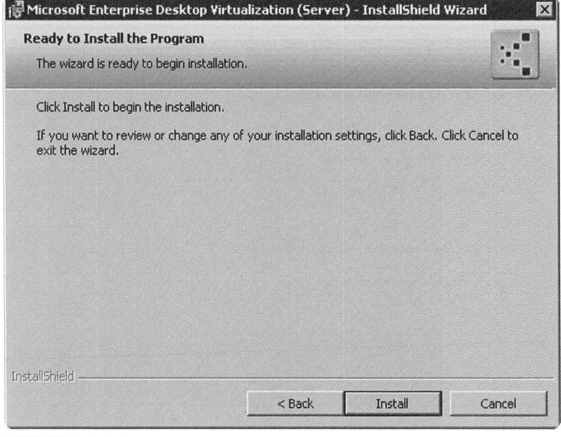

■ **FIGURE 15.52** Ready to Install.

for us to predict exactly how and why you will be using virtualization, we can only provide some general tips on optimization in the steps below.

1. With your Virtual PC 2007 VM shut down and highlighted in the Virtual PC Console window, click the *Settings* button to open the configurable options. It is recommended that you disable floppy disk drives and undo-disks.
2. Start the VM and install any applications that you need to include in the final image.
3. Navigate to the Power Options Properties window found in the Control Panel under Performance and Maintenance. Confirm that sleep and hibernation are both disabled; in fact they may be missing altogether.
4. It is important that you also disable the automatic restart feature of Windows Startup and Recovery, as shown in Figure 15.53. System properties are also found in the Control Panel under Performance and Maintenance.

Warning

For a VM image to function properly with MED-V it needs to have been built using a Microsoft Volume License Key.

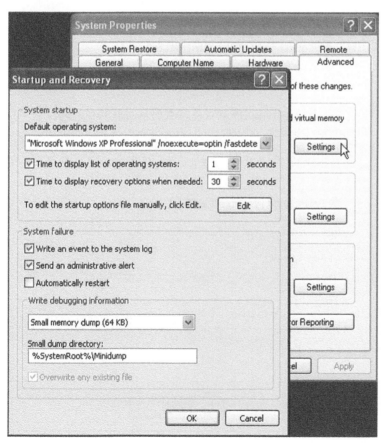

■ **FIGURE 15.53** Startup and Recovery.

5. Launch the Virtual PC 2007 VM that you created and confirm that it has .NET Framework 2.0 SP1 or higher installed. If not, the easiest way to obtain the latest .NET version is via the Windows Update Web site, http://update.microsoft.com. It is also a good idea to apply any other outstanding updates while you are at it.

6. Copy the MED-V workspace .MSI file from your MDOP 2009 DVD to the virtual drive of the VM. The needed file is named MED-V_Workspace_1.0.72.msi and is located in the MED-V \Installers folder. Once copied, launch the MSI to initiate the install. Click *Next* at the welcome screen, accept the license agreement (after you read it), and click *Next* again. Another click, this time on *Install*, will get things moving. When complete, leave the *Launch VM Prerequisites Tool* box checked and click *Finish*, as shown in Figure 15.54.

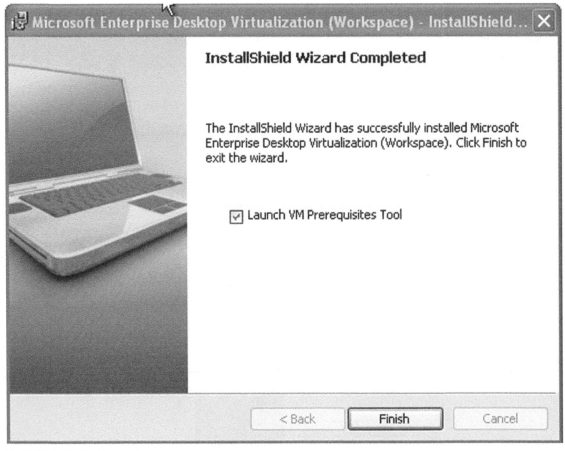

■ **FIGURE 15.54** Wizard Completed.

7. The MED-V VM Prerequisite Wizard will step you through several options for features and functionality that you can leave on or turn off based on your needs, while avoiding putting an unnecessary drain on your PCs resources. As the window displays in Figure 15.55, click *Next* to start.

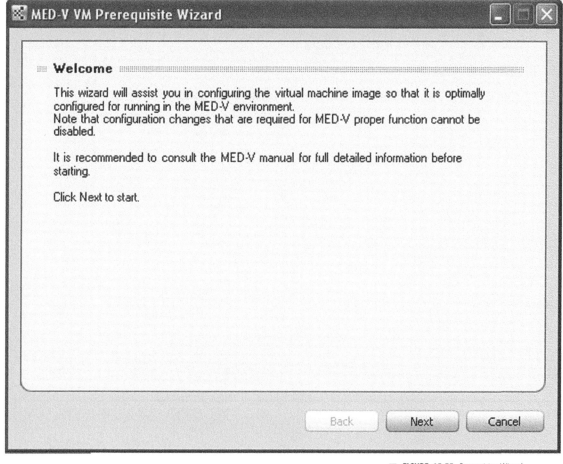

■ FIGURE 15.55 Prerequisite Wizard.

8. As you step through each screen, shown in Figures 15.56–15.58, you are most likely better off accepting the defaults, but if there are some settings that you think you need to change, do not be too afraid to do so. The wizard will not allow you to break the workspace. This is why you will see many of the options are grayed-out and unchangeable.

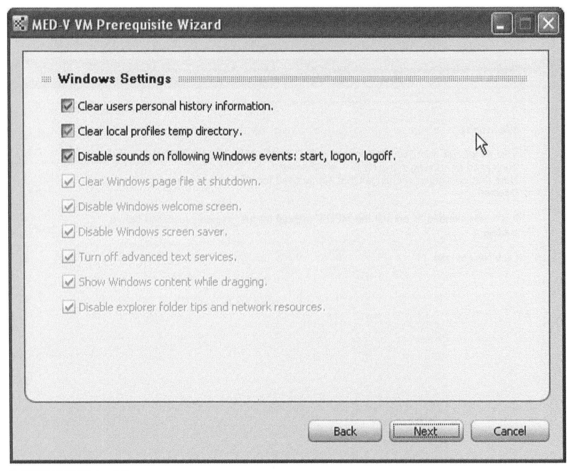

■ **FIGURE 15.56** Windows Settings.

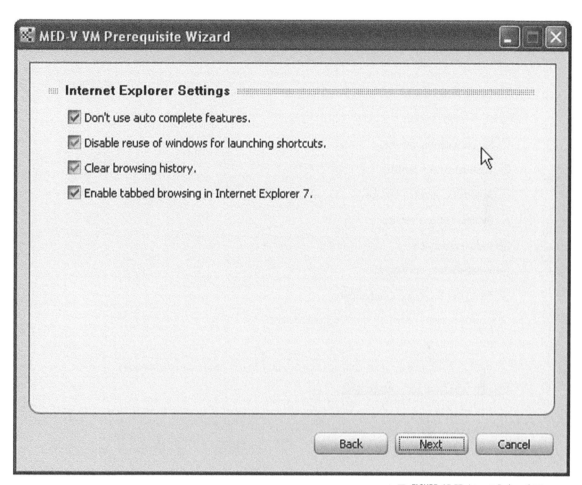

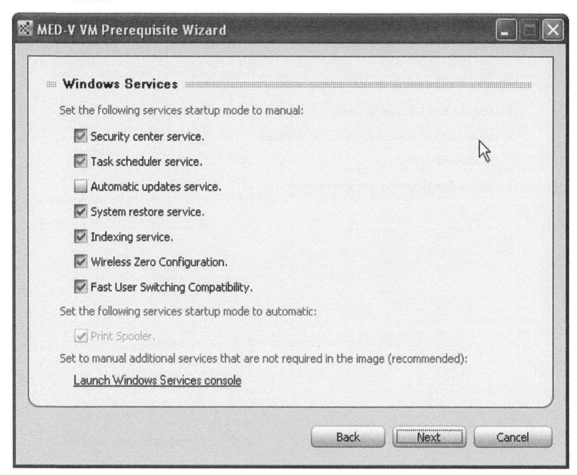

9. Shown in Figure 15.59, the wizard gives you the opportunity to set up the image to auto log-on. If that interests you from an ease of using standpoint, check the box and enter the user name and password.
10. You have now finished creating a Virtual Machine Image. Next we will build a MED-V image from the new workspace.

Warning

Be sure to consider the security ramifications of enabling auto log-on. Use this only for kiosks or other shared devices and only when the auto log-on account has very limited permissions to system or network resources.

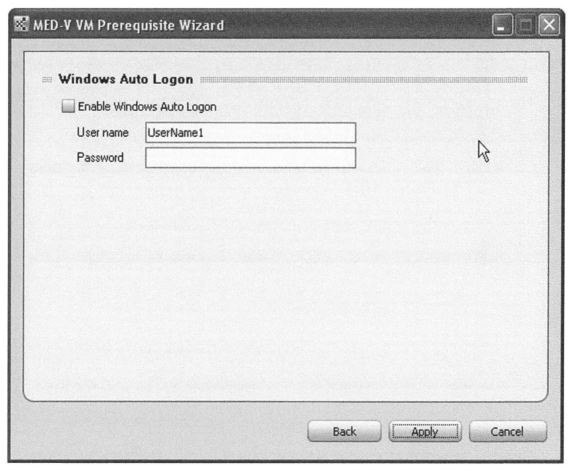

■ **FIGURE 15.59** Windows Auto Logon.

CREATING A MED-V IMAGE

Once created, a MED-V image can be wrapped up in a MED-V package and uploaded to an image repository for web-based distribution. You can also deploy a package via other distribution tools, such as Systems Management Server (SMS) or System Center Configuration Manager (SCCM).

1. Launch the MED-V Management Console. Near the top of the console you will find a button labeled *Images*, as shown in Figure 15.60, click it.

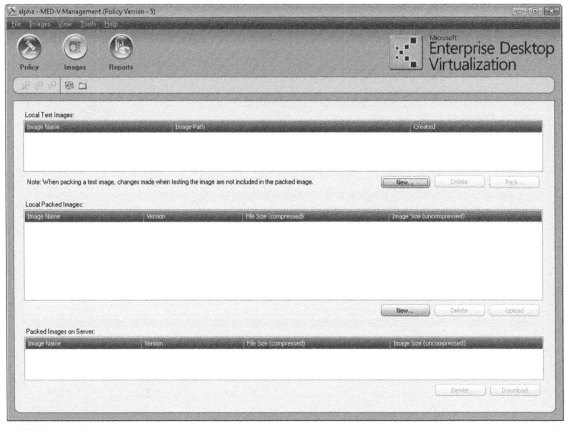

■ **FIGURE 15.60** MED-V Management.

2. The window displayed consists of three sections listing all the MED-V images in their various states of maturity. MED-V images are born in the Local Test Images section which includes all locally stored unpacked images. Once an image is packed it will be displayed in the Local Packed Images window. The final state for an image is when it has been packed and uploaded to the server. Such images are listed in the Packed Images on Server section.

Let us move on by clicking the *New...* button in the Local Test Images section of the console. Leverage the *Browse...* button to locate the .VMC file for the Virtual PC image that you just created and type in a name for the new MED-V image in the *Image name* field, as shown in Figure 15.61. When ready click the ever-popular *OK* button.

3. It is important to validate that your image is working before packing it for deployment. Fortunately, the MED-V console provides an easy way to accomplish this. At the top of the window click on the round

■ **FIGURE 15.61** Test Image Creation.

Policy button and then select the *Virtual Machine* tab, as shown in Figure 15.62. Use the dropdown arrow next to the *Assigned Image* field to select your recently created image. If it does not appear on the list, you may need to click the *Refresh* button located to the right of the dropdown arrow.

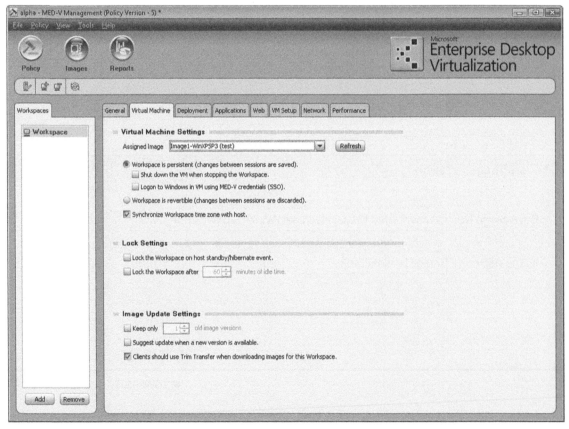

■ **FIGURE 15.62** Virtual Machine Settings.

Now decide what type of workspace you need, persistent or revertible, by selecting the appropriate check box. Persistent workspaces record all changes made to them by the user and saves them between sessions. A revertible workspace discards all user changes and reverts back to the original image each time it is launched.

4. Now that you are about ready to execute your test, save your settings by clicking the *Save changes* button on the console toolbar, as shown in Figure 15.63.

■ **FIGURE 15.63** Save changes.

5. From your Start Menu, select MED-V and enter your credentials to start the new virtual Workspace. Once presented with a dialog box similar to the one in Figure 15.64 click *Use Test Image*.

6. Your workspace and image should now open up and present you with the fruit of all of your hard work. Go ahead and thoroughly test your applications and kick the tires. If you need to make adjustments to the image, you now have the knowledge to do so and can refer back to earlier sections of this chapter for help.

Warning

Changes made within a virtual image during testing are not saved between sessions. If you need to make changes to the Virtual PC image, do not attempt to do so while you are still testing the MED-V deployment. You will need to stop the workspace first and then open the Virtual PC image with the Virtual PC app.

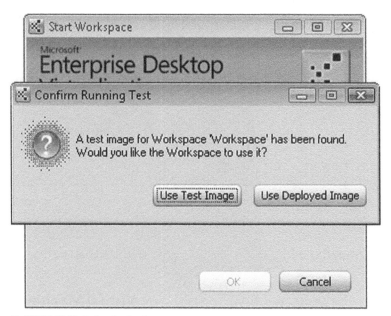

■ **FIGURE 15.64** Confirm Running Test.

7. If you are satisfied with your MED-V image, pack it. Return to the MED-V Management console and click the *Images* button at the top of the window, as shown in Figure 15.65. Click the *New...* button under the Local Packed Images section of the window.

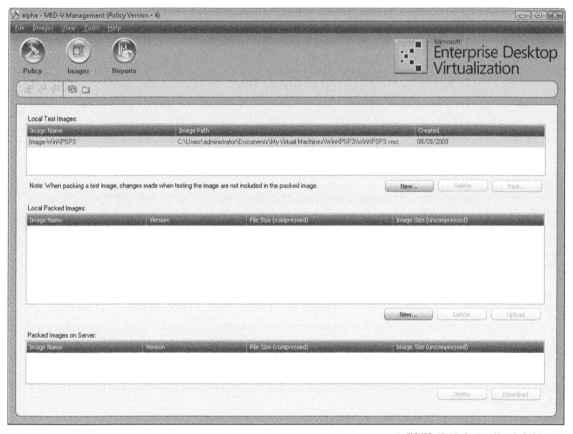

■ **FIGURE 15.65** Create a New Packed Image.

8. Use the *Browse...* button to navigate to the same .VMC file that you have been working with and assign it a name in the *Image name* field, as shown in Figure 15.66.

9. You are prompted to click *OK* once the packing is complete. You should see your packed image presented along with additional information such as its size, as in Figure 15.67.

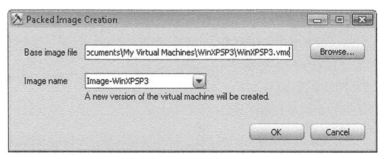

■ **FIGURE 15.66** Packed Image Creation.

■ **FIGURE 15.67** Packed Image Complete.

We have only covered MED-V basics. We could likely fill another book just detailing this robust product. Additional information can be found on the Web at http://technet.microsoft.com/en-us/library/ff433567.aspx.

SUMMARY

Microsoft virtualization is a collection of solutions designed to protect and enhance personal and enterprise computing. Virtual PC segregates desktop operating environments while MED-V enables easy implementation of images.

In addition to basic virtualization capabilities, Microsoft also provides backward compatibility by including Windows XP with certain Virtual PC licenses.

When creating a virtualization strategy, do not stop with the datacenter. There are also plenty of opportunities on your desktops.

Migrating virtual machines from Virtual Server 2005

The act of migrating a virtual machine from Virtual Server 2005 to Hyper-V is a simple process. The following steps outline the method recommended by Microsoft.

1. Launch the existing virtual machine within Virtual Server 2005 and collect the following machine settings:
   a. Memory Amount
   b. Disk Type\Size
   c. CPU Configuration
   d. Virtual Network Configuration
   e. Network Adapter Settings; IP Address, DNS, etc.
2. Update your virtual machine in terms of patches. There may be patches specific to virtual machine functionality, for example, if your virtual machine is running Windows 2003, Service Pack 2 is required prior to migrating to Hyper-V. Be sure to include all critical Microsoft patches and any application patches that may be available.
3. Hyper-V *Integration Services* replaces the *Virtual Machine Additions* components in Virtual Server, so uninstall these prior to migration. You can uninstall these components using the following steps:
   a. Within the virtual machine itself, go to the Control Panel and launch *Add\Remove Programs*.
   b. Click *Virtual Machine Additions* and choose *Remove*.
   c. Reboot the virtual machine when uninstall completes so it can fully complete the process, and before moving on to Step 4.
4. At this point you should perform a backup; however, you see fit for the virtual server. This will vary depending on the server's purpose and your preference—file system, file system and operating system, etc. Once your backup is complete, you will need to shut down the virtual machine fully, not in a saved state—shutting down the virtual machine in a saved state will not allow you to manage your undo disks. You will need to discard your Undo Disks prior to the migration.

Warning
You cannot use a SCSI disk to boot a virtual machine in Hyper-V, so if the startup disk of the virtual machine to be migrated is not IDE, you will need to change this prior to migrating.

Warning
Although it is not recommended, you can wait to uninstall the *Virtual Machine Additions* components after you migrate the virtual machine to Hyper-V, but only on *Virtual Machine Additions* version 13.813 and later. Attempting to do this with older versions may fail and cause corruption in your newly migrated virtual machine.

Undo Disks and Differencing Disks are similar; however, differencing disks are associated with a single virtual hard disk (VHD), not the virtual machine like the Undo Disks. Therefore, the differencing disks can follow the virtual machine through the migration if you choose.

5. You are now ready to check the Hardware Abstraction Layer (HAL) for compatibility. Hyper-V installed an APIC MP HAL when it installs *Integration Services* on the virtual machine, if you choose to move the virtual machine to Hyper-V without changing the HAL first, you will be prompted to upgrade when you start the install of *Integration Services*. Microsoft recommends changing this prior to your migration. To do this, follow these steps:

   a. Restart the virtual machine and perform steps b and c within the virtual machine to be migrated.

   b. Open *MSConfig.exe*, click the *Boot* tab, and then select *Advanced Options*.

   c. Select the *Detect HAL* check box, click *Ok*, and restart the virtual machine.

6. Having completed all of the preceding steps, you can now shut down the virtual machine to be migrated.

7. Virtual Server 2005 utilizes a series of files for a virtual machine. Depending on the virtual machine itself, the files will be one or more of the following type: *.vmc, *.vhd, *.iso, *.vfd. You will only have one *.vhd file and that is the only one you need to migrate.

8. From here you can use this single *.vhd file to create your new virtual machine in Hyper-V. You may have a virtual server that utilizes multiple VHDs in Virtual Server 2005, you can follow the steps above to migrate each of those disks into Hyper-V.

Is there a difference in migrating Windows Server 2003 VM or Vista VMs? How is the migration process different from the Import and Export functions?

Case studies

THE CASE OF THE UNEXPECTED UPGRADE

Unprepared, Inc. has 300 manufacturing locations scattered across the United States. Their business is making widgets that they then distribute regionally from each plant. Each plant runs 24×7 and employs around 70 people (none of which are IT personnel). Supporting those workers are 20 computers deployed at each location and shared across three shifts. The primary application in use in the field is Widget Builder Pro v1.0 or WBPv1 for short. This program plays an integral part in their manufacturing process and they can afford very little downtime or they will miss shipping commitments and loose business to their competitors.

Unprepared, Inc.'s software vendor has announced that support for WBPv1 will end in 90 days and all customers need to upgrade to WBPv2. If customers do not upgrade they will no longer be supported when they have issues and new patches for WBPv1 will not be provided. To make matters worse the hardware requirements of the new version significantly exceeds the capacity of the 3-year-old Windows XP SP3 computers in place.

Management has decided that the cost and level of effort to deploy 600 new computers to run WBPv2 is not feasible and that running in an unsupported state is not acceptable. They now turn to the IT department to make things right and keep the business running.

The situation:

- New software will not run on existing computers.
- Upgrading 600 computers is not feasible.
- Running unsupported is not an option.

The conclusion that the IT department of Unprepared, Inc. made.

Terminal Services to the rescue!

After consulting with the vendor to ensure that they would support running WBPv2 under Terminal Services, the IT department went to work building their plan. Due to the number of users that would be running the program and the criticality of its availability, it was obvious that they would need a farm of servers. But how many servers would be needed to handle the load. The software vendor gave them some help by providing a general server specification and a number of users each server would support. Thinking it best to start small, validate, and then expand they put together their recommendation. They would start their TS farm with three servers and 10 pilot locations. They would build and deploy an .msi package that would seize the file association for the .wbp file from the locally installed WBPv1 to the remote-based WBPv2. They would deploy to each of the pilot locations one at a time taking both quantitative performance figures from their monitoring tools and subjective user experience interviews. Weighing these statistics and opinions along with the vendor guidelines they laid out an expansion plan so that management would understand when more hardware would be needed and what it would cost.

Well the rollout was a success, the downtime was minimal, they were never out of support with the software vendor, and the IT department at Unprepared, Inc. was heralded as heroes. OK, we all know that even the best plan still requires a lot of hard work to achieve its goals and that IT is rarely held up as heroes. However, it is part of the job that we all signed up for.

THE CASE OF MIGRATING A LEGACY HARDWARE PLATFORM TO APP-V OR HYPER-V

BigCompany, Inc. has a very old hardware platform supporting an outdated software application that has become critical to business functionality. Past attempts to upgrade the hardware or software have failed for various reasons; inability to get the proper amount of downtime, fear of breaking the application being hosted and being unable to get proper vendor support for the application.

There are two approaches that can be considered in this situation. In option one BigCompany utilizes App-V to create a virtualized instance of the outdated application. Doing so allows the engineers to take the time to properly install, configure, and validate the functionality of the application without having to interfere in the day-to-day operations occurring on the outdated hardware platform actively running in the production environment. Once the legacy application is validated in its newly "virtualized" form, it can easily be published to a current hardware platform running any flavor of Microsoft operating system. This approach allows for both hardware and software redundancy in the event of an emergency.

The second approach would be for BigCompany to fully virtualize the legacy server, complete with the software application already installed and configured. Doing so would also provide both hardware and software redundancy, with the only limitation (*as compared to the App-V approach*) being the ability to move the software application between various servers if needed.

THE CASE OF SUPPORTING A LARGE APPLICATION IN A WIDESPREAD ORGANIZATION

BigCompany, Inc. has recently decided to make the version of Office Suite used by their employees to be consistent across the enterprise. However, due to networking and other infrastructure limitations, the traditional SMS delivery method is considered NOT to be an option for delivering the current Office Suite to all of the workstations that require it.

BigCompany has already begun designing their Dynamic Data Center to include application virtualization. The implementation of App-V allows BigCompany to package the latest Office Suite in a way that allows them to publish the application across the enterprise utilizing BITS and proper package creation. They include in the package the functionality to migrate the data and then uninstall previous versions of the Office Suite as part of the deployment of the App-V package to the workstation. Not only does this approach allow for the full deployment of the Office Suite to their entire enterprise, but it also allows for much easier updating of the Office Suite going forward by only having to update a single source and allowing it to replicate out to all of the workstations in a BITS controlled and silent fashion.

THE CASE OF MANAGING A GROWING DATA CENTER

GrowingUp, Inc. has been increasingly successful since its formation not so long ago. The CIO of GrowingUp realizes that his data center will continue to grow as business continues to be successful. He also understands how quickly data center growth can make the management of critical systems and their data a losing battle for his engineers and their managers. The CIO makes the decision to plan ahead for future growth and management.

Creating a task force of engineers and technical leads, the CIO is able to properly design and implement a fully dynamic data center that will allow not only for proper growth, but also the proper monitoring of that growth and the systems and data involved. The results are a truly dynamic data center that is easily auditable and reportable, not only to the engineers who designed it, but also internal and external audit and regulatory organizations.

THE CASE OF LIMITED CAPACITY

Undersized, Inc. was in a pickle. It needed to implement new accounting and payroll systems, but had nearly reached the capacity of their data center and could only add a few more servers. The two new applications would require 18 servers be added in order to support production, development, and testing environments. Undersized, Inc. had plenty of floor space open, but no employees had thought about the company's power and cooling resources until they were faced with the grim prospect of pulling additional power and adding more air-handling units. The costs promised to be enormous and were not forecast into the company's annual budget.

The IT department at Undersized, Inc. needed to devise a plan quickly that would support the new applications, not exceed the capacity of its data center, and be far less expensive than upgrading its power and cooling infrastructure.

The accounting and payroll applications were very similar in their hardware requirements. Each would require a database server and two application servers per instance. Two applications, times three instances (production, development, and testing), times three servers left them with a need for 18 new servers, but capacity for only six. Faced with the challenge of getting more out of less the IT team turned to thoughts of virtualization with Hyper-V. They worked closely with the software vendors to define their recommended requirements for memory and processors. They also confirmed that the vendors would support running their applications in a virtual environment.

The plan that they created was to reduce their new server count down to five machines. They decided to implement two production database servers, one for each application. This was based on performance concerns expressed by the software vendors with regards to virtualizing these machines. However, everyone was in agreement that the development and testing database servers could be run as Hyper-V virtual machines. They further concluded that all of the applications servers, production, development, and testing could be virtualized with Hyper-V as well. Basing their infrastructure needs on the vendors supplied hardware recommendations and with plans to thoroughly validate in their own environment, their design called for deploying three Hyper-V servers to run all of the virtual machines.

Ultimately, Undersized, Inc. was able to deploy the new applications within the confines of its data center by leveraging virtualization with Hyper-V to reduce the needed hardware footprint.

Appendix

C

Windows Server 2008 R2 Delta Changes

INTRODUCTION

In this chapter, we will review the Windows Server 2008 R2 delta changes. The changes in this chapter are those that occurred between Windows Server 2008 R1 (RTM) and Windows Server 2008 R2 releases. If you have experience in administering Windows Server 2008, this chapter will help you quickly gain an understanding of new enhancements offered in the R2 release.

NETWORKING CHANGES

Windows Server 2008 R2 includes several new networking features to provide a better end-user experience and increase the security of your network. Two of the biggest network changes include the new services DirectAccess and BranchCache. We will introduce you to both of these services and additional network enhancements in this section.

DirectAccess

DirectAccess is a new feature introduced in Windows Server 2008 R2 and Windows 7. DirectAccess provides end users with constant, secure connectivity to the corporate network anytime an Internet connection is available and without the need for traditional VPN client software installed. This connection not only gives end users easy access to the company network but also provides systems such as configuration management and software distribution servers access to the PC. This is a win-win feature for end users and IT departments alike. DirectAccess is accomplished by creating a secure tunnel between the Windows 7 workstation and the Windows Server 2008 R2 network.

BranchCache

BranchCache is a new feature in Windows Server 2008 R2 that allows branch offices to cache files from file servers and intranet Web sites locally to a branch office. With BranchCache enabled, the first time a file is accessed it is copied across the wide-area network (WAN) and opened on the local computer. A cached copy is then saved on a server designated as the local cache or another client computer. The next time a computer tries to access the remote file; it is accessed via the branch office cache location instead of pulling the file across the WAN a second time. Figure C.1 depicts a graphical overview of how hosted BranchCache works. BranchCache requires Windows Server 2008 R2 servers and Windows 7 clients.

VPN Reconnect

VPN Reconnect is a feature that allows Windows 7 clients to automatically reconnect a dropped VPN connection due to intermittent loss of Internet connectivity. For example, you may be connected to an airport wireless network with multiple wireless access points. Typically, moving from one access point to another could intermittently drop your Internet connection. This would result in you having to reconnect your VPN client, including reentering your username and password. A Windows 7 client

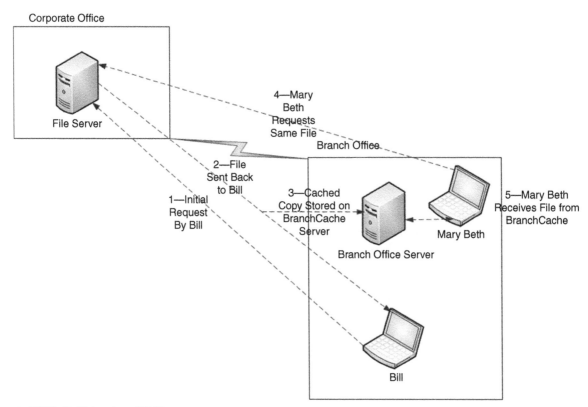

■ **FIGURE C.1** Windows Server 2008 R2 BranchCache.

using VPN Reconnect would automatically reestablish the VPN connection without you having to reenter your username and password. VPN Reconnect requires a Windows 7 clients and VPN connectivity via Windows Server 2008 R2 Routing and Remote Access Services.

DNS cache locking

Windows Server 2008 R2 introduces several new features to enhance the security of DNS. One of these features is DNS cache locking, which allows an administrator to configure how often cached DNS entries are updated. When a Windows DNS server performs a recursive query, it caches a copy of the result locally. This allows future queries to be updated via cache instead of requiring the DNS server to perform the same query again. One of the risks of using this technology is the possibility of cache poisoning. This is where malicious DNS entries are brought into a

DNS server's cache, which could redirect clients to malicious Web sites. DNS cache locking can help combat this risk by allowing the administrator to set a percentage of the time to live of the record as the amount of time required before the cached copy can be updated. For example, the DNS administrator could set the cache locking to 80% of the time to live. This would mean that cached DNS records could not be updated until 80% of the time to live had passed. This is a global change per DNS server, meaning it cannot be set per zone or record. You can update the DNS Cache locking percentage using the registry key HKEY_LOCAL_MACHINE\SYSTEM\CurrentControlSet\Services\DNS\Paramenters. A restart of the DNS service is required for any changes to take effect.

DNS Security Extensions

DNS Security Extensions (DNSSEC) is a new standards-based technology to help increase DNS security by using public key/private key technology to sign DNS records. A DNS server performing a recursive query of signed DNS zones will also receive a public key from the authoritative DNSSEC-enabled DNS Server. The DNS server performing the query can use the public key to verify the validity of the results being returned. DNSSEC is supported by Windows Server 2008 R2 servers and Windows 7 clients.

Firewall profiles per network connection

Windows Server 2008 R1 and Windows Vista introduced the concept of Network Location. The Windows firewall could have different settings for different network types. For example, while connected to the domain network, the server could have more ports opened and less strict firewall rules than when connected to a public network such as the Internet. Servers with multiple network adapters, connected to multiple networks could only use one profile, so the least restrictive profile would have to be used. Windows Server 2008 R2 resolves this issue by allowing administrators to use individual firewall profiles for each network connection. This prevents you from having to lower firewall security for public networks while allowing all necessary connectivity for trusted networks.

ACTIVE DIRECTORY CHANGES

Active Directory (AD) was first introduced with the release of Windows 2000 Server. Most of the core functionality has remained the same through Windows Server 2003, Windows Server 2008, and now Windows Server

2008 R2. However, with each release, Microsoft has made some performance improvements and added new features. In this section, we will take a look at some of the new AD features in Windows Server 2008 R2.

AD Recycle Bin

AD now includes an undelete option known as the Recycle Bin. The AD Recycle Bin acts a lot like the Windows recycle bin we are all very familiar with. The AD Recycle Bin stores objects for 180 days (by default) after they are deleted from AD. This allows for easy full fidelity recovery of deleted AD objects using PowerShell commands. The main requirement to use this feature is that your AD forest should be in Windows Server 2008 R2 native mode, and all domain controllers in the domain need to be running Windows Server 2008 R2. Let us take a closer look at the AD recycle bin.

Offline Domain Join

Offline Domain Join is a new feature in Windows Server 2008 R2 and Windows 7 that allows you to join a computer to an AD domain without having connectivity to a domain controller. The offline domain join is a three-step process:

1. The *djoin* command line tool is run on a Windows 7 or Windows Server 2008 R2 computer that is joined to the domain. The djoin/provision option is used to provision a computer account for the computer for which you want to perform an offline domain join. This generates a file to be used by the computer that will be joining the domain.
2. The file is copied to the computer that will be joining the domain via offline domain join. The *djoin* command is run with the /requestODJ parameter. This will copy the offline domain join file to the Windows directory and instruct the computer to join the domain on boot.
3. Boot the computer when connected to the network hosting the AD domain. The domain join process will automatically join the computer to the domain.

The offline domain join process can be very useful when you are automatically deploying a large number of computers, or if you want to give someone the ability to join a computer to the domain, without them needing special privileges in AD. The following will walk you through the process to perform an offline domain join.

In this process, we will be using two computers. LABDC1 will be the domain controller hosting the contoso.com domain. Srv1 will join the LABDC1 domain using the offline domain join process.

1. Log on to the domain controller (LABDC1).
2. Open a command prompt and enter the command [Code] djoin/provision/domain contoso.com/machine Srv1/SaveFile C:\djoinprovision.txt [Code] (see Figure C.2). This command is telling the computer to run the djoin provisioning process for the contoso.com domain. Create a djoin file for the server Srv1 and save it as C:\djoinprovision.txt. After running the command, you should receive confirmation that the offline domain join file was created successfully.
3. You now need to copy the file to the computer you want to join to the domain. You can use any method you prefer to copy the file. We just need to have it on the machine that we want to join to the domain.
4. Log on to the server we want to join to the domain (Srv1). Check the computer properties to ensure the computer is a member of a workgroup and not joined to the domain (see Figure C.3).

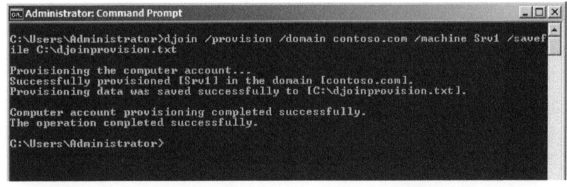

```
C:\Users\Administrator>djoin /provision /domain contoso.com /machine Srv1 /savef
ile C:\djoinprovision.txt

Provisioning the computer account...
Successfully provisioned [Srv1] in the domain [contoso.com].
Provisioning data was saved successfully to [C:\djoinprovision.txt].

Computer account provisioning completed successfully.
The operation completed successfully.

C:\Users\Administrator>
```

■ **FIGURE C.2** Provision computer and create offline domain join file.

Computer name, domain, and workgroup settings		
Computer name:	SRV1	🛡 Change settings
Full Computer name:	SRV1	
Computer description:		
Workgroup:	WORKGROUP	
Windows activation		

■ **FIGURE C.3** Computer properties.

5. Open a command prompt and run the command [Code] djoin/ requestODJ/loadfile C:\djoinprovision.txt/Windowspath C:\Windows (see Figure C.4). This command is telling the computer that on next boot, it should join the domain using the information provided in the file C:\djoinprovision.txt. You should see a success message and a notice stating you must reboot the computer for it to complete the offline domain join process.

6. You can now power down or reboot the computer as you normally do after joining a computer to a domain. At this point, the computer is joined to the domain and needs to reboot for changes to take effect on the local machine.

7. Log on to the computer and view computer properties to verify it was indeed joined to the domain (see Figure C.5).

AD Best Practices Analyzer

AD now includes a Best Practices Analyzer (BPA). BPAs for other Microsoft products have been around for several years. The most popular of these is the Exchange Server BPA. BPAs do exactly as their name

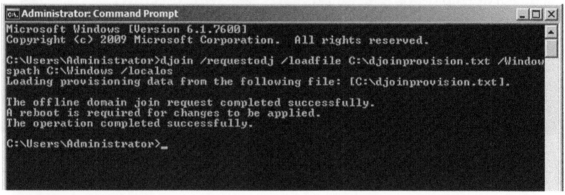

■ **FIGURE C.4** Perform offline domain join process.

Computer name, domain, and workgroup settings		
Computer name:	Srv1	Change settings
Full computer name:	Srv1.contoso.com	
Computer description:		
Domain:	contoso.com	

■ **FIGURE C.5** Computer joined to domain.

implies. The BPA will scan your servers and analyze software configurations. It will then compare those configurations to a list of best practices provided by the Microsoft product group responsible for that particular piece of software. As an AD administrator, you should not only run the AD BPA after deploying AD, but on a regular basis post installation or when significant configuration changes have been made to your environment. Let us explore the AD BPA in more detail.

1. The AD BPA is automatically installed with the AD Domain Services Role. You can access the BPA by selecting the AD node in Server Manager, then scrolling down to the BPA as seen in Figure C.6.
2. To run the BPA click the *Scan this Role* link. This will start a scan of the AD Domain services on the server.
3. After the scan completes, results of the scan will be displayed inside the BPA window. You can immediately see any noncompliant configuration settings or warnings under the noncompliant tab. You can also click on any alert to see full details of the issue and how to resolve it (see Figure C.7).
4. You can click the *Compliant* tab if you want to see the rules that were run in which the system was in compliance with best practices configurations.
5. The BPA can be rerun at any time from Server Manager. Run this tool and remediate any issues on a regular basis to ensure your AD domain remains highly reliable and healthy.

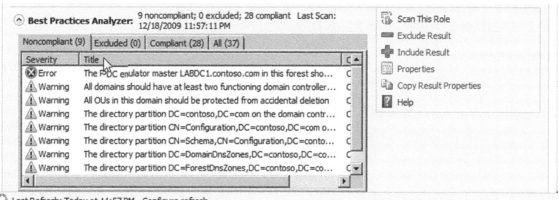

■ **FIGURE C.6** AD Best Practices Analyzer.

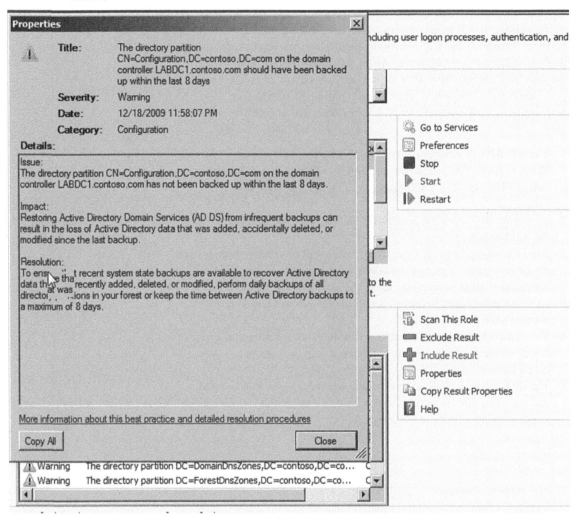

FIGURE C.7 AD BPA Warning.

AD Web services

Windows Server 2008 R2 AD includes Web services that provide remote management capabilities for AD. The AD Web services are primarily built to allow administrators to remotely administer AD using PowerShell. This allows you to send PowerShell commands to a remote domain controller from your local PC or other management server. Additionally, the AD Web services provide a way for developers to write applications that use the Web services to interact with AD.

Managed Service Accounts

Many applications and network services require the use of service accounts. These accounts are typically dedicated to a specific application and have passwords set to never expire. This requirement ensures no accidental service disruption due to a password expiring. However, this requirement poses a security problem, especially for organizations that must comply with various government regulations. Microsoft has addressed this issue with a new feature known as Managed Service Accounts. Managed Service Accounts allows the AD to automatically manage the passwords and Service Principal Names (SPNs). AD will automatically manage and change the password on a regular basis and ensure the service using the account gets the password update. A managed service account is created using the New-ADServiceAccount PowerShell cmdlet.

AD Administrative Center

The new AD Administrative Center (see Figure C.8) provides a way for administrators to perform regular management tasks via an easy-to-use interface built on top of PowerShell. This means that as an administrator you can use the graphical user interface (GUI) to perform a task and the

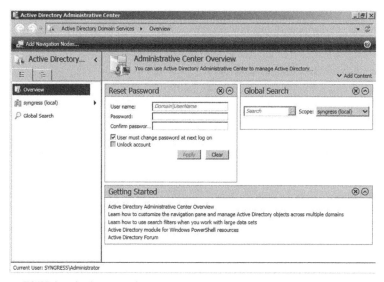

■ **FIGURE C.8** AD Administrative Center.

GUI then makes a call to a PowerShell script or cmdlet to complete the requested task. Most of the functions you perform in AD Users and Computers (ADUC) can be performed in the new AD Administrative Center-rich GUI. Whether you are a new or seasoned Windows administrator, you will want to check out the new AD Admin Center.

ADAC provides enhanced features such as the ability to manage multiple domains from a single pane of glass, a comprehensive search, and an integrated password reset tool. You may choose to use this tool over ADUC for many of the common day-to-day administration tasks for AD, such as resetting passwords or creating new user accounts. ADAC is accessed from the Administrative Tools folder in the Start Menu.

AD Module for PowerShell

Windows Server 2008 R2 is the first Microsoft server operating system to include PowerShell as part of the standard OS installation. To go along with the built-in PowerShell functionality, Windows Server 2008 R2 includes a series of cmdlets to administer AD via PowerShell. Using the AD Module for PowerShell, you can use PowerShell to administer user, computers, groups, domains, and domain controllers.

The AD Module for PowerShell allows you to perform many of the core AD tasks from the PowerShell command line. By using PowerShell you can easily automate common tasks or save scripts for future use. PowerShell also allows you to more easily update hundreds or thousands of accounts with a few simple commands. The following types of tasks can be performed within PowerShell with the AD module loaded:

- User and Computer Account Administration
- Create and Administer Groups
- Create and Administer Managed Service Accounts
- Create and Administer Organizational Units
- Create and Administer Password Policies
- Manage the Forest or Domain
- Manage Domain Controllers
- Search for and Modify Objects in the Domain

Whether you are a "command line junkie" or new to PowerShell, the new module for AD could easily become one of your primary administrative tools. It could end up saving your hours of time by automating updates and streamlining the process to update mass numbers of objects. You can access the AD Module for PowerShell from the Administrative Tools folder in the Start Menu.

Read-Only SYSVOL for Read-Only Domain Controllers

In Windows Server 2008 R1 (RTM) the SYSVOL folder was writable on Read-Only Domain Controllers (RODC). Windows Server 2008 R2 now makes the SYSVOL folder read-only on RODCs.

FILE AND PRINT SERVICES CHANGES

Windows Server 2008 R2 introduces some new features and enhancements for file and print services. These new features provide better security, stability, and end-user experience. In this section, we will explore some of these new features and how you might use them on your network.

Read-Only DFSR Replicas

Windows Server 2008 R2 allows administrators to set DFSR-based replicated folders to read-only. Using this feature, you can set up a central share with read-write access and provide read-only replicas to remote servers. This can allow administrators to easily publish files to various geographic locations, but ensure that remote users are only viewing files and cannot make updates to the remote copies.

File Classification Infrastructure

File classification is a new feature included in Windows Server 2008 R2. File Classification Infrastructure (FCI) allows administrators to classify files based upon folder or file type. Using these classification capabilities, administrators can then run reports or set retention policies on the file classes. Additionally, Windows Server 2008 R2 can automatically move files to an archive location after their retention periods have expired. This feature is added by installing the Windows Server 2008 R2 role service.

Print driver isolation

Windows Server 2008 R2 introduces a new print server reliability feature. Print driver isolation ensures that print driver functions run within their own processes. Prior to Windows Server 2008 R2, the driver functions and Windows print spooler ran in the same Windows process. If a poorly developed print driver crashed, it could bring down the entire print spooler service, resulting in the entire print server being unavailable. Using print driver isolation, an unreliable print driver no longer has impact on the print spooler's process. This ensures the print server remains online in the event an unreliable print driver fails.

Note

Print driver isolation may sound like a small change, but it has a great impact on large organizations that have large print servers.

Network Scanner Management

The new distribute scan management features in Windows Server 2008 R2 provide management and workflow features for network-based scanners. Using scan management you can administer network scanners across your network from a single-pane-of-glass interface. Additionally, you can setup network scanners to perform workflow functions for scan jobs. For example, a user could logon to a network scanner and scan a legal document. The network scanner could then send the document to a scan management server which could then route the document to a file server or SharePoint document library automatically.

INTERNET INFORMATION SERVER (IIS) CHANGES

With the release of Windows Server 2008 R2, Microsoft has included a dot release of IIS bringing the version to 7.5. IIS 7.5 on Windows Server 2008 R2 includes new administrative and security enhancements to further evolve and secure the popular Web server.

Request Filtering Module

The Request Filtering Module is introduced as an add-on extension for IIS 7.0 to allow administrators to block Web requests deemed harmful. Request filtering provides additional security to IIS by limiting the types of requests and commands that can be sent to IIS via the Web browser. IIS 7.5 now includes the module as a standard part of the Web server role.

Best Practices Analyzer

IIS 7.5 now includes a Best Practices Analyzer (BPA). You should run the BPA after initial configuration and on a regular basis thereafter to ensure your IIS deployment is healthy and optimally configured. We will look at the IIS BPA in greater detail later in this chapter.

PowerShell module

As with most roles in Windows Server 2008 R2, IIS 7.5 includes a PowerShell module allowing administrators to perform most administrative functions from the PowerShell command line. Administrators can use PowerShell to quickly perform IIS administrative tasks as well as automate the configuration of IIS for fast and standardized deployment of IIS Web servers.

Support for Managed Service Accounts

Windows Server 2008 R2 AD allows administrators to create Managed Service Accounts. Managed Service Accounts allow administrators to change the password of a service account without having to update each service using that particular account. IIS 7.5 application pools provide support for Managed Service Accounts. For example, an IIS application pool could be running under the account IIS_Service. For security purposes, an administrator needs to change the password on this account. The administrator simply has to change the password of the AD account. Once the password has been changed, the IIS application pool will automatically update the password field to reflect the new password without administrator interaction.

Hostable Web Core

The IIS engine itself can be hosted by other systems and applications. This gives developers the ability to include Web server functionality within their applications without having to write their own server. By using APIs they can leverage IIS directly inside their application code.

.NET support on server core installs

Windows Server 2008 R1 allowed IIS to be installed on a core install but did not support .NET. Windows Server 2008 R2 and IIS 7.5 now support the use of .NET in IIS Web applications running on a server core install of the operating system. .NET Framework versions 2.0, 3.0, 3.5.1, and 4.0 are supported.

Hyper-V changes

Windows Server 2008 R2 includes several new enhancements to Hyper-V virtualization services. These enhancements include live migration, hot adding and removal of virtual disks, new processor features, and support for jumbo frames on virtual machines (VMs).

Live migration

Windows Server 2008 R2 includes a much welcomed feature to enhance the process of moving VMs from one Hyper-V host to another. Windows Server 2008 R1 includes a feature known as Quick Migration, which suspends VMs and quickly transfers them to another host. This process does, however, cause a brief outage to any VMs being moved. When using quick migration to move a VM, some applications on that VM may time-out and need to be restarted due to their sensitivity to network or machine disruptions.

Live migration allows Hyper-V to overcome these limitations when moving VMs by removing the need for them to be temporarily suspended thus removing downtime for applications running on the VM being moved. Live migration uses a process to transfer memory pages from the current host to the destination host and then simply transfers ownership of the VM's virtual disks to the destination host. The Live migration process is depicted in Figure C.9.

Live migration allows administrators to easily, on the fly, add new hosts to a Hyper-V cluster instantly increasing the resources needed for VM workloads. Live Migration can also be used to allow administrators to service hosts during normal business hours without impacted business services and applications. For example, an administrator might want to add additional memory to a Hyper-V host. He could use Live Migration to move any active VMs from the host to another host in the cluster. He could then turn off the host to add additional memory. After adding memory, the administrator could use Live Migration to move the VM workloads back to the host.

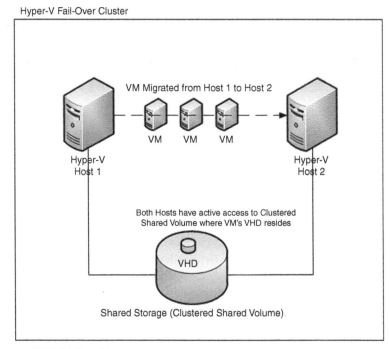

■ **FIGURE C.9** Hyper-V Live migration process.

Live migration requires that Hyper-V be deployed on a Windows Server 2008 R2 Fail-over cluster. Additionally, live migration requires a dedicated network adapter on each Hyper-V host for migration traffic. It is also recommended that processors on all hosts are from the same manufacturer and of the same processor family. This ensures all processor features can be used.

Processor enhancements

Windows Server 2008 R2 Hyper-V includes several new processor enhancements including support for 32 processor cores per physical host. Hyper-V can also take advantage of Windows Server 2008 R2 Core Parking features. Hyper-V moves VM CPU loads to the fewest required number of processor cores allowing Windows to suspend the cores not being used. As workloads require more CPU resources, the cores are no longer suspended and Hyper-V moves VM workloads to those cores.

Storage enhancements

Windows Server 2008 R2 Hyper-V adds new storage features which allow administrators to easily add and remove VM storage. Hyper-V now allows administrators to add or remove virtual and physical storage hot, while the VM is still running. This feature allows administrators to easily reconfigure VM storage without requiring downtime. For example, assume a production SQL server needs additional storage space for more databases. As the administrator you can add a new virtual disk drive to store new databases without taking the server offline.

REMOTE DESKTOP SERVICES (FORMERLY KNOWN AS TERMINAL SERVICES) CHANGES

With the release of Windows Server 2008 R2, Terminal Services has been renamed Remote Desktop Services. If you have experience in administering Terminal server in previous operating systems, you should be aware of the new Windows Server 2008 R2 names of various Terminal Server technologies. Table C.1 lists the old versus new name for common Remote Desktop Services and admin tools.

Along with a new name, Microsoft has also added several new features to further enhance Remote Desktop Services. In this section, we will explore some of the feature changes to the various components of Remote Desktop Services.

Note
Though it is recommended that all hosts in a Hyper-V cluster have the same processors, Windows Server 2008 R2 Hyper-V includes a new feature known as processor compatibility mode. Processor compatibility mode allows you to include computers with various processor types in a Hyper-V cluster. Processor compatibility mode turns off features of newer processors so that all processors in the cluster use the same features as the processor with the least number of features. This allows you to add older hosts to Hyper-V clusters, but also will cause newer hosts to run with a reduced set of processor features.

Table C.1 Common Remote Desktop Services and Admin Tools

Windows Server 2008 and Prior Name	Windows Server 2008 R2 Name
Terminal Services	Remote Desktop Services
Terminal Services Manager	Remote Desktop Services Manager
Terminal Server .	Remote Desktop Session Host
Terminal Services Configuration	Remote Desktop Session Host Configuration
Terminal Services Licensing	Remote Desktop Licensing
Terminal Services Licensing Manager	Remote Desktop Licensing Manager
Terminal Services Gateway	Remote Desktop Gateway
Terminal Services Gateway Manager	Remote Desktop Gateway Manager
Terminal Services Session Broker	Remote Desktop Connection Broker
Terminal Services RemoteApp Manager	RemoteApp Manager
Terminal Services Web Access	Remote Desktop Web Access

Remote Desktop Session Host

The Remote Desktop Session Host role includes several new features to provide a better administration experience as well as increased security for Remote Desktop Services deployments. Changes to Remote Desktop Session Host include:

- *Client Experience Configuration*—You can now centrally manage Remote Desktop audio/video redirection and Windows Aero interface options for Remote Desktop clients. These client experience features can be configured when adding the Remote Desktop Session Host role.
- *Roaming User Profile Cache Management*—Larger Remote Desktop Services deployments may have hundreds or even thousands of users logging into Remote Desktop Servers. It is common to see cached copies of profiles using a lot of storage space on Remote Desktop Servers. To help control the disk space usage of cached profiles, a GPO can be applied to Remote Desktop Servers placing a quota on the amount of disk space that can be used by cached profiles. If the quota is reached, the server will delete profiles of users with the oldest last logon until the profile cache falls below the quota.
- *Remote Desktop IP Virtualization*—Remote Desktop IP Virtualization allows administrators to create a pool of IP addresses allowing each

remote desktop session to have a unique IP address. This feature is useful for applications that may require each instance to have a unique IP or when troubleshooting and you need to track the IP of a particular session on a remote desktop server.

- *Enhanced CPU Scheduling*—Remote Desktop Services now includes a processor scheduling feature known as Fair Share Scheduling. This feature distributes CPU resources evenly across each Remote Desktop Session ensuring one user session does not impact the performance of another user's session. This scheduling is done automatically by the remote desktop server and does not require configuration.

Remote Desktop Virtualization Host

The Remote Desktop Virtualization Host is a new role included with Windows Server 2008 R2 Remote Desktop Services and provides a fully featured Virtual Desktop Infrastructure (VDI) solution for Windows. Remote Desktop Virtualization Host services allow administrators to setup pools of Hyper-V VMs that can be logged onto by users. Users can be assigned unique machines or assigned the next available machine in the pool. This gives users fully featured desktop computers accessible via a remote connection.

RemoteApp and Desktop Connection

Windows Server 2008 R2 further extends the features of RemoteApp to VDI-based Virtual desktops. Windows Server 2008 R1 allows administrators to use RemoteApp to make access to Terminal Services-based applications seamless to end users. Users can launch an application shortcut from their local computer or terminal, and that application appears to launch locally instead of displaying a remote desktop session to the terminal server.

Windows Server 2008 R2 in conjunction with Windows 7 publishes available RemoteApp applications and Desktop Virtualization Host-based VMs to the Start Menu of Windows 7 clients. This allows end users to easily access applications and virtual desktops they have access to by simply opening them from the Start Menu on their local computer.

Remote Desktop Connection Broker

The Remote Desktop Connection Broker in Windows Server 2008 R2 now extends the broker capabilities to virtual desktops in a Remote Desktop Virtualization Host. As with previous versions of the sessions broker, the Remote Desktop Connection broker provides load balancing and ensures users reconnect to existing sessions after a disconnect. The Remote Desktop Connection Broker connects users to the new RemoteApp and Desktop Connection feature.

Remote Desktop Gateway

The Remote Desktop Gateway feature includes several new enhancements over the previous Terminal Services Gateway. The new Remote Desktop Gateway includes the following new features:

- Gateway Level Idle and Session Timeouts
- Logon and System Messages
- Pluggable Authentication
- Network Access Protection Remediation

Gateway Level Idle and Session Timeouts

This feature allows administrators to configure idle and session timeouts on the gateway itself. By setting these timeouts administrators can ensure unused sessions are disconnected and active users are forced to periodically reconnect.

Logon and System messages

Administrators can now configure special message windows to be displayed to users when connecting to a Remote Desktop Services Gateway. System messages can be used to provide active users with important notifications such as information regarding system outages. The Logon message can be used to provide users important notifications every time they logon. These can be useful to advertise new applications or services available via the gateway.

Pluggable authentication

Pluggable authentication allows developers to write custom authentication modules for Remote Desktop Gateways. This can be used to further enhance Remote Desktop Gateway services by providing such features as Two-Token authentication.

Network Access Protection Remediation

Network Access Protection (NAP) Remediation features allow computers connecting via a Remote Desktop Gateway remediate any noncompliant security settings prior to connecting to the network. This ensures even computers connecting via Remote Desktop Gateways comply with corporate NAP policies.

Remote Desktop Web Access

Remote Desktop Web Access was first introduced in Windows Server 2008 R1 as Terminal Server Web Access providing users with a portal to view and connect to available RemoteApp-based applications within a Web browser. The new Remote Desktop Web Access feature includes the following enhancements over Terminal Service Web Access:

■ Security Trimmed RemoteApp Filtering
■ Forms-based authentication (FBA)
■ Public and Private Computer Options
■ Single Sign-on

Security trimmed RemoteApp filtering

Windows Server 2008 R1 Terminal Services Web Access displays any RemoteApp Web applications available on the system to all end users. This allows users to see RemoteApps even if they do not have access to them. Windows Server 2008 R2 Remote Desktop Web Access now security trims the interface so that users only see RemoteApp shortcuts they have access to.

Forms-based authentication

Remote Desktop Web Access now offers the ability to provide FBA. This provides a more user friendly logon page which users may be used to from other applications such as Outlook Web Access (OWA) in Microsoft Exchange.

Public and private computer options

Users can now specify what type of computer they are connecting from when logging into Remote Desktop Web Access. This provides more strict security settings when logging in from a public computer such as a kiosk.

Single sign-on

When using Terminal Server Web Access in Windows Server 2008 R1, users were prompted twice to logon to RemoteApps via the Web interface. They would be prompted once to access the Web access server and a second time when launching the application. Remote Desktop Web Access number provides single sign-on so that users only need to initially logon to the Web access site. Credentials are then passed to the RemoteApp automatically.

Remote Desktop Client experience

Several new features have been added to further enhance the Remote Desktop experience for Windows 7 client computers. Windows 7 clients connecting to a Windows Server 2008 R2 server gain these additional features:

- *Multiple Monitor Support*—Remote Desktop Services now support multiple monitors for Windows 7 clients. This allows RemoteApps to take advantage of multiple monitors in the same manner as if they were running applications on the local computer.
- *A/V Playback*—Remote Desktop Services now redirects Windows Media Player-based A/V content to the client computer where it is played locally using that client computer's memory and CPU to view the content locally.
- Windows 7 Aero—Remote Desktop Sessions support Windows 7 Aero features when the connecting client is a Windows 7 computer.

Remote Desktop Services PowerShell module and Best Practice Analyzer (BPA)

Remote Desktop Services now comes with more management features and options including a PowerShell module and BPA. Using PowerShell administrators can perform most Remote Desktop Services administration via a PowerShell command prompt.

The BPA helps administrators verify their Remote Desktop Services configuration is following best practices and that there are no misconfigurations that could negatively impact the deployment.

HIGH AVAILABILITY AND RECOVERY CHANGES

Windows Server 2008 R2 includes several features to further enhance high availability and backup services. These include new features such as PowerShell support for clustering and the ability to backup individual files and folders with Windows Backup.

Fail-over cluster PowerShell support

Fail-over clusters can now be set up and administered using PowerShell 2.0. This not only includes the new cmdlets for Fail-over clustering but also the ability to remotely send commands to cluster services via PowerShell 2.0. With the added support for PowerShell, the cluster.exe command line utility is being deemphasized and may not be available in future releases of Windows.

Cluster Shared Volumes

Fail-over clustering supports the use of cluster shared volumes (CSVs). These are volumes that can be accessed by multiple nodes of the cluster at the same time. This brings new benefits to Hyper-V deployments by providing Live Migration and reduced number of LUNs required. Earlier in this chapter we discussed how Live Migration allows you to move VMs between two hosts in a fail-over cluster with no downtime. CSVs are what make this process possible.

Since previous versions of Windows could only have one host actively accessing the LUN, a fail-over would cause all VMs stored on a LUN to fail-over. Prior to Windows Server 2008 R2, Microsoft recommended that each VM in a fail-over cluster be assigned its own LUN to ensure that a single VM could fail-over. For many deployments, this resulted in a lot of LUNs being assigned to each Hyper-V host. Windows Server 2008 R2 removes this restriction using CSVs, allowing both hosts to access the volume at the same time and enabling a single VM on a LUN to fail-over without requiring other VMs on that same LUN to do the same.

Improved Cluster Validation

Windows Server 2008 introduced the Cluster Validation Wizard. By using this wizard administrators could easily verify and setup a cluster ensuring it was in a supported configuration. If the cluster passed the validation wizard it was considered to be in a correct configuration. Windows Server 2008 R2 adds additional tests to further ensure a cluster can be validated using the Cluster Validation Wizard.

Support for additional Cluster aware services

The Remote Desktop Connection Broker and DFS Replication (DFSR) can both be configured on a fail-over cluster to provide high availability and redundancy to these services.

Ability to back up individual files and folders

Windows Server 2008 R1 (RTM) backup did not have the ability to select individual files and folders to be backed up. This was a feature offered in previous versions of Windows such as Windows Server 2003. Windows Server 2008 R1, however, only provided the ability to back up a full volume. Windows Server 2008 R2 has brought back the feature to allow administrators to selectively choose which files and folders to include in a backup set.

SECURITY CHANGES

Windows Server 2008 R2 introduces new features to help ensure your network is more secure and protected. These new features include additions to existing services and entire new applications and roles. In this section, we will discuss some of the security enhancements offered by the R2 release of Windows Server 2008.

DNSSEC support

As previously mentioned in this chapter, Windows Server 2008 R2 provides support for the standards-based DNSSEC. This technology is not proprietary to Microsoft and is being adopted by many DNS solution providers. DNSSEC helps ensure DNS zones are more secure by offering public/private key signing of zones to help prevent man-in-the-middle attacks.

AppLocker

AppLocker is a new feature available in Windows Server 2008 R2 and Windows 7 to restrict which applications and scripts users can install on the system. AppLocker allows administrators to create rules based upon file version, file name, publisher, and other attributes of the application. Using AppLocker administrators can decrease the chances of malicious applications being installed and executed on systems they manage.

Changes to Network Access Protection

Windows Server 2008 R2 NAP now allows administrators to implement multiple System Health Validators (SHV). This allows different SHVs to be applied to different network policies. For example, an administrator could configure an SHV that requires that computers have all current windows updates and antivirus software to be installed. This SHV could then be applied to computers connected to the corporate network. The administrator could then configure a second SHV to require only antivirus software be installed and apply it to a network policy for computers connecting remotely such as via VPN.

Windows Server 2008 R2 also includes the ability to create Network Policy Server (NPS) templates. Administrators can now configure NPS settings and save them as a template. The template can then be used to deploy NPS policies without having to recreate all settings each time a new policy is needed.

Managed Service Accounts

It is a well-known best practice that account passwords should be changed on a regular basis. For years, administrators have struggled with performing password changes on service accounts because changing a password usually meant making configuration changes to the service itself. For example, by changing a password on a service account for an IIS Application Pool, the administrator would then need to logon to the Web server, open IIS Manager, and change the password settings of each application pool in which that password had been set. This not only caused huge administrative overhead, but sometimes resulted in forgotten app pools and Web applications experiencing service disruptions. As mentioned earlier in this chapter Windows Server 2008 R2 now provides the ability to setup Managed Service Accounts. Managed Service Accounts allow an administrator to change a service account password without impacting services such as IIS application pools being impacted. If an administrator changes the managed service account password, the IIS application pool will automatically update its configuration with the new password.

New security auditing features

Microsoft has further expanded auditing capabilities in Windows Server 2008 R2. These include:

- Global Object Access Auditing
- Reason for access reporting
- New audit categories can be enabled via GPO

Global Object Access Auditing

In Windows Server 2008 R2, an administrator can globally audit object access to the file system or registry. This allows you to globally monitor access to changes to the system no matter what settings are configured at the file and folder level.

Reason for Access Reporting

This feature allows you to review why a particular account was allowed or denied access to an object. For example, if a user was a member of a group that gave them access to a particular file, Reason for Access Reporting would indicate that this access was given because the user was a member of a group that was given access.

POWERSHELL CHANGES

Windows Server 2008 R2 includes the new PowerShell 2.0, providing new features including remote management capabilities. Administrators can now send PowerShell commands to a server from a remote workstation or other server. Additionally, Windows Server 2008 R2 includes an expanded set of cmdlets to manage Windows Servers. In this section, we will take a look at some of the new features of PowerShell 2.0 on Windows Server 2008 R2.

Integrated Scripting Environment and debugger

Windows Server 2008 R2 includes the new Integrated Scripting Environment (ISE) and fully functional debugger. The ISE is a GUI interface that provides script writers an easy way to create, edit, and validate PowerShell scripts. Using the ISE you can also run the new debugger to perform common debug tasks such as the ability to step through code and add break points. If you write PowerShell scripts you may want to familiarize yourself with the new ISE and debugger environments.

Background jobs

PowerShell now allows you to run commands in the background. This allows you to continue to work in the shell while a command is running. For example, you could issue a PowerShell command that could change a setting on 1000 AD accounts. Due to the number of accounts being updated the command may take several minutes to complete. PowerShell will now allow you to continue issuing other PowerShell commands while the process to update the AD accounts completes.

Transactions

PowerShell now allows you to create transactions that can run a batch of scripts or commands as a single process giving you the ability to commit or rollback mass changes. This is much like the behavior of SQL transactions.

Cmdlets for server administration

Windows Server 2008 R2 includes a large number of cmdlets for administering Windows Servers. In fact an administrator can perform most administrative functions on a Windows Server 2008 R2 server using

PowerShell 2.0. Providers and cmdlets have been written for most server roles giving administrators the ability to automate common tasks and rapidly make configuration changes to hundreds or thousands of servers at once.

SUMMARY

In this chapter, we discussed the major changes released between Windows Server 2008 R1 (RTM) and Windows Server 2008 R2. This chapter provides current Windows Server 2008 administrators a quick guide for identifying the new features and changes in Windows Server 2008 R2 from the previous operating system release. This chapter also provides reference to previous chapters allowing you to easily find content related to a new feature now available in R2.

Notes from the Field

ServerManageCmd and PowerShell

ServerManagerCmd was introduced in Windows Server 2008 R1 (RTM) as a powerful command line utility to perform many common administrative tasks. Most of the ServerManagerCmd commands are now available in PowerShell 2.0 on Windows Server 2008 R2. With this in mind, Microsoft is deemphasizing the use of ServerManagerCmd and the utility may not be included in future releases of the operating system.

Index

Note: Pagenumbers followed by *f* indicate figures and followed by *t* indicate tables.